THE
GREAT
INITIATES

THE
GREAT
INITIATES

A Study of the Secret History of Religions

BY ÉDOUARD SCHURÉ

Translated from the French by Gloria Rasberry
Introduction by Paul M. Allen

HARPER & ROW, PUBLISHERS

SAN FRANCISCO

Cambridge		London
Hagerstown		Mexico City
Philadelphia		São Paulo
New York		Sydney

1817

Authorized English Translation by permission of the Librairie Académique
Perrin, Paris, France

This book is published in France under the title *Les Grands Initiés*

Library of Congress Cataloging in Publication Data

Schuré, Édouard, 1841-1929.
    The great initiates.

    Translation of Les grands initiés.
    Includes bibliographical references and index.
    1. Religions.   I. Title.
BL80.S33   1980   291   79-3597
ISBN 0-06-067125-4

80   81   82   83   84   10   9   8   7   6   5   4   3   2   1

Dedicated
to the Memory of
Margherita Albana Mignaty
by The Author

"The soul is the key to the Universe."

"I am convinced that the day will come
when psychologists, poets and philosophers
will speak the same language, and
will understand one another."

—Claude Bernard

*These words were chosen by Édouard Schuré
as the motto for the Introduction to the first
French edition of this book in 1889.*

CONTENTS

9

CONTENTS

Édouard Schuré and *The Great Initiates*

THIS first American edition of Édouard Schuré's *The Great Initiates* marks another chapter in the eventful history of a remarkable book. According to a recent report, since its first publication in Paris in 1889 it has gone through 220 new editions. It is estimated that it has been purchased by approximately 750,000 persons, and—counting its translations into many other languages, including Russian—it has been read by somewhere between three and four million people. Today, without advertising effort beyond a brief listing in the trade catalogue of the Paris publisher, the French edition continues to sell about 3,000 copies annually.

Compared with the record of many modern American bestsellers, these figures may not seem particularly impressive. However, the fact that after seventy-two years *The Great Initiates* is still read and continues to sell in appreciable quantities, shows that many people in various parts of the world still enjoy this book.

Perhaps one of the reasons for this continued interest in *The Great Initiates* is that it is certain to make a very definite impression upon the reader. He may or may not enjoy it, but he will not easily forget it. Readers the world over recall their first meeting with Schuré's *Great Initiates* with pleasure and appreciation, even after a lapse of many years.

In a certain sense, *The Great Initiates* is a pioneer work. It was born out of the author's deep experience and observation of life. It is a protest against what he called "a false idea of truth and progress" current in his time, and in ours as well. It is his constructive answer to "the stagnation, disgust and

11

impotence" resulting from a one-sided view of life, a per-
nicious evil still at work in human affairs today.

The Great Initiates encompasses long centuries of man's
life on earth, and reflects his great search—the greatest search
of all—the quest for the spirit. The book describes the motiva-
tions behind external history, the growth of man's religious
striving, the rise and fall of cultures, and indicates their importance for us today. It reflects the lives and deeds of men
of extraordinary stature, "the fire-pillars in the dark pilgrimage
of mankind," Carlyle called them. In these pages one witnesses
spiritual adventure of a depth and intensity rarely experienced
by creative human beings, even in their most exalted moments.
This aliveness, this freshness, this excitement of discovery
which breathes through *The Great Initiates* may well explain
its continuing popularity after nearly three-quarters of a
century.

Edouard Schuré was born in the old cathedral city of Strasbourg on January 21, 1841. As a young boy he experienced
certain events which, as he described them many years later,
"left traces upon my thoughts, to which my memory returns
ever and again." The result of these events he called "inner
vision, evoked by impressions of the external world."

The first of these experiences occurred shortly after the
death of his mother, when he and his father visited a resort in
Alsace. On the walls of one of the buildings the ten-year-old
boy saw a remarkable series of frescoes, depicting the world of
undines, sylphs, gnomes and fire-spirits. Before these representations of what men of the Middle Ages called the Elemental
Beings, here shown in vivid, wonderful artistic form, the boy
was transported, as it were, into another world, the world of
creative fantasy. Like a talisman, the pictures awakened the
magic forces of wonder in the child's soul. The artist's creative

fantasy called to the fantasy slumbering within the boy, and the result was a new perception. For, as Carlyle wrote, "Fantasy, being the organ of the Godlike, man thereby—though based, to all seeming, on the small Visible,—does nevertheless extend down into the infinite deeps of the Invisible, of which Invisible, indeed, his Life is properly the bodying."

From this time, "the infinite deeps of the Invisible" seemed to draw the boy ever and again into the cathedral at Strasbourg. There, in the hush of the crypt, the majesty of the great nave, the glory of the music, the awe-inspiring mystery of the service, the holy calm of the candle-flames, the wreathing fragrance of incense smoke ascending into the dimness, he felt a kind of inner satisfaction, a longing fulfilled. Something of the spirit of the great mystics, Meister Eckhart and Johannes Tauler, whose lives were connected with this place, touched the soul of the boy, and he felt the transforming peace of the Friends of God of Strasbourg. Finally the moment came when the world of the spirit opened itself before his enraptured eyes. It is perhaps prophetic of his future activity that again it was a work of art that was the external cause of this second milestone on Édouard Schuré's path to the spirit.

One afternoon he was sitting in a corner of the lofty gallery of the cathedral, gazing in deep absorption at the light streaming through a great rose window. Like Dante when face to face with the Celestial Rose of the Paradise, the boy beheld the Figure of the Risen Christ, surrounded by an aureole of sublime glory. In that instant, cathedral, men, women—all his earthly surroundings—vanished, swallowed up in a heavenly influx. From that moment, for the rest of his long life, Édouard Schuré was convinced that his destiny was linked with the service of the divine world.

Not long after the death of his father, which occurred when Schuré was fourteen, he visited Paris, and saw for the first time the classical sculptures in the Louvre. The beauty of the Venus di Milo, of Dionysus, of the wounded Amazon, penetrated deeply into the boy, awakening in him a love and appreciation for the world of ancient Greece, which was to play so significant a role in his later work. In these sculptures Schuré became aware of the fact that a divine beauty can be made manifest in physical substance through the magic of art.

At about this same time Schuré read a description of the Eleusinian Mysteries of ancient Greece, and the inner pictures this evoked were so vivid, so compelling, that he dedicated himself to the task of recreating the sacred drama of Eleusis for modern humanity. For Schuré was convinced that through the experiencing of such a drama, men of modern times can acquire a totally new conception of the relationship between the spiritual striving of the ancient world and the religious conceptions of today.

Parallel with these experiences of soul and spirit, Schuré's early years were devoted to formal education. Eventually he received his degree in law at the University of Strasbourg, but he never entered into practice. He visited Germany, remaining there for a few years, during which time he wrote *Histoire du lied,* published in 1868. In this book he expressed his love for music and poetry, which had been enhanced by his personal acquaintance with Richard Wagner, then living in Munich. Schuré counted his relationship with Wagner as one of the three most important friendships of his life. In his *Richard Wagner, son oeuvre et son idee* (1875), Schuré recorded his deep appreciation of Wagner's efforts to reconstruct in modern times and in contemporary musical form pictures from the spiritual history of humanity. Because of this book and many articles he wrote on the same theme, Schuré is remembered as a pioneer in developing an appreciation of Wagner's work on the part of the French public.

Shortly after his return from his travels in Germany, Schuré married the sister of his friend, the composer Nessler. He and his wife moved to Paris, where Schuré continued his writing and studies, making friends with some of the most important men and women in the cultural life of France of his time.

With the outbreak of the Franco-Prussian War of 1870, Schuré and his wife went to Italy. In Florence he continued working on his Wagner book, entering whole-heartedly into the life of the literary and artistic circles of the city. There Schuré made the second great friendship of his life.

One day Malvida von Meysenbergs, the devoted admirer and helper of the philosopher, Friedrich Nietzsche, introduced Édouard Schuré to a Greek lady, Margherita Albana Mignaty. The meeting made a profound impression upon Schuré, an impression he was to recall clearly in the last year of his life: "When I saw those great sunny radiant eyes directed questioningly upon me, I felt my consciousness almost desert me, for my whole being seemed called upon to reveal itself."

In the presence of this beautiful woman, so reminiscent of the women of the classical Greece he so deeply loved, Schuré once again found access to the spiritual world opening within him. In Margherita Albana Mignaty he discovered a soul to whom the unseen world was as immanent as the physical. This direct relationship with the spiritual world was the result of the death of her child, which had taken place some years before.

Through their many conversations, Schuré's own spiritual perception broadened and deepened beyond anything he had previously imagined. He referred to her as his Muse, and saw in her "a spirit that moves mountains, a love which awakens and creates souls, and whose sublime inspiration burns like a radiant light." On one occasion he asked her how she acquired

15

such precise knowledge of the spiritual history of mankind, such intimate details concerning long-forgotten antiquity. Her reply was profoundly simple: "When I wish to penetrate to the very depths of a subject, I shut myself in my room and reveal myself to myself."

Through the inspiration of Margherita Albana Mignaty, "as a testimony of a faith acquired and shared," *The Great Initiates* came into being. In the introduction to his *Le Théâtre initiateur, son passe, son present, son avinir,* based on a series of lectures Schuré gave before the Société de Géographie in Paris early in 1925, he wrote:

"Many years ago I happened to be at Florence, working at a poem on Empedocles, the philosopher-magician of Agrigentum, who ended his triumphant career by suicide on Mount Etna . . . Every morning I went to the Uffizi library to consult the ancient authors who had dealt with the Mysteries of Eleusis to which, from earliest youth, I had been irresistibly attracted. The municipal library, standing in the heart of Florence, behind the Museum, on the banks of the Arno, not far from the Palazzio Vecchio which proudly erects its slender campanile, sentinel-like, above the elegant city—all this was a favorable setting for my meditations. One day, lost in the labyrinth of the mysteries contained in the pages of Plato and Porphyry, Iamblichus and Apuleius, my inner vision suddenly extended its bounds beyond the horizon.

"What fascinated me in the history of Empedocles was the torturing riddle of the Beyond, as it presents itself to the individual man through his emotional life. But what terrifying vistas are produced by this enigma when stated for the whole of humanity! What is mankind's origin? What is humanity's destination? From what abyss has humanity escaped, only to plunge into what annihilation, or into what Eternity? What relation does mankind bear to the cosmic powers working behind the apparent chaos of the universe, in order to produce so marvelous a harmony? In the dense darkness where the alarming materialism of our age wallows, it is no longer a matter of merely restoring the link between the visible and the invisible for individuals, but of demonstrating how fruitful is the working of the omnipotent Beyond in the history of all humanity.

"With these thoughts a new and ardent desire came to birth within me. I was filled with the impulse to trace the connection between the revelation of Eleusis and that of the Christ.

"In order to build a bridge between the lost Paradise and earth plunged in darkness, was it not necessary to reconstruct the living chain of the various religions, to restore to Hellenism and Christianity their original unity, to reconcile once again the whole tradition of East and West? At that instant, as in a flash I saw the Light that flows from one mighty founder of religion to another, from the Himalayas to the plateau of Iran, from Sinai to Tabor, from the crypts of Egypt to the sanctuary of Eleusis. Those great prophets, those powerful figures whom we call Rama, Krishma, Hermes, Moses, Orpheus, Pythagoras, Plato and Jesus, appeared before me in a homogeneous group. How diverse in form, appearance and color! Nevertheless, through them all moved the impulse of the eternal Word. To be in harmony with them is to hear the Word which was in the Beginning. It is to know and experience the continuity of inspiration in history as an historical fact.

"Could not this lightning vision, this moment of consciousness become a new bridge to traverse the abyss separating earth from heaven? It was as if I had found my *Novum Organum*. This work, coming to me from the very center of things, was sufficient to last me for the rest of my life, and far more. A new life opened, filled with work on *The Great Initiates* and the inspiring help of Margherita Albana Mignaty."

Today, when one reads page after page of fascinating details and vivid impressions drawn from the spiritual life of mankind, one may believe that the whole of *The Great Initiates* flowed easily and rapidly from the pen of the author. Nothing could be further from the truth. Though Schuré's achievement ultimately brought him great joy, the writing of *The Great Initiates* was an arduous effort. His penetration into the spiritual world involved a constant inner struggle, and the entire task of writing the book required ten years of strenuous work.

After Schuré's return to Paris he continued his work on *The Great Initiates* and also became a regular contributor of articles on the history of religions, the drama, and on general cultural subjects to the *Revue des Deux Mondes* and the *Nouvelle Revue*. He wrote on the Greek dramas, the Druids, Joan of Arc and other great figures of French history, the poetry of Shelley, the magic of Merlin, and repeatedly on the work of Richard Wagner. In August, 1876 Schuré traveled to Bayreuth to attend the first complete performance of Wagner's *Der Ring des Niebelungen*, given in the newly-constructed Festival Theater, under the direction of Hans Richter. Among the people of many countries who flocked to Bayreuth for this great cultural event was the philosopher, Friedrich Nietzsche. Schuré met Nietzsche, and had many conversations with him.

Like Nietzsche, Schuré revolted against the crass materialism of the nineteenth century which was rampant everywhere. As he wrote, "Science is concerned only with the physical and material world; ethical philosophy has lost the leadership of the minds of men; religion . . . no longer is supreme in the social life: ever great in charity, it no longer radiates the spirit of faith." The arid concepts of the scientific world of his time, expressed in the work of men like Claude Bernard, the physiologist, Berthelot, the chemist, Auguste Comte and Herbert Spencer, the positivist philosophers, Emile Duerckheim, the sociologist, and Hyppolite Taine, the psychologist—to name but a few—repelled him. On the other hand, observation had convinced Schuré that for the sake of temporal advantage the Church had sacrificed its former high estate, had compromised its position. In place of true faith and love, he observed the theological skepticism of men like David Friedrich Strauss, who described the Resurrection of the Christ as *ein welthistorischer humbug,* and Ernst Renan, the ex-seminarist, who exclaimed about Christianity, "O divine comedy!" In Schuré's view such exclamations, greeted with appreciation by many cultured men of the time, were the spirit of Antichrist incarnate. His firm conviction was, "Today neither the Church, imprisoned in its dogma, nor science, locked up inside matter, any longer knows how to make men whole. Science need not change its method, but it must broaden its scope; Chrisianity need not change its tradition, but it must understand its origins, its spirit and its significance."

The giants of French literature in the nineteenth century, with their rejection of any evidence of the existence of the spiritual world and their utter refusal to recognize inspiration as a source of creative work, gave Schuré great concern. He observed that "Art and literature have lost the sense of the divine. A large part of our youth has become interested in what its new masters call Naturalism, thus degrading the beautiful name of Nature, for Naturalism is the systematic negation of the soul and the spirit." Thus in the naturalistic writing of Anatole France, Emile Zola and others like them, Schuré detected an infectious illness gnawing at the vitals of the cultural and spiritual life of his time. Proof positive, in his eyes, was Zola's insistence that the work of the novelist must be based "upon the scientific methods of psychology," which meant the death-blow to creative life as Schuré understood it.

Schuré was convinced that without a total reorientation in terms of the spirit, a complete renewal of outlook in regard to science, art and religion, the man of the nineteenth century faced a deterioration of his physical capacities, a dulling of his soul activities and a serious weakening of his spiritual faculties. For Schuré, the wonderful achievements of technical science, the so-called progress in art and the "higher criticism" which explained the Gospels on the solid basis of materialism, since one and all turned their backs upon the true relationship of man and the spiritual world, was but an accumulating of wrath against the day of wrath.—And when one considers where the once acclaimed materialism of the last century has led, when one considers the terrible harvest of war, the unspeakable suffering which has accrued from it to untold millions in our own time, can one doubt for a moment that Schuré was right?

In the autumn of 1887 came the news of the death of Margherita Albana Mignaty. Some time before, in writing of her impending decease, as token of their continuing oneness, she had promised to bequeath to Schuré her Lamp, her Lyre and her Torch. In a dream Schuré understood these symbols to mean the light of her spirit, the melodious instrument of her soul, and the undying flame of her love, which would accompany him always in his creative work. His continued productivity in the after-years, his constant love for her and his undiminished sense of her nearness were precious tokens to Schuré that his Muse had kept her promise, even beyond death. To the very end of his long life, her spiritual presence was his constant comfort, his strength, his consolation in sorrow, his joy and inspiration, and with deepest reverence, appreciation and gratitude he often spoke of all that she meant, of all that she had brought to him...

Two years after her death Édouard Schuré's *The Great Initiates* was published, and he dedicated the book to her memory with the declaration,

> ". . . Without you, this book would never
> have appeared . . . you hovered over it . . .
> you nurtured it, and you blessed it with
> a hope divine..."

"In 1889, when it first appeared, my *Great Initiates* was greeted by the press with icy silence. Nevertheless, after a short time, subsequent editions multiplied and kept increasing from year to year. At first the ideas appeared startling to the majority of readers. They evoked the distrust of both University and Church, but neither this nor the coldness of most of our critics hindered the book's success. Slowly and surely *The Great Initiates* continued on its way through the gloom, winning its success by its own strength. Letters of interest and appreciation poured in from all parts of the world, coming to me from five continents. During the (First) World War innumerable letters accumulated at my home, the most sincere of them from the battlefront. Since that time there has been such an acceleration in the sale of the work that one day my eminent friend, Andre Bellesort, said to me, 'You have not only won *your* public, but *the* public!' "

These lines were written by Schuré in 1926 when the 91st edition of *The Great Initiates* was passing through the press. He concluded: "Since *The Great Initiates* has continued on its upward path despite tradition and prejudice, I must conclude that there is a vital power in its principal idea. This idea is none other than a clear and determined reconciliation between science and religion, whose dualism has sapped the foundations of our civilization, and threatens us with the worst catastrophes. This reconciliation can be effected only by a new composite view of the visible and invisible world by means of spiritual insight and inner vision. Only the certainty of the immortal soul can form a solid basis for earthly life, and only the concord of the great religions, brought about by a return to their common Source of inspiration, can secure the brotherhood of peoples and the future of mankind."

Of what Schuré called the three most significant friendships of his life, the first was with Richard Wagner, the second with Margherita Albana Mignaty, and the third with Rudolf Steiner. Through Wagner's music dramas Schuré found his connection with the mystery character of ancient myth and legend. Through Margherita Albana Mignaty he acquired the inspiration and insight to create *The Great Initiates*. Through his friendship with Rudolf Steiner, for the first time in his life he found himself in the physical presence of a man whose spiritual stature and insight were akin to those figures he had described in his book. Therefore, in a certain sense, Schuré's relationship with Steiner was a kind of fulfillment of the spiritual-artistic task he had undertaken with the writing of *The Great Initiates*.

In his memoirs Schuré recalled that it was in 1902 that "Marie von Sivers (later Marie Steiner) had written to me for the first time about Rudolf Steiner, the man whose knowledge exceeded everything which until then had been considered esoteric by men."

In May, 1906, Édouard Schuré and Rudolf Steiner met for the first time when the latter visited Paris to give a course of eighteen lectures on matters of spiritual knowledge. Schuré recalled that "From all I had heard from Marie von Sivers and had read elsewhere, I had indeed expected a man who might have the same goal as myself. However, I was rather indifferent when Rudolf Steiner came to meet me.

"Then—as he stood in the doorway and looked at me with eyes which revealed an understanding of infinite heights and depths of development, and his almost ascetic countenance, expressing and instilling kindness and boundless confidence— he made a tremendous impression upon me (*une impression foudroyante*). Such an impression I had experienced only twice before in my life, and then much less strongly, with Richard Wagner and with Margherita Albana Mignaty. Immediately two things became clear to me, even before Rudolf Steiner started to speak.

"For the very first time I was certain that an initiate stood before me. For a long while I had lived in spirit with initiates of the past, whose history and development I had attempted to describe. And here at last, one stood before me on the physical plane.

"A second thing also became clear to me in this very brief moment, as we forgot everything about us, and only looked into each other's eyes: I was certain that this man standing before me was to play an important role in my life."

As for the lectures themselves, Schuré recalled that Steiner's "warm, convincing speech, illuminated by continuous clear thinking, impressed me immediately . . . When he spoke about the appearances and happenings in the supersensible world, it was as if he was completely at home there. In familiar language he told us what took place in those unfamiliar regions . . . He did not describe; he *saw* the objects and happenings, and made them visible in such a way that those cosmic events appeared to one like real objects on the physical plane. When one listened to him, one could have no doubt of his spiritual insight, which was as clear as physical vision, only much more comprehensive."

Later, Schuré published his extensive notes of Steiner's Paris lectures in order, as he wrote, "to venerate anew the incomparable master, to whom I owe one of the greatest enlightenments of my life."

Among the audiences attending Steiner's course of lectures in Paris at this time, filling the hall to overflowing, were people from England, Holland, Germany, Switzerland and Russia. Writers well known in the Russian literature of the period were present, including the poets K. D. Balmont and N. M. Minski, the novelist, Dimitri S. Mereshkovski and his wife, Znadia N. Hippius.

In his autobiography, *The Course of My Life,* Steiner wrote of these Paris lectures of 1906: "In this cycle of lectures I gave what I felt to be 'mature' within me of the leading elements of spiritual knowledge pertaining to the nature of the human being . . . This knowledge was among the most profoundly moving inner experiences of my soul . . ."

The first performance of Schuré's drama, *The Mystery of Eleusis,* was given at Munich in May, 1907. Steiner related that "Long before, Marie von Sivers had translated Schuré's reconstruction of the Eleusinian drama. I arranged it as to language for dramatic presentation." The performance took place on Whitsunday, and all the details of the production: the acting, costume design and scenic effects had been executed under Steiner's direction.

Schuré was present at the performance, and wrote that "What I had seen and represented unconsciously, Steiner recognized and confirmed. He saw in this *Mystery of Eleusis* the starting-point of true dramatic art . . . and confirmed not only the form of my drama, but also the treatment and words. I can hardly express what inner satisfaction I felt when Steiner made this clear to me, and further, what encouragement I received to continue the work I had been doing. For it is one of those very cherished moments in the creative life of the artist when he meets someone who recognizes and knows that he is drawing what he says from spiritual vision . . ."

In 1909 Steiner staged a production of Schuré's play, *The Children of Lucifer*, written in 1900. Marie von Sivers had translated the play into German, and Schuré, who witnessed its first presentation, was very much pleased with the whole undertaking. Like many another author, Schuré had his experience with an inquisitive audience on this occasion: "After the performance, I was overwhelmed with questions. People asked where I had found this or that, and why I had written this or that in such a way. And I well remember how Rudolf Steiner stood by my side and looked at the questioners as if he wished to help me out of my embarrassment. Of course I could not say where I had got all this and why it was so and not otherwise. And no one understood that better than Rudolf Steiner."

The year 1909 is also important in the relationship between Schuré and Steiner, for it was then that Marie von Sivers' translation of *The Great Initiates—Die Grosse Eingeweiten—* was published by the firm of Max Altmann in Leipzig. In the introduction to this book, Rudolf Steiner wrote in part: "Schuré is convinced that there is a future for spiritual culture . . . His artistic creativity rests upon this faith, and this book has grown out of it. It speaks about the 'Great Illuminated,' the Great Initiates, who have looked deeply into the background of things, and from this background have given great impulses for the spiritual development of mankind. It traces the great spiritual deeds of Rama, Krishna, Hermes, Pythagoras and Plato, in order to show the unification of all these impulses in Christ . . . The light streaming from Schuré's book enlightens those who wish to be firmly rooted in the spiritual sources from which strength and certainty for modern life can be drawn. One who understands the religious needs of our time will be able to recognize the benefits Schuré's book can provide in this area particularly. It offers historic proof that the essence of religion is not to be separated from the concept of 'initiation' or 'illumination.' The need for religion is universally human. A soul that assumes it can live without religion is caught in a deep self-deception. But these needs can be satisfied only by the messengers of the spiritual world, who have attained the highest level of development. Religion ultimately can reveal the greatest verities to the simplest hearts. Thus its starting-point lies where fantasy lays aside the cloak of illusion and becomes imagination, so that the highest reality is disclosed to the soul, and where the search for truth becomes inspiration, at which stage not the reflected light of thoughts, but the primordial light of ideas, speaks. Inasmuch as Schuré describes the great founders of religion as the highest initiates, he presents the religious development of mankind from its deepest roots. One will understand the essence of 'initiation' of the future when one gains an insight into this through the great religious phenomena of the past.

"Today there is much talk about the limits of human knowledge. It is said that this or that must be hidden from man because with his understanding he cannot penetrate beyond a certain point. In future one will recognize that a person's limits of understanding will widen to the extent that he develops himself. Things that seemed unknowable enter into the realm of knowledge when man unfolds his capacities for knowledge which slumber within him. Once one has gained confidence in such a widening of the human capacities for knowledge, he has already entered upon the path, at the end of which stand the Great Initiates.

"Schuré's book is one of the best guides for finding this path in our day. It speaks about the deeds of the Illuminated. These deeds can be recognized in the spiritual history of mankind, and this book traces the path from these deeds to the souls of the Illuminated themselves...

"When people can become convinced that the spiritual impulses of the past, which continue to live on in their souls, have originated from the faculty of spiritual insight, then they will be able to work their way to the recognition that this faculty can also be attained today.

"One who can trace the spiritual life of the present, not merely on the surface, but in its depths, will be able to observe how, after the ebbing away of materialistic streams, sources of the spiritual life open up from many directions. Whoever observes this clearly will not question the transitory necessity of materialism. He will know that this materialism had to develop in these last centuries because the fruits of external culture were possible only under its one-sided influence. But such a person will also see the dawning of a new age of spirituality.

"In Schuré's *Great Initiates* we believe we have one of the best symptoms of this approaching spiritual age. We include the author of this book among those who boldly step forward into the dawn of this age. The strength which flows from searching into the souls of the Great Initiates has given him the daring and the freedom necessary to write such a courageous book as the one before us."

In 1911 a second German edition of *The Great Initiates* appeared, and Steiner wrote in the introduction, "Édouard Schuré, the profound portrayer of *The Great Initiates,* appeals to souls who yearningly lift their eyes to the great guides of human intuition, in order that they may fill themselves with the ideas which have been revealed in the course of history. These ideas can awaken within every human being a premonition of the solution of the riddles of existence.

"Today we possess a rich, scholarly literature concerning many of the personalities about whom Schuré speaks in this book . . . but Schuré's brilliant description gives something essentially different than this literature. A personality speaks through this book, penetrating with intuitive eyes into the activity of the soul powers which embody themselves in man. This personality has the capacity to lift the reader to the horizon of eternal ideas, whose realization is the true history of mankind."

In May, 1914 Rudolf Steiner again visited Paris for a brief series of lectures. On this occasion he went out to the town of Chartres with Édouard Schuré in order to visit the wonderful Gothic cathedral, one of the glories of human artistic achievement. In his memoirs Schuré relates that "We had stood for a long time in the right aisle of the church. He had remained rather quiet. Then, as we were going out, he related to me wonderful things about John, about the Gospel of St. John, and went back suddenly to Plato and Aristotle. I could not escape the impression that he had met these figures again in the cathedral. These and other impressions remain unforgettably with me, and since that time they have admonished me to return to my own path, which from that moment has been quite clearly that of the Christian inspiration."

From this intimate picture, one can understand that his friendship with Rudolf Steiner was a highly decisive turning-point in the life of Édouard Schuré. His premonition upon first meeting Steiner, that the latter "was to play an important role" in his life, was amply fulfilled.

ÉDOUARD SCHURÉ

Two months after their Chartres visit, the shadows of world conflict passed over Europe, and Schuré and Steiner were separated by the tragic events which followed. However, in the midst of the war, a third German edition of *The Great Initiates* was called for, and again Steiner wrote a brief introduction, dating it, "Berlin, July, 1916." Indicating that "the thoughts of *The Great Initiates* find a sympathetic response in the stream of development which is connected with Herder and Goethe," with characteristic insight and awareness of the need for objectivity, particularly at a moment in history when national feelings tended to cloud men's judgments, Steiner concluded, "The content of Schuré's book definitely belongs to those universal spiritual values which stand over and above what separates nations."

In another context, Steiner referred to *The Great Initiates*: "The thoughts contained in this book have strongly influenced the souls and minds of the present time, but only the future will show the whole extent of this influence." In conclusion, he prophesied that the day would come when "this book will be considered an extremely valuable contribution to the spiritual content of our age."

Édouard Schuré is reported to have said that he considered the section on the Christ in *The Great Initiates* "the weakest part of the book." This realization came to him when he translated Rudolf Steiner's *Christentum als Mystische Tatsache*, Christianity as a Mystical Fact, into French. From Steiner's book Schuré experienced the esoteric depth and grandeur of the Deed of the Christ in its significance for the whole of earth evolution. Schuré wrote that in Steiner's work he found "a confirmation of the fundamental place of Christ in history. He is shown to be the manifestation of the divine Word

29

through man. Steiner places Him as the axis and center in the development of mankind . . . The divine Word, the Christ, dwelt above humanity from the Beginning . . . But only gradually has He drawn near mankind in the course of the latter's development. He illuminated prophets like Krishna, Buddha, Hermes, Moses, but He completely manifested Himself only when He incarnated on the physical plane in the personality of Jesus of Nazareth."

In Rudolf Steiner's Science of the Spirit, or Anthroposophy, Édouard Schuré found full and satisfying amplification of these thoughts.

At the conclusion of his *L'Evolution divine*, Schuré looks forward to what science, art and religion will be in times to come. He envisions a Christianity of the future which is in the highest sense artistic, because it includes within itself all the creations of art, basing them upon the most selfless, most sublimely artistic Deed of Love ever fulfilled upon earth: the Mystery of Golgotha and Resurrection. Then Schuré concludes, "This religion will be explained and supported by a new science, which might be called *the Science of the Spirit*. The aim of the latter will be to seek from the principles and causes that lie behind all phenomena, and to ascend from the visible to the invisible, from the material to the spiritual. With this object in view, the Science of the Spirit will strive to build up a synthesis of the sciences of physical observation by cultivating, through the discipline of initiation, the faculties of imagination, inspiration and intuition that are necessary for the perception of the soul and spiritual worlds . . . Art will be the inspired interpreter, the hierophant and the torch-bearer of integral Science and universal Religion . . ."

In his book *The Great Initiates* Édouard Schuré makes his contribution toward the fulfillment of this prophecy. For he

ÉDOUARD SCHURÉ

is a pioneer in depicting for modern times man's eternal striving for knowledge of his origin, evolution and destiny in the light of the eternal spirit.

—Paul M. Allen

Alvastra,
South Egremont, Massachusetts,
June, 1961.

RAMA

The Aryan Cycle

*Zoroaster asked Ormuzd, the Great Creator,
"Who is the first man with whom you conversed?"*

*Ormuzd answered, "Noble Yima, the one who was in command of the Courageous.
I told him to watch over the worlds which belong to me, and I gave him a saber of gold and a sword of victory."
And Yima moved forward on the way of the sun and assembled the courageous men in the famous Airyana-Vaeja, created pure.*
—Zend Avesta (Vendidad-Sadé 2nd Fargard)

O Agni, Holy Fire! Purifying fire! You who sleep in the wood, and ascend in shining flames on the altar, you are the heart of sacrifice, the fearless wings of prayer, the divine spark hidden in everything, and the glorious soul of the sun!
—Vedic Hymn

1

The Races of Mankind
and the Origins of Religion

"HEAVEN *is my Father,* it engendered me. I have this entire celestial circle as my family. *My Mother is the noble Earth.* The highest part of its surface is her womb; *there the Father makes fruitful the womb of the one who is his wife and daughter.*"

Thus the Vedic poet sang four or five thousand years ago, before an earth altar where a fire of dry herbs flamed. A profound divination, a sublime consciousness is expressed in these strange words. They contain the secret of the double origin of mankind. Anterior to and superior to the earth is the divine archetype of man; celestial is the origin of his soul. But his body is the product of earthly elements fecundated by a cosmic essence. The embraces of Uranus and the Great Mother, in the language of the Mysteries, signify the showers of souls or of spiritual monads which come to fertilize terrestrial seeds; they are the organizing principles without which matter would be only an inactive and diffused mass. The highest part of the earth's surface, which the Vedic poet calls the womb of the earth, designates the continents and mountains, cradles of the races of man. As for Heaven, *Varuna,* the *Uranus* of the Greeks, this represents the invisible order, super-physical, eternal and intellectual; it embraces the entire infinity of space and time.

In this chapter we shall consider only the terrestrial origins of humanity according to esoteric traditions, confirmed by modern anthropological and ethnological science.

The four races which share the globe today are daughters of varied lands. Successive creations, slow elaborations of the earth at work, the continents have emerged from the seas at great intervals of time, which the ancient priests of India called interdiluvian cycles. During thousands of years, each continent produced its flora and fauna, culminating in a human race of a different color.

The southern continent, engulfed by the last great flood, was the cradle of the primitive red race of which the American Indians are but the remnants, descended from the troglodytes, who reached the top of the mountains when their continent sank. Africa is the mother of the black race, called the Ethiopian by the Greeks. Asia gave birth to the yellow race, preserved in the Chinese. The last arrival, the white race, came from the forests of Europe, between the tempests of the Atlantic and the laughter of the Mediterranean. All human types are the result of mixtures, combinations, degeneracies or selections of these four great races. In the preceding cycles, red and black races ruled successively with powerful civilizations which have left traces in Cyclopean structures as well as in the architecture of Mexico. The temples of India and Egypt had traditions concerning these vanished civilizations.—In our cycle the white race is predominant, and if one calculates the probable antiquity of India and Egypt, one will find that its preponderance dates back seven or eight thousand years.[1] (See Notes, page 505)

RAMA

According to Brahmanic traditions, civilization probably began on our globe five thousand years ago, with the red race on the southern continent, while all of Europe and part of Asia were still under water. These myths also speak of an earlier race of giants. Gigantic human bones, whose formation resembles the monkey more than man, have been found in caves of Tibet. These creatures were related to a primitive humanity, intermediate, and still akin to animal life, possessing neither articulated speech, social organization, nor religion. For these three things always appear at the same time, and this is the meaning of that remarkable bardic triad which says, "Three things come into existence at the same time: God, light and freedom." With the first stammering of speech, society is born and the vague hint of a divine order appears. It is the breath of Jehova in the mouth of Adam, the word of Hermes, the law of the first Manu, the fire of Prometheus. A God trembles in the human faun. The red race, as we have said, inhabited the southern continent, now engulfed, called *Atlantis* by Plato, in keeping with Egyptian traditions. A great earthquake destroyed part of this continent, and scattered the remainder. Several Polynesian races, as well as the Indians of North America and the Aztecs whom the Spanish conquerors found in Mexico, are the survivors of this ancient red race whose civilization, lost forever, had its days of glory and material splendor. All these people carry in their souls the incurable melancholy of old races which die without hope.

After the red race, the black race dominated the globe. One must look for the superior species, the best of the race, in the Abyssinian and the Nubian, in whom is preserved the type of this race at its height. The latter invaded southern Europe in prehistoric times, and were driven back by the inhabitants. Their trace has been completely erased from our popular traditions. During the period of their supremacy, they had

religious centers in Upper Egypt and in India. Their Cyclopean cities crenelated the mountains of Africa, the Caucasus
and Central Asia. Their social organization was an absolute the-
ocracy. At the top were priests who were feared like the gods;
at the bottom were groveling tribes without any acknowledged
family. The women were slaves. These priests possessed profound knowledge, the principle of the divine unity of the
universe, and the worship of the stars which, under the name of
Sabeanism, spread among the white peoples.[2] But between the
knowledge of the priests and the crude fetishism of the masses,
there was no middle ground, no idealistic art, no vivid mythology. Moreover, they possessed an already scientific industry,
especially the art of handling huge stones by means of the
ballista, and of melting metals in immense furnaces, at which
they used prisoners of war. Among this race, strong in physical
resistance, passionate energy and the capacity for affection,
religion therefore was the reign of power, through terror. The
nature of God hardly affected the consciousness of these child-
like peoples except in the form of a dragon, a terrible antediluvian animal which the kings had painted on their banners,
and the priests carved on the portals of their temples.

If the sun of Africa helped give birth to the black race, it can
be said that the glaciers of the arctic regions witness the advent
of the white race. The latter are the Hyperboreans of whom
Greek mythology speaks. These sandy-haired, blue-eyed men
came from the north through forests illuminated by the aurora
borealis, accompanied by dogs and reindeer, directed by bold
leaders and guided by clairvoyant women. Shaggy hair of gold,
and eyes of azure: these were their predetermined colors. This
race is to invent the worship of the sun and of the sacred fire,
and will bring into the world the longing for heaven. Sometimes these people will rebel against heaven to the point of

wishing to climb up to it; at other times they will bow before its splendors in absolute adoration.

Like the others, the white race also had to tear itself away from the savage state before becoming aware of itself.—Its distinctive characteristics are the love of individual freedom, reflective sensitivity which creates the power of sympathy, and supremacy of the intellect, which gives the imagination an idealistic and symbolic turn.—Spiritual sensitivity brought about affection—man's preference for but one wife; from this came this race's tendency toward monogamy, the conjugal principle and the family.—The need for freedom, coupled with that of sociability created the clan, with its elective principle. Visionary imagination created ancestor worship, which forms the root and center of religion among white people.

The social and political principle is manifest the day some half-savage men, besieged by an enemy people, instinctively assemble and choose the strongest and most intelligent among them to defend and lead them. On that day society is born. The chief is a king in embryo; his companions are future noblemen. The deliberating old men, unable to march, already form a kind of senate or assembly of elders.—But how was religion born? It has been said that it arose out of the fear of primitive man, face to face with nature. But fear has nothing in common with reverence and love. It does not unite fact and idea, visible and invisible, man and God. As long as man did nothing but tremble before nature, he was not yet man. He became man when he seized the link which connected him with the past and future, with something superior and beneficent, and when he worshiped that mysterious unknown. But how did he worship for the first time?

Fabre d'Olivet offers a supremely astute and thought-provoking hypothesis on how ancestor worship must have been established among the white race.[3] In a quarrelsome clan, two rival warriors are arguing. Raging, they are about to fight, and are already grappling with one another. At that moment, a dishevelled woman throws herself between them and separates them. Her eyes are aflame; her voice has the tone of authority. In panting, cutting words she says that in the forest she has just seen the ancestor of the race, the victorious warrior of yesteryear, the *Heröll*, appear before her. He does not wish two brother warriors to fight, but to unite against the common enemy. "The ghost of the great ancestor, the *Heröll*, told me so," exclaims the excited woman. "He spoke to me; I saw him!" What she says, she believes. Convinced, she convinces. Moved, astonished, and as though overcome by an invincible force, the reconciled rivals regard this inspired woman as a kind of divinity.

Such inspirations, followed by abrupt changes, must have occurred frequently and in many diverse forms in the prehistoric life of the white race. Among savage people it is the woman who, in her excitable sensitivity, first senses the spiritual, affirms the unseen.

Let us now consider the unexpected and enormous consequences of an event similar to the one about which we are speaking. In the clan, in the tribe, everyone is talking about the marvelous event. The oak tree where the inspired woman saw the vision, becomes sacred. She is taken back to it, and there, under the hypnotic influence of the moon, which plunges her into a visionary state, she continues to prophesy in the name of the great ancestor. Soon this woman and others like her, standing on rocks in the middle of forest glades, at the sound of the wind and the distant ocean, call forth the diaphanous souls of ancestors before quivering crowds who, charmed by magic incantations, see them or think they see them amidst the mists drifting in the moonlight. Ossian, the last of the great Celts, will summon Fingal and his companions in the gathering clouds. Thus at the very origin of social life, ancestor worship is established among the white race. The great ancestor becomes the god of the tribe. This was the beginning of religion.

But this is not all. Around the prophetess old men group themselves and observe her in her deep sleep and in her prophetic ecstacies. They study her divers states, examine her revelations, interpret her oracles. They observe that when she prophesies in the visionary state, her face is transfigured. Her speech becomes rhythmical, and her raised voice pronounces her oracles as she sings a serious and meaningful melody.[4] From this come the lines, verses, poetry and music, whose origins are considered divine among the people of the Aryan race. The idea of revelation could occur only with respect to facts of this kind. At the same time we see religion and worship, priests and poetry arise.

In Asia, Iran and India, where peoples of the white race established the first Aryan civilization, mixing with people of different colors, men quickly gained ascendancy over women in religious insight. There we no longer hear anyone speak except wise men, Rishis and prophets. Woman, subjugated, submissive, is no longer priestess except in the home. But in Europe the trace of the important role of woman is found among peoples of the same origin who remained savage for thousands of years. It appears in the Scandinavian Pythoness, in the Voluspa of the Edda, in the Celtic Druidesses, in the women diviners who accompanied the Germanic armies and decided the day of battle,[5] and even in the Thracian Bacchantes who survive in the legend of Orpheus. The prehistoric clairvoyant is continued in the Pythia of Delphi.

The first prophetesses of the white race are organized in Druidess schools under the supervision of informed elders or Druids, men of the oak tree. At first they were only doers of good deeds. Through their intuition, their divination and their enthusiasm, they gave a great impetus to the race. But rapid corruption and tremendous abuses of this institution were inevitable. Feeling that they were mistresses of the destinies of the people, the Druidesses wanted to rule the latter at any cost. Lacking inspiration, they tried to reign by terror. They demanded human sacrifices, making these the essential element of their cult. In this, the heroic instincts of their race worked in their favor. The people were courageous, their warriors held death in contempt; at the first call they came voluntarily and bravely threw themselves beneath the knives of bloodthirsty priestesses. Through human hecatombs the latter hurried the living to join the dead as messengers, for it was believed that in this manner one gained the protection of the ancestors. This activity on the part of the prophetesses and Druids became a fearful means of domination.

This is the first example of the perversion the noblest instincts of human nature inevitably undergo when they are not controlled by a wise authority or guided toward the good by a higher conscience. Left to the mercy of ambition and individual passion, inspiration degenerates into superstition, courage into ferocity, the sublime ideal of sacrifice into an instrument of tyranny and of sinister and cruel exploitation.

But the white race was only in its violent, wild youth. Passionate in the spiritual sphere, it had yet to undergo many other and more bloody crises. It had just been awakened by the attacks of the black race, which was beginning to invade the south of Europe. This was an unequal struggle from the beginning. The half-savage whites, just emerging from their forests and their lacustrine homes, had no other means of defense than their spears and stone-tipped arrows. The blacks had iron weapons, armor of brass, all the resources of their industrial civilization and their Cyclopean cities. Defeated in the first encounter, the white captives became the slaves of the black men, who forced them to quarry stone and to carry crude ore into their furnaces. Escaped captives brought back to their own country the customs, skills and fragments of the science of their conquerors. They learned two things from the black men: the smelting of metals, and holy writing, that is, the art of recording certain ideas by means of mysterious hieroglyphic signs which they inscribed on the skins of beasts, on stone, or the bark of the ash tree. From this we get the runes of the Celts. Smelted, forged metal was the instrument of war; sacred writing was the origin of science and of religious tradition. The struggle between the white and black races wavered back and forth for many centuries from the Pyrenees to the Caucasus, and from the Caucasus to the Himalayas. The salvation of the white men was in their forests. There, like wild animals, they could hide themselves, reappearing at a suitable moment. Emboldened, disciplined and better armed as the centuries progressed, they finally took revenge, overthrew the cities of the black men, drove them from the coasts of Europe, later invading North Africa and Central Asia, then inhabited by black peoples.

The mixture of the two races was effected either by peaceful colonization or by military conquest. Fabre d'Olivet, that wonderful seer of the prehistoric past of mankind, starts with this idea in order to set forth a clear view of the origin of the people called the Semitic and also of the Aryans. Wherever the white colonists yielded to the black peoples, accepting their rule and receiving religious initiation from their priests, there Semitic peoples such as the pre-Menes Egyptians, the Arabs, the Phoenicians, Chaldeans and Jews probably came into being. The Aryan civilizations, on the other hand, probably were formed where the white men ruled the black men as a result of war or conquests—as in the case of the Iranians, Hindus, Greeks and Etruscans. In addition, among *Aryan peoples* we also include all the whites who remained in a savage and nomadic state in antiquity such as the Scythians, the Getae, the Celts, and later the Germans.

In this way the basic diversity between religions and sacred writing of these two great categories of nations can be explained. Among the Semites, where the intellectuality of the black race originally predominated, over and above the popular idolatry a tendency toward monotheism can be observed. The principle of the oneness of the hidden, absolute and formless God was one of the essential dogmas of the priests of the black race and of their secret initiation. Among the white men who were conquerors or who remained of pure blood, one observes on the contrary, a tendency toward polytheism, mythology and personification of divinity, stemming from their love of nature and their impassioned ancestor worship.

The main difference between the style of writing of the Semites and the Aryans probably resulted from the same cause. Why do all Semitic people write from right to left, and why do all Aryan people write from left to right? The reason Fabre d'Olivet gives is as curious as it is original. It calls before our eyes a real vision of the forgotten past.

Everyone knows that in prehistoric times no writing at all was done by the general masses of the people. The custom only spread with phonetic script, or the art of representing the sounds of words by letters. But hieroglyphic script, or the art of representing things by arbitrary signs, is as old as human civilization. And always in those primitive times, such writing was the privilege of the priesthood, since it was considered a sacred thing, a religious function, and originally a divine inspiration. When, in the Southern Hemisphere, the priests of the black or southern race drew their mysterious signs on animal skins or on stone slabs, they used to face the South Pole, the lines of their handwriting directed toward the east, the source of light. Therefore they wrote from right to left. The priests of the white or Nordic race learned writing from the black priests and at first wrote like them. But when the sense of their origin was developed in them, along with national consciousness and racial pride, they invented their own signs, and instead of facing the south, the country of the black men, they faced the north, the country of their ancestors, while continuing to write in the direction of the east. Their characters then ran from left to right, the direction of Celtic runes, of Zend, Sanskrit, Greek, Latin, and all writings of the Aryan races. The letters move toward the rising sun, the source of terrestrial life, but the people face the north, the country of their ancestors and the mysterious source of the aurora borealis.

The Semitic and the Aryan currents are the two rivers upon which all our ideas, mythology, religion, art, science and philosophy have come to us. Each of these streams carries with it a different conception of life; the reconciliation and balance of the two would be truth itself. The Semitic current contains absolute and superior principles: the idea of unity and universality in the name of a supreme Principle which, in its application, leads to the unification of the human family. The Aryan current contains the idea of ascending evolution in all terrestrial and supra-terrestrial kingdoms, and its application leads to an infinite diversity of developments in the richness of nature and the many aspirations of the soul. Semitic genius descends from God to man; Aryan genius ascends from man to God. One is represented by the punishing archangel who descends to earth, armed with sword and thunder; the other by Prometheus, who holds in his hand the fire snatched from heaven and surveys Olympus with his glance.

We bear these two geniuses within us. We think and act under the influence of the one or the other in turn. But they are not harmoniously blended within us. They contradict and fight each other in our inner feelings, in our subtle thoughts, as well as in our social life and institutions. Hidden beneath many forms which can be summarized under the generic terms *spirituality* and *naturalism,* they control our discussions and struggles. Irreconcilable and invincible, who will unite them? And yet the progress, the salvation of mankind depends upon their reconciliation and synthesis. For this reason, in this book we would like to go back to the source of the two streams, to the birth of the two geniuses. Beyond the conflicts of history, the wars of cults, the contradictions of sacred texts, we shall enter the very consciousness of the founders and prophets who gave religions their initial impetus. From above, these men received keen intuition and inspiration, that burning light which leads to fruitful action. Indeed, synthesis pre-existed in them. The divine ray dimmed and darkened with their successors, but it reappears, it shines whenever a prophet, hero or seer returns to his life origin. For only from this point of departure does one see the goal; from the shining sun, the path of the planets.

Thus revelation in history is continuous, graduated, multiform, like nature, but identical in its source, *one* like Truth, unchangeable as God.

In following back along the Semitic stream, by way of Moses we come to Egypt, whose temples, according to Manetho, embodied a tradition thirty thousand years old. In tracing back along the Aryan stream, we come to India, where as a result of the conquest of the white race, the first great civilization developed. India and Egypt were the two great mothers of religions. They knew the secret of the great initiation. We shall enter their sanctuaries.

But their traditions will carry us back even further to an earlier period when the two rival geniuses of which we spoke, appear united in a primeval innocence and a marvelous harmony. This is the primitive Aryan period. Thanks to the wonderful achievements of modern science, thanks to philology, mythology and comparative ethnology, today we are able partly to envision this period. It is outlined in the Vedic hymns, which nevertheless, in their patriarchal simplicity and sublime purity, are but a reflection. It was a virile and serious age, resembling nothing less than the Golden Age dreamed of by the poets. Grief and strife are by no means absent, but within men is a confidence, a strength and a serenity which mankind has never recaptured.

In India, thought will become more profound, feelings will be refined. In Greece, passions and ideas will be clothed in the charm of art and the magic cloak of beauty. But no poetry surpasses certain Vedic hymns in moral loftiness, in eminence and intellectual breadth. In them breathes the feeling of the Divine in nature, the Unseen surrounding it and the great Unity pervading the whole.

How was such a civilization born? How did such a superior intellectuality develop in the midst of wars between races and the battle against nature? Here the investigations and conjectures of contemporary science stop. But the religious traditions of people, interpreted according to their esoteric meaning, go further and allow us to imagine that the first concentration of the Aryan nucleus in Iran took place through a kind of selection. This latter was worked out in the very center of the white race, under the leadership of a conquering lawmaker who gave his people a religion and a law in harmony with the genius of the white race.

The holy book of the Persians, the *Zend-Avesta,* speaks of this ancient legislator under the name of Yima, and Zoroaster, in founding a new religion refers to him as the first man to whom Ormuzd, the living God, spoke. Jesus Christ refers to Moses in the same manner.—The Persian poet Firdausi calls this same lawmaker Djem, the conqueror of black men.—In the Hindu epic, the *Ramayana,* he appears under the name

47

Rama, is dressed like an Indian king, is surrounded by the splendors of a progressive civilization, but he retains his two distinctive characteristics of reforming conqueror and initiate. —In the Egyptian traditions, the time of Rama is indicated by the reign of Osiris, Lord of Light, which precedes the reign of Isis, Queen of Mysteries.—Finally, in Greece, the ancient hero-demigod was honored under the name Dionysius, which comes from the Sanskrit *Deva Nahusha,* the divine restorer. Orpheus even gave this name to the divine Intelligence, and the poet Nonnus sang of the conquest of India by Dionysius, according to the tradition of Eleusis.

Like radii of the same circle, all these traditions indicate a common center. By following their path one can reach it. Then, long before the India of the Vedas, before the Iran of Zoroaster, in the early dawn of the white race, one sees the first creator of the Aryan religion emerging from the forests of ancient Scythia, crowned with his twin tiara of conqueror and initiate, and bearing in his hand the mystical fire, the holy fire which will illumine all races.

It is to Fabre d'Olivet that the honor is due for having discovered this personality.[6] He marked out the bright path which leads to him, and in following this path I, in turn, shall attempt to call him forth.

2

The Mission of Rama

Four or five thousand years before our time, dense forest still covered ancient Scythia, which extended from the Atlantic Ocean to the Arctic Seas. This continent, which the black men had seen develop island by island, they called, "land emerging from the waves." How this land contrasted with their white soil, bleached by the sun, this Europe of green coasts, with humid, deeply indented bays, of dreamy rivers, somber lakes, and of mists, forever clinging to the sides of its mountains! On the grassy, uncultivated plains, vast like the pampas, one heard nothing but the call of deer, the roaring of buffalo and the gallop of the great herds of wild horses, shaking their manes in the wind. The white man who lived in the forests of ancient Scythia was no longer a cave man. Already he could call himself master of this land. He had invented flint knives and hatchets, bow and arrow, sling and bowstring. Finally he had found two battle companions, two excellent, incomparable, lifelong friends: the dog and the horse. The domesticated dog, having become the faithful guardian of his forest home, gave a sense of security to his house. In taming the horse, man had conquered the land and subjugated the other animals; he had become the king of space. Mounted on wild horses, these sandy-haired men rode like the lightning. They killed the bear, the wolf, the aurochs and frightened the panther and the lion who lived in our forests at that time.

Civilization had begun; the embryonic family, the clan and the tribe existed. Everywhere the Scythians, sons of the Hyperboreans, erected huge menhirs to their ancestors.

When a leader died, his arms and horse were buried with him so that, it was said, the warrior could ride across the clouds and chase the dragon of fire in the other world. Hence the custom of sacrificing the horse, which plays such an important role in the Vedas and among the Scandinavians. Religion thus began in the worship of ancestors.

The Semites found the one God, the universal Spirit, in the desert, on the mountain tops, in the immensity of stellar space. The Scythians and the Celts found their gods in the form of many spirits, in the heart of their forests. There they heard voices; there they experienced the first thrills of the Unseen, visions of the great Beyond. This is why the forest—delightful or dreadful—has remained dear to the white race. Charmed by the music of the leaves and the magic of the moon, in the course of the ages, men always return to it as to a fountain of youth, the temple of the great mother Hertha. There sleep men's gods, their loves, their lost Mysteries.

From the most remote times, visionary women prophesied under trees. Each tribe had its great prophetess, like the Voluspa of the Scandinavians, with her school of Druidesses. But these women, at first nobly inspired, became ambitious and cruel. The good prophetesses changed into evil magicians. They instituted human sacrifices, and the blood of their *Herôlls* flowed continuously over the dolmens, to the sinister chants of the priests and the approving shouts of the ferocious Scythians.

Among these priests was a young man in the prime of life; his name was Ram. Though he had been destined for the priesthood, his contemplative soul and penetrating mind rebelled against this bloody cult.

The young Druid was gentle and serious. Early in life he had shown remarkable knowledge of plants, their marvelous powers, the distilling and preparation of their juices, as well as the study of stars and their forces. He seemed to divine, to see far-off things. Hence his premature authority over the older Druids. A kindly greatness emanated from his words and his being. His wisdom contrasted with the madness of the Druidesses, those screechers of curses who pronounced their inauspicious oracles during convulsions of delirium. The Druids had called him "the one who knows," and the people called him "the inspired one of peace."

Nevertheless, Ram, striving after divine science, had travelled over all of Scythia and the southern countries. Fascinated by his personal knowledge and his modesty, the priests of the black men had revealed a part of their secret knowledge to him. When he returned to the northern country, Ram was frightened at seeing the cult of human sacrifices increasing more and more among his people. He saw in it the ruin of his race. But how could he fight this custom propagated by the arrogance of the Druidesses, the ambition of the Druids, and the superstition of the people? Then another calamity befell the white men, and Ram thought he saw in it heaven's punishment of the sacrilegious cult. From their expeditions into the southern countries and from their contact with the black men, the white men had brought back a terrible disease, a kind of plague. It infected men through the bloodstream, through the sources of life. The entire body became covered with black spots. The breath became foul, the swollen limbs, eaten by ulcers, became deformed, and the sick person died in excruciating pain. The breath of the living and the smell of the dead spread the plague widely. And white men, stupefied, fell and died by the thousands in their forests, abandoned even by birds of prey.

Deeply sorrowful, Ram vainly looked for a means of salvation.

He was in the habit of meditating under an oak tree in a glade. One evening, during which he had pondered for a long time over the evils of his race, he fell asleep at the foot of the tree. In his sleep it seemed to him that a loud voice was calling him by name, and he thought he awakened. Then he saw before him a man of majestic height, clothed like himself in the white robe of the Druids. He carried a rod, around which a snake was coiled. The astonished Ram was about to ask the stranger what it meant, but the latter, taking him by the hand, made him stand up and showed him a beautiful branch of mistletoe on the very tree at the foot of which he had been resting. "O Ram!" he said, "There is the remedy you seek." Then he took from his breast a little gold pruning knife, cut the branch, and gave it to him. He murmured a few words about the way to prepare the mistletoe, and disappeared.

Then Ram awakened fully, feeling very deeply comforted. An inner voice told him that he had found salvation. He prepared the mistletoe according to the instructions of the divine friend with the golden sickle. Then he made a sick man drink this brew in a fermented liquor, and the patient was cured. The marvelous healings he brought about made Ram famous in all Scythia. He was summoned everywhere for healing work. When consulted by the Druids of his tribe, he shared his discovery with them, adding that it must remain the secret of the priestly caste in order to insure its power. Ram's disciples, traveling over all Scythia with branches of mistletoe, were considered divine messengers and their master a demigod.

This event marked the origin of a new cult. From this time on, the mistletoe became a sacred plant. Ram perpetuated its fame by instituting the holiday of Noel, or of the new salvation, which he placed at the beginning of the year, calling it the Night Mother of the universe, or of the great renewal. As for the mysterious being whom Ram had seen in a dream and who had shown him the mistletoe, in the esoteric tradition of the white men of Europe he is called *Aesc-heyl-hopa,* which means "hope for salvation is in the forests." The Greeks called him Aesculapius, the genius of medicine who holds the magic rod in the form of a caduceus.

Nevertheless, Ram, "the inspired one of peace," had broader plans. He wanted to cure his people of a moral wound more disastrous than the plague. Chosen chief of the priests of his tribe, he issued an order that all the schools of the Druids and Druidesses were to stop making human sacrifices. This news spread to the ocean, hailed as a joyful event by some, as an outrageous sacrilege by others. Their power threatened, the Druidesses began to scream curses upon the presumptuous man, to hurl death sentences against him. Many Druids who saw in human sacrifices their only means of power, joined them. Ram, extolled by a large group, was hated by others. But rather than withdraw from the battle, he aggravated it by establishing a new symbol.

At that time each white tribe had its rallying sign in the form of an animal which symbolized its chosen qualities. Some of the chiefs nailed cranes, eagles or vultures to the framework of their wooden houses; others, the heads of wild boars or buffalo. This is the origin of the coat-of-arms. But the chosen emblem of the Scythians was the bull, which they called Thor, the sign of brute force and violence. Ram took the figure of the ram, the courageous, peaceful leader of the flock, in place of the bull, and made it the rallying sign of his followers. This emblem, established in the midst of Scythia, became the signal for a great clamor and an actual revolution in men's thought. The white people divided into two camps. The very soul of the white race was split in half, in order to free itself from animality, so that it might climb the first step of the invisible sanctuary which leads to divine mankind. "Death to the Ram!" shouted Thor's supporters. "War on the Bull!" shouted Ram's friends. A fearful war was imminent.

In the face of this threat, Ram hesitated. If war were let loose, would this not intensify the evil and force his race to destroy itself? At this moment he had another dream.

The stormy heaven was filled with dark clouds which swept over the mountains and moved above the bending trees of the forest. Standing on a rock, a wild-haired woman was about to strike a fine warrior who was tied before her. "In the name of the ancestors, Stop!" shouted Ram, throwing himself upon the woman. The Druidess, threatening her adversary, gave Ram a look as piercing as the blade of a knife. But the thunder rolled in the thick clouds, and amidst a flash of lightning a dazzling figure appeared. The forest paled before it. The Druidess fell as if thunderstruck, and the bonds of the captive having been broken, he looked at the shining giant with a gesture of defiance. Ram did not tremble, for in the features of the apparition he recognized the divine being who had already spoken to him beneath the oak tree. This time he appeared more beautiful, for his entire body shone with light. And Ram saw that he was in an open temple with broad columns. In the place of the sacrificial stone, an altar was raised. Nearby stood the warrior whose eyes still feared death. The woman lying on the flagstones, appeared to be dead. And now the heavenly genius carried a torch in his right hand; in his left hand was a cup. He smiled benevolently, saying, "Ram, I am pleased with you. Do you see this torch? It is the sacred fire of the divine Spirit. Do you see this cup? It is the cup of Life and Love. Give the torch to the man, the cup to the woman." Ram did as his genius commanded him. Hardly was the torch in the man's hand and the cup in the woman's, than the fire lighted of itself on the altar, and both shone transfigured in the light, like the divine husband and wife. At the same time the temple grew larger; its columns mounted to heaven; its vault became the firmament. Then, carried by his dream, Ram saw himself borne to the top of a mountain under the starry sky. Standing near him, his genius explained the meaning of the constellations, and in the flaming signs of the zodiac Ram read the destinies of mankind.

"Wonderful spirit, who are you?" Ram asked the genius. And the genius replied, "I am called *Deva Nahusha*, divine Intelligence. You will spread my light over the earth, and I shall always come at your call. Now, be on your way. Go!" And with his hand, the genius pointed toward the East.

3

Exodus and Conquest

In this dream, as in a flash of lightning, Ram saw his mission and the great destiny of his race. From that moment he no longer hesitated. Instead of igniting the spark of war among the peoples of Europe, he decided to take the best of his race into Asia. He announced to his people that he would institute the cult of the sacred fire, which would bring about mankind's happiness; that human sacrifices would be abolished forever; that ancestors would be invoked no longer by bloodthirsty priestesses beside savage rocks dripping with human blood, but in each home, by husband and wife joined in a single prayer, in a hymn of adoration, near the fire which purifies. Yes, the visible fire of the altar, symbol and conductor of the invisible celestial fire, would unite family, clan, tribe and all peoples—a center of the living God on earth. But in order to reap this harvest, it was necessary to separate the good grain from the tares; it was necessary for the bravest to prepare themselves to leave Europe in order to conquer a new land, a virgin country. There he would issue his law; there he would establish the cult of the regenerating fire.

This proposal was received enthusiastically by a young people, yearning for adventure. Lighted fires, kept burning for several months on the mountains, were the signal for the mass migration of all who wished to follow the Ram. The tremendous migration, directed by that great shepherd of peoples, slowly started to move, departing in the direction of Central Asia. Among the Caucasus Mountains were several Cyclopean strongholds of the black men which had to be captured. In memory of these victories, the white people later carved huge rams' heads in the rocks of the Caucasus.

Ram proved himself worthy of his great mission. He smoothed out difficulties, read thoughts, predicted the future, healed the sick, calmed the rebels, set courage aflame. Thus the heavenly powers which we call Providence willed the rule of the northern race on earth, and by means of Ram's wisdom, cast shining light upon its path. Lesser inspired leaders had already rescued this race from its savage state. But Ram, who first conceived of social law as an expression of divine law, was truly a straightforward, inspired man of the highest order.

He made friends with the Turanians, old Scythian tribes who inhabited upper Asia, and led them in the conquest of Iran, where he completely repelled the black men, for he intended that a people of unmixed white race would inhabit Central Asia and become a center of light for all others. He founded the city of Ver, which Zoroaster called an admirable city. He taught men how to till and sow seed in the soil; he was the father of cultivated wheat and of the vine. He created classes according to occupations and divided the people into priests, warriors, laborers and artisans. In the beginning, the classes were not at all rivals. The hereditary privilege, source of hatred and jealousy, was introduced only later. He forbade slavery as well as murder, stating that slavery was the cause of all evils. As for the tribe, that primitive grouping of the white race, he preserved it as it was, allowing it to elect its leaders and judges.

Ram's crowning work, the pre-eminently civilizing instrument created by him, was the new role he gave to woman. Until that time, man had considered woman either as a wretched slave whom he overburdened and brutally mistreated, or as the turbulent priestess of the oak tree and rock, from whom he sought protection and who ruled him in spite of himself—a fascinating, dreadful sorceress whose oracles he feared and before whom his superstitious heart trembled. Human sacrifice was woman's revenge against man, when she sank the knife into the fierce male tyrant's heart. Outlawing this horrible cult and reëstablishing woman in man's estimation in her divine function as wife and mother, Ram made her the priestess of the hearth, the guardian of the sacred fire, the equal of her husband, the one who joined with him in calling upon the souls of the ancestors.

Like all great legislators, Ram did nothing more than develop and organize the great instincts of his race. In order to enhance and beautify life, Ram ordained four great yearly festivals. The first was that of the spring or of generations. It was dedicated to the love of husband and wife. The festival of summer or of harvest belonged to the sons and daughters, who offered the fruit of their labor to the parents. The festival of autumn feted fathers and mothers; they then gave fruit to their children as a sign of rejoicing. The holiest and most mysterious of festivals was Noel, or the great sowing-time. Ram dedicated it both to new-born children, the fruits of love conceived in spring, and to the souls of the dead, to the ancestors. A point of connection between the visible and the invisible, this religious observance was both a farewell to souls in flight, and a mystical greeting to those who returned to be reincarnated in the mothers, to be reborn in children. On this holy night, the ancient Aryans assembled in the sanctuaries of Airyana-Vaeia as they had formerly in their forests. With fires and chants they celebrated the renewal of the earthly and solar year, the germination of nature in the heart of winter, the trembling of life before the abyss of death. They sang of the universal kiss of heaven given to earth, and the triumphant birth of the new sun from the great Night-Mother.

Thus Ram linked human life with the cycle of the seasons and with the movements of the stars. At the same time he emphasized its divine significance. Because he founded such productive institutions, Zoroaster called him "the leader of peoples, the most blessed monarch." This is why the Hindu poet Valmiki, who places the ancient hero in a much more recent period, surrounded by the luxury of a more advanced civilization, nevertheless preserves in him the characteristics of such a high ideal. "Rama with lotus blue eyes," said Valmiki, "was lord of the world, master of his soul, and the object of men's love. He was the father and mother of his subjects. *He knew how to bestow upon all beings the bond of love.*"

Once settled in Iran, at the gates of the Himalaya Mountains, the white race was not yet ruler of the world. It was necessary that its vanguard push onward into India, the main center of the black men, ancient conquerors of the red and yellow races. The *Zend-Avesta* speaks of this march of Rama[7] on India. The Hindu epic makes it one of its favorite themes. Rama was the conqueror of the land which the Himavat encircles, the land of elephants, tigers and gazelles. He ordered the first attack, and led the first thrust of this colossal battle in which two races unconsciously contended for the scepter of the world. Poetic tradition of India, elaborating upon the secret traditions of the temples, transformed their struggle into a fight between black and white magic. In his war against the peoples and kings of the land of the Jambus, as it was then called, Ram or Rama, as the Orientals named him, employed means which appear miraculous simply because they are beyond the ordinary capacities of mankind. Other great initiates attain similar results, due to their knowledge and manipulation of the hidden forces of nature. Here tradition shows Rama causing streams to burst forth in the desert, finding in these unexpected resources a kind of balm whose use he taught; elsewhere he puts an end to an epidemic with a plant called *homa* (Greek *amomon*, Egyptian *persea*) from which he extracted a healing essence. This plant became sacred among his followers, replacing the mistletoe of the oak tree, preserved by the Celts of Europe.

Rama made use of all kinds of magic spells against his enemies. The priests of the black men ruled only by means of a decadent cult. In their temples they were in the habit of keeping enormous snakes and pterodactyls, rare survivors of antediluvian animals, which were worshiped like gods, and which terrified the masses. They made these snakes eat the flesh of captives. Sometimes Rama appeared unexpectedly in these temples with torches, driving out, frightening and subduing both serpents and priests. Sometimes he appeared in the midst of his enemies, exposed and defenseless among those who sought his death, departing again without anyone having dared touch him. When those who had allowed him to escape were questioned, they answered that upon meeting his gaze they were petrified, or that, while he was speaking, a mountain of brass was placed between them and him and they could not see him. Finally, as a consummation of his work, the epic tradition of India attributed to Rama the conquest of Ceylon, last refuge of the black magician Ravana, on whom the white magician showered down fire, first having formed a bridge over the sea by means of an army of monkeys closely resembling some primitive tribe of bimanous savages, led and inspired by this great charmer of nations.

4

The Last Will
of the Great Ancestor

THROUGH his strength, genius and kindness, say the sacred books of the Orient, Rama became master of India and spiritual king of the earth. Priests, kings and people bowed down before him as before a heavenly benefactor. Under the sign of the ram his missionaries spread afar the Aryan law which proclaimed equality of conquerors and conquered, the abolition of human sacrifice and slavery, respect for the woman in the home, the worship of ancestors and the institution of the sacred fire, visible symbol of the nameless God.

Rama had grown old. His beard had become white, but the strength had not left his body and the majesty of the pontiffs of truth reposed on his forehead. The kings and the representatives of the people offered him absolute authority. He requested one year to think it over, and again had a dream. The genius who inspired him, spoke to him in his sleep.

He saw himself once more in the forests of his youth. He had become young again, and was wearing the linen robe of the Druids. The moon was shining. It was the holy night, the

Night-Mother, when people await the rebirth of the sun and the year. Rama was walking under the oak trees, listening to the voices of the forest. A beautiful woman came to him. She was wearing a magnificent crown. Her hair was the color of gold, her skin the whiteness of snow, and her eyes had the deep luster of the sky after a storm. She said to him, "I was the savage Druidess; through you I have become the radiant wife. And now my name is Sita. I am the woman glorified by you. I am the white race; I am your wife. O, my master and my king, is it not for my sake that you crossed rivers, charmed peoples and deposed kings? This is the reward. Take this crown in your hand, put it on your head and rule the world with me." She knelt humbly and submissively, offering him the crown of the earth. Its precious stones radiated a thousand lights, the rapture of love smiled in the woman's eyes and the soul of the great Rama, shepherd of the peoples, was touched. But, above the forests, Deva Nahusha, his genius, appeared and said to him, "If you place that crown upon your head, divine Intelligence will leave you; you will see me no longer. If you clasp this woman in your arms, she will die of your happiness. But if you refuse to possess her she will live happy and free on earth, and your invisible spirit will reign over her. Choose! Either listen to her or follow me." Sita, still kneeling, looked at her master, her eyes overflowing with love, pleadingly awaiting his answer. Rama remained silent for a moment. He looked deep into Sita's eyes, considering the gulf which separates complete possession from an everlasting farewell. But feeling that supreme love is supreme abnegation, he placed his liberating hand on the white woman's forehead, blessed her, and said, "Farewell! You are free. Do not forget me!"

Immediately the woman disappeared like a lunar phantom. Young Aurora raised her magic wand above the ancient forest. The king became old again. A shower of tears bathed his white beard, and from the depths of the woods a mournful voice called "Rama, Rama!"

But Deva Nahusha, the genius shining with light, exclaimed, "Come to me!" And the divine spirit carried Rama off to a mountain in the north of Himavat.

After this dream which showed him the fulfilment of his mission, Rama assembled the kings and representatives of the people, saying to them, "I do not desire the supreme power you offer me. Keep your crowns and observe my law. My task is finished. I am retiring forever with my fellow initiates to a mountain of Airyana-Vaeia. From there I shall watch over you. Guard the sacred fire! If it should happen to die out, I shall reappear among you as a judge and terrible avenger!" After this he withdrew with his intimate followers to Mount Albori between Balk and Bamyan, and entered into a retreat known to the initiates alone. There he taught his disciples what he knew of the earth and the Great Being. Then they went out to carry into Egypt and as far as Occitania the sacred fire, symbol of the divine unity of things, and the horns of the ram, emblem of the Aryan religion. These horns became the insignia of initiation and later of priestly and royal power.[8] From a distance Rama continued to watch over his people and over his beloved white race. The last years of his life were spent in arranging the calendar of the Aryans. We owe the signs of the zodiac to him. It is the last work of the patriarch of the initiates, a strange book, written with stars in heavenly hieroglyphics in the immeasurable, boundless firmament, by the Ancient of Days of our race. In establishing the twelve signs of the zodiac, Ram attributed a triple meaning to them. The first referred to the powers of the sun during the twelve months of the year; the second, to a certain extent told his own story; the third indicated the secret means he had used to attain his goal. This is why the signs, read in reverse order, later became the secret emblems of progressive initiation.[9] He ordered his friends to keep his death secret and to continue his work by perpetuating their brotherhood. For centuries people believed that Rama, wearing the tiara of ram's horns, was still alive on the holy mountain. In Vedic times the Great Ancestor became Yama, the judge of the dead, the psychopomp Hermes of the Hindus.

5

The Vedic Religion

THROUGH his genius for organizing, the great initiator of the
Aryans had created in Central Asia and Iran, a people, a society, a living impulse which was to radiate in all directions.
The colonies of the primitive Aryans spread into Asia and
Europe, carrying with them their customs, cults and gods. Of
all the colonies, the branch of the Aryans of India most closely
resembles the primitive Aryans.

The sacred books of the Hindus, the Vedas, have a threefold
value for us. First, they lead us to the home of the ancient, pure
Aryan religion, of which the Vedic hymns are brilliant rays. In
addition, they give us the key to India. Finally, they show us an
initial crystallization of basic ideas of esoteric doctrine and of
all Aryan religions.[10]

Let us confine ourselves to a brief sketch of both the exterior
and the heart of the Vedic religion.

There is nothing simpler and greater than this religion, in
which an intense naturalism is mixed with a transcendant spirituality. Before sunrise, a man—the head of a family—is stand-

65

ing before an earth altar where a fire, lighted with two pieces of wood, burns. At one and the same time this man is father, priest and king of the sacrifice. "While Dawn disrobes," as a Vedic poet says, "like a woman leaving her bath:—Dawn who has woven the loveliest of cloths," the leader repeats a prayer, an invocation to *Usha* (the Dawn), to *Savitar* (the Sun), and the *Asuras* (the spirits of life). The mother and sons pour the fermented liquors of the *asclepus,* the *soma,* into *Agni,* the fire, and the rising flame carries to the invisible gods the purified prayer spoken by the patriarch and the heart of the family.

The state of mind of the Vedic poet is far removed from both Hellenic sensualism (I refer to the popular cults of Greece, not the doctrine of the Greek initiates) and from the Judaic monotheism which worships the formless, omnipresent Lord.

For the Vedic poet, nature resembles a transparent veil, behind which move imponderable divine forces. These powers are the forces he calls upon, worships and personifies, but without being deceived by his metaphors. For him Savitar is less sun than Vivasvat, the creative power of life, who animates man and who moves the solar system. Indra, the divine warrior, crossing the sky in his gilded chariot, hurling thunder and making the clouds burst, personifies the powers of this same sun in atmospheric life, in "the great transparency of the atmosphere." When they call upon Varuna, the Greek Uranus, god of the vast, luminous sky, who embraces everything, the Vedic poets go even higher. "If Indra represents the active, militant life of heaven, Varuna represents its unchangeable majesty. Nothing equals the magnificence of the descriptions the hymns give of him. The sun is his eye, the sky his clothing, the hurricane his breath. It is he who established heaven and earth on unshakeable foundations, and who keeps them separate. He made everything and preserves everything. No one can touch the works of Varuna, no one fathoms him, but he knows all and sees all that is and will be. In the heights of heaven he lives in a palace with a thousand doors; he watches the path of the birds in the air and of ships on the seas. From that point, from the height of his golden throne with its brass foundation, he surveys and judges the deeds of men. He is the preserver of order in the universe and in society; he punishes the guilty; he is merciful to the man who repents. And to him the anguished cry of remorse is raised; before his presence the sinner comes to rid himself of the weight of his error. Elsewhere Vedic religion is ritualistic, sometimes highly speculative. With Varuna it goes down into the depths of consciousness and realizes the notion of holiness." In addition, it elevates itself to the pure idea of one God who permeates and overlooks the great All.

Nevertheless, the imposing pictures the Vedic hymns unroll in great quantity like bountiful rivers, present to us only the exterior sheath of the Vedas. With the conception of *Agni*, the divine fire, we are very close to the core of the doctrine and its esoteric, transcendent foundation. In fact, *Agni* is the cosmic agent, the principle of the universe, par excellence. "It is not only the terrestrial fire of lightning and the sun. Its true domain is the unseen, mystical heaven, temporary dwelling-place of the eternal light and of the first principles of all things. Its births are infinite, whether it bursts forth from the piece of wood in which it sleeps like the embryo in the womb, or whether as a 'child of the waves,' it issues with the noise of thunder from celestial rivers where the *Acvins* (celestial horsemen) engendered it with *aranis* of gold. *Agni* is the eldest of the gods, ruler in heaven as well as on earth, and he officiated in the abode of Vivasvat (the sky or sun) long before Matharicva (the lightning) brought him to mortals and Atharvan and the Angiras, ancient high priests, appointed him here below as protector, host and friend of men. Master and generator of the sacrifice, *Agni* becomes the bearer of all mystical speculations of which sacrifice is the purpose. *He engenders the gods,* he organizes the world, he produces and preserves universal life; in short, he is *cosmogonic power.*

"*Soma* is the teardrop of *Agni.* In reality it is the drink of a fermented plant poured as a libation to the gods during the sacrifice. But, like *Agni,* it has a mystical existence. Its supreme abode is in the depths of the third heaven where Surya, daughter of the sun, filtered it, and where Pushan, food-giving god, bound it. It is from there that the Falcon, a symbol of lightning, or *Agni* himself went and snatched it from the heavenly Archer, from Gandharva its guardian, and brought it to men. The gods drank it and became immortal; men also will become immortal when they drink it in the home of Yama, dwelling-place of the happy. In the meantime, here below it gives them vigor and fullness of life; it is ambrosia and the water of youth. It nourishes, permeates plants, invigorates the semen of animals, inspires the poet and provides wings for prayer. *Soul of heaven and of earth, of Indra and Vishnu, with Agni, it forms an inseparable couple; this couple that lighted the sun and stars.*"

The conception of Agni and Soma contains the two essential principles of the universe, according to esoteric doctrine and all living philosophy. Agni is the *Eternal Masculine,* the creative intellect, pure spirit; Soma is the *Eternal Feminine,* the soul of the world, or the ethereal substance, womb of all the visible and invisible worlds before the eyes of the flesh, and finally nature, or subtle matter in its infinite transformations.[11] And the perfect union of these two beings constitutes the supreme being and essence of God.

From these two major ideas springs a third and no less fecund one. The Vedas make of *the cosmogonic act a perpetual sacrifice.* In order to produce all that exists, the supreme being sacrifices himself; he divides himself in order to emerge from his unity. This sacrifice therefore is considered the vital point of all the functions of nature. This idea, surprising at first, very profound when one considers it further, contains in embryo the entire theosophic teaching of the evolution of God in the world, the esoteric synthesis of polytheism and monotheism. It will lead to the Dionysiac teaching of the fall and redemption of souls, which will have full expression in Hermes and Orpheus. From this will arise the doctrine of the Holy Word, proclaimed by Krishna and fulfilled by Jesus Christ.

The fire sacrifice with its ceremonies and prayers, the unchangeable center of the Vedic cult, thus becomes the reflection of this great cosmogonic act. The Vedas attach a capital importance to prayer, to the form of invocation which accompanies sacrifice. For this reason they make a goddess of prayer, Brahmanaspati. Faith in the evocative and creative power of human speech, accompanied by a powerful activity of the soul or an intense projection of will is the source of all cults, and the reason for the Egyptian and Chaldean doctrine of magic. For the Vedic and Brahmanic priests, by means of fire, chants and prayers, called upon the Asuras, the invisible Lords, and the Pitris or souls of ancestors, whom they believed seated themselves upon the grass during the sacrifice, attracted by the fire, the songs and the prayers. The science relating to this aspect of the cult involves the hierarchy of spirits of every rank.

As for the immortality of the soul, the Vedas confirm this with unmistakable clarity. "There is an immortal side to man; that is the one, O Agni, which you must warm with your rays and quicken with your fires. O Jatavedas, in the glorious body, formed by you, carry it to the world of the godly." The Vedic poets not only indicate the destiny of the soul, but are also concerned with its origin. "Where were souls born? There are those who come to us and return, who return and come back again." That in brief is the doctrine of reincarnation, which will play a major role in Brahmanism and Buddhism, among the Egyptians and the Orphics, in the philosophy of Pythagoras and Plato, the mystery of mysteries, the secret of secrets.

After this, how can one not recognize in the Vedas the broad lines of an organic religious system, a philosophic concept of the universe? In them is not only the profound intuition of anterior intellectual truth, superior to the observation, but also unity and breadth of vision in the understanding of nature and in the coordination of its phenomena. Like a beautiful rock crystal, the consciousness of the Vedic poet reflects the sunshine of eternal truth, and in this brilliant prism shine all the rays of a universal theosophy. The principles of the eternal teaching are even more visible here than in the other sacred books of India and in the other Semitic or Aryan religions, because of the extraordinary directness of the Vedic poets and the clarity of this primitive religion, so lofty and so pure. At that time, the distinction between the mysteries and popular worship did not exist. But in carefully reading the Vedas, behind the father of the family or the officiating poet of the hymns, one already perceives another more important person. One glimpses the Rishi, the wise man, the initiate, from whom he received the truth. One also observes that this truth was transmitted by an uninterrupted tradition which dates back to the beginnings of the Aryan race.

Thus, then, is the Aryan people launched in its conquering, civilizing career along the Indus and Ganges. Rama's invisible genius, the knowledge of things divine, Deva Nahusha rules over it. Agni, the sacred fire, flows in its veins. A rose-tinted aura surrounds this age of youth, power and virility. The family is established, the woman respected. Priestess of the home, sometimes she herself composes and sings the hymns. "May this wife and husand live one hundred autumns," said a poet. They love life, but they also believe in the after-life. The king lives in a castle on a hill which overlooks the village. In war he is set upon a splendid chariot, clothed in shining armor, wearing a tiara; he shines like the god Indra.

Later, when the Brahmans have established their authority, near the magnificent palace of the *maharaja* or great king, one sees the stone pagoda from which come the arts, the poetry and drama of the gods, pantomimed and danced by sacred dancers. Castes exist for the moment, but not in a strict sense and without absolute boundaries. The warrior is priest, and the priest, warrior; more often he is the chief or king's officiating priest.

Now here comes an individual, poor in appearance but with a rich future. His hair and beard are unkempt, he is half-clothed in red rags. This *muni*, this recluse, lives near the holy lakes, in a wild place where he gives himself to meditation and the ascetic life. From time to time he comes to admonish the leader or king. Often he is pushed aside and disobeyed, but he is respected and feared. Already he exercises a terrible power.

Between the king on his gilded chariot, surrounded by warriors, and the almost naked *muni*, having no weapons other than his thought, his speech and his gaze, a battle will take place. And the conqueror will not be the king; it will be the recluse, the almost fleshless, emaciated beggar, because he will have knowledge and strength.

The story of this battle is the same as that of Brahmanism, as later it will be that of Buddhism. In it is summed up almost all of India's history.

KRISHNA

India and Brahmanic Initiation

He who creates worlds without ceasing is threefold. He is Brahma, the Father; he is Maya, the Mother; he is Vishnu, the Son; Essence, Substance and Life, each includes the others, and all three are one in the Ineffable.

—Brahmanic Doctrine, Upanishads

Thou carriest within thee a sublime Friend whom thou knowest not. For God dwells in the inner part of every man, but few know how to find Him. The man who sacrifices his desires and his works to the Beings from whom the principles of everything stem, and by whom the Universe was formed, through this sacrifice attains perfection. For one who finds his happiness and joy within himself, and also his wisdom within himself is one with God. And, mark well, the soul which has found God is freed from rebirth and death, from old age and pain, and drinks the water of Immortality.

—Bhagavad-Gita

6

Heroic India
The Sons of the Sun
and The Sons of the Moon

From the conquest of India by the Aryans emerged one of the most glorious civilizations the earth has ever known. The Ganges and its tributaries saw great empires and vast capitals arise, like Ayodhya, Hastinapura and Indrapechta. The epic accounts of the *Mahabharata* and the popular cosmogonies of the Puranas, which include the oldest historical traditions of India, speak dazzlingly of royal opulence, of heroic grandeur and of the chivalrous spirit of those vanished times. Nothing more proud nor yet more noble can be imagined than one of those Aryan kings of India standing on his war chariot and commanding armies of elephants, horses and infantrymen. A Vedic priest consecrates his king before the assembled crowd in this manner: "I have brought you into our midst. All of the people want you. Heaven is firm, earth is firm; these mountains are firm; may the king of families be firm also." In a later code of laws, the *Manava-Dharma-Sástra,* one reads, "These masters of the world who, eager to get rid of one another, unleash their strength in battle without flinching, after their death go directly to heaven." In fact, they consider themselves descendants of the gods and believe themselves their rivals, ready to become gods themselves. Filial obedience, military valor, with a sense of unselfish protection for all, is man's ideal. As for woman, the Hindu epic, humble servant of the Brahmans, hardly ever depicts her except with the qualities of the faithful wife. In their poems neither the Greeks nor the peoples of the North have portrayed such delicate, noble and exalted wives as the passionate Sita or the gentle Damayanti.

What the Hindu epic does not tell us is the deep mystery of the mixture of races and the slow incubation of religious ideas which brought about profound changes in the social organization of Vedic India. The Aryans, pure-blooded conquerors, found themselves in the presence of very mixed and inferior races, where the yellow and red types intermixed with blacks in many nuances. The Hindu civilization thus appears as a mighty mountain, at its base a melanian race, mixed bloods on its sides, pure Aryans on its summit. Since the separation of the caste was not rigid in primitive times, many mixtures took place among these peoples. The purity of the conquering race changed more and more with the centuries, but to this day one sees the predominance of the Aryan type in the higher classes and the melanian type in the lower classes. And, from the lower levels of Hindu society, like the miasmas of the jungle mixed with the odor of wild beasts, always arose a burning vapor of passions, a mixture of languor and ferocity. Superabundant black blood gave India her special color. It attenuated and weakened the race. The miracle is that despite this mixing and so many changes, the dominant ideas of the white race could be preserved at the peak of this civilization.

This, then, is the ethnic base of India: on the one hand, the genius of the white race with its moral sense and sublime metaphysical aspirations; on the other, the genius of the black race with its passionate energy and solvent strength. How is this double genius expressed in the ancient religious history of India? The oldest traditions speak of a solar dynasty and a lunar dynasty. The kings of the solar dynasty claim their descent from the sun. The others considered themselves to be sons of the moon. But this symbolic language concealed two opposing religious concepts and meant that these two categories of sovereigns were related to two different cults. The solar cult attributed the male sex to the God of the universe. Around it was grouped all that was purest in the Vedic tradition: the science of the sacred fire and of prayer, the esoteric conception of the supreme God, respect for woman, ancestor worship, elected and patriarchal royalty. The lunar cult attributed the feminine sex to divinity, under whose sign the religions of the Aryan cycle have always worshipped nature, even blind, unconscious nature in its violent, terrible manifestations. This cult leaned toward idolatry and black magic, preferred polygamy and tyranny, supported by the passions of the masses. The battle between the sons of the sun and the sons of the moon, between the Pandavas and Kuravas, is the theme of the great Hindu epic, the *Mahabharata,* a kind of summary in perspective of the history of Aryan India before the definitive formation of Brahmanism. This battle abounds in spirited combats and strange, endless adventures. In the middle of this gigantic epic, the Kuravas, the lunar kings, become the conquerors. The Pandavas, noble children of the sun, guardians of the pure rites, are dethroned and banished. As exiles they hide in the forests, seeking refuge among the anchorites, wearing clothing made of bark, and leaning on hermits' sticks.

Will the baser instincts triumph? Are the powers of darkness, represented in the Hindu epic by the black Rakshasas, to be victorious over the enlightened Devas? Will tyranny crush the elite beneath its chariot of war, the cyclone of evil passions destroy the Vedic altar and extinguish the sacred fire of the ancestors? No. India is only at the beginning of her religious evolution. She will display her metaphysical and organizing genius in the establishment of Brahmanism. The priests who served the kings and chiefs under the name of *purohitas,* those placed in charge of the fire sacrifice, had already become their advisors and ministers. They had great wealth and considerable prestige. But they would not have been able to give to their caste that sovereign authority, that position above attack, even from royal power itself, without the aid of another group of men who personify the spirit of India in its most original and profound sense. These are the anchorites.

From time immemorial these ascetics dwelt in retreats in the depth of the forests, beside rivers, or in the mountains near sacred lakes. They were sometimes found alone, sometimes assembled into brotherhoods, but always united in a single spirit. One recognizes in them the spiritual kings, the real masters of India. Heirs of the ancient wise men, the Rishis, they alone held the secret interpretation of the Vedas. In them lived the spirit of asceticism, hidden knowledge and transcendant powers. In order to obtain this wisdom they endured everything in the form of hunger, cold, burning sun, the terror of the jungles. Defenseless in their wooden huts, they live in prayer and meditation. With their voice, their gaze, they summon or drive away serpents, and calm lions and tigers. Happy is one who obtains their blessing, for he will have the Devas as friends! Woe to one who abuses or kills them, for their curse, say the poets, follows the guilty one to his third incarnation! Kings tremble at their threats, and, strangely enough, these ascetics themselves cause the gods to be afraid. In the *Ramayana,* Visvamitra, a king who became an ascetic, acquires such power through his strictness and meditation that the gods tremble for their lives. Then Indra sends him the most captivating of the Apsaras, who comes to bathe in the lake in front of the saint's hut. The anchorite is seduced by the celestial nymph; a hero is born from their union, and for several thousand years the existence of the universe is assured. Beneath these poetic exaggerations one senses the true superior power of the anchorites of the white race who, with acute divination and strong will, rule the turbulent soul of India from the depths of their forests.

From the midst of the brotherhood of anchorites was to emerge the priestly revolution that made India the most formidable of theocracies. The victory of spiritual power over temporal power, of the anchorite over the king, out of which the power of Brahmanism was born, came in the guise of a reformer of the first rank. By reconciling the two warring groups, the white race and the black race, the solar cults and the lunar cults, this divine being was the true creator of the national religion of India. Moreover, through his teaching this powerful genius introduced a new idea of immense significance into the world: the holy word, or divinity manifest in man. This first of the Messiahs, this eldest of the sons of God, was Krishna.

His legend is principally interesting in that it sums up and dramatizes all Brahmanic doctrine. But it has remained scattered and unformed in tradition because the Hindu genius entirely lacks plastic force. The confusing and mythical account of *Vishnu-Pourana* nevertheless contains some historic facts about Krishna which are of a personal and striking nature. On the other hand, the *Bhagavad-Gita,* that wonderful fragment interpolated into the great poem, the *Mahabhârata,* which the Brahmans consider one of their most sacred books, contains in all purity the doctrine attributed to him. It was while reading these two books that the face of the great religious initiator of India appeared before me with the power of a living person. Therefore, I shall relate the story of Krishna, drawing upon these two sources, one of which represents popular tradition, the other, that of the initiates.

7

The King of Madura

A T the beginning of the *Kali-Yuga Age,* around the year 3,000
B.C., according to the chronology of the Brahmans, the
thirst for gold and power invaded the world. For several centuries, the ancient sages say, Agni, the celestial fire which forms
the glorious body of the Devas and purifies the souls of men, had
spread its ethereal effluences over the earth. But the burning
breath of Kali, goddess of desire and death, who comes out of
the abysses of the earth like a fiery exhalation, then passed over
all hearts. Justice had reigned with the noble sons of Pandu,
solar kings who obeyed the voices of the wise men. As victors
they pardoned the conquered, and treated them as equals. But
since the children of the sun had been exterminated or driven
from their thrones, and their few descendants were hiding
among the anchorites, injustice, ambition and hatred had
gained the upper hand. Changeable and deceitful like the nocturnal body which they had taken as their symbol, the lunar
kings engaged in a merciless war among themselves. Neverthe-

less, one had succeeded in overcoming all the others by means of terror and unusual powers.

In northern India, on the banks of a wide river, a powerful city flourished. It had twelve pagodas, ten palaces and one hundred gates flanked with towers. Multicolored banners floated over its high walls, resembling winged serpents. This was proud Madura, impregnable like Indra's fortress. Kansa reigned there with a crafty mind and an insatiable soul. He allowed only slaves around him; he thought he owned only what he had subjugated, but what he possessed seemed nothing to him, compared with what remained to be conquered. All the kings who recognized the lunar cult paid him homage. But Kansa dreamed of conquering all India, from Lanka to the Himavat. In order to execute this plan, he allied himself with Kalayeni, master of the Vyndhia Mountains, the powerful king of the Yavanas, men with yellow faces. As one of the goddess Kali's followers, Kalayeni had dedicated himself to the mysterious arts of black magic. He was called the friend of the Rakshasis, nocturnal demons, and the king of serpents because he used the latter to frighten his people and his enemies. At the far end of a dense forest was the goddess Kali's temple, carved in a mountain. It was a great dark cave of unknown depth; the entrance was guarded by giants with animal heads, carved in the rock. There they led those who wished to pay homage to Kalayeni, in order to obtain from him some secret power. He would appear at the entrance of the temple in the midst of a host of monstrous snakes that entwined themselves around his body and rose up at the command of his scepter. He forced his tributaries to kneel before these serpents whose heads, twisted into knots, hung over his. At the same time he muttered a mysterious formula. It was said that those who performed this rite and worshipped those serpents obtained tremendous gifts and everything they desired. But they fell irrevocably under Kala-

yeni's power. Far or near, they remained his slaves. If they tried
to disobey him or escape him, they thought they saw the terrible
magician, surrounded by his reptiles, arise before them; they
saw themselves encompassed by the serpents' hissing heads, and
were paralyzed by their spell-binding eyes. Kansa asked Kalayeni for his support. The king of the Yavanas promised him
dominion over the earth, provided he would marry his daughter.

Proud as an antelope and supple as a serpent was the daughter of the magician king, the beautiful Nysumba, with golden
pendants and ebony breasts. Her face resembled a dark cloud
with nuances of bluish reflections from the moon; her eyes
were like two lightning flashes, her warm lips like the pulp of a
red fruit with white seeds. One might have thought she was
Kali herself, the goddess of desire. Soon she reigned as mistress
over Kansa's heart, and breathing upon all his passions, turned
them into a glowing furnace. Kansa had a palace filled with
women of every color, but he listened only to Nysumba.

"If I may have a son from you," he told her, "I shall make
him my heir. Then I shall be master of the earth; I shall no
longer fear anyone."

But Nysumba did not have a son, and she became angry. She
was jealous of Kansa's other wives, whose love had been more
fruitful. She made her father increase the number of sacrifices
to Kali, but her womb remained sterile like sand beneath the
torrid sun. Then the king of Madura ordered that the great sacrifice of fire be made before all the city, and that all the Devas
be invoked. Kansa's wives and the people attended with great
ceremony. Kneeling before the fire, the chanting priests called
upon the great Varuna, Indra, the Aswini and the Maruts.
Queen Nysumba approached and threw a handful of perfumes
into the fire with a gesture of challenge, as she uttered a magic
formula in an unknown language. The smoke thickened, the

flames swirled and the frightened priests cried out, "O Queen, those are not the Devas, but the Rakshasas who passed over the fire! Your womb will remain sterile!"

Kansa approached the fire and said to the priests, "Tell me, then, of which of my wives will the master of the world be born?"

At that moment Devaki, the king's sister, came near the fire. She was a pure, unpretentious virgin, who had spent her childhood spinning and weaving, living as in a dream. Her body was on earth, but her soul seemed forever in heaven. Devaki knelt humbly, begging the Devas to give her brother and beautiful Nysumba a son. The priest looked at the fire and then at the virgin. Suddenly he cried out in complete amazement, "O king of Madura, none of your sons will be master of the world! He will be born in the womb of your sister who is kneeling here!"

Great were Kansa's dismay and Nysumba's anger at these words. When the queen was alone with the king she said, "Devaki must die at once!"

"How," asked Kansa, "could I cause my sister to die? If the Devas are protecting her, their vengeance would fall upon me!"

"Then," said Nysumba in a rage, "let her reign in my place and let your sister bring into the world the one who will cause you to die in shame! But I no longer wish to reign with a coward who is afraid of the Devas. I am returning home to my father, Kalayeni!"

Nysumba's eyes cast oblique flames, the pendants shook on her shiny dark neck. She rolled upon the ground, and her beautiful body twisted like a raging serpent. Kansa, fearful of losing her, and captivated by a terrible desire, was eaten by a new passion.

"Very well," he said, "Devaki will die, but do not leave me!"

A gleam of triumph shone in Nysumba's eyes; a rush of blood brought color back to her sepia face. She jumped up and encircled the conquered tyrant with her supple arms. Then, caressing him lightly with her ebony breasts from which emanated potent perfumes, and touching him with her burning lips, she whispered in a soft voice, "We shall offer a sacrifice to Kali, goddess of desire and death, and she will give us a son who will be master of the world!"

But that same night in a dream the *purohita*, the priest of sacrifice, saw king Kansa drawing his sword against his sister. Immediately he went to the virgin Devaki, told her that mortal danger threatened her, and ordered her to flee to the anchorites without delay. Devaki, directed by the priest of the fire, disguised as a penitent, left Kansa's palace and the city of Madura without anyone observing her. Early in the morning the soldiers looked for the king's sister in order to put her to death, but they found her room empty. The king questioned the guards of the city. They answered that the gates had remained closed all night long. But in their sleep they had seen the dark walls of the fortress break under a ray of light, and a woman leave the city, following that ray. Kansa realized that an invincible power was protecting Devaki. From that moment, fear entered his heart and he began to hate his sister with a mortal hatred.

8

The Virgin Devaki

WHEN Devaki, dressed in clothing made of strips of bark which hid her beauty, entered the vast solitudes of the giant forest she staggered, exhausted from fatigue and hunger. But as soon as she felt the shade of the awesome forest, tasted the fruit of the mango tree and inhaled the freshness of a stream, she took on new life, like a blossoming flower. First she passed beneath tremendous arches formed by massive tree trunks, whose branches planted themselves in the soil again, multiplying their arcades infinitely. For a long time she walked, sheltered from the sun, as in a dark pagoda without an exit. The buzzing of the bees, the cry of the amorous peacocks, the song of the kokels and of a thousand birds, drew her still further on. And still larger became the trees, the forest denser and more entangled. Tree trunks crowded close beside tree trunks, foliage descended over foliage to form cupolas and growing pylons. Sometimes Devaki walked through corridors of greenery which the sun flooded with light, and where tree trunks lay overturned by the storm. Sometimes she paused beneath arbors of mango trees and asokas, from which cascaded garlands of lianas and a profusion of flowers. Deer and panthers leaped in the thickets; frequently buffalo made the branches snap, or a band of monkeys would pass shrieking through the foliage. She walked through scenes like this for the whole day. Toward evening, above a grove of bamboos she saw the motionless head of a wise elephant. He looked at the virgin with an intelligent, protective air, raising his trunk as if to greet her. Then the forest became light, and Devaki saw a landscape of deep peace and celestial, paradisical charm.

A pond strewn with lotus and water lilies spread out before her; its heart of blue opened into the great forest, like another sky. Bashful storks dreamed motionless upon its banks, and two gazelles were drinking from its waters. On the other side, in the shelter of the palms stood the hermitage of the anchorites. A soft pink light bathed the lake, the forest and the dwelling of the holy Rishis. Against the horizon the white summits of Mount Meru rose above the ocean of forests. The breath of an invisible river gave life to the plants while the softened thunder of a distant waterfall was wafted on the breeze like a caress or a melody.

At the edge of the pond Devaki saw a boat. Standing near it, a man of mature age, an anchorite, seemed to be waiting. Silently he gestured to the virgin to get into the boat, and he took up the oars. As the little boat moved forward, stroking the water lilies, Devaki saw a female swan swimming over the pond. In a bold flight a male swan came through the air and began to describe large circles around her. Then he descended upon the water near his companion, shaking his snow white plumage. At this spectacle, Devaki trembled greatly without knowing why. But the boat had touched the opposite shore, and the lotus-eyed virgin found herself before Vasichta, leader of the anchorites.

Sitting on a gazelle's skin, clothed in the hide of a black antelope, Vasichta had the venerable appearance of a god rather than a man. For sixty years he had eaten only wild fruit. His hair and beard were as white as the summit of the Himavat, his skin was transparent, and the gaze of his dim eyes was turned inward in meditation. Upon seeing Devaki, he arose and greeted her.

"Devaki, sister of the famous Kansa, you are welcome in our midst. Guided by Mahadeva, the supreme master, you have left the world of sorrows for that of happiness. For here you are near the holy Rishis, masters of their senses, content with their destiny and seeking the path to heaven. We have waited long for you, as the night waits for the dawn. For we are the eyes of the Devas fixed on the world. We live in the densest of forests. Men do not see us, but we see men and we observe their actions. The dark age of desire, blood and crime is raging over the world. We have chosen you for the task of deliverance, and the Devas have chosen you through us. For it is in the womb of woman that the ray of divine splendor must take on human form."

At that moment the Rishis were leaving the retreat for evening prayer. The aged Vasichta ordered them to bow down to the ground before Devaki. They bowed low as Vasichta continued, "This one will be the mother of all of us, for from her will be born the spirit which is to regenerate us." Then, turning to her, he said, "Go, my child. The Rishis will lead you to a neighboring lake where the penitent sisters live. You will dwell among them, and the mysteries will be fulfilled."

Devaki went to the retreat surrounded by lions. There she was to live with the devout women who feed tame gazelles and devote themselves to ablutions and prayers. Devaki took part in their sacrifices. An aged woman gave her secret instructions. These penitents had been commanded to dress her in exquisite scented fabrics like a queen and to let her wander alone in the open forest. And the forest, filled with perfumes, voices and mysteries attracted the young woman. Sometimes she met processions of old anchorites returning from the river. Upon seeing her they knelt before her and then continued on their way. One day near a stream covered with pink lotus, she noticed a young anchorite in prayer. He stood up at her approach, cast a long, sad look at her and walked away in silence. And the serious faces of the old men, the image of the two swans and the look of the young anchorite haunted the virgin in her dreams.

Near the stream was a tree of unknown age, with wide branches, which the holy Rishis called "the tree of life." Devaki liked to sit in its shade. Often when she fell asleep there, she was visited by strange visions. Voices sang behind the foliage, "Glory to thee Devaki! He will come, crowned with light, that pure fluid emanating from the great soul, and the stars will become dim before his splendor. He will come, and life will defy death, and he will rejuvenate the blood of all beings. He will come, sweeter than honey and amrita, purer than the spotless lamb and a virgin's mouth, and all hearts will be overwhelmed in love. Glory, glory, glory be to you Devaki!"

Were these the anchorites? Were these the Devas, who sang like this? Sometimes it seemed to her that a distant power or a mysterious presence, like an invisible hand suspended over her, forced her to sleep. Then she fell into a deep, sweet, inexplicable slumber, out of which she awakened bewildered and disturbed. She turned around as if to look for someone, but she never saw anyone. But several times she found roses strewn on her bed of leaves, and a crown of lotus in her hands.

One day Devaki fell into a deeper ecstasy. She heard heavenly music like an ocean of harps and divine voices. Suddenly the sky opened into depths of light. Thousands of magnificent beings were looking at her and in the brightness of a flashing ray of light, the sun of suns, Mahadeva, appeared to her in human form. Then having been *overshadowed* by the Spirit of the worlds, she lost consciousness, and oblivious of earth, in a boundless felicity, she conceived the holy child.[12]

When seven moons had described their magic circles around the sacred forest, the chief of the anchorites summoned Devaki. "The will of the Devas has been fulfilled," he said. "You have conceived in purity of heart and in divine love. Virgin and mother, we greet you. A son will be born of you, who will be the savior of the world. But your brother Kansa is looking for you to kill you, along with the tender fruit you carry in your womb. You must escape him. The brothers will lead you to the shepherds who live at the foot of Mount Meru, beneath scented cedars, in the pure air of the Himavat. There you will bring into the world your divine child, and you shall call him Krishna, the holy one. But see that he knows nothing of his origin and yours; never speak to him about it. Go without fear, for we are watching over you."

And Devaki went away to the shepherds of Mount Meru.

9

Krishna's Youth

AT the foot of Mount Meru stretched a fertile valley, green with pastures and surrounded by vast forests of cedar trees, where the pure air of Himavat sighed gently. In this high valley lived a tribe of herdsmen over which the patriarch Nanda, friend of the anchorites, ruled. Here Devaki found refuge from the persecutions of the tyrant of Madura, and here in Nanda's home she brought her son, Krishna, into the world. Except Nanda, no one knew who the stranger was nor where this son came from. The women of the area simply said, "It is a son of the Gandharvas,[13] for Indra's musicians must have been present at the love-making of this woman who resembles a celestial nymph, an Apsara." The marvelous child of this unknown woman grew up among the flocks and shepherds under the care of his mother. The shepherds called him "The Radiant One" because his presence alone, his smile and his big eyes had a way of spreading joy. Animals, children, women, men, everyone loved him and he seemed to love everyone, smiling at his mother, playing with the lambs and the young children of his own age, or speaking with the old men. The child Krishna was fearless, full of daring and performed astonishing feats. Sometimes he was found in the woods lying on the moss, wrestling with young panthers and holding their mouths open, without their daring to bite him. Above all things and all beings, Krishna adored his young mother, so beautiful and so radiant, who spoke to him of the heaven of the Devas, of heroic battles and of the wonderful things she had learned from the anchorites. And the shepherds who led their flocks beneath the cedars of Mount Meru would say, "Who is this mother, and who is this son? Although she is dressed like our women, she looks like a queen. The amazing child was raised with ours, yet he does not look like them. Is he a genius? Is he a god? Whoever he is, he will bring us happiness."

When Krishna was fifteen years old, his mother Devaki was summoned by the leader of the anchorites. One day she disappeared without saying goodbye to her son. When he saw her no longer, Krishna went to look for the patriarch Nanda and asked him, "Where is my mother?"

Nanda answered, bowing his head, "My child, do not question me. Your mother has gone on a long journey. She has returned to the country from which she came, and I do not know when she will return."

Krishna said nothing at all, but he lapsed into such a deep reverie that all the children kept away from him as if gripped by a superstitious fear. Krishna deserted his friends, left their games, and, lost in his reflections, went alone to Mount Meru. He wandered for several weeks. One morning he came to a high, wooded peak where his view reached over the chain of the Himavat Mountains. Suddenly near him he saw a tall old man in the white robe of an anchorite, standing under the giant cedars in the morning light. He seemed one hundred years old. His snow-white beard and his bare head shone with majesty.

The lively child and the centenarian gazed at each other for a long time. The eyes of the old man rested benignly upon Krishna, but Krishna was so startled at seeing him that he remained silent in admiration. Although Krishna saw him for the first time, it seemed as if he knew this aged man.

"Whom do you seek?" the old man asked at last.

"My mother."

"She is no longer here."

"Where shall I find her?"

"With Him who never changes."

"But how shall I find Him?"

"Seek."

"And shall I see you again?"

"Yes, when the daughter of the serpent incites the son of the bull to crime, then you will see me again in a purple light. Then you will kill the bull, and you will crush the head of the serpent. Son of Mahadeva, know that you and I are but one in Him. Seek, always seek."

And the old man extended his hand in a gesture of benediction. Then he turned and took a few steps under the high cedars in the direction of the Himavat. Suddenly it seemed to Krishna that the old man's form became transparent and disappeared with a luminous vibration in the shimmering glow of the fine-needled branches.[14]

When Krishna came down from Mount Meru, he appeared to be transformed. A new energy emanated from his being. He gathered his companions together and told them, "Let us fight the bulls and snakes; let us defend the good and subdue the wicked!" With bow in hand and sword at his side, Krishna and his companions, sons of the shepherds, now transformed into warriors, began to beat the forests, fighting the wild beasts. In the depths of the woods one could hear the roaring of hyenas, jackals and tigers, and the young men's cries of truimph over the defeated animals. Krishna killed and tamed lions; he made war on kings and freed oppressed peoples. But sadness remained in the depths of his heart. This heart had but one deep, mysterious desire; he longed to find his mother and to see the strange, august old man again. He asked himself, "Did he not promise me that I would see him again when I crushed the head of the snake? Did he not tell me that I would find my mother again with Him who never changes?" But it was useless for him to fight, conquer, kill—he had not seen the majestic old man nor his own glorious mother.

One day he heard people speak about Kalayeni, king of the serpents, and he asked to fight with his most terrible serpent in the presence of the black magician. It was said that this creature, trained by Kalayeni, had already eaten hundreds of men, and that its glance could paralyze the most courageous with fear. Krishna saw a long, greenish-blue reptile come from the depths of Kali's dark temple at Kalayeni's call. The serpent slowly raised its thick body, distended its red crest, and its piercing eyes lit up in its monstrous head, covered with shiny scales. "This serpent," said Kalayeni, "knows many things. It is a powerful demon. It will tell them only to the one who kills it, but it kills those who fail. It has seen you; it is looking at you; you are in its power. All that is left for you to do is worship it or die in a senseless struggle." Krishna was indignant at these words, for he felt that his heart was like the tip of a lightning bolt. He looked at the snake, then threw himself upon it, seizing it beneath the head. Man and serpent rolled on the steps of the temple. But before the serpent could encircle him in its coils, Krishna cut off its head with his sword.

Disentangling himself from the still writhing body, the young conqueror triumphantly raised the head of the serpent in his left hand. But this head was still alive. It kept looking at Krishna, and said, "Why did you kill me, son of Mahadeva? Do you think you will find truth by killing the living? Foolish one, you will only find it in dying yourself. Death is in life, life is in death. Beware the daughter of the serpent and spilt blood. Be careful! Be careful!" With these words, the serpent died. Krishna let the head fall and went away, filled with horror. But Kalayeni said, "I have no power over this man; Kali alone can subdue him with a spell."

After a month of ablutions and prayers on the banks of the Ganges, having purified himself in the light of the sun and in the thought of Mahadeva, Krishna returned to his native country, among the shepherds of Mount Meru.

The autumn moon showed its shining orb above the cedar forests and the night air was perfumed with the scent of wild lilies in which the bees had hummed all day long. Sitting beneath a large cedar tree at the edge of a meadow, weary of the vain battles of earth, Krishna dreamed of heavenly combats and of the boundless heaven itself. The more he thought of his glorious mother and the august old man, the more his childish exploits seemed despicable and the more celestial things came to life within him. A consoling charm, a divine recollection flooded his entire being. Then a hymn of thankfulness to Mahadeva arose from his heart and overflowed from his lips in a sweet, divine melody. Attracted by this wonderful song, the Gopis, daughters and wives of the shepherds, left their houses. The first, having spied the heads of their families coming home, returned immediately after having pretended to pick flowers. Some came nearer, calling, "Krishna! Krishna!" Then, very ashamed, they ran away. Gradually becoming bolder, the women surrounded Krishna in groups like timid, curious gazelles, charmed by his melodies. But, lost in his dream of the gods, he did not see them. More and more enchanted by his song, the Gopis began to grow impatient at not being noticed. Nichdali, Nanda's daughter, with eyes closed, had fallen into a kind of ecstasy. But Sarasvati, her sister, bolder than she, quietly moved near Devaki's son, pressed against his side and said in a soft voice, "O Krishna, don't you see that we are listening to you, that we can no longer sleep in our homes? Your melodies have cast a spell upon us. O adorable hero, we are captivated by your voice, and can no longer do without you!"

"O keep singing!" a young girl said. "Teach us to sing!"

"Teach us dancing," said a woman.

And Krishna, coming out of his dream, looked favorably upon the Gopis. He spoke kind words to them and, taking their hands, made them sit on the grass near the huge cedars, in the bright moonlight. Then he told them what he had seen within himself. He told them the story of the gods and heros of Indra's wars and of the exploits of the divine Rama. The women and young girls listened, captivated. These tales lasted until dawn. When pink Aurora arose behind Mount Meru and the kokilas began to chirp beneath the cedars, the Gopi girls and women furtively returned to their homes. But the next night, as soon as the crescent moon appeared, they returned more eagerly than ever. Seeing that they were enchanted by his narratives, Krishna taught them to sing and to portray in gestures the sublime actions of the heros and the gods. To some he gave vinas with strings which vibrate like souls, to others resounding cymbals like the hearts of warriors, to others drums which imitate thunder. And choosing the most beautiful, he inspired them with his thoughts. With arms extended, walking and moving about in a divine dream, the sacred dancers portrayed the majesty of Varuna, the anger of Indra killing the dragon, or the despair of abandoned Maya. Thus the battles and everlasting glory of the gods, which Krishna saw within himself, came to life again in these happy, transfigured women.

One morning the Gopis had scattered. The sound of their musical instruments and their singing, laughing voices had faded in the distance. Krishna, who had remained alone under the huge cedar tree, saw Sarasvati and Nichdali, Nanda's two daughters, coming toward him. They sat down beside him. Sarasvati, throwing her arms around Krishna's neck, making her bracelets jingle, said to him, "In teaching us the sacred songs and dances you have made us the happiest of women; but we shall be the most unhappy ones when you have left us. What will become of us when we shall see you no longer? O, Krishna, marry us! My sister and I will be your faithful wives, and our eyes will not have the pain of losing you." While Sarasvati spoke thus, Nichdali closed her eyes as if she were falling into an ecstasy.

"Nichdali, why do you close your eyes?" Krishna asked.

"She is jealous," answered Sarasvati, laughing. "She does not wish to see my arms around your neck."

"No," replied the blushing Nichdali, "I am closing my eyes in order to look at your image, which is engraved deep inside me. Krishna, you can leave, but I shall never lose you!"

Krishna became thoughtful. Smiling, he loosened Sarasvati's arms which were passionately wound about his neck. Then he looked at the two women and embraced them. First he kissed Sarasvati's lips, then Nichdali's eyes. In these two long kisses, young Krishna seemed to explore, to taste all the pleasures of earth. Suddenly he trembled, saying, "You are beautiful, O Sarasvati! You, whose lips have the perfume of amber and all the flowers! You are adorable, O Nichdali! You, whose eyelids veil intense eyes, and who know how to look within yourself! I love you both . . . But how could I marry you, since my heart would have to be divided between you?"

"O, he will never be in love!" said Sarasvati spitefully.

"I shall love only with an everlasting love."

"And what is required for you to love in that way?" asked Nichdali tenderly.

KRISHNA

Krishna had stood up. His eyes were aflame. "To love with an everlasting love?" he asked. "Daylight must disappear. Thunder must fall upon my heart, and my soul must flee beyond myself into the heights of heaven!"

While he spoke it seemed to the young girls that he increased in height. Suddenly they were afraid of him and returned home sobbing. Krishna took the road to Mount Meru alone. The following night the Gopis met for their games, but they waited for their teacher in vain. He had disappeared, leaving them only an essence, a perfume from his being: the sacred songs and dances.

10

Initiation

IN the meantime, having learned that his sister, Devaki, had lived among the anchorites, and not having been able to find her, King Kansa began to persecute them and hunt them like wild beasts. They had to take refuge in the remotest and wildest part of the forest. Then their leader, old Vasichta, though one hundred years of age, set out to speak to the king of Madura. The guards saw with amazement a blind old man led by a gazelle which he kept on a leash, appear at the gates of the palace. Out of respect for the Rishi, they allowed him to pass. Vasichta approached the throne where Kansa was sitting beside Nysumba, and said, "Kansa! King of Madura! Woe to you, daughter of the serpent, who breathes hate into him! The day of your punishment is near. Devaki's son is alive! He will come, covered with armor of impenetrable scales, and will drive you from your throne in shame. Now tremble and live in fear; that is the punishment the Devas allot you!"

The warriors, guards and servants knelt before the holy centenarian as he departed, led by his gazelle, no one daring to touch him. But from that day, Kansa and Nysumba dreamed of secret ways to bring about the death of the leader of the anchorites. Devaki was dead, and no one except Vasichta knew that Krishna was her son. Nevertheless, the news of the latter's feats had reached the king's ears. Kansa thought, "I need a strong man to protect me. The one who killed Kalayeni's great serpent will not be afraid of the anchorite." Accordingly, Kansa called the patriarch, Nanda, and said, "Send me the young hero, Krishna, so I may make him the driver of my chariot and my first counsellor."[15] Nanda informed Krishna of the king's command, and Krishna answered, "I shall go." He thought to himself, "Can the king of Madura be the One Who never changes? Through him I shall find out where my mother is."

Kansa, observing Krishna's strength, skill and intelligence, was pleased with him and entrusted him with the care of his kingdom. But Nysumba, upon seeing the hero of Mount Meru, trembled throughout her whole body with an impure desire, and her cunning mind shaped a secret plan, inspired by a criminal thought. Unknown to the king she had the driver of the chariot summoned to her apartments. As a magician she possessed the art of instantly becoming young again by means of potent philters. Devaki's son found the ebony-breasted Nysumba lying almost naked upon a bed of velvet. Gold rings bound her ankles and arms and a crown of precious stones sparkled upon her head. At her feet burned a copper censer, from which issued a cloud of perfumes.

"Krishna," said the daughter of the serpent king, "your countenance is smoother than the snows of Himavat, and your heart is like the tip of a bolt of lightning. In your innocence you shine above the kings of earth. Here no one has recognized you; even you do not know yourself. I alone know who you are. The Devas have made you master of men; I alone can make you master of the world. Are you willing?"

"If it is Mahadeva who is speaking through you," Krishna said, looking grave, "you will tell me where my mother is, and where I shall find the tall old man who spoke to me beneath the cedars of Mount Meru."

"Your mother?" asked Nysumba with a smile of disdain, "It certainly is not I who will tell you; as for that old man, I do not know him. Foolish one, you continue to dream and do not see the earthly treasures I am offering you! There are kings who wear crowns who are not kings. There are sons of shepherds who bear royalty on their foreheads and who do not know their strength. You are young; you are handsome. Hearts belong to you. Kill the king in his sleep, and I shall place the crown upon your head, and you will be master of the world. For I love you and you were predestined for me. I so wish, and I so command!"

As she spoke, the queen raised herself, domineering, fascinating, terrible as a beautiful snake. Sitting upright on her couch, she cast a flame of such dark fire into Krishna's limpid eyes that he trembled. Hell appeared in those glances. He saw the abyss of the temple of Kali, goddess of desire and death, where snakes writhed in an everlasting agony. Then suddenly Krishna's eyes seemed like two swords. They pierced the queen through and through, and the hero of Mount Meru cried out, "I am faithful to the king who chose me as protector! As for you, know that you will die!"

Nysumba gave a piercing scream and rolled over on her couch, biting the velvet covering. All her artificial youth had faded; she had become old and wrinkled once again. Krishna went away, leaving her to her anger.

Tortured night and day by the anchorite's words, the king of Madura said to the driver of his chariot, "Since the enemy has set foot in my palace I no longer sleep in peace. An infernal magician named Vasichta, who lives in a dense forest came and left his curse on me. Since that time I no longer breathe; the old man has poisoned my days. But with you who fear nothing, I do not fear him. Come with me to the accursed forest! A spy who knows all the paths will lead us to him. As soon as you see him, run to him and strike him without allowing him to say a word to you, or look at you. When he is mortally wounded, ask him where the son of my sister Devaki is, and what his name is. The peace of my kingdom hangs on this mystery."

"Calm yourself," Krishna said, "I was not afraid of Kalayeni nor of Kali's serpent. Who can make me tremble now? However powerful this man may be, I shall find out what he is hiding from you!"

Disguised as hunters, the king and his driver rode in a swift chariot, drawn by spirited horses. The spy who had explored the forest followed behind them. It was the beginning of the rainy season. The rivers were rising, growing plants covered the roads, and the white line of storks was seen on the tops of the clouds. When the men neared the sacred wood the horizon darkened, the sun hid itself, the air was filled with a copper-colored mist. From the stormy sky clouds hung like horns over the wild foliage of the forest.

"Why," Krishna asked the king, "has the heaven suddenly darkened and the forest become so black?"

"Well do I know," said the king of Madura. "It is Vasichta, the evil recluse, who is darkening the sky and arming the accursed forest against me. But Krishna, are you afraid?"

"Let the sky change its face and the earth its color! I am not afraid!"

"Then, Forward!"

Krishna lashed the horses with his whip and the chariot dove beneath the thick shade of the baobabs. It moved forward for a time at an amazing speed. But the forest became still wilder and more frightening. Lightning flashed, thunder roared.

"Never," said Krishna, "have I seen the sky so dark and the trees twisting in this way. Your magician is powerful!"

"Krishna, slayer of serpents, hero of Mount Meru, are you afraid?"

"Let the earth quake and the sky crumble! I am not afraid!"

"Then keep going!"

Again the daring driver whipped the horses and the chariot continued on its way. Now the storm became so dreadful that the giant trees bent and the quaking forest roared like the howling of a thousand demons. Lightning struck near the travelers; a shattered baobab blocked the way; the horses stopped and the earth trembled.

"Your enemy must be a god," said Krishna, "since Indra himself is protecting him."

"We are approaching the goal!" cried the king's spy. "Look at that path of green! At the end of it is a wretched hut. It is there that Vasichta, the great *mouni* lives, feeding birds, feared by wild animals and protected by a gazelle. But not for a kingdom shall I take one step more!"

At these words, the king of Madura became white. "He's there? Really? Behind those trees?" Clinging to Krishna, he whispered in a low voice, while his whole body trembled, "Vasichta! Vasichta, who is plotting my death is there! He sees me from his secret retreat. . . . His eye is following me! Save me from him!"

"Yes, by Mahadeva!" said Krishna, getting out of the chariot, "I want to see the one who causes you to tremble like this!"

For a year the aged Vasichta quietly had awaited death in his hut, hidden in the thickest part of the sacred forest. Before the death of his body he was freed from his fleshly prison. His eyes were blind, but he saw with his soul. His skin hardly felt heat and cold, but his spirit lived in a perfect unity with the sovereign Spirit. Praying and meditating without ceasing, he saw things of this world only in the light of Brahma. A faithful disciple brought him grains of rice, on which he lived. The gazelle who ate from his hand warned him of the approach of wild beasts. Then he drove the latter away by whispering a mantram and by extending his bamboo staff with its seven nodes. As for men, whoever they were, by means of his gaze he saw them when they were still several miles away.

Krishna, walking along the dark path, suddenly found himself before Vasichta. The leader of the anchorites with legs crossed was sitting on a mat, leaning against the post of his hut in a deep calm. From the eyes of the blind man came the inner glimmer of the seer. As soon as Krishna saw him, he recognized him. "The majestic old man!" He felt a sensation of joy; reverence entered his soul. Forgetting the king, his chariot and his kingdom, he knelt on one knee before the saint and worshipped him.

Vasichta seemed to see him. His body, leaning against the hut, sat up with a slight trembling; he extended both arms to bless his guest and his lips murmured the sacred syllable, *AUM!*[16]

Meanwhile, Kansa, hearing no outcry and not seeing his driver return, slipped furtively along the path and stood petrified with astonishment upon seeing Krishna kneeling before the holy anchorite. The latter turned his blind eyes toward Kansa. Raising his staff, he said,

"O king of Madura, you are coming to kill me! Greetings! For you will free me from the pain of this body. You wish to know where is the son of your sister Devaki, who is to dethrone you. Here he kneels before me and before Mahadeva; he is Krishna, your own charioteer! How foolish and cursed you are, since your most fearful enemy is this very one here! You have brought him to me, so that I can tell him that he is the chosen one. Tremble! You are lost, for your infernal soul will indeed be the prey of demons!"

Stupefied, Kansa listened. He did not dare look the old man in the face. Pale with rage, seeing Krishna still kneeling, he took his bow and arching it with all his might, discharged an arrow at Devaki's son. But his arm had trembled; the arrow swerved and sank deep into Vasichta's chest. With his arms extended in the form of a cross, Vasichta appeared as though waiting for the arrow in a kind of ecstasy.

A cry was heard, a terrible cry.—It was not from the heart of the old man, but from Krishna's. He had heard the arrow hum past his ear, and then he had seen it sink into the saint's flesh.... And it seemed to Krishna that it had sunk into his own heart, so closely had his soul become identified with the Rishi's at that moment. With that sharp arrow all the pain of the world pierced Krishna's soul, tearing it to its core.

Nevertheless, Vasichta, with the arrow in his chest and without changing position, was still moving his lips. He murmured, "Son of Mahadeva, why do you cry out? Killing is vain! The arrow cannot reach the soul and the victim is the conqueror of the assassin. Be victorious, Krishna, destiny is being fulfilled! I am returning to Him Who never changes. May Brahma receive my soul! But you, his elect, savior of the world, stand up! Krishna! Krishna!"

And Krishna stood up, his hand on his sword; he wanted to strike the king, but Kansa had fled.

Then a flash rent the dark sky and Krishna fell to earth, thunderstruck, paralyzed by a blinding light. While his body remained inert, his soul, united with that of the old man through power and sympathy, ascended into space. Earth, with its rivers, seas and continents disappeared like a black ball, and both souls arose to the seventh heaven of the Devas, to the Father of Beings, to the Sun of Suns, to Mahadeva, the Divine

Intelligence. They were plunged into an ocean of light, which opened before them. In the center of the sphere Krishna saw Devaki, his radiant mother, his glorified mother, who with an ineffable smile stretched forth her arms and drew him to her breast. Thousands of Devas came to bathe in the radiance of the Virgin Mother, as in a fountain of light. And Krishna felt permeated with love from Devaki. Then from the heart of his shining mother his being radiated throughout all the heavens. He felt that he was the Son, the divine soul of all beings, the Word of Life, the Creative Word, Superior to universal life, nevertheless he pervaded it through the essence of grief, through the fire of prayer and the happiness of a divine sacrifice.[17]

When Krishna came to himself, thunder still rolled in the sky, the forest was dark and torrents of rain were falling upon the hut. A gazelle was licking the bloodstained body of the slain ascetic. "The majestic old man" was but a corpse. But Krishna arose as if revived. An abyss separated him from the world and its vain appearance. He had lived the great truth; he understood his mission.

As for Kansa, filled with terror he was fleeing through the storm in his chariot, and his horses galloped as if flogged by a thousand demons.

11

The Teaching of the Initiates

KRISHNA was greeted by the anchorites as the anticipated, predestined successor to Vasichta. They performed the *srada* or funeral ceremony for the holy old man in the sacred forest, and Devaki's son received the staff with its seven nodes as a sign of command, after having performed the sacrifice of fire in the presence of the three eldest anchorites who knew the three Vedas by heart. Then Krishna withdrew to Mount Meru to think upon his teaching and the way of salvation for all men. His meditation and austerities lasted seven years. At the end of that time he felt that he had subdued his earthly nature through his divine nature, and that he had become sufficiently identified with the son of Mahadeva to merit the name, the son of God. Then only did he call to him the anchorites, young and old, in order to reveal his teaching to them. They found Krishna purified and matured; the hero had changed into the saint; he had not lost his lion's strength, but he had gained the gentleness of the dove. Among those who hastened to Krishna, the first to come to him was Arjuna, a descendant of the solar kings, one of the Pandavas dethroned by the Kuravas, or lunar kings. Young Arjuna was full of fire, but was easily discouraged and inclined to doubt. He became deeply attached to Krishna.

Seated under the cedars of Mount Meru, facing the Himavat, Krishna began to speak to his students about truths inaccessible to men who live in slavery to the senses. He taught them the doctrine of the immortal soul, its rebirths and its mystic union with God. The body, he said, covering of the soul which makes its home there, is a finite thing, but the soul which inhabits the body is invisible, imponderable, incorruptible and eternal. Earthly man is threefold, like the divinity he reflects: spirit, soul and body. If the soul unites with the spirit, it attains *Satwa,* wisdom and peace; if it remains wavering between spirit and body, it is ruled by *Raja,* passion, and goes from object to object in a fatal circle; if it gives itself over to the body, it falls into *Tama,* irrationality, ignorance and temporary death. Every man can observe this in himself and in those around him.

"But," asked Arjuna, "what is the fate of the soul after death? Does it always obey the same law, or can it escape it?"

"It never escapes it, but always obeys it," answered Krishna. "This is the mystery of rebirth. As the depths of heaven open to the lights of the stars, so the depths of life are illumined in the light of this truth. When the body is dissolved, when *Satwa,* wisdom, has the upper hand, the soul flies to the regions of those pure beings who have knowledge of the Most High. When the body experiences this dissolution while *Raja,* passion, rules, the soul comes again to live among those who have become attached to the things of earth. Likewise, if the body is destroyed when *Tama,* ignorance, predominates, the soul, overshadowed by matter is again attracted by irrational beings.[18]

"That is right," said Arjuna. "But tell us now, in the course of centuries what becomes of those who have followed wisdom, and who go to live in the divine worlds after death?"

"Man, overtaken by death during devotion," answered Krishna, "having enjoyed the rewards of his virtues in the higher regions for several centuries, finally returns again to inhabit a body in a holy and respectable family. But that kind of regeneration in this life is very difficult to obtain. The man so born again finds himself with the same degree of application and advancement as regards the understanding that he had in his first body, and again he begins to work in order to perfect himself through devotion."

"So then," said Arjuna, "even the good are required to be born anew, to begin the life of the body again! But tell us, O Lord of Life, for the one who seeks after wisdom is there no end at all to everlasting rebirths?"

"Listen," said Krishna, "to a very great and deep secret, to the sovereign, sublime, and pure mystery. In order to reach perfection it is necessary to acquire *knowledge of oneness,* which is above wisdom; it is necessary to lift oneself to the divine Being who is above the soul and even above intelligence. Now this divine being, this sublime friend, is in each one of us. For God dwells within every man, but few know how to find Him. And this is the way to salvation. Once you have seen the Perfect Being Who is above the world and within you, resolve to leave the enemy which takes the form of desire. Overcome your passions. The joys of the senses are like the matrices of sorrows to come. Not only do good, but be good. Let the motive be in the deed, not in the reward. Renounce the fruit of your works, but let each of your acts be like an offering to the Supreme Being. The man who sacrifices his desires and works to the Being in Whom the beginnings of all beings originate, and by Whom the universe was formed, obtains perfection through his sacrifice. Spiritually integrated, he attains that spiritual wisdom which is above the cult of offerings, and experiences a divine happiness. For one who finds his happiness and his joy within himself and within himself finds light as well, is at one with God. Now, hear this: The soul which has found God is freed from rebirth and death, from old age and pain and drinks the water of immortality."

Then Krishna explained his teaching to his students and through inner contemplation he lifted them gradually to the sublime truths which had been unfolded to him in the experience of his vision. When he spoke of Mahadeva, his voice became more serious, his countenance was illuminated. One day, filled with curiosity and boldness, Arjuna said to him, "Let us see Mahadeva in his divine form! Cannot our eyes behold him?"

Then Krishna, standing, began to speak about the Being Who breathes in all beings, the Being with a hundred thousand forms, innumerable eyes, faces turning in all directions, and Who nevertheless is greater than they by all the heights of infinity; Who in His motionless, limitless body contains the moving universe with all its divisions. "If in the heavens the splendor of a thousand suns glittered at the same time," said Krishna, "this would hardly resemble the splendor of the only All-Powerful." While he thus spoke of Mahadeva, such light streamed from Krishna's eyes that his students could not bear its brightness, and knelt at his feet. Arjuna's hair stood up on his head, and bowing deeply, he said, "Master, your words frighten us and we cannot bear the sight of the Great Being you portray before our eyes. It overwhelms us."

Krishna continued, "Listen to what He tells you through me. You and I have had several births. Mine are known only to me, but you do not know yours. Although by my nature I am not subject to birth or death, and although I am the master of all creatures, nevertheless, since I command my being, I become visible through my own power. Every time virtue wanes in the world and vice and injustice are victorious, I become visible, and thus I appear from age to age for the salvation of the righteous, the destruction of the wicked and the reestablishment of virtue. One who really knows my nature and my divine work, upon leaving his body does not return to a new birth, but comes to me."

Speaking thus, Krishna looked upon his students with tenderness and kindness. Arjuna cried out, "Lord! You are our Master, you are the son of Mahadeva! I see him in your kindness, in your ineffable charm, even more than in your terrible brightness! It is not in the overpowering heights of infinity that the Devas seek you and want you! It is in human form that they love and adore you. Neither penitence nor almsgiving, nor the Vedas, nor sacrifice are worth a single one of your glances. You are truth! Lead us to the fight, to the battle, to death! Wherever it is, we will follow you!"

Smiling and enraptured, the students pressed closer to Krishna, saying, "Why didn't we recognize it sooner? Mahadeva is speaking through you!" Krishna answered, "Your eyes were not open. I have given you the great secret. Tell it only to those who can understand it. You are my chosen ones. You see the purpose; the crowd sees only the end of the road. And now let us preach to the people the way of salvation!"

12

Triumph and Death

Having taught his students on Mount Meru, Krishna accompanied them along the banks of the Jamaina and Ganges in order to convert the people. One evening on the outskirts of a city, the crowd gathered around him. What he preached to the people above all was charity toward one's neighbor. "The evils with which we torment our neighbor," he said, "follow us, just as our shadow follows our body. Works which have love for one's fellow man as a basis are those which must be pursued by the righteous, for they are those which will weigh most on the heavenly scale. If you go only among the good, your example will be useless; do not be afraid to live among the wicked in order to lead them back to the good! The virtuous man is similar to the huge banyan tree whose beneficent shade gives freshness of life to the plants surrounding it!" Sometimes Krishna, whose soul now overflowed with a perfume of love, spoke of abnegation and sacrifice in a gentle voice and with appealing illustrations. "Just as earth supports those who tread upon her with their feet and tear up her womb while tilling the soil, so

we must return good for evil.—The good man must fall under
the blow of the wicked as the sandalwood tree scents the hatchet
which strikes it when it is hewn down." When the demi-savants,
infidels and arrogant asked him to explain the nature of God,
he answered in sentences like these: "Man's knowledge is but
vanity; all his good actions are illusion when he does not know
how to relate them to God. One who is humble in heart and
spirit is beloved of God; he does not need anything else. Infinity
and space alone can understand infinity; only God can understand God."

These were not the only new things in his teaching. He
captivated and won people with what he said about the
living God, about Vishnu. He taught that the Master of the
Universe had incarnated more than once among men. He had
appeared successively in the Seven Rishis, in Vyasa and in
Vasichta. He would appear again. But Vishnu, according to
Krishna, liked to speak sometimes through the mouths of the
humble, through a beggar, a repentant woman, a little child.
He told the people the parable of Durga, the poor fisherman,
who had found a little child dying of hunger under a tamarind
tree. The good Durga, although crippled by pain and burdened
with a large family which he did not know how he could feed,
was moved with pity for the little child and took him home.
Now the sun had set, the moon was rising over the Ganges, the
family had said the evening prayer and the little child murmured in a low voice, "The fruit of the cataca purifies water;
thus good deeds purify the soul. Take your nets, Durga. Your
boat is floating on the Ganges." Durga lowered his nets and they
were weighed down by the great number of fish. The child had
disappeared. "Thus," said Krishna, "when man forgets his own
misery for another's, Vishnu reveals himself and makes him
happy in his heart!" By such stories Krishna preached the cult

of Vishnu. Each man was amazed to find God so near his heart, when the son of Devaki spoke.

The reputation of the prophet of Mount Meru spread over India. The shepherds who had seen him grow up and had witnessed his first exploits, could not believe that this holy man was the impetuous hero they had known. Old Nanda was dead, but his two daughters, Sarasvati and Nichdali, whom Krishna loved, were still alive. Their destinies had been very different. Sarasvati, annoyed at Krishna's departure, had sought forgetfulness in marriage. She had become the wife of a man of noble caste, who had married her for her beauty, but later he had repudiated her and sold her to a *vaysia,* or merchant. Sarasvati had left this man out of contempt, to become a woman of low repute. Then one day, desolate in heart, heavy with remorse and displeasure, she returned to her country and went secretly to find her sister, Nichdali. The latter, forever thinking of Krishna as if he were present, had not married at all and lived as a servant with her brother. When Sarasvati told her of her misfortunes and shame, Nichdali answered, "My poor sister! I forgive you, but my brother will not. Krishna alone can save you!"

A flame shone in Sarasvati's lifeless eyes. "Krishna!" she exclaimed. "What has he become?"

"A saint, a great prophet. He preaches on the banks of the Ganges."

"Let us find him!" cried Sarasvati. And the two sisters set out, the one stained with passion, the other perfumed with innocence. Yet both were consumed by the same love.

Krishna was teaching his doctrine to the warriors or *Kshatryas,* for he alternately taught the Brahmans, the men of military caste, and the people. To the Brahmans he explained with the calm of mature years the deep truths of divine knowledge; before the rajahs he extolled with the fire of youth the virtues of

warriors; to the people he spoke with the simplicity of childhood, of charity, resignation and hope.

Krishna was seated at a feast in the home of a famous leader
when two women asked to be presented to the prophet. They
were allowed to enter because of their penitents' dress. Sarasvati
and Nichdali knelt at Krishna's feet. Sarasvati cried out, shed-
ding a flood of tears, "Since you left us, I have spent my life in
wrongdoing and in sin; but if you will, Krishna, you can save
me!"

Nichdali added, "O Krishna, when I saw you before, I knew
I would love you forever; now that I find you again in all
your glory I know that you are the son of Mahadeva!" And both
of them kissed his feet.

The rajahs said, "Holy Rishi, why do you allow these common women to insult you with their foolish words?"

Krishna answered, "Let them pour out their hearts. They are
worth more than you, for this one has faith, and that one, love.
Sarasvati, the sinner, is saved as of now because she believed in
me, and Nichdali, in her silence has loved truth more than you
with your shouting. Be it known that my radiant mother who
lives in Mahadeva's sun will teach Nichdali the mysteries of
eternal Love when all of you will be plunged in the darkness of
lower lives!"

From that day on, Sarasvati and Nichdali became closely
attached to Krishna and followed him with his disciples. Inspired by him, they taught other women.

Kansa still reigned in Madura. Since the murder of old
Vasichta, the king had not found peace on his throne. The
prophecy of the anchorites had come true. Devaki's son was
alive! The king had seen him, and at his gaze he had felt his
power and royalty disappear. Like a dry leaf he trembled for
his life, and often, in spite of his guards, he would turn around
suddenly, expecting to see the young hero, terrible and radiant,

standing at his door. For her part, Nysumba, tossing on her couch in her apartments, dreamed of her lost powers. When she learned that Krishna, now a prophet, was preaching on the banks of the Ganges, she persuaded the king to send a troop of soldiers to bring him back captive.

When Krishna saw the soldiers he smiled and said, "I know who you are and why you come. I am ready to follow you to your king, but first, let me tell you about the King of Heaven who is mine!" And he began to speak about Mahadeva, his splendor and his revelations. When he had finished, the soldiers presented their arms to Krishna, saying, "We shall not take you as a prisoner to our king, but we shall follow you." And they remained with him.

When he learned this, Kansa was very frightened.. Nysumba said to him, "Send the finest soldiers in the kingdom!"

This was done, and they came to the city where Krishna was teaching. They had promised not to listen to him, but when they saw the radiance of his countenance, the majesty of his carriage and the respect the crowd showed him, they could not help hearing him. Krishna spoke to them of the inner servitude of those who do evil, and the heavenly freedom of those who do good. The Kshatryas were filled with joy and surprise, for they felt relieved of a tremendous burden. "Truly you are a great magician," they said, "for we had sworn to lead you to the king in chains, but it is impossible for us to do this since you have freed us from ours."

They returned to Kansa and said to him, "We cannot bring this man to you! He is a great prophet and you have nothing to fear from him."

The king, seeing that all was useless, had his guard increased and iron chains put on all the gates of his palace. Nevertheless, one day he heard a great noise in the city and shouts of joy and triumph. The guards came and exclaimed, "It is Krishna entering Madura! The people are forcing the gates; he is breaking the iron chains!" Kansa wanted to flee, but the guards themselves compelled him to remain on his throne.

Followed by his students and a great number of anchorites, Krishna was making his entry into Madura. The city was decked with flags and in the midst of a turbulent host of people who resembled a sea disturbed by the wind, Krishna entered the city beneath a shower of garlands and flowers. Everyone acclaimed him. The Brahmans stood grouped under the sacred banana trees before the temples in order to greet Devaki's son, the conqueror of the serpent, the hero of Mount Meru, but above all, the prophet of Vishnu. Followed by a brilliant procession, hailed as liberator by the people and the *kshatryas,* Krishna appeared before the king and queen.

"You have reigned only with violence and evil," said Krishna to Kansa, "and you deserve a thousand deaths because you killed the holy elder, Vasichta. Nevertheless, you will not die yet. I want to prove to the world that it is not in killing that one triumphs over one's conquered enemies, but in forgiving them!"

"Evil magician," said Kansa, "you have stolen my crown and my kingdom! Kill me!"

"You speak like a madman," said Krishna, "for if you died in your present state of irrationality, hardness and crime, you would be lost irrevocably in the other life. If, on the other hand, you begin to understand your folly and repent in this one, your punishment will be less in the other, and through the intercession of pure spirits, one day Mahadeva will save you."

Nysumba whispered into the king's ear, "Fool! Take advantage of his pride! While one is alive, the hope for vengeance remains!"

Krishna understood what she had said without having heard it. He looked at her severely, but with great pity. "O wretched one, always your poison! Corrupter, black magician, you have nothing in your heart but the venom of serpents! Extirpate it, or one day I shall be forced to crush your head!— And now you will go with the king to a place of penitence to expiate your crimes under the supervision of the Brahmans.''

After these events, with the consent of the noblemen and people of the kingdom, Krishna consecrated Arjuna, his disciple, the most illustrious descendant of the solar race, as king of Madura. He gave supreme authority to the Brahmans, who became the king's advisors. He himself remained leader of the anchorites, who formed the superior council of Brahmans. In order to remove this council from attacks, he had a fortified city built for them and himself in the mountains. It was protected by a high wall, and was called Dvarka. In the center of this city was placed the temple of the initiates, the most important part of which was hidden underground.[19]

But when the kings of the lunar cult learned that a king of the solar cult had again ascended the throne of Madura and that through him the Brahmans were to become masters of India, they formed a powerful league among themselves in order to overthrow him. Arjuna gathered around him all the kings of the solar cult, of the white Aryan, Vedic tradition. From the heart of the temple of Dvarka, Krishna observed and guided them. The two armies found themselves face to face, and the decisive battle was imminent. But Arjuna, his master no longer near him, was troubled and his courage weakened. One morning at daybreak Krishna appeared in the tent of the king, his disciple. "Why," asked the master severely, "have you not begun the battle, which is to decide whether the sons of the sun or the sons of the moon will reign on earth?"

"Without you I cannot do it," answered Arjuna. "Look at these two great armies, these multitudes who are about to kill each other!"

From the height where they stood, the lord of spirits and the king of Madura looked upon the two great armies drawn up opposite each other. The leaders' gilded coats of mail shone in the sun; thousands of cavalrymen, horses and elephants awaited the battle signal. At that moment the leader of the enemy army, the oldest of the Kuravas, blew his great shell, whose sound resembled the roaring of a lion. At once on the vast battlefield was heard the neighing of horses, the confused noise of arms, drums and trumpets. There was a great uproar. Arjúna had only to mount his chariot, drawn by white horses, and to blow his sea shell of celestial blue, in order to give the battle signal to the sons of the sun. But here was the king, overcome by pity and discouragement. "Upon seeing this multitude about to attack each other, I feel my limbs weaken, my mouth is parched, my body trembles, my hair stands on end, my skin burns, my head swims. I see evil signs! No good can come from this massacre! What shall we do with kingdoms, pleasures and even with life? Those very men for whom we want kingdoms, pleasures and joys are standing there ready to fight each other, forgetting their lives and their possessions. Teachers, fathers, sons, grandfathers, uncles, grandsons, relatives are going to slaughter one another. I do not wish to kill them in order to reign over this earth! What pleasure can I find in killing my enemies? Once the traitors are dead, evil will fall upon us!"

"How," asked Krishna, "has this plague of fear gripped you? It is unworthy of a sage; it is the source of infamy, alienating us from heaven! Do not be a weakling! Stand on your feet!"

But Arjuna, overcome with discouragement, sat in silence. Finally he said, "I shall not fight."

Then Krishna, ruler of spirits, continued with a slight smile, "O Arjuna, I called you king of sleep so that your spirit might always watch, but your spirit has fallen asleep and your body has conquered your soul! You weep over those for whom one

118

should not mourn, and your words lack wisdom. Wise men weep neither for the living nor for the dead. You and I and those leaders of men have always existed, and we shall never cease to exist in the future. Just as the soul experiences childhood, youth and old age in this body, so will it experience it in other bodies. A man of discernment is not disturbed about it. Son of Bharat, bear pain and pleasure with the same spirit! Those whom they no longer affect deserve immortality. Those who see the real essence see the eternal, everlasting truth, which is above soul and body. Truth lives through everything, is above destruction. No one can destroy the indestructible. All these bodies will not last, and you know it. But seers know also that the incarnate soul is everlasting, indestructible and infinite. Therefore you must fight, descendant of Bharat!

"Those who believe that the soul can kill or that it is killed, are equally mistaken. The soul does not kill, neither is it killed. It is not born, it does not die and cannot lose this being which it always has had. Just as an individual throws away old clothing to put on new, so the incarnate soul casts off one body to take on others. Sword does not cut it, nor does fire burn it, water wet it, nor air wither it. It is waterproof, incombustible, durable, strong, eternal. The soul passes through everything unharmed. Therefore you should worry neither about death nor about life, O Arjuna! For one who is born, death is certain; for one who dies, birth is sure. Face your duty without flinching; for a *kshatrya* nothing is better than a fair fight. Happy are the warriors who find in battle an open door to heaven! But if you do not wish to fight this just battle, you will sink into sin, giving up your duty and reputation. All beings will speak of your everlasting infamy, and infamy is worse than death for one who has been honored!"

At these words of the master, Arjuna was seized with shame, feeling his royal blood surge up, along with his courage. He leaped into his chariot and gave the battle signal. Then Krishna said farewell to his followers and left the battlefield, for he was certain of the victory of the sons of the sun.

However, Krishna had perceived that in order to cause the defeated ones to accept his religion, it was necessary to win their souls. This would be a more difficult victory than that with arms. Just as the holy Vasichta had died, pierced by an arrow in order to reveal supreme truth to Krishna, so Krishna had to die voluntarily from the arrows of his moral enemy in order to plant in the heart of his adversary the faith he had preached to his students and to the world. He knew that the former king of Madura, far from doing penance, had taken refuge with his father-in-law, Kalayeni, king of the serpents. Kansa's hatred, constantly aroused by Nysumba, caused Krishna to be followed by spies, seeking the appropriate moment to strike him. But Krishna felt that his mission was ended and only required the supreme seal of sacrifice in order for it to be fulfilled. Therefore he stopped evading and paralyzing his enemy with the power of his will. He knew that if he ceased to protect himself with this hidden power, the long awaited blow would strike him in the darkness. But the son of Devaki wished to die far from men, in the solitude of Himavat. There he would feel nearer his radiant mother, the sublime old man and the sun of Mahadeva.

Therefore Krishna went to a retreat which was hidden in a lonely place at the foot of the lofty summits of the Himavat. None of his students had fathomed his plan. Only Sarasvati and Nichdali read it in their teacher's eyes by means of the divination which exists in woman and in love. When Sarasvati understood that Krishna wished to die, she threw herself at his feet, kissed them passionately and cried, "Master, do not leave us!"

Nichdali looked at him and said quietly, "I know where you are going. Since we love you, let us follow you!"

Krishna said, "In my heaven, love can be refused nothing. Come!"

After a long journey the prophet and the holy women reached the huts grouped about the tall, bare cedar, on a snow-capped rocky mountain. On one side, arose the immense domes of the Himavat; on the other, in the depths, were a maze of lower mountains; in the distance stretched the plain of India, lost in a dream-like, golden mist. In this retreat lived several penitents, dressed in bark clothing, their hair uncut and twisted in a knot, their beards long, bodies dirty and dusty, their limbs withered by the wind and the hot sun. Some were little more than dried skin on a dry skeleton. Upon seeing this sad place Sarasvati cried, "Earth is far away, and heaven is silent. Lord, why have you brought us to this spot, forsaken by God and men?"

"Pray," replied Krishna, "if you want earth to come near and heaven to speak to you."

"With you, heaven is always present," said Nichdali, "but why does heaven wish to leave us?"

"It is necessary," answered Krishna, "that the son of Mahadeva die, pierced by an arrow, in order that the world may believe his word."

"Explain this mystery to us!"

"You will understand it after my death. Let us pray."

For seven days they engaged in prayer and ablutions. Often Krishna's face became transfigured and was shining. On the seventh day, toward sunset, the two women saw archers coming up to the retreat.

"Here are Kansa's archers who are looking for you," said Sarasvati. "Master, defend yourself!"

Krishna, kneeling near the cedar tree, did not cease praying. The archers came and looked at the women and the penitents. They were rough soldiers with yellow and black skins.

Seeing the ecstatic form of the saint, they were speechless. At first they tried to draw him out of his ecstasy by throwing stones at him, but nothing could make him abandon his immobility. Then the soldiers seized him and tied him to the trunk of the cedar tree. Krishna let this be done as if he were in a dream. The archers took their positions at a distance and began to shoot at him. When the first arrow pierced him, Krishna cried out, "Vasichta, the sons of the sun are victorious!" When the second arrow quivered in his flesh, he said, "My radiant mother, let those who love me enter with me into your glory!" At the third, he simply said, "Mahadeva!" And then with the name of Brahma, he gave up his spirit.

Krishna's body was burned by his followers in the holy city of Dvarka. Sarasvati and Nichdali threw themselves into the fire so they could join their teacher. The crowd thought they saw Mahadeva arise out of the flames in a body of light.

After these events became known, a great part of India embraced the cult of Vishnu, which reconciled the solar and lunar cults in the religion of Brahma.

13

The Radiance of the Solar Word

S UCH is the legend of Krishna, reconstructed in its organic whole and placed in historical perspective.

It sheds a vivid light on the origins of Brahmanism. Naturally it is impossible to establish on the basis of actual documents that behind the myth of Krishna is a real person. The threefold veil which covers the evolution of all oriental religions is thicker in India than elsewhere. For the Brahmans, absolute masters of Hindu society, sole guardians of its traditions, often remolded and transformed them in the course of ages. But they faithfully preserved all the basic elements, and if their sacred teaching has changed with the centuries, its core has never been touched. Therefore, unlike many European scientists, we do not explain a figure like Krishna by saying that it is "a fairy tale drawn out of a solar myth, with a philosophic fantasy to cap it all." We do not believe that this attitude explains how a religion was established which has lasted thousands of years, has produced a marvelous poetry and several great philosophers, has resisted the strong attack of Buddhism,[20] the Mongol and Mohammendan invasions and the English conquest, preserving even in its extreme decadence, the feeling for its unknown and exalted origin. A great man is always involved in the origin of a great institution. Considering the dominant role of the character of Krishna in epic and religious tradition, his human elements on the one hand and his constant identification with God manifest, or Vishnu, on the other, it behooves us to believe that he was the creator of the Vishnu cult which gave Brahmanism its power and its prestige. It is therefore logical to admit that in the midst of the religious and social chaos which the invasion of naturalist and passional cults made in primitive India, an enlightened reformer appeared who revived the pure Aryan doctrine with the idea of the Trinity and the Divine Word made manifest, who put the seal on his work by the sacrifice of his life, thus giving India her religious soul, her national impress and her definitive organization.

Krishna's importance will appear still greater and of a truly universal nature if we recognize that his doctrine contains two basic ideas, two organizing principles of religious and esoteric philosophy. I am speaking of the organic doctrine of the immortality of the soul or progressive lives through reincarnation, and his teaching of the Trinity or the Divine Word revealed in man. I have but briefly indicated the philosophical import of this major concept which, when thoroughly understood, brings about life-giving results in all domains of science, art and life. In conclusion, I shall confine myself to a historical remark.

The idea that God, Truth, Infinite Beauty and Goodness are revealed in conscious man with a redemptive power which rises to the heights of heaven through the power of love and sacrifice—this idea, fecund above all others, appears for the first time in Krishna. It is personified at the moment when, forsaking its Aryan youth, humanity is about to sink deeper and deeper into the worship of matter. Krishna reveals the idea of the Holy Word; humanity will no longer forget it. Humanity will thirst even more for redeemers and sons of God as it realizes its decadence more keenly. After Krishna, the Solar Word shines powerfully in the temples of Asia, Africa and Europe. In Persia, it is Mithras, reconcilor of the luminous Ormuzd and somber Ahriman; in Egypt, it is Horus, son of Osiris and Isis; in Greece, it is Apollo, god of the sun and the lyre; it is Dionysius, awakener of souls. Everywhere the solar god is a mediating god, and light is also the Word of Life. Is it not also from this that the Messianic idea comes? Be this as it may, it is through Krishna that this idea entered the ancient world; it is through Jesus that it will spread over the entire earth.

In the remainder of this secret history of religions, I shall show how the teaching of the divine Trinity is linked to that of the soul and its evolution, and how and why they are implied in and complement one another. Let us say at once that their point of contact forms the vital center, the glowing crux of esoteric doctrine. In observing the great religions of India, Egypt, Greece and Judea merely externally, one sees only discord, superstition, chaos. But, investigate the symbols, question the Mysteries, look for the basic teaching of the founders and prophets, and harmony will be observed. By varied and often indirect roads one will finally recognize that to fathom the arcana of one of these religions is to fathom the arcana of all the others. Then a strange phenomenon comes about. Bit by bit, but in a widening circle, one sees the doctrine of the initiates shine in the center of religions like a sun, while each single religion appears as a different planet. With each of them we change atmosphere and celestial orientation, but it is always the same sun which lights our way. India, the great dreamer, plunges us along with herself into the dream of Eternity. Grandiose Egypt, of deathly austerity, invites us to the journey beyond the grave. Enchanting Greece transports us to magic festivals of life and gives her Mysteries the character of alternating charm and terror, and of her eternally passionate soul. Finally, Pythagoras scientifically formulates esoteric teaching, gives it perhaps the fullest and soundest expression it has ever had, for Plato and the Alexandrians were but its popularizers.

In the jungles of the Ganges and the solitudes of the Himalayas we have seen the source of this esoteric teaching.

HERMES

The Mysteries of Egypt

O blind soul, arm yourself with the torch of the Mysteries and in terrestrial night you will discover your luminous reflection, your heavenly soul. Follow this divine guide, letting him be your Genius. For he holds the key to your past and future lives.
—Call to the Initiates, from *The Book of the Dead*

Listen to your inner selves and look into the infinity of space and time. There reverberate the song of the stars, the voice of the numbers and the harmony of the spheres.

Each sun is a thought of God, each planet a mode of that thought. In order that you may know divine thought, O souls, you painfully descend along the paths of the seven planets and their seven heavens and ascend once again.

What do the stars do? What do the numbers say? What do the spheres revolve? O souls that are lost and saved, they relate, they sing, they revolve—your destinies!
—Fragment from *Hermes*

14

The Sphinx

I N comparison with Babylon, mournful metropolis of despotism, in the ancient world Egypt was a veritable citadel of
sacred knowledge, a school for its most illustrious prophets, a
shelter and a laboratory for the noblest traditions of humanity.
Thanks to great excavations and remarkable research activities,
the ancient Egyptians are better known to us today than any of
the civilizations which preceded Greece, for Egypt reveals to us
its history, written on pages of stone. Its monuments are being
excavated, its hieroglyphs are being deciphered, but the deepest arcanum of its history is yet to be fathomed. This arcanum is
the esoteric teaching of its priests. This teaching, scientifically
cultivated in the temples, prudently veiled in its Mysteries, reveals to us simultaneously the soul of Egypt, the secret of its
politics and its preponderant role in the history of the universe.

Our historians speak of Pharaohs in the same manner as of
the despots of Nineveh and Babylon. For them, Egypt is an absolute and conquering monarchy like Assyria, differing from
the latter only in that it lasted several thousand years longer. Do

they realize that in Assyria royalty crushed the priesthood in order to make of it a tool, whereas in Egypt the priesthood disciplined royalty and never abdicated even in the worst times, standing up to kings, driving out despots and always governing the nation—and this with an intellectual superiority, a profound and hidden wisdom which no teaching body has ever equalled in any country or in any age? I can hardly believe that they do, for rather than draw innumerable conclusions from this essential fact, our historians have hardly seen it and do not seem to attach any importance to it. However, one must be an archeologist or linguist to understand that the implacable hatred between Assyria and Egypt comes from the fact that these two peoples represented two opposite principles in the world, and that the Egyptian people owed their long survival to a religious and scientific framework stronger than all revolutions.

From the Aryan epoch, throughout the troubled era which followed Vedic times to the Persian conquest and the Alexandrian age, (that is, over a period of more than five thousand years) Egypt was the stronghold of pure and exalted teachings, whose totality constitutes the science of principles, and which can be called the esoteric orthodoxy of antiquity. It was possible for fifty dynasties to succeed one another, for the Nile to deposit its alluvium over entire cities, for the Phoenician invasion to flood the country and be repelled;—in the midst of history's ebb and flow, beneath the seeming idolatry of its external polytheism, Egypt preserved the ancient foundations of esoteric theology and its priestly organization. It stood firm against the centuries like the pyramid of Gizeh, half-sunk beneath the sands, but intact. Thanks to this immobility of the sphinx, keeping its secret, to this resistance in granite, Egypt became the axis around which the religious thought of humanity revolved in its passage from Asia to Europe. Judea,

Greece and Etruria were so many spirits of life which formed different civilizations. But from whom did they draw their basic ideas, if not the living storehouse of ancient Egypt? Moses and Orpheus created two opposite and remarkable religions, one with its rigid monotheism, the other with its dazzling polytheism. But in what mold was their genius formed? Where did one of them find the power, energy, boldness to recast a half-savage people like brass in a furnace, and where did the other find the magic to make gods speak to the soul of its fascinated barbarians like a well-tuned lyre? In the temples of Osiris, in ancient Thebes, which the initiates called the city of the sun or the solar ark because it contained the synthesis of divine science and all the secrets of initiation.

Every year at the summer solstice when the floods of rain fall in Abyssinia, the Nile changes color and takes on that tint of blood, about which the Bible speaks. The Nile swells until the autumnal equinox conceals the outline of its banks. But standing upon their granite plateaus beneath the blinding sun, temples carved in the heart of the rock, necropoles, pylons and pyramids reflect the majesty of their ruins in the Nile, now transformed into a sea. Thus the Egyptian priesthood passed through the centuries accompanied by its organization and symbols, secrets which for a long time were impenetrable to science. In these temples, these crypts, these pyramids developed the famous teaching of the Word of Light, of the universal Word which Moses enclosed in his golden ark and of which Christ was to be the living torch.

Truth is unchangeable in itself, it alone outlives everything, but it changes its habitations, its forms and its manifestations. "The light of Osiris" which once lighted the depths of nature and the heavenly vault for the initiates is extinguished forever in the abandoned crypts. Hermes' saying to Asclepios was fulfilled: "O Egypt! Egypt!—In future generations there will remain only incredible tales about you, and nothing will be left but words carved in stone."

Nevertheless, it is a ray from that mysterious sun of the sanctuaries which we would like to bring to life once again by following the secret path of ancient Egyptian initiation, insofar as the esoteric institution itself and the fleeting reflection of the ages will allow.

But before entering the temple let us glance at the great phases through which Egypt passed before the age of the Hyksos.

Almost as old as the framework of our continent, the earliest Egyptian civilization dates back to the ancient red race.[21] The colossal sphinx of Gizeh near the great pyramid, is its handiwork. From the time when the Delta (later formed by the alluvium of the Nile) did not yet exist, the huge symbolic animal lay upon its granite hill, before the chain of the Lybian Mountains, looking at the sea, dashing against its feet where today the sands of the desert are spread. The sphinx, that first creation of Egypt, became the latter's principal symbol, its distinctive mark. The oldest human priesthood carved it, a picture of calm and of the awe-inspiring majesty of nature. A man's head emerges from a bull's body with lion's paws, and folds its eagle wings at its sides. It is terrestrial Isis, a portrayal of the living unity of nature's kingdoms, for the ancient priesthoods knew and taught that in the great order of evolution, human nature emerges from animal nature. In this composite of bull, lion, eagle and man are also contained the four animals of Ezekiel's vision, representing the four constituent elements of the microcosm and macrocosm: water, earth, air and fire, the foundations of esoteric science. This is why, in subsequent centuries when the initiates saw the sacred animal lying on the steps of the temples or in the recesses of crypts, they felt this mystery come to life within them and they silently folded the wings of their spirits over inner truth. For before Oedipus, they knew that the answer to the riddle of the sphinx is Man, the microcosm, the divine agent who includes within himself all the elements and forces of nature.

The red race therefore, has left no other trace of itself than the sphinx of Gizeh, irrecusable proof that in its own way it had posed and solved the great problem.

15

Hermes

THE black race which succeeded the southern red race in dominion over the world, made Upper Egypt its main sanctuary. The name Hermes-Toth, that mysterious first initiator of Egypt into the sacred doctrine, doubtless refers to an initial, peaceful mixture of the white race and the black race in the regions of Ethiopia and Upper Egypt, long before the Aryan period. Hermes is a generic name like Manu and Buddha. It designates man, a caste and a god at the same time. As a man, Hermes is the first and great initiator of Egypt; as a caste, Hermes is the priesthood, the depositary of esoteric traditions; as a god, Hermes is the planet Mercury, including in its sphere a category of spirits and divine initiators; in brief, Hermes presides in the supraterrestrial region of celestial initiation. In the spiritual economy of the world all these things are bound together by secret affinities as by an invisible thread. The name Hermes is a talisman which sums them up, a magic sound which calls them forth. Hence its prestige. The Greeks, disciples of the Egyptians, called him Hermes Trismegistus, or three times great, because he was considered king, legislator and priest. He typifies a period when priesthood, magistracy and royalty were united in a single governing body. Manetho's Egyptian chronology calls this period the reign of the gods. At that time there was neither papyrus nor phonetic writing, but sacred ideography already existed; the science of the priesthood was inscribed in hieroglyphs on the columns and walls of the crypts. Considerably improved, it later passed into the temple libraries. The Egyptians attributed to Hermes forty-two books dealing with esoteric science. The Greek book known by the name *Hermes Trismegistus,* indeed includes altered but infinitely valuable fragments of ancient theogony which is like the *fiat lux* from which Moses and Orpheus received their first enlightenment. The doctrine of the fire-principle and of the word-light contained in the *Vision of Hermes* will remain the climax and center of Egyptian initiation.

We shall attempt to rediscover this vision of the masters, this mystic rose which blooms only in the darkness of the sanctuary and in the arcana of the great religions. Certain of Hermes' words, stamped with ancient wisdom, are well adapted to prepare us for this. "None of our thoughts," said he to his disciple, Asklepius, "can conceive of God, nor can any language define Him. The incorporeal, invisible and formless cannot be comprehended by our senses. What is eternal cannot be measured with the short measure of time; God therefore is ineffable. God indeed can transmit to a few elect the ability to rise above natural things in order to perceive some radiation of His supreme perfection, but these elect find no words to translate into every-day language the non-material vision which has made them tremble. They can explain to humanity the secondary causes of the creations which take place before their eyes as images of universal life, but the First Cause remains hidden, and we shall not succeed in understanding it except by experiencing death." Thus spoke Hermes about the unknown God on the threshold of the crypts. The disciples who entered with him into their depths learned to know Him as a living being.[22]

The book speaks of his death as of the departure of a god. "Hermes saw the totality of things, and having seen he understood, and having understood he had the power to manifest and to reveal. What he thought, he wrote; what he wrote, he hid in great measure, keeping wisely silent and speaking at the same time so that all the world to come might seek these things. And thus, having commanded the gods, his brothers, to act like participants in a funeral procession, he ascended to the stars."

If it is absolutely necessary, one can isolate the political history of peoples, but one cannot isolate their religious history. The religions of Assyria, Egypt, Judea and Greece are understood only when one grasps their point of connection with the ancient Indo-Aryan religion. Considered separately, they are but so many puzzles and pantomimes. Viewed together and from above, they represent a superb evolution, where all the elements control and explain each other. In short, the history of a religion will always be limited, superstitious and false; nothing is true except the total religious history of all mankind. At this level one no longer feels anything but the currents which encircle the globe. The Egyptian people, of all humanity the most independent and isolated from external influences, could not escape this universal law. Five thousand years before our time, the light of Rama, kindled in Iran, shone upon Egypt and became the law of Ammon-Ra, the solar god of Thebes. This establishment enabled him to brave many revolutions. Menes was the first king of justice, the first Pharaoh to carry out this law. He was careful not to take from Egypt her former theology, which was his also. He simply confirmed and expanded it by adding to it a new social organization. The priests were given the task of instruction as a first council; judges were assigned to another; government to both; royalty was conceived of as their task, and subject to their control; the relative independence of the nomes of provinces was the foundation of society. This can be called the government of the initiates. As a keystone it had a synthesis of sciences known under the name of Osiris (O-Sir-Is), intellectual lord. The great pyramid was its symbol, as was the mathematical gnomon. The Pharaoh who received his initiation-name from the temple, who exercised sacerdotal and royal art on the throne, was therefore a far different person from the Assyrian despot whose arbitrary power rested upon crime and blood. Pharaoh was the crowned initiate, or at least the pupil and instrument of the initiates. For centuries the Pharaohs were to defend the law of the Ram, which then represented the rights of justice and international arbitration, against then despotic Asia and anarchic Europe.

Around the year 2,000 B.C. Egypt underwent the most dreadful crisis a people can experience: that of foreign invasion and partial conquest. The Phoenician invasion was itself the result of the great religious schism in Asia which had aroused the masses to insurrection. Led by shepherd-kings called Hyksos, this invasion rolled its flood over the Delta and Middle Egypt. The schismatic kings brought with them a corrupt civilization, Ionian indolence, the luxury of Asia, the customs of the harem and crude idolatry. The life of Egypt was threatened, its culture and its universal mission were endangered. But Egypt possessed a spirit of life, that is, an organized body of initiates, depositaries of the ancient knowledge of Hermes and Ammon-Ra. And what did that spirit do? It withdrew to the heart of its sanctuaries, it gathered itself together, the better to resist the enemy. The priesthood outwardly bowed before the invasion and recognized the usurpers who brought the law of the Bull and the cult of Apis. But, hidden in the temples like a sacred depositary, the two councils kept their science and traditions, the ancient pure religion, and with it the hope of a restoration of the former dynasty. It is at this period that the priests propagated among the people the legend of Isis and Osiris, of the dismemberment of the latter and his subsequent resurrection through his son Horus, who would find his scattered limbs, carried away by the Nile. The imagination of the people was stimulated by the pomp of public ceremonies. Their love for the old religion was maintained by acting out the misfortunes of the goddess, her lamentation over the loss of her celestial husband and the hope she placed in her son Horus, the divine mediator. But at the same time the initiates deemed it necessary to place esoteric truth beyond attack by covering it with a threefold veil. The spreading of the popular cult of Isis and Osiris corresponds with the inner scientific organization of the greater and lesser Mysteries. Moral tests were invented, the oath of silence was required, and the penalty of death strictly inflicted upon the initiates who divulged the least detail of the Mysteries. Thanks to this strict organization, Egyptian initiation became not only the haven of esoteric doctrine, but also the crucible of the revival of Egypt and the school for future religions. While the crowned usurpers ruled in Memphis, Thebes was slowly preparing the regeneration of the people. From his temple, from his solar ark, came the savior of Egypt, Amos, who routed the Hyksos after nine centuries of domination, restoring Egyptian science and the male religion of Osiris to their rightful place.

Thus the Mysteries saved the soul of Egypt under foreign tyranny, for the good of mankind. For such was then the strength of their discipline, the power of their initiation, that they contained Egypt's best moral force and highest spiritual achievements.

Ancient initiation rested upon a concept of man, both healthier and nobler than ours. We have dissociated the training of the body, soul and spirit. Our physical and natural sciences, progressive in themselves, set aside the principle of the soul and its diffusion in the universe; our religion does not satisfy the needs of the spirit; our medicine wishes to know neither soul nor spirit. Modern man seeks pleasure without happiness, happiness without knowledge and knowledge without wisdom. The ancients did not allow one to separate these things. In every domain they took into account man's threefold nature. Initiation was a gradual training of every human being toward the lofty heights of the spirit, from which one can survey life. "In order to attain mastery," said the sages of that age, "man needs a total remolding of his physical, moral and spiritual being. But this remolding is only possible through the simultaneous exercise of the will, intuition and reason. Through the complete cooperation of these three, man can develop his faculties to an incalculable degree. The soul has senses which are asleep; initiation awakens them. Through profound study and constant application, man can put himself in conscious touch with the hidden forces in the universe. Through a great effort he can attain direct spiritual perception, can open to his vision paths of the after-life and can make himself capable of advancing along these paths. Only then can he say he has conquered fate and here on earth has acquired his divine freedom. Only then can the initiate become an initiator, prophet and theurgist, that is, a seer and creator of souls. For only one who controls himself can control others; only one who is free can set free."

The ancient initiates thought in this manner. The greatest among them lived and acted accordingly. Therefore initiation was something very different from an empty dream and far more than a simple scientific precept; it was the creation of a soul through itself, its development to a higher level and its efflorescence in the divine world.

Let us place ourselves in the age of the Rameses during the time of Moses and Orpheus, around the year 1300 B.C., and attempt to reach the heart of Egyptian initiation. The sculptured monuments, Hermes' books and the Jewish and Greek tradition enable us to call the progressive stages of initiation to life again and to form an idea of the highest revelation of Egyptian spiritual development.

16

Isis — Initiation — The Trials

IN the time of the Rameses, Egyptian civilization was shining in the fullness of its glory. The Pharaohs of the twentieth dynasty, pupils and sword-bearers of the sanctuaries, bore the battle against Babylon like real heros. The Egyptian archers harassed the Lybians, Bodons and Numdis to the center of Africa. A fleet of four hundred sailboats pursued the league of the schismatics to the mouth of the Indus. Better to withstand the attack of Assyria and its allies, the Rameses had laid out strategic routes as far as Lebanon, and had built a system of forts between Mageddo and Karkemish. Endless caravans moved through the desert from Radasieh to Elephantine. Architectual activity continued without a break and occupied workers from three continents. The nypostyle room of Karnak, each pillar of which reaches the height of the Vendome Column, was repaired; the Temple of Abydos was adorned with sculptural wonders, and the Valley of the Kings with grandiose monuments. Building went on at Bubast, Luksor and Speos Ibsambul. At Thebes a victory pylon commemorated the taking of Kadesh. At Memphis the Rameseum arose, surrounded by a forest of obelisk statues and gigantic monoliths.

In the midst of this feverish activity, this glittering life, more than one foreigner seeking the Mysteries, coming from the distant shores of Asia Minor, the Mountains of Thracia, landed in Egypt, attracted by the reputation of its temples. When he arrived in Memphis, he was struck with amazement. Monuments, spectacles, public festivals, all gave him the impression of wealth and grandeur. After the ceremony of royal consecration, which took place in the secrecy of the sanctuary, he would see the Pharaoh leave the temple before the crowd and climb upon his shield carried by twelve flag-bearing officers of his staff. Before him twelve young Levites carried the royal insignia on gold-braided cushions: the ruler's sceptre with a ram's head, the sword, bow and collection of arms. Behind him came the royal household and the priestly schools, followed by the initiates in the major and minor Mysteries. The pontiffs wore the white tiara and their chests glowed with the fire of symbolic jewels. The dignitaries of the crown wore decorations of the Lamb, Ram, Lion, Lily and Bee, suspended from massive chains, intricately worked. The guilds brought up the rear of the procession with their emblems and flying banners. At night magnificently decorated boats carried the royal orchestras over artificial lakes. On the boats dancers and musicians were outlined in hieratic poses.

But this overwhelming pomp was not what the traveler was seeking. A desire to penetrate the secret of things, a thirst for knowledge, is what brought him from so far away. He had been told that magi and hierophants, in possession of divine science, lived in the sanctuaries of Egypt. He too wanted to fathom the secret of the gods. He had heard a priest of his country speak of *The Book of the Dead,* of its mysterious scroll which was placed beneath mummies' heads like a *viaticum,* and which related in symbolic form the voyage of the soul after death, according to the priests of Ammon-Ra. With avid curiosity and a certain inner fear mixed with doubt, he had followed this long voyage of the soul into the after-life, witnessing expiation in a burning region, the purification of its sidereal covering, its encounter with the evil pilot seated in a boat with his head turned aside, and with the good pilot who looks forward. He observed the soul's appearance before the forty-two terrestrial judges, its justification by Toth and finally its entry and transfiguration in the light of Osiris. We can imagine the power of this book, as well as the total revolution that Egyptian initiation sometimes effected upon human minds, from this passage of *The Book of the Dead:*

"This chapter was found at Hermopolis in blue writing on an alabaster stone, at the feet of the god Toth (Hermes) in the time of King Menkara, by Prince Hastatif, when he was on a trip to inspect the temples. He carried the stone into the royal temple. O great secret! He no longer saw, he no longer heard, when he read that pure and holy chapter; he no longer went near any woman and no longer ate meat or fish."

But what truth was there in this disturbing account, in these hieratic pictures, behind which glistened the terrible mysteries of after-life? "Isis and Osiris know," he was told. But who were these gods about whom one spoke only with one's finger upon one's lips? It was to learn this that the stranger knocked at the door of the great temple of Thebes, or of Memphis.

Servants led him beneath the portico of an inner court, whose great pillars seemed like gigantic lotus supporting the solar ark, the Temple of Osiris, with their strength and purity. The hierophant approached the new arrival. The majesty of his countenance, the tranquillity of his face, the mystery of his dark, impenetrable eyes, filled with an inner light, were already enough to disquiet the postulant. That gaze pierced like an awl. The stranger felt that he was facing a man from whom it would be impossible to hide anything. The priest of Osiris questioned the newcomer about the city of his birth, his family and the temple which had instructed him. If in this brief but penetrating examination he was considered unworthy of the Mysteries, a silent but irrevocable gesture pointed to the door. But if the hierophant found in the aspirant the sincere desire for truth, he asked him to follow him. They passed through porticos and inner courts, then through a corridor carved in the rock, open to the sky and bordered with stelae and sphinxes, until they reached a small temple which served as an entrance to the underground crypts. The door was disguised by a life-sized statue of Isis. The goddess, seated in an attitude of meditation and contemplation, held a closed book in her lap. Her face was veiled. Beneath the statue one could read, "No mortal has lifted my veil."

"This is the door to the hidden sanctuary," said the hierophant. "Look at these two columns. The red one represents the ascension of the spirit into the light of Osiris. The black one signifies its captivity in matter, and this fall can continue into annihilation. Whoever approaches our science and teaching risks his life. Madness or death is what the weak or the wicked find; the strong and the good alone find life and immortality. Many reckless ones have entered this door, and have not come out alive. It is an abyss which leads only the fearless to the daylight once again. Therefore, consider carefully what you are about to do, the dangers you will face, and if your courage is not equal to every ordeal, give up the quest. For once this door is closed behind you, you will no longer be able to turn back."

If the stranger persisted in his wish, the hierophant would lead him into the outer court and commend him to the temple servants, with whom he was required to spend a week, obliged to perform the most menial tasks, listening to the hymns and performing ablutions. He had to observe the strictest silence.

When the evening of the ordeals arrived, two *neocoros,* or assistants, led the candidate for the mysteries to the door of the secret sanctuary. They entered a dark corridor without any visible exit. On the two sides of this dismal room, in the torchlight, the stranger saw a row of statues with men's bodies and animals' heads,—lions, bulls, birds of prey, and serpents— which seemed to watch his progress while they mocked him. At the end of this sinister passage, which was crossed in complete silence, a mummy and a human skeleton stood opposite each other. And with a silent gesture, the two *neocoros* showed the novice a hole in the wall in front of him. It was the entrance to a corridor so low that it could be entered only by crawling on hands and knees.

"You can still turn back," said one of the assistants. "The door of the sanctuary is not yet closed. If you do not turn back now, you must continue on your way and cannot return."

"I shall go forward," said the novice, summoning all his courage.

He was then given a little lighted lamp. The *neocoros* turned around and closed the door of the sanctuary with a loud bang. The novice could no longer hesitate; he had to enter the corridor. Hardly had he eased through by crawling on his knees when he heard a voice at the end of the tunnel, saying, "Fools who covet knowledge and power perish here!" Because of a strange acoustical phenomenon, this sentence was repeated seven times by echoes at various points. Nevertheless, he had to move forward; the corridor became wider, but inclined downward more sharply. At last the daring traveller found himself before a shaft which led into a hole. An iron ladder disappeared into the latter; the novice took a chance. As he hung upon the lowest rung of the ladder, his frightened gaze looked downward into a terrifying abyss. His poor naphtha lamp which he gripped convulsively in his trembling hand, cast its dim light into endless darkness. What should he do? Above him,—impossible return; below,—a drop into the blackness of awful night. In his distress he noticed a crevice on his right. Stretching forward with one hand on the ladder, and his lamp held out with the other, he saw steps. A staircase! Safety! He climbed upward, escaping the abyss. The staircase cut through the rock in the form of a spiral. Finally, the aspirant found himself in front of a bronze grating leading into a great hall, supported by huge caryatids. On the wall could be seen two rows of symbolic frescoes. There were eleven groups on each side, softly lighted by the crystal lamps which the beautiful caryatids bore in their hands.

A Magus called a *pastophor,* a guardian of sacred symbols, opened the grating for the novice and welcomed him with a kind smile. He congratulated him upon having successfully passed the first test. Then, leading him across the hall, he explained the sacred paintings. Under each of these paintings was a letter and a number. The twenty-two symbols represented the twenty-two first Mysteries and constituted the alphabet of secret science, that is, the absolute principles, the universal keys which, employed by the will, become the source of all wisdom and power. These principles were fixed in the memory by their correspondence with the letters of the sacred language and with the numbers associated with these letters. Each letter and each number expressed in this language a ternary law, having its repercussion in the *divine world,* the *intellectual world,* and the *physical world.* Just as the finger touching the string of a lyre causes a note of the scale to resound and all its harmonics to vibrate, so the spirit which contemplates all the virtualities of a number, the voice which utters a letter with the knowledge of its meaning, evokes a power which echoes in the three worlds.

Thus the letter *A* which corresponds to number *1,* expresses *in the divine world,* Absolute Being from which all beings emanate; *in the intellectual world,* the unity, origin, and synthesis of numbers; *in the physical world,* Man, the head of related beings, who, through expansion of his faculties, rises into the concentric spheres of infinity. The arcanum was represented among the Egyptians by a Magus in a white robe, a scepter in his hand and wearing a gold crown. The white robe meant purity, the scepter, authority and the gold crown, universal light.

The novice was far from understanding everything he heard that was strange and new, but great perspectives opened before him at the words of the *pastophor* before the beautiful paintings, which looked at him with the impassive gravity of the gods. Behind each of them he glimpsed a series of thoughts, and pictures suddenly were called forth. He surmised for the first time *the interior* of the world through the mysterious chain of causes. Thus, from letter to letter, from number to number, the teacher explained to the pupil the meaning of the arcana, and led him past *Isis Urania* to the *Chariot of Osiris,* past the *Thunderstruck Tower* to the *Flaming Star,* and finally to the *Crown of the Magi.* "Mark well," said the *pastophor,* "what this crown means: all will which is joined to God in order to manifest truth and to effect justice after this life, enters into participation with divine power over beings and things, attaining the everlasting reward of liberated spirits." While listening to the teacher's words, the neophyte experienced a mixture of surprise, fear and rapture. These were the first lights of the sanctuary, and the truth seen in part, appeared to him to be the light of a divine recollection.

But the trials were not over. When he finished speaking, the *pastophor* opened a door leading to another long, narrow corridor, at the end of which glowed a red-hot furnace. "Why that is death!" exclaimed the novice, looking at his guide fearfully.

"My son," said the *pastophor*, "death frightens only weak minds. I once crossed this fire like a bed of roses." And the gate of the hall of secrets closed behind the postulant. Upon approaching the fiery furnace, he saw it reduced to an optical illusion created by a light interlacing of resinous wood placed over iron lattice work in quincunxes. A path through the middle allowed him to pass by quickly. The *trial by water* followed the *trial by fire*. The aspirant was forced to go through a stagnant black pool, lighted by naphtha flames which flashed up behind him in the room of fire. After this, two assistants led him, still trembling, into a dim grotto where a soft couch could be dimly seen, lighted by the mysterious flickering of a bronze lamp hanging from the vault. He was dried, his body was bathed in exquisite essences, he was dressed in fine linen and was left alone after being told, "Rest and wait for the hierophant."

Weak with fatigue, the novice stretched himself upon the sumptuous bed. After his varied emotions this moment of calm seemed sweet. The sacred paintings he had seen, all those strange faces, the sphinx, the caryatids, again passed before his eyes. But why did one of the paintings keep coming back to him like an hallucination? Again and again he saw arcanum X represented by a wheel suspended on its axis between two columns. On one side sits Hermanubis, genius of good,—handsome as a young Ephebe; on the other, Typhon, genius of evil, falls head downward into the abyss. Between the two, on top of the wheel, sits a sphinx holding a sword in its paw.

The tones of lascivious music which seemed to come from outside the grotto, caused this picture to fade. The sounds were light and undefinable, of a sad, penetrating languor. A metallic tinkling reached his ear, mixed with vibrations of the harp and the sounds of a flute, along with panting sighs like a torrid breathing. Wrapped in a dream of fire, the stranger closed his eyes. Upon reopening them, he saw an overwhelming vision of life and infernal seduction a few steps away from his bed. A Nubian woman, clothed in transparent dark-red gauze, a necklace of amulettes at her neck, similar to the priestesses of Mylitta, was standing there embracing him with her glance, holding a cup crowned with roses in her left hand. She was of the type whose intense, strong sensuality embodies all the powers of the female animal: high, prominent cheekbones, nostrils dilated, full lips like a delicious ripe fruit. Her dark eyes shone in the dusk. The novice had lept to his feet in astonishment, not knowing whether he should tremble or rejoice, instinctively crossing his hands on his chest. But the slave moved toward him, slowly lowering her eyes. In a low voice she murmured, "Are you afraid of me, noble stranger? I bring you the reward of conquerors, the forgetfulness of troubles, the cup of happiness." The novice hesitated; then, as though overcome with lassitude, the Nubian woman sank upon the bed, enveloping the stranger in a pleading look as in a humid flame. Woe to him if he did not defy her, if he bent over that mouth, if he became drunk with the heavy perfumes arising from these bronzed shoulders! Once he had touched that hand and had placed his lips upon that cup, he was lost. He turned upon his bed, entwined in a burning grasp . . . But after the wild satisfying of his desire, the liquid he had drunk plunged him into a deep sleep. When he awoke, he found himself alone and in anguish. The lamp cast a ghost-like light upon his disordered bed. A man was standing before him; it was the hierophant. He said to him:

"You were victorious in the first trials. You triumphed over death, fire and water, but you have not learned to conquer yourself. You who seek the heights of the mind and knowledge succumbed to the first temptation of the senses and fell into the abyss of matter. One who is a slave to the senses lives in darkness. You preferred darkness to light; therefore remain in darkness. I warned you of the dangers to which you were exposing yourself. You saved your life, but you have lost your freedom. You are to remain a slave of the temple, under penalty of death."

If, on the other hand, the aspirant had overturned the cup and repelled the temptress, twelve *neocoros* armed with torches would have come to lead him triumphantly into the sanctuary of Isis where Magi, ranked in a semi-circle and dressed in white, awaited him in a plenary assembly. In the depths of the temple he would see the colossal statue of Isis in cast metal, splendidly lighted, a gold rose at her breast, and wearing a crown of seven rays. She held her son Horus in her arms. The goddess and the hierophant clothed in velvet, would receive the newcomer, and under the most awesome oaths, make him pledge silence and submission. Then he greeted him in the name of the entire assembly as a brother and future initiate. Before the august teachers, the disciple of Isis thought himself in the presence of the gods. Grown beyond himself, he entered for the first time into the sphere of truth.

17

Osiris — Death and Resurrection

NEVERTHELESS he was admitted only to the threshold. Long years of study and apprenticeship began. Before rising to Isis Uranus, he had to know terrestrial Isis, had to learn the physical sciences. His time was divided between meditations in his cell, the study of hieroglyphics in the halls and courts of the temple, as large as a city, and in lessons from his teachers. He learned the science of minerals and plants, the history of man and peoples, medicine, architecture and sacred music. In this long apprenticeship he had not only to *know,* but to *become.* He had to acquire strength through renunciation. The ancient wise men believed that man possesses truth only if it becomes a part of his innermost being, a spontaneous deed of his soul. But in this intense work of assimilation, the pupil was left to himself. His teachers did not help him in anything, and often he was amazed at their coldness and their indifference. He was carefully supervised, he was subjected to inflexible rules, absolute obedience was required of him, but nothing was revealed to him beyond certain limits. His uncertainties and his questions were answered by "Wait and work." Then, sudden revolts, bitter regrets and horrible suspicions surged up in him. Had he become the slave of bold impostors or black magicians who were subjugating his will to an infamous purpose? Truth was fleeing, the gods were abandoning him, he was alone, a prisoner of the temple. Truth appeared to him in the form of a sphinx. The sphinx said to him, "I am Doubt!" And the winged beast, with its head of an impassive woman and its lion's paw, carried him away to tear him apart in the burning desert sand.

But hours of calm and divine forbearance followed these nightmares. Then he understood the symbolic meaning of the trials he had gone through upon entering the temple. For, alas! The dark well into which he had almost fallen was less dark than the abyss of unfathomable truth; the fire he had passed through was less to be feared than the passions which still burned his flesh; the black, freezing water into which he had to plunge was less cold than the doubt into which his mind sank and became engulfed in his evil moments.

In one of the halls of the temple, arranged in two rows, were those same sacred paintings which had been explained to him in the crypt during the night of ordeals, and which represented the twenty-two arcana. These arcana, which could be partly seen at the threshold of esoteric science, were the very pillars of theology, but it was necessary to have gone through the entire initiation in order to understand them. Since then none of the leaders had spoken to him of them again. He was allowed only to walk in this room and meditate upon the signs. He spent long, solitary hours there. Through these figures, pure as light, serious as Eternity, invisible and impalpable truth slowly entered the heart of the neophyte. In the silent society of these quiet, nameless divinities, each of which seemed to preside over a sphere of life, he began to feel something new: First, a descent into the depths of his being, then a sort of detachment from the world, which made him soar above things. Sometimes he asked one of the Magi, "One day will I be allowed to smell the rose of Isis, to see the light of Osiris?" He was told, "That does not depend upon us; truth is not given. Either one finds it in oneself, or one does not find it. We cannot make an adept of you; you must become one yourself. The lotus grows under the river a long time before it blossoms. Do not rush the blossoming of the divine flower! If it is to come, it will appear in its own time. Work and pray!"

And the disciple returned to his studies and to his meditation with a quiet joy. He enjoyed the strict, sweet charm of the solitude where a breath of the Being of Beings passes. Thus the months and years flowed by. He felt a slow transformation, a complete metamorphosis taking place within him. The passions which had attacked his youth moved away from him like ghosts, and the thoughts which now encircled him were kind, like immortal friends. What he experienced now was the swallowing up of his earthly self and the birth of another, purer, more ethereal self. In this mood he would fall prostrate before the steps of the closed sanctuary. Then there was no longer any revolt, no desire of any kind, no regret in him. There was only a perfect surrender of his soul to the gods, a complete oblation to truth. "O Isis," he would say in his prayer, "since my soul is but a teardrop from your eyes, may it fall as dew upon other souls, and in dying may I feel their perfume arise to you! Here am I, ready for the sacrifice!"

After one of these silent prayers, the disciple in a semi-ecstasy saw the hierophant standing near him like a vision from the sun, enclosed in the warm colors of sunset. The master seemed to read all the disciple's thoughts, to penetrate the entire drama of his inner life.

"My son," he said, "the time is approaching when truth will

be revealed to you, for already you have had a foretaste of it in going down into your innermost depths, and there finding the life divine. You are to enter the great, ineffable communion of the initiates, for you are worthy of it by the purity of your heart, by your love of truth and your power of self-denial. But no one crosses Osiris' threshold except by way of death and resurrection. We shall accompany you into the crypt. Be not afraid, for you are already one of our brothers!"

At dusk the priests of Osiris, bearing torches, accompanied the new adept into the lower crypt, supported by four pillars, placed upon sphinxes. In a corner was an open marble sarcophagus.[23]

"No man," said the hierophant, "escapes death, and every living soul is destined to resurrection. The adept goes through the tomb alive, that afterward he may enter into the light of Osiris. Lie down, therefore, in this coffin and wait for the light! Tonight you will go through the door of Fear and you will reach the threshold of Mastery."

The initiate lay down in the open sarcophagus. The hierophant extended his hand over him in blessing and the procession of initiates left the cave in silence. A little lamp placed on the ground flickeringly lights the four sphinxes which support the thick columns of the crypt. A choir of deep voices is heard, low and muffled. Where does it come from? It is the funeral chant! He is breathing his last; the lamp casts a final light, then is extinguished entirely. The adept is alone in the darkness. The coldness of the tomb falls upon him, freezing all his limbs. Gradually he experiences the painful sensation of death and falls into a lethargy. His life passes before him in successive scenes like something unreal and his earthly consciousness becomes more and more vague and diffuse. But as he feels his body disintegrate, the ethereal part, the fluid of his being, is disengaged. He enters into an ecstasy . . .

HERMES

What is that shining, far distant point which appears imperceptible against the black background of the shadows? It is coming closer, it is growing larger, it is becoming a five-pointed star, whose rays include all the colors of the rainbow, and which shoots into the darkness discharges of magnetic light. Now there is a sun which attracts it into the brightness of its incandescent center. Is it the magic of the masters which produces this vision? Is it the invisible which becomes visible? Is it a foreboding of celestial truth, the flaming star of hope and immortality? It is disappearing, and in its place a flower blooms in the night, a flower not of matter, but sensitive and endowed with soul! It opens before him like a white rose; it spreads its petals, he sees its living leaves tremble and its shining calyx blush.—Is this the flower of Isis, the Mystical Rose of Wisdom which enclosed Love in its heart? But now it is evaporating, like a cloud of perfume. Then the ecstatic one feels flooded with a warm, caressing breeze. Having assumed strange forms, the cloud condenses and becomes a human figure, the figure of a woman, the Isis of the hidden sanctuary, but younger, smiling and radiant. A transparent veil is wrapped around her and her body shines through it. In her hand she holds a scroll of papyrus. She softly approaches, leans over the initiate lying in his tomb, and says, "I am your invisible sister; I am your divine soul, and this is the book of your life. Its written pages contain your past lives, its blank pages, your future lives. One day I shall unroll all before you. You know me now. Call, and I shall come!" As she speaks, a ray of tenderness streams from her eyes. . . . O presence of my angelic counterpart, ineffable promise of the divine, wondrous fusion in the impalpable Beyond! . . .

But everything bursts; the vision fades. With a horrible rending, the adept feels himself hurled into his body as into a corpse. He returns to a state of conscious lethargy; bands of iron fetter his limbs; a terrible weight presses upon his brain;

he awakens . . . Standing before him is the hierophant, accompanied by the Magi. They surround him, make him drink a cordial, and he arises.

"You are resurrected!" exclaims the prophet. "Come and celebrate with us the *agape* of the initiates, and tell us of your journey in the light of Osiris. For henceforth you are one of us."

Let us accompany the hierophant and the new initiate to the observatory of the temple, in the warm splendor of an Egyptian night. It is there that the head of the temple gave the recent adept the great revelation, by relating to him *The Vision of Hermes*. This vision was not written on any papyrus. It was indicated in symbolic signs on the stelae of the secret crypt, known to the one prophet. From pontiff to pontiff, the explanation was orally transmitted.

"Listen carefully," said the hierophant. "This vision includes the eternal history of the world and of all things."

18

The Vision of Hermes

ONE day Hermes fell asleep after having reflected upon the origin of things.[24] A heavy torpor took hold of his body, but as the latter became numb, his spirit ascended into space. Then it seemed to him that an immense being, without definite form, called him by name.

"Who are you?" asked Hermes, startled.

"I am Osiris, Sovereign Intelligence, and I can unveil everything. What do you wish?"

"To look at the source of beings, O divine Osiris, to know God!"

"You will be satisfied."

Immediately Hermes was flooded with a blissful light. Upon its diaphanous waves the captivating forms of all beings passed. But suddenly the terrifying shadows of sinuous shapes descended upon him. Hermes was plunged into a humid chaos filled with smoke and a dismal moaning. Then a voice arose from the abyss. It was *the cry of light*. Suddenly a faint fire burst forth from the humid depths and reached the ethereal heights.

Hermes arose with it, and found himself once again in space. In the abyss the chaos became ordered; the choirs of the stars stretched out over his head, and *the voice of the light* filled infinity.

"Did you understand what you saw?" Osiris asked Hermes in his dream, suspended between earth and heaven.

"No," replied Hermes.

"Well then, you will know. You have just seen what is for all time. The light you first saw is divine intelligence, which contains everything, including the archetypes of all beings. The gloom into which you were plunged is the material world where men of earth live. But the fire which you saw flame forth from the depths, is the Divine Word. God is the Father, the Word is the Son, their union is Life."

"What wondrous sense has opened within me?" asked Hermes. "I no longer see with the eyes of the body, but with those of the spirit. How is this?"

"Child of dust," said Osiris, "it is because the Word is within you! What in you hears, sees, acts,—is the Word itself, the sacred fire, the Creative Word."

"Since that is so," said Hermes, "let me see the life of the worlds, the way of souls, whence man comes and whither he returns."

"Let it be as you desire."

Hermes again became heavier than a stone and fell through space like an aerolite. Finally he saw himself at the top of a mountain. It was night; earth was dark and bare; his limbs seemed heavy as iron.

"Lift up your eyes and behold!" said Osiris' voice.

Then Hermes saw an amazing sight. Infinite space and the starry heaven enveloped him in seven luminous spheres. In a single glance Hermes saw the seven heavens above him like seven transparent, concentric globes, whose sidereal center he occupied. The last had the Milky Way as an enclosure. In each sphere a planet with a Genius of different form, sign and light revolved. While the awestruck Hermes viewed their scattered efflorescence and their majestic movements, the voice said to him:

"Look, listen, and understand. You see the seven spheres of all life. Through them the fall of souls takes place, and also their ascension. The seven Genii are the seven rays of Word-Light. Each of them governs a sphere of the Spirit, a sphere of the life of souls. The one nearest you is the Genius of the Moon with disquieting smile and wearing a silver sickle. He presides at births and deaths. He disengages souls from bodies and draws them into his ray.—Over him, pale Mercury shows descending or ascending souls the way with his staff, which contains knowledge.—Higher still, bright Venus holds the mirror of Love where souls alternately forget and recognize each other. Above her the Genius of the Sun raises the triumphal torch of Everlasting Beauty.—Yet higher, Mars brandishes the sword of Justice.—Sitting on his throne over the azure sphere, Jupiter holds the scepter of supreme power, which is Divine Intelligence.—At the boundary of the world, under the signs of the zodiac, Saturn bears the globe of Universal Wisdom."[25]

"I see," exclaimed Hermes, "the seven regions which make up the visible and invisible world. I see the seven rays of the Word-Light, of the only God, Who penetrates and governs them by these rays. But, O my Master, how is the journey of man made through all these worlds?"

"Do you see," asked Osiris, "glowing seeds fall from the regions of the Milky Way in the seventh sphere? They are the seeds of souls. They live like light-vapors in the region of Saturn, happy, without care, not knowing their happiness. But in falling from sphere to sphere they are clothed in ever heavier coverings. In each incarnation they acquire a new corporeal sense, in conformity with the environment in which they are living. Their vital energy increases, but as they enter denser sheaths they lose the memory of their heavenly origin. Thus is effected the descent of the souls which come from the divine ether. More and more captivated by matter, more and more intoxicated by life, like a shower of fire they rush with trembling voluptuousness through regions of pain, love and death, into their earthly prison, where you yourself are moaning, held by the charged center of the earth, where divine life seems to you a vain dream."

"Can souls die?" asked Hermes.

"Yes," answered the voice of Osiris. "Many perish in the fatal descent. The soul is the daughter of heaven and its journey is a test. If in its wild love of matter it loses the memory of its origin, the divine spark which was in it and which would have become brighter than a star, returns to the ethereal region, a lifeless atom, and the soul disintegrates in the whirlpool of crude elements."

At these words of Osiris, Hermes trembled, for a roaring storm enveloped him in a black cloud. The seven spheres disappeared beneath thick vapors. He saw human specters uttering strange cries, carried away and torn to pieces by phantoms of monsters and animals, amidst groans and endless blasphemies.

"This," said Osiris, "is the fate of irremediably base and wicked souls. Their torture ends only with their destruction, which is the loss of all consciousness. But see, the vapors disperse, the seven spheres reappear beneath the firmament! Look this way! Do you see that host of souls trying to climb back into the lunar region? Some are pushed down to earth like flocks of birds in the blast of the storm. With a great stirring of wings others reach the higher sphere which draws them into its revolving. Once they have arrived they recover the vision of divine things. But now they are not content with reflecting the latter in a dream of powerless bliss. They become infused with the lucidity of conscience lighted by grief and with the strength of will acquired in battle. They become luminous, for they possess the divine in themselves and reflect it in their acts. Therefore, strengthen your soul, O Hermes, and quiet your clouded mind by watching these distant flights of souls mount to the seven spheres and scatter like hosts of sparks! For you too can follow them; it is sufficient to will it, in order to lift oneself. See how they gather into divine choirs, each under its chosen Genius! The most beautiful live in the solar region, while the most powerful rise as far as Saturn. Some even rise to the Father, themselves becoming powers among Powers. For there where everything ends, everything eternally begins, and the seven spheres intone in unison, 'Wisdom! Love! Justice! Beauty! Splendor! Knowledge! Immortality!' "

"That," said the hierophant, "is what ancient Hermes saw, and what his successors handed down to us. The words of the wise man are like the seven notes of the lyre which contain all music, together with the numbers and laws of the universe. Hermes' vision resembles the starry sky whose endless depths are strewn with constellations. For the child, it is only a vault with golden nails; for the wise man, it is infinite space where worlds revolve with their rhythms and wondrous cadences. This vision contains the eternal numbers, evocative signs and magic keys. The more you learn to consider and understand it, the more you will see its boundaries widen, for the same organic law governs all the worlds."

And the prophet of the temple expounded the sacred text. He explained that the doctrine of Word-Light represents divinity in *the static state,* in its perfect equilibrium. He pointed out its threefold nature, which at the same time is intelligence, strength and matter; spirit, soul and body; light, word and life. Essence, manifestation and substance are three terms which reciprocally imply one another. Their union constitutes the divine and intellectual principle *par excellence,* the laws of ternary unity which dominate creation from the highest to the lowest.

Having thus led his disciple to the ideal Center of the universe, to the generating Principle of being, the master expanded him over time and space and showed him a multitude of efflorescences. For the second part of the vision represents divinity *in the dynamic state,* that is, in active evolution. In other words, it involves the visible and invisible universe, the living heaven, the seven spheres attached to the seven planets, which symbolize seven principles, seven different conditions of matter and spirit, seven varied worlds which each man and each generation must pass through in their evolution amidst a solar system. The seven Genii, or the seven cosmogonic gods signified the seven higher, directing spirits of all the spheres, themselves arisen from an ineluctable evolution. Each great god, therefore, was for an ancient initiate the symbol and patron of legions of spirits which reproduced his type in a thousand variants and which in their sphere could exert an influence upon man and earthly things. The seven Genii of Hermes' vision are the seven Devas of India, the seven Amshapands of Persia, the seven mighty Angels of Chaldea, the seven Sephiroth[26] of the *Kabbala,* and the seven Archangels of the Christian *Apocalypse.* And the great septenary which enfolds the universe not only vibrates in the seven colors of the rainbow and in the seven tones of the musical scale, but it is also evident in the being of man, who is threefold in essence but seven-fold in his evolution.[27]

"Thus," said the hierophant in conclusion, "you have come to the threshold of the great arcanum. Divine life appeared to you in the form of phantoms of reality. Hermes acquainted you with the invisible heaven, the light of Osiris, the hidden God of the universe, who breathes in millions of souls, animates the wandering globes and vitalizes bodies in labor. Now it is up to you to move forward, choosing your path in order to climb to pure Spirit. For you belong henceforth to *the resurrected living.* Remember that there are two principal keys to knowledge. This is the first: 'The outside is like the inside of things; the small is like the large; there is but a single law, and he who works is One. Nothing is small, nothing is large in the divine economy.' This is the second: 'Men are mortal gods, and gods are immortal men.'—Happy is the one who understands these words, for he possesses the key to everything. Remember that the law of mystery conceals the great truth. Total knowledge can be revealed only to our brothers who have gone through the same tests as we. It is necessary to mete out truth according to individual capacities; one must veil it for the weak, whom it would drive mad, and hide it from the wicked, who can grasp only bits with which they make weapons of destruction. Seal it in your heart and let it speak in your works. Knowledge will be your strength; faith, your sword; silence, your impenetrable armor."

The revelations of the prophet of Ammon Ra, which opened to the new initiate such broad horizons in himself and the universe, doubtless produced a deep impression when they were spoken atop the observatory of a temple of Thebes, in the clear calm of an Egyptian night. The pylons, the rooftops and white terraces of the temples lay sleeping far below among the dark masses of the nopal and tamarind trees. In the distance, monoliths, colossal statues of the gods, were sitting like incorruptible judges on their silent lake. Three pyramids, geometric figures of the tetragram and the sacred septenary, were fading on the horizon, their triangles scarcely seen in the delicate, grey mist. The vast firmament was filled with stars. With what new eyes he looked at these stars, pictured for him as future abodes! When at last the golden boat of the moon emerged from the dark mirror of the Nile, which disappeared on the horizon like a long bluish serpent, the neophyte thought he saw the boat of Isis which sails upon the river of souls, carrying them to the sun of Osiris. He remembered *The Book of the Dead,* and the meaning of all these symbols now became clear to him. After what he had seen and learned, he could well believe that he was in the twilight kingdom of Amenti, the mysterious place of pause between terrestrial and celestial life, where the dead, at first sightless and speechless, little by little find again both vision and voice. He too was going to make the great journey, the journey through infinite worlds and existences. Hermes had absolved him and deemed him worthy. He had told him the solution of the great riddle: "A single soul, the great soul of Everything, in dividing itself gave birth to all the souls which struggle mightily in the universe."

Armed with this great secret he climbed into Isis' boat. It set sail. Lifted into the ethereal spaces, it floated into interstellar regions. Already the broad rays of a tremendous dawn spread themselves over the blue sails of the celestial horizon. Already the choir of glorious spirits, of the Akhimu-Seku who have reached eternal rest, were singing, "Arise, Ra Hermakuti! Sun of Spirits! Those who are in your boat are in exaltation! They utter exclamations in the boat of millions of years! The great, divine cycle is overflowing with joy in giving glory to the sacred boat. Rejoicings take place in the mysterious chapel. O Arise, Ammon Ra Hermakuti!—Sun which creates itself!" And the initiate responded with the proud words, "I have reached the land of truth and justification. I am resurrected like a living god. I share the glory of the choir of the gods who inhabit the heaven, for I am one of them!"

Such proud thoughts and such bold aspirations well might

haunt the soul of the adept in the night following the mystical ceremony of resurrection. The next day on the avenues of the temple in glaring daylight, the night seemed to him no more than a dream, but what an unforgettable dream,—that first trip into the impalpable and invisible! Again he read the inscription of the statue of Isis, "No mortal has lifted my veil." But a corner of the veil had been raised, nevertheless, but only to drop immediately, and he had awakened in the land of the tombs. Ah, how far he was from the envisioned goal! For the journey is a long one, in *the boat of millions of years!* But at least he had partly seen the final goal.

Even though his vision of the other world may have been only a dream and a childish picture of his imagination, still clouded by the mist of earth, nevertheless could he doubt that other consciousness he had felt unfold in him, that mysterious *counterpart,* that celestial self which had appeared to him in its astral beauty like a living form, and which had spoken to him in his sleep? Was it a soul-sister, was it his Genius, or was it only a reflection of his inner spirit and a foretaste of his future being? Marvel and Mystery! One thing was certain: it was a reality, and if this soul was but his, it was real. What would he not do to find it again! He would live millions of years before he would forget that divine hour when he had seen his other, his pure and radiant self![28]

The initiation was completed. The adept was a consecrated priest of Osiris. If he was an Egyptian he remained connected with the temple; if a foreigner, sometimes he was allowed to return to his homeland, there to establish a cult or to fulfill a mission. But before leaving he solemnly swore to maintain absolute silence about the secrets of the temple. Never was he to betray to anyone what he had seen or heard, nor to reveal the teaching of Osiris except under the triple veil of mythological symbols or Mysteries. If he broke this pledge, violent death would overtake him sooner or later, however far away he was. But silence had become the shield of his strength.

After his return to Ionia, to his restless city, observing the impact of raging passions among this multitude of men who lived like madmen, without knowing themselves, often he recalled Egypt, the pyramids, the Temple of Ammon Ra. Then the dream of the crypt would return to him, and as, back there, the lotus floats upon the waves of the Nile, so always this shining vision arose above the mire and troubled river of this life. At designated times he heard the voice of the shining vision, and it was the voice of heavenly light, awakening in his being an intimate harmony as it said to him, "The soul is a veiled light. When it is neglected, it becomes dark and is extinguished. But when the consecrated oil of love is poured upon it, it shines forth as an immortal lamp!"

MOSES

The Mission of Israel

"*There was nothing that was veiled for him, and he covered with a veil the essence of everything he had seen.*"
—Inscription beneath the Statue of Phtahmer, high priest of Memphis, in the Louvre.

"*The most difficult and most obscure of the sacred books, Genesis, contains as many secrets as words, and each word conceals several others.*"
—Saint Jerome

"*Child of the past and bearer of the future, this book (the first ten chapters of Genesis), heir of all the knowledge of the Egyptians, bears seeds of the future sciences. It possesses what nature possesses that is deepest and most mysterious, what the mind can conceive of miracles, and what the spirit contains that is most sublime.*"
—Fabre d'Olivet, *The Hebraic Tongue Restored.*

19

Monotheistic Tradition and the Patriarchs of the Desert

R EVELATION is as ancient as conscious humanity. The fruit of inspiration, it arises out of the night of time. If one examines carefully the sacred books of Iran, India and Egypt, one will assure oneself that the basic ideas of esoteric teaching form its hidden but deep foundation. In esoteric teaching is found the invisible soul and the generating element of these great religions. All powerful initiators have perceived in one moment of their lives the radiance of central truth, but the light which they drew from it was refracted and colored according to their genius, their mission, their particular time and place.

We have experienced the Aryan initiation with Rama, the Brahmanic with Krishna and that of Isis and Osiris with the priests of Thebes. After all this, shall we deny that the non-material element of the Supreme God, which constitutes the basic tenet of monotheism and the unity of nature, was known to the Brahmans and priests of Ammon-Ra? Doubtless they did not picture the world as born in an instantaneous act, by a whim of Divinity, as do some theologians. But wisely and gradually, by way of emanation and evolution, they traced the visible from the invisible, the universe from the unfathomable depths of God. Male and female dualism came from primitive oneness, the living trinity of man and the universe from creative dualism, and so forth. The holy numbers made up the eternal work, the rhythm and tool of Divinity. Contemplated with more or less clarity and power, they evoked in the soul of the initiate the internal structure of the world through his being just as the exact note obtained by means of a bow from a glass covered with sand traces in miniature the harmonious forms of vibrations which fill the vast kingdom of the air with their sonorous waves.

But the esoteric monotheism of Egypt never passed outside the sanctuaries. Its sacred science remained limited to a small minority. The enemies from outside began to break in upon this ancient rampart of civilization. During the period we have come to, the 12th century B.C., Asia was sinking into the cult of matter. Already India was moving with rapid strides toward her decadence. A great empire had arisen on the banks of the Tigris and Euphrates. Babylon, that colossal and mighty city, astonished the nomadic peoples who roamed about it. The rulers of Assyria proclaimed themselves lords of the four kingdoms of the world and strove to establish the boundaries of their dominions at the very ends of the earth itself. They crushed peoples, deported them in hordes, conscripted them and pitted them against one another. Neither the rights of men, human respect, nor religious principle, but personal, unbridled desire was the law of the followers of Ninus and Semiramis.

The knowledge of the Chaldean priests was profound, but much less pure, less lofty and less efficacious than that of the Egyptian priests. In Egypt, authority was given to science.

The priesthood always exercised a moderating influence upon royalty. The Pharaohs remained pupils of the priests and never became hateful despots, as did the rulers of Babylon. In Babylon, on the contrary, the priesthood from the beginning was merely a tool of tyranny. In a bas-relief of Nineveh, Nimrod, a stocky giant, is seen strangling with his muscular arm a young lion which he holds pressed against his chest. Here is a self-explanatory symbol. This is how the monarchs of Assyria strangled the Iranian lion, the heroic people of Zoroaster, assassinating their pontiffs, ruining the schools of the Magi, holding their kings for ransom. If the Rishis of India and the priests of Egypt caused Providence to reign on earth by their wisdom, at least to a certain degree, it can be said that the reign of Babylon was one of Fate, that is, of blind and brutal force. Babylon thus became the tyrannical center of universal anarchy, the inflexible eye of the social hurricane which enveloped Asia, the terrible eye of Fate, forever open, lying in wait for nations, in order to devour them.

What could Egypt do against this invading flood? Already the Hyksos had almost swallowed her up. She withstood them bravely, but could not resist forever. Six more centuries, and the Persian cyclone, following the Babylonian tornado, would sweep away Egypt's temples and Pharaohs. Moreover, Egypt, which possessed the genius of initiation and conservation in the highest degree, never sought expansion or exercised propaganda. Must the accumulated treasures of its science be lost? Indeed the greatest part was buried, and when the Alexandrians came they could find only fragments. Two peoples of different genius, nevertheless, lighted their torches in Egypt's sanctuaries,—torches with different rays, with which one people illumined the heights of heaven, and the other enlightened and transfigured the earth: Israel and Greece.

The importance of the people of Israel in the history of humanity is readily apparent from the very beginning, for two reasons. First, it represents monotheism; second, it gave birth to Christianity. But the providential aim of the mission of Israel appears only to one who uncovers the symbols of the Old and New Testaments and perceives that they conceal the entire esoteric tradition of the past, though under a form often altered —especially as regards the Old Testament—by the numerous editors and translators, the majority of whom did not know the original meaning of the texts. The role of Israel becomes clear when one discovers that these people form the indispensable link between the old and the new cycle, between the East and the West. A result of the monotheistic idea is the unification of humanity under the same God and under a single law. But as long as theologians make a childish idea of God, and as long as men of science simply ignore Him or deny Him, the moral, social and religious unity of our planet will be only a pious desire or a postulate of religion and science, which are powerless to effect it. On the other hand this organic unity appears possible when one recognizes esoterically and scientifically in the divine principle the key to the world and to life, to the evolution of man and society.

Finally, Christianity, that is to say, the religion of Christ, appears in its exalted and universal nature only as it unveils to us its esoteric essence. Only then does it reveal itself as the result of all that preceded it, in that it contains the principles, the goals and the means leading to the complete regeneration of mankind. Only in revealing to us its ultimate mysteries will Christianity become what it truly is: the religion of promise and fulfillment, that is, of universal initiation.

Moses, the Egyptian initiate and priest of Osiris, was indisputably the organizer of monotheism. Through him this principle, until then hidden beneath the threefold veil of the Mysteries, came out of the depths of the temple and entered the course of history. Moses had the courage to establish the highest principle of initiation as the sole dogma of a national religion, and the prudence to reveal its consequences to only a small number of initiates while imposing it upon the masses through fear. In so doing, the prophet of Sinai evidently had before him distant vistas which extended far beyond the destinies of his people. The establishment of the universal religion of mankind is the true mission of Israel, which few Jews other than its greatest prophets have understood. In order for this mission to be fulfilled, the swallowing up of the people who championed it was implied. The Jewish nation was dispersed and annihilated. The idea of Moses and the Prophets has lived and increased. Enlarged and transfigured by Christianity, taken up by Islam, although on a lower plane, it was to make inroads upon the barbaric West and was to influence Asia herself once again. Henceforth it would be useless for mankind to rebel and struggle against itself in convulsive efforts; mankind was to revolve around this major idea like the nebula around the sun which organizes it. This was the tremendous work of Moses.

For this undertaking, the most colossal since the prehistoric migration of the Aryans, Moses found an already prepared instrument in the tribes of the Hebrews, particularly in those settled in Egypt in the valley of Goshen, living there in servitude under the name of *Beni-Jacob*. In the founding of a monotheistic religion he had as forerunners those nomadic and peaceful rulers whom the Bible presents to us in the figures of Abraham, Isaac and Jacob.

Let us look at these Hebrew patriarchs. We shall then try to separate the figure of their great prophet from the mirages of the desert and the dark nights of Sinai, where the thunder of the legendary Jehovah rumbles.

These Ibrim, these untiring nomads, these everlasting exiles were known for centuries, even for thousands of years. Brothers of the Arabs, the Hebrews like all Semites, were the result of an ancient mixture of the white with the black race. They had been seen traveling back and forth through northen Africa under the name of *Bodons,* those men without shelter and without bed, who pitched their tents in the vast deserts between the Red Sea and the Persian Gulf, between the Euphrates and Palestine. Ammonites, Elamites or Edomites, these nomads all looked alike. For transportation, the ass or the camel; for a house, the tent; their only property, wandering herds like themselves, forever feeding on foreign soil. Like their ancestors the Ghiborim, like the first Celts, these restless people hated carved monuments, the fortified city, forced labor and the temple of stone. Nevertheless, the mighty cities of Babylon and Nineveh with their gigantic palaces, their Mysteries and their debauchery, worked an invincible charm upon these semi-savage peoples. Lured into these prison-houses of stone, captured by the soldiers of the kings of Assyria, conscripted into their armies, they sometimes wallowed in the orgies of Babylon. At other times the Israelites allowed themselves to be seduced by the Moabite women, those bold enticers with dark skin and shining eyes. The latter drew them into the adoration of stone and wood idols and the frightful worship of Moloch. But suddenly the thirst for the desert again seized them, and they fled. Returning to the rugged valleys where only the roaring of wild beasts is heard, to the vast plains where one is guided only by the lights of the heavenly constellations, beneath the cold gaze of those stars their ancestors had worshipped, they were ashamed of themselves. If then a patriarch, an inspired man, spoke to them of the one God, of Elelion, of the Elohim, of Sabaoth, the Lord of Hosts, Who sees all and punishes the guilty, these over-grown, wild children bowed their heads and, kneeling in prayer, allowed themselves to be led like lambs.

Little by little this idea of the great Elohim, of the one all-powerful God filled their souls, as in the Padan-Harran twilight blends everything in the landscape into the infinite line of the horizon, drowning colors and distances in the splendid evenness of the firmament and transforming the universe into a single mass of shadows arched over by a scintillating dome of stars.

What were the patriarchs like? Abram, Abraham, or Father Orham, was a king of Ur, a Chaldean city near Babylon. The Assyrians, according to tradition, pictured him sitting in an armchair, with a kindly manner. This very old individual who has figured in the mythological history of all peoples, since Ovid mentions him, is the same as the man the Bible represents as migrating from the land of Ur into the land of Canaan, at the command of the Eternal: "The Everlasting appeared to him and said unto him: I am the Almighty God; walk before me and be thou perfect . . . I will establish my covenant between me and thee and thy seed for an everlasting covenant, to be a God unto thee, and to thy seed after thee" (*Genesis* 17: 1, 7). This passage, translated into modern language, means that a very old Semitic leader named Abraham who probably had received the Chaldean initiation, felt compelled by an inner voice to lead his tribe toward the West, and imposed upon it the cult of the Elohim.

The name Isaac, according to the prefix *Is*, seems to indicate an Egyptian initiation, while that of Jacob and Joseph reveals a Phoenician background. Be that as it may, it is probable that the three patriarchs were the three leaders of different peoples who lived in different eras. Long after the time of Moses Israelite tradition grouped them into a single family. Isaac became the son of Abraham, and Jacob, the son of Isaac. This manner of representing intellectual paternity by physical paternity was frequently used in ancient priesthoods. From this traditional genealogy a major fact stands out: The presence of the monotheistic cult among the patriarch-initiates of the desert. The fact that these men had inner experience of spiritual revelations in the form of dreams or visions even in the waking state, is in no way contrary to esoteric science, nor to that universal psychic law which rules souls and worlds. In the Bible narrative these facts have assumed the naive form of visits from angels to the patriarchs in their tents.

Did these patriarchs have a clear understanding of the spirituality of God and the religious goals of mankind? Without doubt they did. Inferior in positive science to the Magi of Chaldea as well as to the Egyptian priests, they probably surpassed them in moral stature and that breadth of soul which is brought about by a free, nomadic life. For them the sublime order that the Elohim cause to hold sway in the universe is translated into the social order of family worship, respect for their wives, passionate love for their sons, protection for the entire tribe, hospitality toward strangers. In short, these great fathers are natural arbiters between families and tribes. Their patriarchal staff is a scepter of equity. They exercise a civilizing authority and breathe gentleness and peace. Here and there, esoteric thought can be seen penetrating into the patriarchal tradition. Thus, when at Bethel Jacob sees in a dream a ladder with the Elohim at the top and angels ascending and descending upon it, one recognizes a popular form, a Judaic adaptation of the vision of Hermes and the doctrine of the descending and ascending evolution of souls.

An historical fact of greatest importance concerning the age of the patriarchs appears to us in two revealing verses. It concerns a meeting of Abraham with a brother initiate. Having made war on the kings of Sodom and Gomorrah, Abraham goes to pay homage to Melchizedek. This king lives in the fortress which later will be Jerusalem. "Melchizedek, King of Salem, had wine and bread brought forth. For he was the priest of

Elohim, the Most High God. And he blessed Abram, saying: 'Blessed be Abram of the Most High God, possessor of heaven and earth.' " (*Genesis* 14:18, 19.) Here then is a king of Salem who is a high-priest of the same God as Abraham. The latter treats him as a superior, as a master, and communes with him in the elements of bread and wine, in the name of Elohim, which in ancient Egypt was a sign of communion between initiates. There was therefore a fraternal link, a sign of recognition and a common goal between the worshippers of Elohim from the border of Chaldea as far west as Palestine and perhaps even extending to a few sanctuaries of Egypt.

This monotheistic pattern needed only an organizer.

Thus, between the winged bull of Assyria and the sphinx of Egypt, which from a distance observe the desert between the crushing tyranny and impenetrable mystery of initiation, advance the chosen tribes of the Abramites, Jacobites and the *Ben-Israel*. They flee the shameless festivals of Babylon; they avert their heads as they pass by the orgies of Moab, the horrors of Sodom and Gomorrah and the monstrous cult of Baal. Under the protection of the patriarch, the caravan follows its rugged route, sprinkled with oases, marked with rare springs and slender palm trees. Like a long ribbon it fades away in the immensity of the desert beneath the scorching heat of the day, beneath the deep red of the setting sun and the cloak of darkness, ruled over by the Elohim. Neither herds, women nor old men know the goal of this eternal journey. But they move forward, accompanying the painful, resigned tread of the camels. Where are they going? The patriarchs know; Moses will tell the people.

20

The Initiation of Moses in Egypt — His Flight to Jethro

RAMESES II was one of the great rulers of Egypt. His son was named Menephtah. In accordance with Egyptian custom the latter received his instruction from the priests in the temple of Ammon-Ra at Memphis, for then the royal art was considered a branch of priestly art. Menephtah was a shy young man, curious and of average intelligence. He had a misdirected love for the esoteric sciences, which later made him the prey of inferior magicians and astrologers. As a student companion he had a young man of remarkable genius and of strange, withdrawn character.

Hosarsiph[30] was Menephtah's cousin, son of the royal princess, sister of Rameses II. Was he an adopted or a natural son? This has never been known.[31] Above all, Hosarsiph was the son of the temple, for he had grown up in the shadow of its columns. Dedicated to Isis and Osiris by his mother, already in adolescence he had been seen acting as a Levite at the crowning of the Pharaoh and in the priestly processions of the great festivals, carrying the ephod, chalice or censers. Inside the temple he stood, grave and attentive, listening to the sacred orchestras, the hymns and the teaching of the priests.

Hosarsiph was of short stature. He had a humble and thoughtful look, a forehead like that of a ram and piercing black eyes with the gaze of an eagle and a disturbing intensity. He had been called "the silent one," so intense and almost always quiet was he. Often he stammered while speaking, as though groping for words or as if he feared to express his thoughts. He appeared shy, but suddenly, like a sharp thunderbolt, a terrible idea would burst forth in a single word, leaving behind it a trail of light. It was then understood that if ever "the silent one" decided to act, he would be frighteningly rash. Already between his eyebrows the fatal crease of men predestined to difficult tasks began to form, and upon his forehead hovered a threatening cloud.

Women feared the gaze of this young Levite, a glance as unfathomable as the tomb, while his face was as impassive as the door of the temple of Isis. One would have said that they had a foreboding of an enemy of the feminine sex in this future representative of the male religious principle in its most absolute and intractable form.

Nevertheless his mother, the royal princess, dreamed of the throne of the Pharaohs for her son. Hosarsiph was more intelligent than Menephtah; he could hope for a usurpation with the support of the priesthood. The Pharaohs, it is true, designated their successors among their sons, but sometimes the priests broke the designation of the prince after the Pharaoh's death. This was done in the interest of the state, for more than once they kept the unworthy or weak from the throne in order to give the scepter to a royal initiate. Already Menephtah was jealous of his cousin; Rameses also kept his eye on him, for he feared the taciturn Levite.

One day Hosarsiph's mother met her son in the Serapeum of

Memphis, an immense plaza dotted with obelisks, mausoleums, small and large temples, victory pylons,—a sort of open air museum of national glories, which was reached by passing through an avenue of six hundred sphinxes. The Levite bowed before his royal mother, touching the earth and, as was the custom, waited for her to speak to him.

"You are about to enter the Mysteries of Isis and Osiris," she told him. "I shall not see you for a long time, O my son! But do not forget that you are of the blood of Pharaohs, and that I am your mother. Look around you. . . . If you wish, one day . . . all this will belong to you!"

And with a broad gesture she pointed to the obelisks, temples, Memphis and the entire horizon.

A smile of disdain passed over Hosarsiph's face, which usually was smooth and unmoving like a mask of bronze.

"Then," said he, "you wish me to rule these people who worship gods with heads of jackals, ibis and hyenas? In a few centuries what will remain of all these idols?"

Hosarsiph stooped, took some fine sand in his hand, letting it trickle to earth between his thin fingers before the eyes of his astonished mother. "As much as that," he said.

"Then you scorn the religion of our fathers and the science of our priests?"

"On the contrary! I am striving for them, but the pyramid is motionless; it must start to walk. I shall not be a Pharaoh, for my country is far from here; it is out there—in the desert!"

"Hosarsiph!" said the princess reproachfully, "Why do you utter blasphemies? A wind of fire brought you into my womb and I well see that a storm will carry you away! I brought you into the world, but I do not know you! In the name of Osiris, who are you then? What are you going to do?"

"Do I myself know? Osiris alone knows; he will tell me perhaps. But give me your blessing, O my mother, so that Isis may protect me and the land of Egypt be kind to me!"

Hosarsiph knelt before his mother, respectfully crossed his hands upon his chest and bowed his head. Taking from her head the lotus flower which she wore according to the custom of the women of the temple, she gave it to him to smell. Realizing that the thoughts of her son would remain an eternal mystery for her, she walked away, whispering a prayer.

Hosarsiph passed the initiation of Isis victoriously. With soul of steel and will of iron, he enjoyed the tests. Of mathematical and universal mind, he displayed a giant's strength in his intelligence and handling of the sacred numbers, whose fecund symbolism and applications were almost infinite. His mind, disdainful of things which are but illusion, and of individuals who pass away, breathed with ease only in the unchangeable elements. From that height he penetrated and mastered everything quietly and surely, without showing desire, rebellion or curiosity.

For his teachers as well as for his mother, Hosarsiph remained an enigma. What frightened them most was that he was solid and inflexible, like a principle. One felt that he could neither be bent nor sidetracked. He followed his secret path like a celestial body its invisible orbit. The pontiff, Membra wondered to what height this concentrated ambition would climb. And he wished to know.

One day Hosarsiph with three other priests of Osiris had borne the golden ark which preceded the priest in great ceremonies. This ark contained the ten most secret books of the temple, dealing with magic and theurgy.

Returning to the sanctuary with Hosarsiph, Membra said to him, "You are of royal blood. Your strength and knowledge are beyond your age. What do you wish?"

"Nothing but this." And Hosarsiph placed his hand on the

holy ark that golden sparrow hawks covered with their shining wings.

"Then you want to become a pontiff of Ammon Ra and prophet of Egypt?"

"No! Only to know what is in these books!"

"How can you know, since no one but a priest can know them?"

"Osiris speaks as he wishes, when he wishes, to whom he wishes. What is enclosed in this ark is but the dead letter. If the living Spirit wishes to speak to me, he will speak to me!"

"To hear the Spirit, what do you intend to do?"

"Wait and obey."

When these answers were brought to Rameses II, they intensified his fear. He was afraid that Hosarsiph aspired to be Pharaoh at the expense of Rameses' son, Menephtah. Consequently the Pharaoh ordered that his sister's son be made a sacred scribe in the temple of Osiris. This important function included a knowledge of symbolism in all its forms, cosmography and astronomy, but it kept him away from the throne. The princess' son applied himself with zeal and perfect submission to his duties as priestly scribe, which included the task of inspector of various *nomas,* or provinces of Egypt.

Did Hosarsiph really possess the pride attributed to him? Yes, if it is because of pride that the imprisond lion raises its head and looks at the horizon beyond the bars of his cage, without even seeing the passersby staring at him. Yes, if it is because of pride that the eagle, held captive by a chain, sometimes trembles through his entire body, and with neck bent and wings spread, gazes at the sun. Like all strong ones who are destined for a great work, Hosarsiph did not believe he was subjected to blind Fate; he felt a mysterious Providence watching over him, leading him to his goals.

While he was a priestly scribe, Hosarsiph was sent on an inspection tour of the Delta. The Hebrews, tributaries of Egypt, who then lived in the valley of Goshen,were subjected to disagreeable tasks. Rameses II was connecting Pelusium and Heliopolis by a chain of forts. All the *nomas* of Egypt were to supply their contingent of laborers for this gigantic work. The *Beni-Israel* were burdened with the heaviest tasks. Above all, they were hewers of stone and makers of brick. Independent and proud, they did not bow as easily as did the natives under the cudgels of the Egyptian overseers, but stood up again muttering and sometimes returning the blows. The priest of Osiris could not curb a secret sympathy for these uncompromising unmanageables, these stiff-necks, whose elders, faithful to the Abrahamic tradition, worshipped the one God; who revered their leaders, their *hags* and their *zakens,* but who kicked back beneath the yoke and protested against injustice.

One day he saw an Egyptian guard strike down a defenseless Hebrew with heavy blows. His heart pounded; he flung himself upon the Egyptian, tore his weapons from him and killed him. This act, carried out in a moment of unselfish indignation, determined his life. Priests of Osiris who committed murder were severely judged by the priestly college. Already the Pharaoh suspected a usurper in his sister's son. The life of the scribe hung by only a thread. He preferred voluntary exile, and to impose his expiation upon himself. Everything urged him to the solitude of the desert, into the vast unknown,—his desire, the presentiment of his mission, and over and above all, that inner, mysterious, yet irresistible voice, which at certain times said, "Go! This is your destiny!"

Beyond the Red Sea and the Sinai Peninsula, in the land of Madian, was a temple which was not under the control of the Egyptian priesthood. This region extended like a green band between the Elamitic Gulf and the desert of Arabia. In the distance, beyond the arm of the sea, one could see the somber mass of Sinai, with its bare peaks. This isolated country, hemmed in between the desert and the Red Sea, protected by a volcanic mass, was sheltered from invasions. The temple there was dedicated to Osiris, but the Almighty God named Elohim, was also worshipped. For this sanctuary of Ethiopian origin served as a religious center for Arabs, Semites and men of the black race who were seeking initiation. Thus, for centuries Sinai and Horeb had been the mystical center of a monotheistic cult. The bare, wild grandeur of the mountain rising up in isolation between Egypt and Arabia, awakened the idea of a single God. Many Semites went there on pilgrimages to worship Elohim. There they would remain for several days, fasting and praying in the caves and passages carved in the sides of Sinai. Before this, they would go to purify themselves and to receive instruction in the temple of Madian.

Here Hosarsiph took refuge.

The high priest of Madian or the Raguel (the watchman of God) at that time was named Jethro. He was a man of black skin.[32] He belonged to the purest type of the ancient Ethiopian race which had ruled Egypt four or five thousand years before Rameses, and had not lost its traditions which date back to the oldest races of the globe. Jethro was neither an inspired man nor a man of action, but was a great sage. The treasures of science were accumulated in his memory and in the stone libraries of his temple, and he was also the protector of men of the desert. Lybians, Arabs, nomadic Semites, eternal wanderers, forever the same with their dim seeking after the one God, represented something changeless in the midst of ephemeral cults and crumbling civilizations. In them one felt as if in the presence of the Everlasting; one found in them the memorial of bygone ages, the great silence of Elohim. Jethro was the spiritual father of these unconquered people, these wanderers, these free men. He knew their soul, he had a foreboding of their destiny. When

Hosarsiph came and asked him for shelter in the name of Osiris-Elohim, he received him with open arms. Perhaps he sensed at once that in this fugitive before him was the man predestined to become the prophet of banished men, the leader of the people of God.

Hosarsiph wanted first of all to submit himself to the expiations the law of the initiates imposed upon murderers. When a priest of Osiris had committed even an unpremeditated murder, he was supposed to lose the benefit of his anticipated resurrection "in the light of Osiris," a privilege he had obtained through the tests of initiation, and which placed him far above the masses. In order to expiate his crime and to find his inner light once again, he had to submit himself to further cruel tests and once more to expose himself to death. After a long fast and with the aid of certain potions the atoning one was plunged into a deep sleep; then he was placed in a cave beneath the temple. He remained there for days, sometimes for weeks.[33] During this time he was to undertake a journey into the other world, into Erebus or the region of Amentis, where float the souls of the dead who are not yet detached from the terrestrial atmosphere. There he had to search for his victim, to undergo the latter's anguish, obtain his pardon and help him to find his way to the light. Only then was he considered to have expiated the murder; only then was his astral body washed of the black stains which the poisoned breath and the curses of his victim had soiled. But from this real or imaginary journey, the guilty one very well might not return, and often when the priests went to awaken the expiator from his sleep, they found nothing but a corpse.

Hosarsiph did not hesitate to undergo this test, and others as well.[34] Under the impress of the murder he had committed, he had understood the unchangeable nature of certain laws of the moral order and the deep disturbance that violating them

leaves in the depth of the conscience. With complete abnegation he offered his being in a holocaust to Osiris, asking for the
strength (if he returned to the earthly light) to reveal the law of
justice. When Hosarsiph emerged from the dreadful sleep in
the crypt of the temple of Madian, he felt himself a transformed
man. His past was as though detached from him; Egypt had
ceased to be his homeland, and the immensity of the desert with
its wandering nomads stretched before him as a new field of
action. He looked at the mountain of Elohim on the horizon,
and for the first time, like a vision of a storm in the clouds of
Sinai, the idea of his mission passed before his eyes: From these
moving tribes he was to mold a fighting people who would represent the law of the supreme God amidst the idolatry of cults
and the anarchy of nations—a people who would bring to future centuries truth, sealed in the golden ark of initiation.

On that day in order to mark the new era which had begun in
his life, Hosarsiph took the name *Moses,* which means, *The
Saved One.*

21

The Sepher Bereshith

MOSES married Zipporah, daughter of Jethro, and sojourned many years with the wise man of Madian. Thanks to the Ethiopian and Chaldean traditions which he found in this temple, Moses was able to complete and master what he had learned in the Egyptian sanctuaries, to study the most ancient cycles of humanity and by the process of induction to plunge into the distant horizons of the future. It was at the home of Jethro that he found two books on cosmogony mentioned in *Genesis: The Wars of Jehovah* and *The Generations of Adam.* He studied them with great care.

It was necessary to gird his loins well for the work he was considering. Before him Rama, Krishna, Hermes, Zoroaster and Fo-Hi had created religions of the people; Moses wished to create a people for the everlasting religion. A strong foundation was necessary for such a courageous, new, gigantic undertaking. For this reason Moses wrote his *Sepher Bereshith,* his *Book of Beginnings,* a concentrated synthesis of the science of the past and a framework for the science of the future, a key to the Mysteries, a torch of the initiates, a rallying-point for the entire nation.

Let us try to see what *Genesis* was, according to Moses' way of thinking. Certainly in his thought *Genesis* radiated a different light, it embraced worlds which were much more vast than the naive conception of the tiny earth which appears in the Greek translation of the *Septuagint,* or in St. Jerome's Latin translation!

The Biblical exegesis of the nineteenth century made fashionable the idea that *Genesis* is not the work of Moses, that this prophet may not even have existed, and that he may have been merely an entirely legendary character invented four or five centuries later by the Jewish priesthood in order to give itself a divine origin. Modern criticism bases this opinion on the fact that *Genesis* is composed of various fragments (Elohistic and Jehovistic) pieced together, and that its present editing is posterior by at least four hundred years to the time when Israel left Egypt. The facts established by modern criticism as regards the time of editing the texts that we possess today are accurate; the conclusions it draws from them are arbitrary and illogical. It does not follow from the fact that the Elohist and Jehovist wrote four hundred years after the Exodus, that they were the inventors of *Genesis* and that they did not work on an earlier document, perhaps poorly understood. From the fact that the Pentateuch gives us a traditional account of the life of Moses, it does not follow that it contains nothing true. The mission of the prophet is explained when he is seen in his native environment, the solar temple of Memphis. Finally, the depths of *Genesis* are revealed only in the light of torches snatched from the initiation of Isis and Osiris.

A religion is not formed without an initiator. The judges, the prophets, all the history of Israel, give proof of Moses; Jesus himself cannot be conceived of without him. Moreover, *Genesis* contains the essence of the Mosaic tradition. Whatever changes it has undergone, beneath the dust of centuries and priestly wrappings the venerable mummy must contain the basic idea, the living thought, the testament of the prophet of Israel.

Israel gravitates around Moses as surely, as inevitably as the earth turns around the sun. But once this is established, it is something else to know what the basic ideas of *Genesis* were, what Moses wanted to will to posterity in this secret testament of the *Sepher Bereshith*. The problem can be resolved only from an esoteric point of view, and is as follows: In his role as an Egyptian initiate, the intellectuality of Moses had to be on a par with Egyptian science which, like ours, accepted the permanence of the laws of the universe, the development of worlds by gradual evolution, and in addition had extensive, exact and rational ideas about the soul and invisible nature. If such was Moses' science—and how could a priest of Osiris not have had it?—how can one reconcile this with the naive ideas of *Genesis* concerning the creation of the world and the origin of man? Might not this story of creation which, when taken literally, makes a modern schoolboy laugh, conceal a profound symbolic meaning? Is there a way to unlock the latter? What is this deep meaning? Where can one find the key to it?

That key is to be found: 1. in Egyptian symbolism, 2. in the symbolism of all the religions of the ancient cycle, 3. in the synthesis of esoteric teaching from Vedic India to the Christian initiates of the early centuries.

The Greek authors relate that the priests of Egypt had three ways of expressing their thoughts. "The first was clear and simple; the second, symbolic and figurative; the third, sacred and hieroglyphic. At their wish, the same work assumed a literal, a figurative or a transcendant meaning. This was the genius of their language. Heraclitus expressed the differences perfectly in designating them as *speaking, signifying* and *concealing.*"

In the theogonic and cosmogonic sciences the Egyptian priests always used the third mode of writing. Their hieroglyphs had three distinct meanings. The last two could not be understood without a key. This enigmatic, concentrated style of writing was related to a fundamental tenet of Hermes' doctrine, according to which one and the same law rules the natural world, the human world and the divine world. This language of extraordinary conciseness, unintelligible to the common man, had a singular eloquence for the adept, for, by means of a single sign it evoked the principles, causes and effects radiating from divinity into blind nature, into the human consciousness and into the world of pure spirits. Thanks to this writing, the initiate embraced the three worlds in a single glance.

Considering Moses' education, there is no doubt that he wrote *Genesis* in Egyptian hieroglyphs with three meanings. He entrusted the keys and oral explanation to his successors. When, in Solomon's time, *Genesis* was transliterated into Phoenician characters, when, after the Babylonian Captivity, Esdras edited it in Chaldaic-Aramaic characters, the Jewish priesthood could make but very imperfect use of these keys. At last, when the Greek translators of the Bible appeared, they had no more than a vague idea of the esoteric meaning of the texts. Despite his serious intentions and his great mind, when St. Jerome prepared his Latin translation from the Hebrew text, he could not fathom the basic meaning, and could he have done so, it was right that he remained silent. Therefore, when we read *Genesis* in our translations, we have only the elementary, inferior meaning. Whether they will or no, the exegetes and theologians themselves, orthodox or free thinkers, see the Hebrew text only through the *Vulgate*. The comparative and superlative meaning, which is the profound and true sense of *Genesis,* escapes them. It remains no less mysteriously hidden in the Hebrew text, which by its roots dips down into the sacred language of the temples, remolded by Moses.

This sacred language is one in which each vowel and each consonant has a universal meaning in harmony with the acoustic value of the letter and the state of consciousness of the man who produced it. For the intuitive this profound meaning sometimes bursts forth like a spark from the text; for the seer it shines in the phonetic structure of the words adopted or created by Moses: magic syllables, where the initiate of Osiris let his thought flow like sonorous metal into a perfect mold. Through the study of this phonetic alphabet which bears the impress of the holy language of the ancient temples, by means of the keys which the *Kabbala* provides, some of which date back to Moses, finally through comparative esoterism, today we are allowed to penetrate into and rediscover the real *Genesis.* Thus the thought of Moses emerges, shining like gold from the furnace of the centuries, from the scoria of a primitive theology and the ashes of negative criticism.[35]

Two examples will shed broad light upon what the sacred language of the ancient temples was, and how the three meanings in the symbols of Egypt and those of *Genesis* correspond to one another. On a great many Egyptian monuments one sees a woman wearing a crown, holding in one hand the *crux ansata,* the symbol of everlasting life; in the other hand she holds a scepter in the form of a lotus flower, the symbol of initiation. This is the goddess ISIS. Now Isis has three different meanings. Literally, she personifies Woman, and from this the universal feminine gender. Comparatively, she personifies the fullness of terrestrial nature, with all its reproductive powers. In the superlative, she symbolizes celestial and invisible nature, itself the element of souls and spirits, spiritual light, intelligible in itself, which initiation alone confers.

The symbol which corresponds to Isis in the *Genesis* text and in the Judeo-Christian mind is EVE, *Heva,* the Eternal Feminine. This Eve is not only Adam's wife, she is also the wife of God. She constitutes three-quarters of His being. For the name of the Eternal IEVE of which we have incorrectly made *Jehovah* and *Javeh,* is composed of the prefix *I* and the name *Eve.* The high priest of Jerusalem pronounced the divine name once a year, enunciating it letter by letter in the following manner: *Yod, hè, vau, hè.* The first expressed the divine thought[36] and the theogonic sciences; the three letters of Eve's name expressed the three orders of nature, the three worlds in which this thought is realized, and then the cosmogonic, psychic and physical sciences which correspond to them.[37] The Ineffable encloses deep within Itself the Eternal Masculine and the Eternal Feminine. Their indissoluble union make for His power and mystery. This is what Moses, sworn enemy of all images of divinity, did not tell the people, but recorded figuratively in the structure of the Divine Name when he explained it to his adepts. Thus in the Judaic cult an esoteric nature is hidden in the very Name of God. The wife of Adam, strange, guilty, charming woman, reveals to us her profound affinities with the terrestrial, divine Isis, the mother of the gods, who manifests through her deep womb the turbulence of souls and stars.

Another example: A character which plays a great role in the story of Adam and Eve is the Serpent. *Genesis* calls it *Nâhâsh.* Now what did the serpent mean in the ancient temples? The mysteries of India, Egypt and Greece reply with a single voice: The serpent arranged in a circle means universal life, whose magic agent is starlight. In a still deeper sense, *Nâhâsh* means the power which puts life in motion, the attraction of self for self. In the latter meaning Geoffroy Saint-Hilaire saw the basis for universal gravity. The Greeks called it Eros, Love, or Desire.—Now apply these two meanings to the story of Adam, Eve and the Serpent, and you will see that the Fall of the first couple, the celebrated original sin, suddenly becomes the vast revealing of divine and universal nature with its kingdoms, its classes and its species, in the tremendous, ineluctable cycle of life.

These two examples have enabled us to glance for the first time into the depths of the Mosaic *Genesis*. We already see in part what cosmogony was for an ancient initiate, and what distinguished it from cosmogony in the modern sense.

For modern science, cosmogony is reduced to a cosmography. One will find in it the description of a portion of the visible universe included in a study dealing with the chain of physical causes and effects in a given area. For example, it will be Laplace's system of the world where the formation of our solar system is hypothesized only on the basis of its present functioning and from matter in movement. It will also be the history of the earth, whose irrefutable evidences are the various strata of the soil. Ancient science was not unaware of this development of the visible universe, and if it had less accurate ideas on it than has modern science, nevertheless intuitively it had formulated the general laws.

But for the sages of India and Egypt this was merely the outer aspect of the world, its reflex movement. They sought the explanation of the world in its inner aspect, in its direct and original movement. They found in it another order of laws which reveals itself to our intelligence. For ancient science, the limitless universe was not dead matter governed by mechanical laws, but was a living whole, endowed with intelligence, soul and will. This great divine being had innumerable organs, corresponding to its infinite faculties. As in the human body movements result from the thinking mind and the acting will, so in the eyes of ancient science *the visible order of the universe was but the reflection of an invisible order,* that is, of cosmogonic forces and spiritual monads, kingdoms, classes and species, which through their perpetual involution into matter produced the evolution of life. Whereas modern science considers only the external, the surface of the universe, the science of the ancient temples had the task to reveal the internal, to discover hidden movements. It did not conclude that intelligence derives from matter, but matter from intelligence. It did not describe the universe as born of the blind dance of atoms, but it generated atoms through the vibrations of the universal soul. In short, it moved in concentric circles, from the universal to the particular, from the Invisible to the visible, from Pure Spirit to organized substance, from God to man. This descending order of powers and spirits in inverse proportion to the ascending order of life and bodies, was the ontology of science, of intelligible principles, and formed the basis of cosmogony.

All the great initiations in India, Egypt, Judea and Greece, those of Krishna, Hermes, Moses and Orpheus knew in varied forms this order of elements, powers, souls and generations which descend from the First Cause, from the Ineffable Father.

The descending order of incarnations is simultaneous with the ascending order of lives, and this alone makes it understandable. Involution produces evolution and explains it.

In Greece the male, or Doric temples, those of Jupiter and Apollo (especially that at Delphi), were the only ones which possessed the essential knowledge of the descending order. The Ionic, or feminine temples had but imperfect knowledge of it. The entire Greek civilization being Ionic, science and the Doric order became more and more veiled. Nevertheless, it is incontestable that its great initiators, its heros and philosophers, from Orpheus to Pythagoras to Plato and from the latter to the Alexandrians, depend upon that order. All recognized Hermes as their master.

Let us return to *Genesis*. According to Moses, that other son of Hermes, the first ten chapters of *Genesis* constituted a real ontology, based upon the order and relationship of beginnings. All that begins must end. *Genesis* simultaneously described evolution in time and creation in Eternity, the only creating worthy of God.

In the section on Pythagoras I shall give a picture of theogony and esoteric cosmogony in a less abstract setting than that of Moses, and closer to the modern mind. In spite of the polytheistic form, in spite of the extreme diversity of symbols, the meaning of this Pythagorean cosmogony, on the basis of Orphic initiation and the sanctuaries of Apollo, will be basically identical with that of the prophet of Israel. In Pythagoras the latter will be as though lighted by its natural complement, the doctrine of the soul and its evolution. The latter was taught in the Greek sanctuaries by means of the symbols of the myth of Persephone. It was also called *The Earthly and Heavenly Story of Psyche*. This narrative, corresponding to what Christianity calls *redemption,* is entirely absent from the Old Testament. This is not because Moses and the prophets did not know about it, but because they considered it too difficult for popular teaching, reserving it for the oral tradition of the initiates. The divine Psyche was hidden for a long time beneath the hermetic symbols of Israel, only that it might be personified in the ethereal, luminous appearance of Christ.

As for the cosmogony of Moses, it unites the incisive brevity of Semitic aptitude with the mathematical precision of Egyptian genius. The style of the narrative reminds one of the forms which decorate the interior of the kings' tombs; erect, cold, severe, they conceal an impenetrable mystery in their sharp bareness. The general effect makes one think of a Cyclopean building, but here and there, like lava flowing between the giant blocks, the thought of Moses bursts forth with the impetuosity of an initiate fire between the trembling verses of the translators. In the first chapters of incomparable grandeur, one feels the breath of Elohim pass by, turning the heavy pages of the universe one by one.

Before leaving them, let us look again at some of the mighty hieroglyphs composed by the prophet of Sinai. Like the door of an underground temple each of them opens upon a gallery of esoteric truths which, with their unflickering lamps, light the succession of worlds and ages. Let us attempt to enter it with the keys of initiation. Let us try to see these strange symbols, these magic formulas in their evocative power as the initiate of Osiris saw them, as they emerged in letters of fire from the furnace of his thought.

In the crypt of Jethro's temple Moses is meditating alone, sitting upon a sarcophagus. About him the walls and pilasters are covered with hieroglyphs and paintings, representing the names and forms of the gods as conceived by all peoples of the earth. These symbols summarize the history of vanished cycles and foretell future ones. A lamp placed upon the ground dimly lights these signs, each of which speaks its language to him. But already he no longer sees anything of the external world; he is seeking within himself the word of his book, the form of his work, the Word which will be Action. The lamp has gone out, but before his inner eye in the night of the crypt flames the name:

IEVE

The first letter, *I*, has the white color of light; the three others shine like a changing fire, in which all the colors of the rainbow revolve. And what a strange life is in these characters!

In the initial letter Moses perceives the masculine principle, Osiris, Creative Spirit *par excellence*.— In Eve he observes reproductive power and the Celestial Isis who is a part of it. Thus the divine faculties which contain all the worlds in their power, unfurl and become regulated in the Heart of God. Through their perfect union, the Father and the ineffable Mother form the Son, the Living Word, which creates the universe. This is the Mystery of Mysteries, hidden from the senses but speaking through the sign of the Everlasting as Spirit speaks to Spirit. And the sacred Tetragrammaton shines with an ever more intense light. Moses sees the three worlds, all the kingdoms of nature and the sublime order of the sciences burst forth in a tremendous effulgence. Then his glowing eye centers upon the masculine sign of the Creative Spirit. It is this that he calls upon so that he may pass through the orders of creation, and draw from the Supreme Will the strength to accomplish his own work after having viewed the work of the Everlasting.

Now in the shadows of the crypt shines another divine name:

ELOHIM

For the initiate this means, "He, the Gods, the God of Gods."[38] It is no longer the Being retiring within itself, dwelling in the Absolute, but the Lord of Worlds, Whose thought spreads out into millions of stars, moving spheres of floating universes. "In the beginning God created the heavens and the earth." But at first these heavens were only the thought of endless time and infinite space, filled with emptiness and silence. "And the spirit of God moved upon the face of the deep."[39] What will come forth from Him first? A sun? An earth? A cloud?—Any substance whatever of this visible world? No! What was born from Him first was *Aur,* light. But that light is not physical light, it is intelligible light, born of the trembling of celestial Isis in Infinity's womb; that universal soul, that starry light, that substance which makes souls, from which they blossom in an ethereal fluid; that subtle element by which thought is transmitted to infinite distances; that divine light which is anterior and posterior to that of all suns. At first it spreads into infinity, for it is the powerful *respir* of God, then it returns to itself in a movement of love, the deep *aspir* of the Everlasting. Upon the waves of the divine ether the astral forms of worlds and beings throb as though covered by a translucent veil. And all this is summarized for the magi-seer in the words he pronounces, and which light up in the darkness in shining characters:

RUA ELOHIM AUR[40]

"Let there be light, and there was light."—The breath of Elohim is light!

From the heart of that first non-material light burst the first six days of creation, that is, the seeds, the principles, the forms, the life-soul of everything. It is the Universe existing in power before the letter and according to the Spirit. And what is the last word of Creation, the formula which summarizes Being in action, the Living Word in which appears the first and last thought of the Absolute Being? It is

ADAM—EVE

The Man-Woman. In no way does this symbol represent (as is taught in our churches and as our exegetes believe) the first human couple of our earth, but God in action in the universe and human kind personified; it represents universal Humanity through all the heavens. "God created man in his own image; male and female created he him." This divine couple is the universal Word, for which *Ieve* reveals His true nature in the worlds. The sphere it originally inhabits and which Moses embraces with powerful thought is not the Garden of Eden, the legendary terrestrial paradise, but the limitless, temporal sphere of Zoroaster, the higher earth of Plato, the universal celestial kingdom, *Heden, Hadama,* the substance of all lands. But what will the evolution of mankind be in time and space? Moses views it in a disguised form in the story of the Fall. In *Genesis,* Psyche, the human soul, is called *Aisha,* another name for *Eve.*[41] Her homeland is *Shamaim,* heaven. She lives there happily in the divine ether, but without knowledge of herself. She enjoys heaven without understanding it. For in order to understand it, it is necessary first to have forgotten it and then to remember it; it is necessary to have lost it and to have found it again. She will know only by suffering; she will understand only by falling. And what a deep and tragic fall, quite different from that of the childish Biblical account of which we read! Drawn to the dark gulf by desire for knowledge, Aisha lets herself fall . . . She ceases being pure soul, having only a sidereal body and living in the divine ether. She is clothed in a material body and enters the circle of births. And her incarnations are not one, but one hundred, one thousand, in bodies which are more and more crude, depending upon the bodies she inhabits. She descends from world to world . . . She descends and forgets . . . A black veil covers her inner eye; in the thick tissue of matter, drowned is the divine consciousness, darkened is the memory of heaven. Pale as a lost hope, a weak recollection of her former happiness shines within her! With this spark she must be born again and must regenerate herself!

Yes, *Aisha* still lives in the naked couple who find themselves defenseless upon a wild earth under a hostile sky where thunder roars. Is Paradise lost? The vastness of the veiled heaven stretches behind and before her!

Moses thus views the generations of Adam in the universe.[42]

Next he considers the destinies of man on earth. He sees the past and present cycles. In earthly *Aisha*—in the soul of humanity—the consciousness of God once had shone with the fire of Agni in the land of Cush on the slopes of the Himalayas.

But now it is about to be extinguished in idolatry, in infernal passions beneath Assyrian tyranny amidst foreign peoples and alien gods who consume one another. Moses pledges himself to rekindle it by establishing the cult of Elohim.

Mankind as a whole, like man as an individual, ought to be the image of *Ieve*. But where are the people to be found who will embody Him, and who will be the living word of humanity?

Then Moses, having imagined his book and his work, having probed the darkness of the human soul, declares war on terrestrial, weak-natured, corrupt Eve. In order to fight her and reform her he calls upon the Spirit, the original, all-powerful Fire, *Ieve*, to whose source he wishes to return. He feels that its effluvia are setting him afire and are tempering him like steel. Its name is the Will.

And in the dark silence of the crypt, Moses hears a voice. It comes from the depths of his consciousness, it flickers like a light, saying, "Go to the mountain of God, to Horeb!"

22

The Vision of Sinai

A DARK mass of granite stands so bare beneath the splendor of the sun that one would think it had been furrowed by lightning and carved by thunder. "This is the summit of Sinai, the Throne of Elohim," say the children of the desert. Facing it is a lower mountain, the rocks of Serbal, also steep and wild. In its sides are copper mines and caverns. Between the two mountains is a dark valley, a chaos of rocks which the Arabs call Horeb, the *Ereb* of Semitic legend. This valley of desolation is gloomy indeed when night falls upon it along with the shadow of Sinai. It is even more gloomy when the mountain is crowned with a mantle of clouds, from which sinister flashes of light dart forth. Then a terrible wind blows down the narrow valley. It is said that here Elohim overthrows those who try to fight Him, casting them into the abyss where torrents of rain pour. The Midianites say that here wander the evil ghosts of giants, the *Refaim*, tumbling the rocks upon those who try to climb the sacred cliffs. Popular tradition still has it that sometimes in the flashing fire the God of Sinai appears in the form of a Medusa head with eagle's wings. Woe to those who see His face! To see Him is to die!

This is what the nomads related in the evening, sitting in their tents, when the camels and the women were asleep. In reality only the boldest of Jethro's initiates climbed to the cavern of Serval and spent several days there in fasting and prayer. It was a place dedicated from time immemorial to supernatural visions, to Elohim, or to luminous spirits. No priest, no hunter would have consented to lead a pilgrim there.

Fearlessly Moses had climbed up past the ravine of Horeb. Courageously he had crossed the valley of death with its chaos of rocks. Like every human effort, initiation has its phases of humility and pride. In climbing the mountain Moses had reached the summit of pride, for he was approaching the summit of human power. Already he felt himself at one with the Supreme Being. The burning red sun hung low over the volcanic massive form of Sinai and purple shadows were lying in the valleys below, when Moses found himself before a cavern where a few terebinths protected the entrance. He prepared to enter, but suddenly he was blinded by a light which enveloped him. It seemed to him that the sun burned about him, that the granite mountains had changed into a sea of flames.

At the entrance to the grotto a blinding light shone upon him. An angel with drawn sword blocked his way. Thunderstruck, Moses fell prone upon the ground. All his pride had been broken. The angel's gaze had pierced him with its light. And then, with that deep sense of things which is awakened in the visionary state, he understood that this being was about to impose serious tasks upon him. He would have liked to escape his mission and creep into the earth like a miserable worm.

But a voice said, "Moses! Moses!" And he answered: "Here am I."

"Come no closer; take off your shoes. For the place where you are standing is holy ground!"

Moses hid his face in his hands. He was afraid to look at the angel again, to face his gaze.

And the angel said to him, "You who seek Elohim, why do you tremble before me?"

"Who are you?"

"A ray of Elohim, a solar angel, a messenger of the One Who is and Who will be."

"What do you command?"

"You shall say to the children of Israel: The Everlasting, the God of your fathers, the God of Abraham, the God of Isaac, the God of Jacob sent me to you, to lead you out of the land of slavery."

"Who am I," asked Moses, "that I should lead the Children of Israel out of Egypt?"

"Go," said the angel, "for I shall be with you. I shall put the fire of Elohim in your heart, and His word upon your lips. For forty years you have been calling upon Him. Your voice has reached Him. Here I seize you in his name! Son of Elohim, you belong to me forever!"

And Moses cried out boldly, "Show me Elohim, that I may see His living fire!"

He raised his head. But the sea of flames had vanished; the angel had fled like lightning. The sun had descended upon the extinguished volcanoes of Sinai; a silence of death spread over the vale of Horeb, and a voice which seemed to roll in the blue, losing itself in infinity, said: "I am, that I am!"

Moses came out of this vision as though dumbfounded. He thought for a moment that his body had been consumed by the fire of ether. But his spirit was stronger. When he went down to Jethro's temple again, he was ready for his task. His living idea walked before him like the angel, armed with the sword of fire.

23

Exodus — The Desert —
Magic and Theurgy

Moses' plan was one of the most extraordinary and courageous that man has ever conceived. He was to tear a people from the yoke of a nation as powerful as Egypt, to take it to the conquest of a country occupied by hostile and better-armed inhabitants, to lead it for ten, twenty, forty years in the desert, to consume it with thirst, to weaken it with hunger, to torment it like a blood-horse under the arrows of the Hittites and Amalakites, ready to cut it to pieces, to isolate it with its Tabernacle of the Lord in the midst of these idolatrous nations, to impose monotheism upon it with a rod of fire and to instill in it such a fear and veneration of this One God that He would become incarnate in its flesh, that He would become its national symbol, the goal of all its aspirations and its reason for being.— Such was the amazing work of Moses.

The Exodus was coordinated and preparations made well in advance by the prophet, the chief Israelite leaders, and Jethro. To put his plan into effect, Moses took advantage of a moment when Menephtah, his former study-companion, now Pharaoh, had to repel the mighty invasion of Mermaiu, king of the Lybians. The entire Egyptian army was occupied on the western borders of the country and could not stop the Hebrews. Thus the mass emigration occurred peacefully.

Now we see the *Beni-Israel* on the march. The long file of caravans, with tents carried on camels' backs and followed by great herds, prepares to go around the Red Sea. They still number only a few thousand men. Later the emigration will grow larger "with all kinds of men," as the Bible says. They will include Canaanites, Edomites, Arabs, Semites of all kinds, attracted and fascinated by the desert prophet, who calls them from all directions and shapes them to his liking. The nucleus of his people is formed of the *Beni-Israel,* straightforward men, but rough, obstinate and rebellious. Their *hags* or their leaders have taught them the cult of the One God. This religion constitutes a high patriarchal tradition among them. But in those primitive and violent natures, monotheism is still only a better and intermittent consciousness. As soon as their evil passions reawaken, the instinct toward polytheism, so natural for man, takes the upper hand. Then they fall back into the superstitions, witchcraft and idolatrous practices of the neighboring peoples of Egypt and Phoenicia. Moses will fight this with Draconian laws.

Around the prophet who leads this people is a group of priests presided over by Aaron, Moses' initiate brother, and by the prophetess Miriam, who already represents feminine initiation in Israel. This group constitutes the priesthood. With them, seventy elected leaders or lay initiates press around the prophet of *Ieve.* Moses will entrust to them his secret doctrine and his oral tradition, will transmit to them a part of his powers and sometimes will make them sharers in his inspirations and visions.

In the midst of this group is carried the golden Ark. Moses

borrowed this idea from the Egyptian temples where it served as the secret place for the theurgic books, but he refashioned it in line with his personal plans. The Ark of Israel is surrounded by four cherubim in gold, similar to sphinxes and resembling the four symbolic animals of Ezekiel's vision. One cherubim has the head of a lion, another, of a bull, the third, of an eagle and the fourth, of a man. These personify the four elements of the universe: earth, water, air and fire, as well as the four worlds represented by the letters of the sacred Tetragrammaton. With their wings the cherubim cover the mercy seat, the throne of God.

This Ark will be the means of producing electrifying and splendid phenomena. The latter will be brought about by the magic of the priest of Osiris. These phenomena, exaggerated by legend, will produce the Biblical accounts. In addition, the golden Ark enclosed the *Sepher Bereshith,* or *Book of Cosmogony,* written by Moses in Egyptian hieroglyphics, and the magic wand of the prophet, called *the rod* by the Bible. Later it will also contain the *Book of the Covenant,* or the law of Sinai. Moses will call the Ark the throne of Elohim, for in it rests sacred tradition,—the mission of Israel, the idea of *Ieve*

What political constitution did Moses give to his people? Here it is necessary to refer to one of the strange passages of *Exodus.* This passage appears older and all the more authentic just because it shows us Moses' weak side, his tendency to priestly pride and theocratic tyranny, being reprimanded by his Ethiopian initiator.

. . . On the morrow, Moses sat to judge the people: and the people stood by Moses from the morning unto the evening.

And when Moses' father-in-law saw all that he did to the people, he said, "What is this thing that thou doest to the people? Why sittest thou thyself alone, and all the people stand by thee from morning unto evening?

MOSES

And Moses said unto his father-in-law, Because the people come unto me to inquire of God:

When they have a matter, they come unto me; and I judge between one and another, and I do make them know the statutes of God and his laws.

And Moses' father-in-law said unto him, the thing that thou doest is not good.

Thou wilt surely wear away, both thou, and this people that is with thee: for this thing is too heavy for thee; thou art not able to perform it thyself alone.

Hearken now unto my voice. I will give thee counsel, and God shall be with thee: Be thou for the people to God-ward, that thou mayest bring the causes unto God:

And thou shalt teach them ordinances and laws, and shalt show them the way wherein they must walk, and the work that they must do.

Moreover thou shalt provide out of all the people able men, such as fear God, men of truth, hating covetousness; and place such over them, to be rulers of thousands, and rulers of hundreds, rulers of fifties, and rulers of tens:

And let them judge the people at all seasons: and it shall be, that every great matter they shall bring unto thee, but every small matter they shall judge: so shall it be easier for thyself, and they shall bear the burden with thee.

If thou shalt do this thing, and God command thee so, then thou shalt be able to endure, and all this people shall also go to their place in peace.

So Moses hearkened to the voice of his father-in-law, and did all that he had said.

It is clear from this passage that in Israel's constitution, established by Moses, the executive power was considered an emanation of judicial power and placed under the control of priestly authority. Such was the government willed by Moses to his successors, at the wise advice of Jethro. It remained the same under the Judges from Joshua to Samuel, until the usurpation by Saul. Under the kings, the disparaged priesthood began to lose the real tradition of Moses, which survived only in the prophets.

We have said that Moses was not a patriot, but a civilizer of peoples, having before him the destinies of all humanity. Israel was but a means for him,—universal religion was his goal, and far above and beyond the nomads his thought went out to future ages. From the departure from Egypt until Moses' death, the history of Israel was but one long struggle between the prophet and his people.

Moses first led the tribes of Israel to Sinai in the barren desert, before the mountain dedicated to Elohim by all the Semites, where he himself had had his revelation. There where his Genius seized the prophet, the latter wanted to take possession of his people and engrave the seal of *Ieve* upon their forehead. This seal was the Ten Commandments, the mighty summary of the moral law, the complement of transcendant truth, enclosed in the hermetic book of the Ark.

Nothing is more tragic than this first dialogue between the prophet and his people. Strange, bloody, terrible scenes took place, which left, as it were, the imprint of a hot iron in Israel's mortified flesh. Beneath the amplifications of Biblical legend one divines the possible reality of the facts.

The elite of the tribes camped on the plateau of Pharan, at the entrance to a wild gorge which leads to the rocks of Serbal. The threatening summit of Sinai overlooks this stony, volcanic, rough terrain. Before the entire assembly Moses solemnly announces that he is going to go to the mountain to consult Elohim, and that he will bring back the Law, written upon a stone tablet. He commands the people to watch and fast, to wait in chastity and prayer. He leaves the Ark, hidden by the tent of the Tabernacle, under the watch of the seventy Elders. Then he disappears into the gorge, taking with him only his faithful disciple, Joshua.

Days pass; Moses does not return. The people are anxious at first, then they murmur, "Why did he lead us into this terrible desert and expose us to the arrows of the Amalakites? Moses promised to lead us to the land of Canaan where milk and honey flow, and here we are dying in the desert! Slavery in Egypt was better than this miserable life! Would to God that we still had the food that we ate back there! If the God of Moses is the true God, let him prove it; let all his enemies be scattered, and let us immediately enter the Promised Land." These complaints increase; the people rebel; even the leaders become involved.

Here comes a group of women who are whispering and murmuring among themselves. They are the daughters of Moab, dark-skinned with supple bodies and full figures, the concubines or servants of several Edomite leaders allied with Israel. They recall that they were priestesses of Astaroth, that they celebrated orgies of the goddess in the sacred forests of their native land. They feel that the time has come to reclaim their empire. They are adorned with gold and wear transparent garments; with a smile on their lips they resemble beautiful serpents coming out of the earth in order to display their sinuous forms and glittering reflections in the sun. They mix with the rebels, captivate them with their shining eyes, encircle them with their arms, resounding with copper bracelets, seducing them with their golden speech: "After all, who is this priest from Egypt, and his God? He will die on Sinai. The *Refaim* have probably thrown him in the abyss. It is not he who will lead the tribes into Canaan! But let the Children of Israel call upon the gods of Moab: Belphegor and Astaroth! They are gods that can be seen, and who perform miracles! They will lead Israel to the land of Canaan!" The mutineers listen to the

Moabite women. They incite one another, and the shout goes up from the multitude: "Aaron, fashion gods for us who will walk before us; as for Moses who made us come up from the land of Egypt, we do not know what has happened to him!"

In vain Aaron tries to calm the crowd. The daughters of Moab call upon the Phoenician priests who have arrived with a caravan. The latter bring wooden statues of Astaroth and raise them upon an altar of stone. Under threat of death the rebels force Aaron to cast a golden calf, one of the forms of Belphegor. The bulls and goats are sacrificed to the foreign gods; the people begin to drink and eat, and, led by the daughters of Moab, the lewd dances begin around the idols to the sound of *nebels, kinnors* and tambourines.

The seventy Elders chosen by Moses for the care of the Ark have tried to stop the disorder, but in vain. Now they are sitting on the ground, their heads covered with sackcloth and ashes. Grouped around the Tabernacle of the Ark, with consternation they hear the savage cries, the voluptuous songs, the invocations to the cursed gods, demons of lust and cruelty. With horror they view this people deep in debauchery and in rebellion against its God. What is to become of the Ark and the Book of Israel if Moses does not return?

But Moses does return. From his long meditation, from his solitude on the mountain of Elohim he brings back the Law, carved upon tablets of stone.[43] Entering the camp he sees the dances, the bacchanal of his people before the idols of Astaroth and Belphegor. Catching sight of the priest of Osiris, the prophet of Elohim, the dancers stop, the alien priests flee, the rebels hesitate. Anger seethes in Moses like a consuming fire. He breaks the tablets of stone, and one feels that in this way he would break this entire people. One knows that God possesses him.

Israel trembles, but the rebels dart looks of hatred and fear toward Moses. One word, one gesture of hesitation on the part of the leader-prophet and the hydra of idolatrous anarchy will lift its thousand heads against him and sink the holy Ark, the prophet, and his idea beneath a storm of stones. But Moses is there, and behind him are the invisible Powers which protect him. He understands that above all it is necessary to build up the spirit of the seventy elect to their rightful stature once again, and through them all the people. He calls upon Elohim-*Ieve*, Male Spirit, the Fire-Principle, in his own heart and in the heights of heaven.

"Let the seventy come to me!" cries Moses. "Let them take the Ark and climb with me to the mountain of God! As for this people, let them wait and tremble! I shall return with the judgment of Elohim upon them!"

The Levites take the golden Ark, covered with its wings, from the tent, and the procession of the seventy disappears with the prophet into the narrow passes of Sinai. One cannot tell who trembles the more, the Levites at what they are going to see, or the people at the punishment Moses leaves hanging over their heads like an invisible sword.

O if only they could free themselves from the terrible grip of this priest of Osiris, this prophet of evil! This is the wish of the rebels. And hastily half of the camp folds the tents, harnesses the camels, and prepares to flee. But a strange twilight, a veil of dust spreads over the sky; a sharp breeze blows over the Red Sea, the desert assumes a wild, red appearance and behind Sinai huge clouds pile up. Finally the sky becomes dark. Gusts of wind bring waves of sand, and lightning causes the whirlwind of clouds enveloping Sinai to burst in torrents of rain. Soon the flashes of lightning and the voice of thunder reverberating through all the gorges of the mountain mass bursts upon the plain in successive reports with a fearful din. The people have no doubt that this is the anger of Elohim, invoked by

Moses. The daughters of Moab have disappeared. The idols are overturned, the leaders kneel, the children and women hide under the camels. All night and all day this continues. Lightning strikes tents, killing men and beasts, and thunder continues to rumble.

Toward evening the tempest subsides, but the clouds continue to roll over Sinai, and the sky is still black. At the entrance to the camp the seventy now reappear, with Moses at their head. And in the dim twilight the faces of the prophet and his elect shine with a supernatural light, as if they have brought with them the reflection of a shimmering and sublime vision. Over the golden Ark, over the cherubim with wings of fire, quivers an electrical ray, like a phosphorescent pillar. At this extraordinary spectacle, the Elders and the people, men and women, kneel at a distance.

"Let those who are for the Lord come to me," commanded Moses.

Three-quarters of the leaders of Israel group themselves around Moses; the rebels remain hidden in their tents. Then the prophet moves forward and orders his faithful to put their swords through the instigators of the revolt and the priestesses of Astaroth, so that Israel may tremble forever before Elohim. He orders this so that Israel may remember the law of Sinai and its first commandment, "I am the Lord thy God which have brought thee out of the land of Egypt, out of the house of bondage. Thou shalt have no other gods before me. Thou shalt not make unto thee any graven image, nor any likeness of any thing that is in heaven above, or that is in the earth beneath, or in the waters under the earth."

By means of this mixture of terror and mystery, Moses imposed his law and his cult upon his people. It was necessary to impress the idea of *Ieve* on their soul in letters of fire, and without these inexorable measures, monotheism would never have triumphed over the invading polytheism of Phoenicia and Babylon.

But what had the seventy seen on Sinai? *Deuteronomy* 33:2 speaks of a tremendous vision, of thousands of saints appearing in the midst of the storm on Sinai, in the light of *Ieve*. Did the wise men of the ancient cycle, the ancient initiates of the Aryas, of India, Persia, and Egypt, all the noble sons of Asia, the land of God, come to assist Moses in his task of exercising a decisive pressure upon the consciousness of his associates? The spiritual Powers who watch over humanity are always present, but the veil separating us from them is rent only at decisive moments and for the few chosen ones.

Moses caused the divine fire and energy of his own will to enter the seventy. They were the first temple before that of Solomon; they were the living temple, the temple on the march, the heart of Israel, the royal light of God.

By means of the visions of Sinai, through the mass execution of the rebels, Moses acquired an authority over the nomadic Semites, whom he held in his iron grip. But similar events, followed by new manifestations of power, had to take place during the journey toward the land of Canaan. Like Mohammed, Moses had to manifest simultaneously the genius of a prophet, of a man of war, and of a social organizer. He had to fight against lassitude, calumny and conspiracies. After the revolt of the people he had to level the pride of the Levite priests who wanted to make their role equal to his, to have themselves considered, like him, as men directly inspired by *Ieve*. On the other hand, Moses had to face the more dangerous conspiracies of a few ambitious leaders like Core, Datan and Abiram, who fomented insurrection in order to overthrow the prophet and proclaim a king, as the Israelites did later with Saul, despite the resistance of Samuel. In this struggle, Moses experiences alternations of indignation and pity, the tenderness of a father and the roarings of a lion against the people who fight among themselves, but who, in spite of all, will submit to him. We find the echo of this in the Biblical dialogues between the prophet and his God, dialogues which seem to reveal what took place in the depths of his consciousness.

In the *Pentateuch*, Moses triumphs over all obstacles because of miracles which are excessively unrealistic. Jehovah, conceived of as a personal God, is always at his call. He appears above the Tabernacle like a shining cloud, which is called *The Glory of the Lord*. Moses alone can enter the Tabernacle; the impure who approach it are struck dead. In the Biblical account the Tabernacle of the congregation, which houses the Ark, plays the role of a gigantic electric battery which once charged with the fire of Jehovah, strikes the masses of the people with lightning. First the sons of Aaron, then two hundred fifty followers of Core and Datan, and finally fourteen thousand people are killed by its discharges. Moreover, at a set hour, Moses brings about an earthquake, which swallows up the three rebel leaders along with their tents and their families. This last account is related in wonderful, grandiose poetry. But it is marked by such exaggeration, by such an obviously legendary character, that it would be childish to discuss its reality. A particularly unreal quality is given to these accounts by the role Jehovah plays as an irascible, changeable God. He is always ready to strike and destroy, while Moses represents mercy and wisdom. Such a childish, contradictory concept of Divinity is no less strange to the consciousness of the initiate of Osiris than to that of a Jesus.

Nevertheless these fantastic exaggerations seem to stem from certain phenomena resulting from Moses' magic powers, and are not without analogy in the tradition of the ancient temples. Here it is possible to express one's thoughts regarding the so-called miracles of Moses in the light of a rational theosophy and esotericism. The production of various forms of electric phenomena at the will of powerful initiates is not only attributed to Moses by antiquity. Chaldean tradition attributed it to the Magi, Greek and Latin traditions, to certain priests of Jupiter and Apollo.[44] In similar cases the phenomena are indeed of an electric nature. But the electricity of the earthly atmosphere would be put in motion by a more subtle and universal force active everywhere, and which the great initiates agreed to attract, to concentrate and to project. This force is called *akasa* by the Brahmans, *the fire element* by the Magi of Chaldea, *the great magic agent* by the Kabbalists of the Middle Ages. From the point of view of modern science it can be called *etheric force*. One can either attract it directly or invoke it through the intermediary of invisible agents, conscious or semi-conscious, of which the earthly atmosphere is full, and which the will of the Magi knows how to control. This theory is in no way contrary to a rational concept of the universe, and it is even indispensable in explaining a large body of phenomena which would remain incomprehensible without it. It is necessary only to add that these phenomena are governed by changeless laws which are always proportioned to the intellectual, moral and magnetic strength of the initiate.

An anti-rational and anti-philosophical event would be the setting in motion of the First Cause of God by any being whatsoever (or the direct activation of this cause by Him), which would amount to an identification of the individual with God. Man only relatively rises to Him through thought or prayer, through action or ecstasy. God exercises His activity in the universe only indirectly, through the Hierarchies, by means of universal and unchangeable laws which express His thought, as it were, through earthly and divine humanity, who partially and proportionately represent Him in the world of space and time.

In harmony with these points of view we think it perfectly possible that Moses, sustained by the spiritual Powers who protected him, and manipulating the etheric force with consummate art, could have used the Ark as a sort of receptacle, a magnetic concentrator for the production of electric phenomena of a lethal nature. He isolated himself, his priests and his trusted friends by clothing of linen and by aromatics, which protected them from the discharges of etheric fire. But these phenomena could only be rare and limited. Priestly tradition tends to exaggerate them. Doubtless for Moses' purposes it was necessary to destroy only a few rebel leaders or a few disobedient Levites by means of the projection of fluid, in order to terrorize and subdue all the people.

24

The Death of Moses

WHEN Moses had led his people to the borders of Canaan, he felt that his task was fulfilled. What was *Ieve*-Elohim for the seer of Sinai? It was divine order, coming from above, passing downward through all the spheres of the universe, and realized on the visible earth in the image of the celestial Hierarchies and eternal truth. No, it was not in vain that he had viewed the face of the Lord, reflected in all worlds. The Book was in the Ark and the Ark, kept by a strong people, was a living temple of the Lord. The worship of the One God was established upon earth; the name of *Ieve* shone in flaming letters in the consciousness of Israel; centuries would pass over the changing soul of humanity, but no longer could they erase the name of the Eternal.

Realizing these things, Moses called upon the Angel of Death. He placed his hands upon Joshua as his successor before the Tabernacle of the assembly, so that the spirit of God might pass upon him. Then he blessed all mankind through the twelve tribes of Israel, and ascended Mount Nebo, followed only by Joshua and two Levites. Already Aaron had been "welcomed to his fathers," and the prophetess Miriam had taken the same road. Moses' turn had come.

What were the thoughts of the centenarian prophet when he saw the camp of Israel disappear, and climbed into the great solitude of Elohim? What did he feel upon letting his eyes pass over the Promised Land, from Gilead to Jericho, city of palms? A true poet, Alfred de Vigny, describing Moses' state of soul at this moment, makes him utter the cry:

> O Lord, I have lived, strong and solitary,
> Let me fall asleep with the sleep of earth!

These beautiful lines say more about the soul of Moses than the commentaries of a hundred theologians. This soul resembles the great pyramid of Gizeh,—massive, bare on the outside, but enclosing great mysteries, bearing in its very center a sarcophagus called by the initiates the Sarcophagus of Resurrection. From that point, through an ascending corridor one perceived the North Star. In similar manner, from its center the impenetrable spirit of Moses looked at the final end of all things.

Indeed, all mighty men have known the solitude that creates greatness; but Moses was more alone than others because his principle was more absolute, more transcendant. His God was the male principle *par excellence*. It was pure Spirit. In order to inculcate it into men, he had to declare war on the feminine principle, on the Goddess Natura, on *Heve,* the Eternal Feminine, who lives in the heart of the earth and in the heart of Man. Unceasingly and mercilessly he had to fight it, not in order to destroy it, but to subdue, to master it. Is it then surprising if nature and Woman, between whom reigns a mysterious pact, trembled before him? Is it then so astonishing if they rejoiced at Moses' departure and waited in order to lift their heads until his shadow had ceased to cast on them the feeling of death? Such things doubtless were present in the thoughts of the seer as he climbed the arid slopes of Mount Nebo. Men could not love him, for he had loved only God. Would his work continue to live? Would his people remain faithful to their mission? Alas! The fatal spiritual insight of the dying, the tragic gift of the prophets, lifts all veils in the final hour! As the spirit of Moses became detached from the earth, he saw the terrible reality of the future; he saw the betrayals of Israel, anarchy rearing its head, royalty following the Judges, the crimes of kings staining the temple of the Lord; his book mutilated, not understood; his thought misinterpreted and disparaged by unenlightened or hypocritical priests; the apostasies of kings; the adultery between Judah and idolatrous nations; the pure tradition, the sacred doctrine, stifled, and the prophets, possessors of the Living Word, persecuted to the farthest reaches of the desert.

Sitting in a cave on Mount Nebo, Moses saw all this within himself. But already Death had spread its wings over his forehead and had placed its cold hand upon his heart. Then this lion heart tried to roar once more. Angered by his people, Moses called down the wrath of Elohim upon the race of Judah. He lifted his heavy arm. Joshua and the Levites helped him and heard with horror these words from the mouth of the dying prophet: "Israel has betrayed its God; let it be scattered to the four winds of the heaven!"

With terror the Levites and Joshua looked at their master, who no longer gave any sign of life. His last word had been a curse. Had he breathed his last breath with it? But Moses opened his eyes just once more, and said, "Return to Israel. When the time is come, the Lord will raise up a prophet like myself from among your brothers, and He will place His Word in his mouth. And this prophet will tell you all that the Lord commands.

And it shall come to pass that whoever will not harken to the words which he shall speak to you, the Lord will require it of him!" (*Deuteronomy* 18:18, 19)

After these prophetic words Moses surrendered his spirit. The solar angel with the sword of fire who first appeared to him on Sinai, was waiting for him. He led him into the deep heart of the celestial Isis, upon the waves of that Light which is the Wife of God. Far from the earthly regions they crossed circles of souls of ever-increasing splendor. Finally the angel of the Lord showed him a Spirit of wondrous beauty and celestial sweetness, but of such radiance and of a brightness so overpowering that his own was but a shadow in comparison. The Spirit did not carry the sword of punishment, but the palm of sacrifice and victory. Then Moses understood that this Spirit would accomplish his work, and would lead men back to the Father through the power of the Eternal Feminine, through Divine Grace and Perfect Love.

Then the Law-giver knelt before the Redeemer; Moses worshipped Jesus Christ.

ORPHEUS

The Mysteries of Dionysus

How they toss about in the immense universe as they whirl and seek each other, these myriad souls which burst forth from the great soul of the World! They fall from planet to planet, and in the abyss mourn the forgotten homeland. . . . They are your tears, Dionysus . . . O Great Spirit, O Divine Liberator, take your daughters back into your heart of light.

—Orphic Fragment.

"Eurydice! O divine light!" cried the dying Orpheus. "Eurydice!" moaned the seven cords of his Lyre, as they broke. And his tossing head, carried away forever on the river of the ages, still calls "Eurydice! Eurydice!"

—Legend of Orpheus

25

Prehistoric Greece —
The Bacchantes —
Appearance of Orpheus

In the sanctuaries of Apollo which possessed the Orphic tradition, a mysterious festival was celebrated at the vernal equinox. This was the time when the narcissus bloomed again near the fountain of Castalia. The tripods and the lyres of the temple vibrated of their own accord, and the invisible god was said to return to the country of the Hyperboreans in a chariot drawn by swans. Then the great priestess, dressed as a Muse and crowned with laurel, her forehead bound with sacred bands, sang before the initiates *The Birth of Orpheus,* the son of Apollo and of a priestess of god. The Muse called upon the soul of Orpheus, father of mystics, musical savior of men. She sang of sovereign Orpheus, immortal and thrice-crowned, in hell, on earth and in heaven, a star upon his forehead, walking among the constellations and the gods.

The mystical chant of the priestess of Delphi referred to one of the many secrets kept by the priests of Apollo, unknown to the masses. Orpheus was the animating genius of sacred Greece, the quickener of its divine soul. His seven-stringed lyre embraces the universe. Each string corresponds to a mood of the human soul and contains the law of a science and an art. We have lost the key to its full harmony, but the different modes have not ceased vibrating in our ears. The theurgic and Dionysian impulse which Orpheus knew how to communicate to Greece, was transmittted by Greece to all Europe. Our age no longer believes in the beauty of life. However, if in spite of all, it maintains a deep recollection, a secret, invincible hope, it owes the latter to this divine, inspired one. Let us hail him as the great initiator of Greece, the ancestor of poetry and music, conceived as revealers of eternal truth.

But before reconstructing the story of Orpheus out of the very heart of the tradition of the sanctuaries, let us describe Greece at the time of his appearance.

The latter took place in the age of Moses, five centuries before Homer, thirteen centuries before Christ. India was sinking into its *Kali-Yuga,* into its age of darkness, and manifested no more than a shadow of its former splendor. Through the tyranny of Babylon, Assyria had unleashed upon the world the scourge of anarchy and now continued to tread Asia underfoot. By means of the science of her priests and the strength of her Pharaohs, Egypt might have resisted this universal collapse, but her activities stopped at the Euphrates and the Mediterranean. In the desert Israel was to raise the principle of the male God and of divine unity through the thundering voice of Moses. But earth had not yet heard its reverberations.

Greece was deeply divided by religion and politics.

The mountainous peninsula, extending its arms into the Mediterranean and garlanded by islands, was populated for thousands of years by a branch of the white race akin to the Getes, the Scythians and the primitive Celts. This race had mingled with and experienced the changes of all previous civilizations. Colonies from India, Egypt and Phoenicia had established themselves upon its shores, covering its promontories and valleys with people, activities and manifold divinities. With sails unfurled, fleets passed beneath the legs of the Colossus of Rhodes, astride the two piers of its port. The Cycladic Sea, where on clear days the navigator always sees some isle or shore against the horizon, was furrowed by the red prows of the Phoenicians and the black hulls of the pirates of Lydia. These vessels carried the riches of Asia and Africa: ivory, decorated pottery, cloth from Syria, golden vases, velvet and pearls, and often women, snatched from some wild coast.

Through these mixtures of races was formed a flowing and harmonious language, a mixture of primitive Celtic, Zend, Sanskrit and Phoenician. This language which painted the majesty of the ocean under the name of Poseidon, and the serenity of the sky under that of Ouranos, imitated all the voices of nature, from the chirping of birds to the roar of the storm. It was multi-colored, like its deep blue sea, with changing skies; it was of many sounds, like the waves which murmur in its gulfs or dash themselves upon its innumerable reefs—*poluphlosboïo Thalassa*, as Homer says.

Accompanying these merchants or pirates were often priests, who directed and commanded them as masters. In their boats they jealously hid a wooden image of a god. Doubtless the image was crudely carved, and the sailors of that time had the same fetishism for it that many of our mariners have for their Madonna. But their priests, nevertheless, were in possession of certain sciences, and the divinity they carried from their temple into a foreign land represented for them a concept of nature, a group of laws, a civil and religious organization. For in those days, all spiritual life stemmed from the temples. Juno was worshipped at Argos, Artemis in Arcadia; in Paphos and Corinth the Phoenician Astarte had become Aphrodite, born out of the foam of the waves. Several initiators had appeared in

Attica. An Egyptian colony had brought to Eleusis the cult of Isis in the form of Demeter, Ceres, mother of the gods. Between the Hymettian mountain and the Pentelicus Erechteus had established the cult of a virgin goddess, daughter of the blue sky, friend of the olive tree and of wisdom. During the invasions, at the first sound of alarm, the population took refuge on the Acropolis, pressing about the goddess as about a living victory.

A few male cosmogonic gods ruled over the local divinities. But, consigned to the high mountains and eclipsed by the brilliant procession of feminine divinities, they had little influence. The solar god, the Delphic Apollo,[45] already existed, but as yet he played only an obscure role. There were priests of Zeus, the Most High, at the foot of the snowy summits of Ida, on the heights of Arcadia and beneath the oaks of Dodona. But the people preferred the goddesses who represented the power of nature, whether seductive or terrible, rather than the mysterious, universal god.

The underground rivers of Arcadia, the mountain caverns, descending into the very bowels of the earth, the volcanic eruptions in the isles of the Aegean Sea, had brought the Greeks to the cult of mysterious earth forces. Thus, in the heights and in the depths, nature was felt, feared and venerated. But since all these divinities had neither a social center nor a religious synthesis, they engaged in desperate wars among themselves. The enemy temples, the rival cities, the people divided by ritual, by the ambition of priests and kings, hated each other, were jealous of each other, fighting each other in bloody battles.

But beyond Greece was wild, rugged Thrace. To the north, chains of mountains, covered with giant oaks and topped with rocks, followed behind each other in waves, spread out in enormous circles, or entangled in knotty massifs. The winds from the south beat upon their grassy sides and often storm clouds swept over their summits.

Shepherds of the valleys and warriors of the plains belonged to this strong white race, to the great stock of the Dorians of Greece. This male race *par excellence* is evidenced in the beauty of its sharpness of features and strength of character. Its ugliness appears in the frightfulness and impressive quality that is found in the head of the Medusa and the ancient Gorgons.

Like Egypt, Israel, Etrurua and all those ancient peoples who received their organization from the Mysteries, Greece had its sacred geography, in which each area became the symbol of a purely spiritual and supraterrestrial region of the soul. Why was Thrace[46] always considered by the Greeks as the holy land *par excellence,* the land of light, the real homeland of the Muses? It is because these high mountains bore the oldest sanctuaries of Kronos, of Zeus and of Ouranos. From them had descended in Eumolpic rhythms, poetry, laws and sacred art. The legendary poets of Thrace give evidence of this. The names Thamyris, Linos and Amphion correspond, perhaps, to real people, but above all they personify, according to the language of the temples, so many kinds of poetry. Each of them celebrates the victory of one theology over another. In the temples of that time history was written only allegorically. The individual was nothing, the doctrine and the work, everything. Thamyris, who sang of the war of the Titans and was blinded by the Muses, announces the defeat of cosmogonic poetry by new modes. Linos, who introduced the melancholy songs of Asia into Greece and was killed by Hercules, reveals the invasion into Thrace by a moving, sad, sensuous poetry which the virile mind of the Dorians of the north at first rejected. At the same time this means the victory of a lunar over a solar cult. On the other hand, Amphion, who, according to allegorical legend put the stones in movement with his songs and built temples with the sounds of his lyre, represents the plastic force that solar doctrine and orthodox Dorian poetry exercised upon the arts of Greece and upon all Hellenic civilization.[47]

How different is the light with which Orpheus shines! He beams across the ages with the personal light of a creative genius, whose masculine soul vibrated with love for the Eternal Feminine, and in its lowest depths that Eternal Feminine, who lives and throbs in a triple form in nature, humanity and Heaven, responded. The worship of the sanctuaries, the tradition of the initiates, the cry of the poets, the voice of the philosophers,—and more than all the others, his work, an organic Greece, testify to his living reality!

In those times, Thrace was involved in an intense and heated struggle. The solar and lunar cults were fighting for supremacy. This war between the worshippers of the sun and moon was not, as one might believe, a vain battle between two superstitions. These two cults represented two theologies, two cosmogonies, two religions and two absolutely opposite social organizations. The Ouranian and solar cults had their temples in lofty and mountainous places, with priests and strict laws. The lunar cults held sway in the forests and the deep valleys; they had women as priestesses, with voluptuous rites, a chaotic practice of occult arts and a love of orgiastic excitement. It was a war to the death between the priests of the sun and the priestesses of the moon. It was a battle of the sexes, an ancient, inevitable battle, open or secret, but eternally waged between the male and female principles, between man and woman. Just as the perfect fusion of masculine and feminine constitutes the very essence and mystery of divinity, so the balance of these two principles alone can produce great civilizations.

Everywhere in Thrace as in Greece, the male gods, cosmogonic and solar, had been consigned to the high mountains and desert places. The people preferred the enticing procession of female divinities, who called forth dangerous passions and the blind forces of nature. These cults attributed the feminine sex to the supreme divinity.

Terrible abuses began to result from this. Among the Thracians the priestesses of the moon or of the threefold Hecate had proved their supremacy in appropriating the old cult of Bacchus and in giving him a bloody and dreadful character. As a sign of their victory they had taken the name Bacchantes, as if to mark their mastery, the supreme reign of woman, her domination of man.

Magicians, seducers and bloody sacrificers of human victims, they had their sanctuaries in wild and remote valleys. By what dark attraction, what burning curiosity, were men and women attracted to these solitudes of luxurious vegetation? Naked figures, lascivious dances in the depth of the forest . . . then laughter, a great outcry . . . and a hundred Bacchantes threw themselves upon the stranger and subdued him. He had to swear submission to them and give himself to their rituals, or perish. The Bacchantes tamed panthers and lions, which they displayed in their festivals. At night, their arms entwined with serpents, they knelt before the threefold Hecate; then, in frenzied dances they invoked Bacchus underground, the double-sexed one with a bull's face.[48] But woe to the stranger, woe to the priest of Jupiter or of Apollo, who came to spy on them! He was torn to pieces.

The primitive Bacchantes were the Druidesses of Greece. Many Thracian leaders remained faithful to the old male cults. But the Bacchantes had found their way to some of the Thracian kings, who added their barbaric customs to the luxury and refinements of Asia. The Bacchantes had seduced them with voluptuousness and conquered them with terror. Thus the gods had divided Thrace into two enemy camps. But the priests of Jupiter and Apollo, on their lonely summits, haunted by thunder, found themselves powerless against Hecate, who was gaining strength in the burning valleys and who began to threaten the very altars of the sons of light.

At that time a young man of royal race and wondrous appeal had appeared in Thrace. He was said to be the son of a priestess of Apollo. His melodious voice had a strange charm. He spoke of the gods in a new rhythm, and seemed inspired. His blond hair, pride of the Dorians, fell in golden waves over his shoulders and the music which flowed from his lips lent a gentle, sad contour to the corners of his mouth. His deep blue eyes shone with power, sweetness and magic. The fierce Thracians fled before his glance, but the women versed in the art of charms said that his blue eyes combined the arrows of the sun and the kisses of the moon. Even the Bacchantes, curious about his beauty, often slunk around him like panthers in love, proud of their dark skins, and smiled at his incomprehensible words.

Suddenly this young man, who was called *the son of Apollo,* disappeared. He was said to be dead, to have descended into hell. However, he had secretly fled to Samothrace, then to Egypt, where he asked shelter from the priests of Memphis. Having gone through their Mysteries, he returned at the end of twenty years, bearing an initiation-name which he had acquired as a result of his ordeals, and had received from his teachers as a sign of his mission. He was now called *Orpheus of Arpha,*[49] which means the one *who heals with light.*

The oldest sanctuary of Jupiter then arose on Mount Kaoukaion. Once its hierophants had been great pontiffs. From the top of this mountain, protected from unexpected attacks, they had reigned over all of Thrace. But since the lower divinities had achieved supremacy, their followers were few and their temple was almost abandoned. The priests of Mount Kaoukaion welcomed the initiate from Egypt as a savior. With his knowledge and his enthusiasm, Orpheus assumed the leadership of the majority of the Thracians, completely changed the cult of Bacchus and subdued the Bacchantes. Soon his influence penetrated into all the sanctuaries of Greece. It was he who established the supremacy of Zeus in Thrace and that of Apollo in Delphi, where he laid the foundations of the council of the Amphyctions, which became the social unit of Greece. Finally, through the creation of the Mysteries, he formed the religious soul of his country. For from the height of initiation, he blended the religion of Zeus with that of Dionysus in a universal concept. The initiates received the pure light of sublime truth through his teachings, and this same light reached the people in a more tempered, but no less beneficial form under the veil of poetry and enchanting festivals.

In this way Orpheus became pontiff of Thrace, high-priest of the Olympian Zeus, and the revelator of the heavenly Dionysus to the initiates.

26

The Temple of Jupiter

NEAR the source of the Ebro rises Mount Kaoukaion. Thick oak forests mantle its sides and a circle of rocks and Cyclopean stones crown its summit. For thousands of years this has been a sacred mountain. Pelasgians, Celts, Scythians and Getes had driven one another out and in turn came here to worship their various gods. But is it not always the same God that man seeks when he climbs so high? If not, why does he so painstakingly build a home in this region of thunder and winds?

A temple of Jupiter now rises in the center of the holy site, massive and unapproachable like a fortress. At the entrance stands a peristyle of four Dorian columns, its enormous shafts outlined against a dark portico.

At the zenith the sky is calm, but the storm still howls over the mountains of Thrace, which extend their valleys and peaks in the distance,—a black ocean churned up by the tempest and streaked with lightning.

It is the hour of sacrifice. The priests of Kaoukaion perform this ritual by fire only. They descend the steps of the temple and light the aromatic wood offering with a torch from the sanctuary. Then the pontiff leaves the temple. Clothed in white linen like the others, he wears a crown of myrtle and cypress. He carries an ebony scepter with an ivory head, and wears a golden belt upon which crystals flash their dark lights, symbols of a mysterious royalty. This is Orpheus.

He leads a disciple, a child of Delphi, by the hand. Pale, trembling and enraptured, the pupil awaits the words of the Great Inspired One, echoing the Mysteries. Orpheus sees this, and to reassure the neophyte, chosen by his warm heart, he gently puts his arm around his shoulders. His eyes smile, but suddenly they are aflame. And while down below the priests move around the altar and sing the hymn of fire, Orpheus solemnly tells the beloved the mystic words of initiation, which rise from the depths of his heart like a divine fluid.

These are the winged words of Orpheus to the young disciple:

"Withdraw deep within yourself in order to lift yourself to the Principle of things, to the Great Triad which flames in the immaculate ether. Consume your body with the fire of your thought; detach yourself from matter like the flame from the wood which it devours. Then your spirit will ascend into the pure ether of Eternal Causes as the eagle rises to Jupiter's throne.

"I shall reveal to you the secret of the worlds, the soul of nature, the essence of God. Hear first the great mystery: A single Being rules in the deep sky and in the abyss of earth, the thundering Zeus, the ethereal Zeus. His are profound counsel, powerful hate and delightful love. He rules in the depths of earth and in the heights of the starry sky. He is the Breath of things, the untamed fire, eternal Male and Female, a King, a Power, a god, a Grand Master!

"Jupiter is divine Husband and Wife, Man and Woman,

Father and Mother. From their sacred marriage, from their everlasting union, unceasingly come fire and water, earth and ether, night and day, the proud Titans, the changeless gods and the floating seed of men.

"The loves of heaven and earth are not known to the uninitiated. The mysteries of husband and wife are unveiled only to divine men. But I wish to state what is true. A little while ago the thunder shook these rocks; lightning fell like living fire and a rolling flame, and the echoes of the mountains roared with joy. But you, you were trembling, not knowing whence this fire comes nor where it strikes. It is the male fire, the seed of Zeus, the creative fire. It comes from the heart and brain of Jupiter; it moves in all beings. When lightning falls, it bursts from his right hand. But we, its priests, know its essence; we avoid and sometimes direct its shafts.

"And now, look at the firmament. See that shining circle of constellations over which the filmy veil of the Milky Way, the dust of suns and worlds, is thrown! Behold Orion flaming, Gemini scintillating, the Lyre shining! That is the body of the divine wife, who is revolving in celestial harmony to the songs of the husband. Look with the eyes of the spirit, and you will see her head inclined, her arms extended, and you will lift her veil, strewn with stars!

"Jupiter is both the divine husband and wife. That is the first Mystery.

"But now, child of Delphi, prepare yourself for the second initiation. Tremble, weep, rejoice, worship! For your spirit is about to plunge into the burning zone, where the great Demiurge unites soul and world in the cup of life. Upon drinking from this intoxicating chalice, all beings forget the divine sojourn and descend into the painful abyss of incarnation.

"Zeus is the great Demiurge. Dionysus is his son, his Word made manifest. Dionysus, radiant spirit, living intelligence, was the splendor of his father's habitation, the eternal palace of ether. One day as he viewed the depths of the heavens through the constellations, he saw reflected in the azure abyss his own image, extending its arms to him. Fascinated by this beautiful phantom, enamored with his double, he hastened to grasp it. But the image constantly fled before him. Finally he found himself in a shadowy, perfumed valley, enjoying the delightful breezes which caressed his body. In a grotto he saw Persephone. Maia, the beautiful weaver, was weaving a veil, upon which one could see pictures of all beings moving to and fro. He stopped before the divine virgin, dumb with rapture. At that moment, the haughty Titans and the free Titanides saw him. The former were jealous of his beauty, and the latter, mad with passion, threw themselves upon him like the furious elements, and tore him to pieces. Then, distributing his limbs among themselves, they boiled them in water. His heart they buried. Jupiter struck the Titans with thunderbolts, and Minerva carried the heart of Dionysus away with her into the ether. There it became a glowing sun. But from the smoke of Dionysus' body came souls of men, ascending toward heaven. Once the pale spirits have rejoined the flaming heart of the god, they will flame like torches, and Dionysus will be revived, more alive than ever, in the heights of the empyrean.

"This is the Mystery of the death of Dionysus. Now listen to the Mystery of his resurrection. Men are the flesh and blood of Dionysus; unhappy men are the scattered members, which seek one another by becoming snared in crime and hate, in pain and love, through thousands of lives. The burning heat of the earth, the abyss of the lower powers, forever attract them nearer to this gulf, always tearing them asunder. But we, the initiates, who know what is above and what is below, are the saviors of souls, the Hermes of men. Like magnets we attract them to us, ourselves in turn attracted to the gods. Thus, by means of heavenly incantations we reestablish the living body of the Divinity. We make the heavens weep and the earth rejoice, and like precious jewels we bear in our hearts the tears of all beings, in order to change them into smiles. God dies in us, and in us he is reborn."

Thus Orpheus spoke. The disciple of Delphi knelt before his master, his arms raised in a gesture of supplication. And the pontiff of Jupiter raised his hand above his head, as he spoke these words of consecration:

"May Ineffable Zeus and Dionysus, three times revelator,— in hell, on earth and in heaven—be kind to your youth, and may he pour into your heart the knowledge of the gods."

Then the initiate left the peristyle of the temple and went to throw storax on the fire of the altar, calling three times upon thunderous Zeus. The priests moved in a circle around him, singing a hymn. Deep in thought, the pontiff-king had remained beneath the portico, his arm resting upon a stele. The disciple returned to him.

"The way leading upward to the gods is rough," said Orpheus, who seemed to answer inner voices rather than his disciple. "A flower-strewn path, next a steep incline, and finally rocks, illumined by lightning flashes, with infinity everywhere. This is the destiny of the seer and prophet on earth! My child, continue on the flower-strewn paths of the plain, and do not seek to go beyond them!"

"My thirst increases as you quench it," said the young initiate. "You have taught me about the essence of the gods. But tell me, great master of the Mysteries, the one inspired by divine Eros, shall I ever be able *to see* them?"

"With the eyes of the spirit," said the pontiff of Jupiter, "but not with those of the body. As yet you know how to see only with the latter. You must undergo long tests or great suffering in order to open the inner eyes."

"You alone know how to open them, Orpheus! With you, what can I fear?"

"Do you wish to attempt it? Listen then!—In Thessaly, in the enchanted valley of Tempe rises a mystic temple, closed to the uninitiated. It is there that Dionysus shows himself to the mystics and seers. In one year from now I shall invite you to his festival. Plunging you into a magic sleep, I shall open your eyes to the divine world. Until then, let your life be virtuous, your soul spotless. For truly the light of the gods frightens the weak and destroys the profaners!

"But come into my house. I shall give you the book you will need for your preparation."

The master and the Delphic disciple returned to the interior of the temple. Orpheus led the pupil into the great *cella* which was set aside for him. There an ever-burning Egyptian lamp, held by a winged genius fashioned of forged metal, glowed. Locked in coffers of scented cedar were many papyrus scrolls, inscribed in Egyptian hieroglyphs and Phoenician characters, as well as books written in the Greek language by Orpheus himself. These contained his magic wisdom and his secret doctrine.[50]

Master and disciple conversed in the *cella* for the greater part of the night.

27

A Dionysan Festival
in the Valley of Tempe

WE are in Thessaly, in the cool valley of Tempe.[51] The holy night dedicated by Orpheus to the Mysteries of Dionysus has come. Led by one of the servants of the temple, the disciple of Delphi walks in a narrow, deep ravine, surrounded by sharp rocks. In the somber night only the murmur of the river between its green banks nearby, can be heard. At last the full moon appears from behind a mountain. Its yellow disk rises above the dark grass and the rocks. Its subtle and magnetic light flows into the depths; suddenly the enchanted valley is filled with an Elysian brightness. In a single instant its grassy depths, its groves of ash and poplar, its crystal streams, its grottos clad in falling ivy, and its winding river encircling islands of trees or rolling under entwined bowers, is revealed. A yellow mist and a delightful sleep envelop the plants. The sighs of nymphs seem to make the mirror of the streams tremble, and faint sounds of a flute are heard from the motionless reeds. The silent incantation of Diana reigns over all. . . .

The disciple of Delphi walks as though in a dream. He

pauses to inhale the delightful aroma of honeysuckle and bitter laurel. But the magic brightness lasts only for an instant. The moon is covered with a cloud. Everything becomes dark; the rocks again assume their threatening forms and flickering lights shine from all sides beneath the dense trees, at the edge of the river, in the depths of the valley.

"Those are the mystics," the aged guide of the temple says. "They are setting out on their way. Each procession has its torch-bearing guide. We shall follow them."

The travellers meet choirs leaving the woods, starting on their journey. First they see the *Mystics of Young Bacchus* pass by: adolescents clothed in long tunics of fine linen, and wearing crowns of ivy. They bear cups of carved wood, symbols of the cup of life. Then follow proud, sturdy young men. These are called *The Mystics of Fighting Hercules:* they wear short tunics which reveal their bare legs; lion's skins are draped over their shoulders and loins, and they wear crowns of olive leaves upon their heads. Next the inspired ones appear, *The Mystics of Dismembered Bacchus*, skins of panthers around their bodies, bands of velvet about their heads, thyrsus in their hands.

Passing near a cavern, they see the *Mystics of Adonis* and of *Subterranean Eros* kneeling upon the ground. They are mourning dead relatives or friends. They sing in a low voice, "Adonis, Adonis! Give us back those you have taken from us, or let us go down into your kingdom!" The wind is swallowed up in the cavern, seeming to stretch itself into the underworld with laughs and mournful rattles of death. Suddenly a mystic turns to the disciple of Delphi and says, "You have crossed the threshold of Adonis; never again will you see the light of the living!" Another brushes past him, uttering these words in his ear: "Shade, you will be the prey of Shades! You who come from the night, return to Erebus!" The disciple of Delphi is frozen with fright. He whispers to his guide: "What does this mean?" The servant of the temple appears to have heard nothing. He only says, "You must pass over the bridge. No one avoids the end."

They cross a wooden bridge spanning the Peneus.

"Where," asks the neophyte, "do these plaintive voices and that mournful chant come from? What are those white shadows which walk in long lines beneath the poplars?"

"They are women who are about to become initiated into the Mysteries of Dionysus."

"Do you know their names?"

"Here no one knows the name of anyone, and each forgets his own. As at the entrance to the holy realm the mystics leave their soiled garments when they bathe themselves in the river, afterward clothing themselves in robes of clean linen, here each leaves his name in order to receive another. For seven nights and seven days, one becomes transformed, one passes into another life. Look at all those processions of women! They are not grouped according to family or country, but according to the god who inspires them."

Young girls file by, wearing crowns of narcissus and dressed in blue peplos. The guide named these *The Companion Nymphs of Persephone.* They carry chests, urns and votive vases. Dressed in red peplos next appear *The Mystic Lovers, The Passionate Wives* and *The Seekers of Aphrodite.* They move into the depths of the dark forest. From it come violent cries, mixed with languishing sobs. Little by little, these die away. Then a passionate chorus arises from the dark myrtle wood, mounting to the sky in slow measures. "Eros, you have wounded us! Aphrodite, you have broken our bones! We have covered our breasts with the skin of the fawn, but we bear on our breasts the bloody marks of our wounds! Our heart is a consuming furnace. Others die of poverty; it is love which consumes us. Devour us, Eros! Eros!—Or deliver us, Dionysus! Dionysus!"

ORPHEUS

Another procession moves forward. These women are clothed entirely in black wool, with long veils trailing behind them; all are overcome with deep mourning. The guide calls them *Persephone's Mourners*. At this place is a great marble mausoleum, covered with ivy. They kneel around it, unbinding their hair, as they utter great cries. To the strophe of desire they respond with the antistrophe of grief. "Persephone," they cry, "you are dead, carried away by Adonis! You have descended into the kingdom of the dead. But we who mourn the beloved are the living dead! Let day not dawn for us again! Let the earth which covers you, O great goddess, give us everlasting sleep, and our shade wander, bound to the beloved shade! Hear us, Persephone! Persephone!"

At these strange scenes, under the contagious delirium of these great sufferings, the disciple of Delphi is overcome by a thousand contradictory and tormenting sensations. He is no longer himself; the desires, thoughts and death agonies of all these beings have become his own desires and agonies. His soul is divided into pieces in order to enter a thousand bodies. A mortal anguish has invaded his being. He no longer knows whether he is man or shade.

Then an initiate of great stature who is passing by, pauses and says, "Peace be to the afflicted phantoms! Suffering women, strive for the light of Dionysus! Orpheus is awaiting you!" All surround him in silence, waving their crowns of asphodels; with his thyrsus he points the way. The women go to drink from wooden cups at a stream. The line forms again, and the procession moves on. The young girls have taken the lead. They sing a threnody with the refrain, "Shake the poppies! Drink the water of Lethe! Give us the flower of desire, and may the narcissus bloom again for our sisters! Persephone! Persephone!"

The disciple walks beside his guide for a long time. He passes over fields where the asphodel grows. He walks beneath the shadow of sadly murmuring poplars. He hears lugubrious songs which glide into the air and come from he knows not where. He sees horrible masks and wax figurines hanging from trees like swaddled children. Here and there boats cross the river, filled with people, silent like dead men. Finally the valley broadens, the sky becomes clear above the high mountains. The dawn appears. In the distance can be seen the dark gorges of Ossa, furrowed with ravines, choked with fallen rocks. Nearer, encircled by mountains, the temple of Dionysus shines upon a wooded hill.

Already the sun has gilded the lofty mountain tops. As they approach the temple, coming from all directions, they see processions of mystics, long lines of women, groups of initiates. Outwardly grave but inwardly excited by a tumultuous hope, all meet at the foot of the hill and ascend the approach to the sanctuary. All greet one another like friends, waving the branches and thyrsi. The guide has disappeared, and the disciple of Delphi finds himself, he knows not how, in a group of initiates, their shining hair encircled with crowns and bands of various colors. He has never seen them before, yet he thinks he knows them. They also seem to be waiting for him, for they greet him as a brother, congratulating him on his safe arrival. Carried along by the crowd as though borne on wings, he climbs to the highest steps of the temple. Suddenly, a blinding flash of light strikes his eyes. It is the rising sun, casting its first arrow into the valley, its gleaming rays flooding this assembly of mystics and initiates grouped on the steps of the temple.

Immediately a choir strikes up a paean of praise. The bronze doors of the temple open and, followed by Hermes and the torch bearer, the prophet, the hierophant, Orpheus appears. The disciple of Delphi recognizes him with a tremor of joy. Clothed in velvet, his lyre of ivory and gold in his hand, Orpheus glows with everlasting youth. He says,

ORPHEUS

"Hail to all of you who have come to be reborn after the sorrows of earth, and who are being reborn at this moment! Come, drink of the light of the temple. You who appear out of the night,—mystics, women, initiates! Come, rejoice, You who have suffered; come, rest, You who have fought! The sun which I invoke above your heads and which will shine in your souls is not the sun of mortals; it is the pure light of Dionysus, the great Sun of the initiates. Through your past sufferings, through the trial which brings you here, you will conquer, and if you believe in the divine words, you already have conquered. For after the long circuit of dark existences you will finally leave the painful circle of births, and all of you will find yourselves as a single body, a single soul, in the light of Dionysus!

"The divine spark which guides us upon earth is in us; it becomes a flame in the temple, a star in the sky. Thus the light of truth grows brighter. Listen to the Lyre of seven strings vibrate, the Lyre of God . . . It causes worlds to move! Listen well! May the sound penetrate you, and may the depths of the heavens open!

"Help for the weak, consolation for the suffering, hope for all! But woe to the wicked, to the uninitiated! They will be confounded! For in the ecstasy of the Mysteries each one sees to the very bottom of the soul of the other! The wicked shall be struck with terror, and the profaners with death.

"And now that Dionysus has shone upon you, I shall invoke celestial and all-powerful Eros. May he be in your loves, in your cries, in your joys! Love, for everything loves—the demons of the abyss and the gods of the ether! Love, for everything loves! But love with light, and not with darkness. Remember your goal during your journey. When souls return to the light they bear all the mistakes of their lives like ugly spots upon their sidereal body . . . And in order to erase them, they must expiate them and return to earth . . . But the pure, the strong enter into the Sun of Dionysus.

"And now, sing the *Evohe!*"

"Evohe!" shout the heralds from the four corners of the temple. "Evohe," and the cymbals sound. "Evohe!" replies the joyful assembly, gathered on the steps of the temple. And the call of Dionysus, the holy call to rebirth, to life, rolls into the valley, repeated by a thousand hearts, sent back by all the echoes of the mountains. And the shepherds in the wild gorges of Ossa and those feeding their herds in the highland forests near the clouds, answer, "Evohe."[52]

28

Evocation

THE festival had faded like a dream; the evening had come. The dances, songs and prayers had vanished in the pink mist. Orpheus and his disciple descended through an underground passage into the sacred crypt, extending into the heart of the mountain, to which the hierophant alone had access. It was here that the inspired of the gods devoted themselves to solitary meditation or with the adepts pursued the great arts of magic and theurgy.

Around them spread a vast cavern. Two torches placed upon the ground only dimly lighted the creviced walls and the shadowy depths. A few steps away a dark fissure opened upward into the sunlight. A warm wind came from it, and extending downward, the crevice seemed to descend into the bowels of the earth. A small altar where a fire of dry laurel burned, and a porphyry sphinx guarded the edge of the opening. Far above at a great height, the cavern opened to the starry sky through a slanting fissure. This pale ray of bluish light seemed like the eye of the firmament itself, plunging into this abyss.

"You have drunk from the streams of holy light," said Orpheus, "you have entered with a pure heart into the heart of the Mysteries. The solemn hour has come when I shall cause you to penetrate to the sources of life and light. Those who have not lifted the thick veil which conceals the invisible wonders from the eyes of men, have not become the sons of the gods.

"Listen, therefore, to the truths which must be kept from the crowd, and which are the strength of the sanctuaries:

"God is One, and always resembles Himself. He reigns everywhere. But the gods are myriad and varied, for Divinity is eternal and infinite. The greatest are the souls of the stars. Suns, stars, earths and moons—each star has its own soul, and all have come out of the celestial fire of Zeus, the Primal Light. Semiconscious, inaccessible, unchanging, they rule the great Whole with their regular movements. And into its ethereal sphere each revolving star leads hosts of demigods or shining souls who once were men, and who, having descended the ladder of the kingdoms, gloriously ascended through the cycles once again, finally to leave the circle of births. It is through these divine spirits that God breathes, moves, appears. They are the breath of His living Soul, the rays of His eternal consciousness. They command the hosts of lesser spirits, which bestir the lower elements; they direct the worlds. Far and near, they surround us and although immortal in essence, they clothe themselves in eternally changing forms according to the people, the age and the region. The impious who deny them, fear them; the devout man worships them without knowing them; the initiate knows them, attracts them and sees them. If I have fought to find them, if I have braved death, if, as is said, I descended into hell, it was to subdue the demons of the abyss, to call the gods from on high to my beloved Greece so that the lofty heaven might become wedded to earth, and the spellbound earth listen to the divine voices! Celestial beauty will become incarnate in the flesh of women, the fire of Zeus will flow in the blood of heroes, and long before returning to the stars, the sons of the gods will be resplendent like the Immortals!

"Do you know what the Lyre of Orpheus is? It is the sound of inspired temples. They have the gods as strings. At their music Greece will become attuned like a lyre, and the marble itself will sing in brilliant cadences and celestial harmonies.

"And now I shall call forth my gods, so that in living form they may appear before you, and may show you, in a prophetic vision, the mystical marriage which I am preparing for the world and which the initiates will witness.

"Lie down in the shelter of this rock. Fear nothing. A magic sleep will close your eyelids. You will tremble at first, and you will see terrible things. But afterward a pleasant light, an unknown happiness, will flood your senses and your being!"

The disciple had already crouched in the niche cut in the form of a couch in the rock. Orpheus threw some aromatics on the altar fire. Then he seized his rod of ebony, tipped with a flashing crystal, placed himself near the sphinx and in a deep voice began the evocation:

"Cybele! Cybele! Great Mother, hear me! Original light, agile ethereal flame, forever bounding through space, embracing the echoes and images of all things! I call upon your flaming chargers of light! O, Universal Soul, Creator of Abysses, Sower of Suns, who let your starry mantle trail in the ether, subtle, hidden light, invisible to the eyes of flesh, Great Mother of Worlds and gods, you who embody eternal archetypes! Ancient Cybele, come to me! Come to me! By my magic rod, by my pact with the Powerful, by the soul of Eurydice, I call you forth, many-bodied wife, gentle and vibrant beneath the fire of the everlasting Male! From the highest of spaces, from the deepest abysses, from all directions, come, make haste! Fill this cavern with your effluvia! Surround the son of the Mysteries with a diamond rampart, and make him see in your deep breast the Spirits of the Abyss, of Earth and of the Heavens!"

At these words, underground thunder shook the depths of the cavern and the whole mountain trembled. A cold sweat froze the body of the disciple. He saw Orpheus through a thickening smoke. At one moment he tried to fight against the dread power which felled him, but his brain was overcome, his will annihilated . . . He suffered the agonies of a drowning man who swallows water by the mouthful, and whose horrible convulsion ends in the darkness of unconsciousness . . .

When he regained consciousness, night surrounded him, a night mixed with a dreadful twilight, yellowish and foul. For a long time he stared before him without seeing anything. Frequently he felt his skin brushed as by invisible bats. Finally, dimly, he thought he saw monstrous forms of centaurs, hydras and gorgons move in the shadows. But the first thing he saw distinctly was the huge figure of a woman sitting upon a throne. She was enveloped in a long veil with funereal folds, sewn with dim stars, and was wearing a crown of poppies.

Her great open eyes watched motionless. Hosts of human phantoms moved around her like tired birds, whispering in a low voice, "Queen of the dead, Soul of earth, O Persephone! We are the daughters of heaven. Why are we in exile in this dark kingdom? O Harvester of Heaven, why have you prisoned our souls, which once flew happily among their sisters in the light, in the fields of ether?"

Persephone answered, "I have gathered the narcissus; I have entered the nuptial bed. I drank death with life. Like you, I groan in darkness."

"When shall we be delivered?" asked the groaning souls.

"When my celestial husband, the divine liberator, comes," answered Persephone.

Then terrible women appeared. Their eyes were bloodshot, their heads crowned with poisonous plants. Around their arms and half-naked bodies coiled serpents which they handled like whips. "Souls, specters, larvae!" they hissed, "do not believe the crazy queen of the dead! We are the priestesses of dark life, servants of the elements and of the monsters below, Bacchantes on earth, Furies in Tartarus! We are your eternal queens, unfortunate souls! You shall not leave the cursed circle of births; we shall make you return with our whips! Writhe forever between the hissing coils of our serpents, in the knots of desire, of hate, of remorse!" And dishevelled, they rushed upon the group of bewitched souls, who began to whirl about in the air beneath their whip lashes like a tempest of dry leaves, uttering long groans.

At this sight, Persephone became pale; she seemed no more than a lunar phantom. She murmured, "Heaven, Light . . . gods . . . a dream! Sleep, eternal sleep!" Her crown of poppies withered, her eyes closed in anguish. The queen of the dead fell into a lethargy upon her throne, and everything disappeared into the darkness.

The vision changed. The disciple of Delphi saw himself in a beautiful green valley. Mount Olympus arose at the end of it. Before a dark cave, beautiful Persephone was sleeping on a bed of flowers. In her hair a crown of narcissus replaced the crown of funereal poppies, while the dawn of a new life spread an ambrosial hue over her cheeks. Her dark tresses fell upon her shoulders of sparkling whiteness, and the roses of her gently lifted breasts seemed to summon the kisses of the winds. Nymphs danced upon the field; small white clouds wandered in the azure. A lyre resounded in a temple . . .

In its golden voice, its sacred rhythms the disciple heard the secret music of things. For from the leaves, waves and caverns came a formless, tender melody, and the distant voices of choruses of initiated women in the mountains reached his ear in broken cadences. Some, bewildered, called upon the gods; others thought they saw them as they fell at the edge of the forests, half-dead with fatigue.

At last the blue opened to the zenith, giving birth to a sparkling cloud out of its breast. Like a bird which hovers a moment, then sinks to earth, the god who holds the thyrsus descended and stood before Persephone. He was radiant; in his eyes beamed the divine delirium of worlds about to be born. For a long time he held her with his gaze; then he lifted his thyrsus over her. The thyrsus brushed her breast; she began to smile. He touched her forehead; she opened her eyes, sat up slowly and looked at her husband. Those eyes, still filled with the sleep of Erebus, began to shine like two stars. "Do you recognize me?" asked the god. "O Dionysus," cried Persephone, "Divine Spirit, Word of Jupiter, Celestial Light which shines in the form of man! Each time you awaken me I think that I am living for the first time; worlds are reborn in my memory; the past and future again become the immortal present, and I feel the universe in my heart!"

At the same time, above the mountains, on the edge of the silver clouds, the gods appeared, leaning curiously toward the earth.

Below, groups of men, women and children coming out of valleys and caves, looked at the Immortals with a celestial rapture. Ardent hymns ascended from the temples, along with waves of incense. Between earth and heaven was being prepared one of those marriages which make mothers conceive heroes and gods. Already a pink hue had spread over the entire countryside; already the Queen of the Dead, the Divine Harvester, again ascended to heaven, borne in the arms of her husband. A purple cloud surrounded them, and the lips of Dionysus were placed upon Persephone's mouth . . . Then a tremendous cry of love came from heaven and earth, as if the holy tremor of the gods passing over the Great Lyre wished to tear all the cords and cast the sounds to the four winds. At the same time, from the divine couple burst a fulguration, a hurricane of blinding light . . . And everything disappeared . . .

For a single moment the disciple of Orpheus felt as if swallowed up in the very Source of all lives, immersed in the Sun of Being. But, plunging into its incandescent furnace, he reappeared with celestial wings and like a flash of light he traversed worlds, at their boundaries finding the ecstatic sleep of Infinity.

When he regained his corporeal senses, he was plunged into black night. A luminous lyre alone shone in the deep shadows. It moved away rapidly, like a star. Then only did the disciple recognize that he was in the crypt of evocation, and that this luminous point was the distant cleft in the cavern, opening to the firmament.

A great form was standing near him. He recognized Orpheus by his long curls and the flashing crystal of his staff.

"Child of Delphi, where are you coming from?" asked the hierophant.

"O Master of Initiates, Celestial Charmer, Wondrous Orpheus, I had a divine dream! Was it perhaps a magic charm, a gift of the gods? What happened? Has the world changed? Where am I now?"

"You have gained the crown of initiation; you have lived my dream. Greece will be immortal!—But let us leave here, for in order for the dream to be fulfilled, I must die and you must live."

29

The Death of Orpheus

Lashed by the tempest, the forests of oak trees roared on the slopes of Mount Kaoukaion; the thunder rolled with all its might upon the bare rocks, making the temple of Jupiter shake to its very foundations. The priests of Zeus were assembled in a vaulted crypt of the sanctuary. Seated upon their bronze seats, they formed a semi-circle. Orpheus was standing in their midst, like one accused. He was paler than usual, but a deep flame appeared in his calm eyes.

The eldest of the priests raised his voice, grave as that of a judge:

"Orpheus, you whom they call son of Apollo, we have named you pontiff and king; we have given you the mystic staff of the sons of God; you rule over Thrace with a priestly and royal skill. You raised up the temples of Jupiter and Apollo in this country, and you made the divine Sun of Dionysus shine in the night of the Mysteries. But do you know what really threatens us? You who know the dread secrets, you who more than once have foretold the future, and who spoke to your disciples from a distance by appearing to them in a dream, you do not know what is taking place around you! In your absence, the savage Bacchantes, the accursed priestesses, have assembled in the valley of Hecate. Led by Aglaonice, the sorceress of Thessalia, they have persuaded the leaders on the banks of the Ebre to reestablish the cult of dark Hecate, and threaten to destroy the temples of the male gods and all the altars of the Most High. Agitated by their burning tongues, led by their flaming torches, a thousand Thracian warriors are encamped at the foot of this mountain. Tomorrow they will attack our temple, incited by the breath of these women clothed in panther skins, greedy for the blood of males. Aglaonice, high-priestess of sinister Hecate, leads them; she is the most fearful of sorceresses, implacable and fierce as a Fury. You must know her! What have you to say?"

"I knew all this," said Orpheus, "and all this had to be."

"Then why have you done nothing to defend us? Aglaonice has sworn to slay us on our altars before the living Heaven which we worship! But what is to become of this temple, its treasures, your wisdom, and Zeus himself if you abandon it?"

"Am I not with you?" asked Orpheus gently.

"You have come, but too late," said the old man. "Aglaonice is leading the Bacchantes, and the Bacchantes are leading the Thracians. Will you repel them with the thunder of Jupiter and the arrows of Apollo? Why do you not call into this enclosure the Thracian leaders who are faithful to Zeus, in order to crush the revolt?"

"It is not by arms, but by the Word that one defends the gods. It is not the leaders whom you must strike, but the Bacchantes. I shall go: I alone. Fear not. No profane person will enter this enclosure. Tomorrow the reign of the bloody priestess will end. And mark well, you who tremble before the horde of Hecate, the celestial and solar gods will be victorious! To you, old man

253

who doubted me, I leave the staff of pontiff and the crown of hierophant."

"What are you going to do?" asked the old man, frightened.

"I am going to rejoin the gods . . . To all of you . . . Farewell . . ."

Orpheus went out, leaving the priests sitting dumb in their seats. In the temple he found the disciple of Delphi, and taking his hand firmly, said,

"I am going to the camp of the Thracians. Follow me."

They walked under the oak trees; the storm was far away. Between the thick branches shone the stars.

"For me the supreme hour has come," said Orpheus. "Others have understood me; you have loved me. Eros is the oldest of the gods, say the initiates; he holds the key to all beings. I have caused you to penetrate to the depth of the Mysteries; the gods have spoken to you, you have seen them. Now, far from men at the hour of his death, Orpheus must leave his beloved disciple the explanation of his destiny, the immortal heritage, the pure flame of his soul."

"Master, I am listening, and I shall obey," said the disciple of Delphi.

"Let us walk along this descending path," said Orpheus. "The hour is near. I wish to surprise my enemies. Follow me. Listen and engrave my words in your memory, but keep them secret."

"They will be imprinted in letters of fire upon my heart; centuries will not erase them!"

"You know now that the soul is the daughter of Heaven. You have beheld your origin and your end, and you are beginning to recollect. When the soul descends into the flesh, it continues to receive the influx from above. And it is through our mothers that this powerful breath first reaches us. The milk of their breasts nourishes our bodies, but it is from their souls that our being is nourished, anguished by the stifling prison of the body. My mother was a priestess of Apollo; my first memories are those of a sacred grove, a solemn temple, a woman carrying me in her arms, enveloping me with her soft hair like warm clothing. Terrestrial objects, human faces, overwhelmed me with a dreadful terror. But immediately my mother embraced me in her arms, I met her glance and it flooded me with a divine recollection of Heaven. But this ray died in the dark gloom of earth. One day my mother disappeared; she was dead. Deprived of her gaze, cut off from her caresses, I was terrified in my solitude. Having seen the blood of sacrifice flow, I held the temple in horror and descended to the dark valleys.

"The Bacchantes were astounded at my youth. From that time Aglaonice has ruled over these voluptuous, savage women. Men and women,—everyone feared her. She breathed dark desire and struck others with terror. This Thessalian sorceress exercised a fatal attraction over all who came near her. Through the skill of infernal Hecate she lured young girls into her haunted valley and instructed them in her cult. Meanwhile, Aglaonice had cast her eyes upon Eurydice. She was overcome with a perverse desire, an unbridled evil lust for this virgin. She wanted to draw this young girl into the cult of the Bacchantes, to subdue her, and give her over to infernal genii after having despoiled her youth. Already she surrounded her with seductive promises, with her nocturnal incantations.

"Drawn into the valley of Hecate by some unknown impulse, one day I was walking through the high grasses of a field covered with poisonous plants. Everything around me breathed the horror of the dark forests haunted by the Bacchantes. Perfumes passed by me in gusts like the warm breath of desire. I saw Eurydice. She was walking slowly toward a grotto as though drawn by an invisible charm. Sometimes from the forest came a faint laugh of the Bacchantes, sometimes a strange sigh. Eurydice would stop, trembling, uncertain, and then continue walking as though drawn by a magic power. Her golden curls flowed over her white shoulders, her narcissus eyes swam with intoxication as she walked toward the mouth of Hell. But I had seen Heaven asleep in her glance. 'Eurydice!' I cried out, seizing her hand, 'where are you going?'

"As though awakened from a dream, she uttered a cry of horror and deliverance at once, and then fell upon me. At that instant the divine Eros subdued us, and with a single look, Eurydice and Orpheus were husband and wife forever.

"Meanwhile Eurydice, who clung to me in her fright, pointed toward the grotto with a gesture of terror. I went nearer and saw a woman sitting within. It was Aglaonice. Near her was a small statue of Hecate in wax, painted red, white and black, and holding a whip. She muttered words of a spell while turning her magic spinning wheel; her eyes, staring into emptiness, seemed to devour her prey. I broke the wheel, trod Hecate underfoot, and looking at the sorceress with a severe glance, cried out, 'By Jupiter! I forbid you to think of Eurydice, under penalty of death! For indeed the sons of Apollo do not fear you!'

"Aglaonice, stupefied, writhed like a serpent and disappeared into her den, casting a look of mortal hatred at me.

"I led Eurydice to the door of my temple. The virgins of Ebre, crowned with hyacinth, sang 'Hymen, Hymeneus!' around us; I knew happiness.

"The moon had changed only three times when a Bacchant, directed by the Thessalian sorceress, presented a cup of wine to Eurydice which would give her, said she, the knowledge of philters and magic herbs. Curious, Eurydice drank it and fell lifeless. The cup contained a fatal poison.

"When I saw the pyre consume Eurydice, when I saw the tomb swallow her ashes, when the last trace of her living form had disappeared, I cried out, 'Where is her soul?' In despair I wandered over all Greece. I asked the priests of Samothrace for her evocation; I looked for her in the bowels of the earth, on Cape Tenarus, but in vain. Finally I came to the Cave of Trophonius. There certain priests lead courageous visitors through a crevice to the lakes of fire which boil in the interior of the earth, letting them see what is happening there. As one walks along the way, one goes into ecstasy and second sight opens. One hardly can breathe, the voice becomes choked, and one can no longer speak except by signs. Some retreat half-way, others persist and die of suffocation; the majority of those who leave the fissure alive become insane. Having seen what no lips must repeat, I climbed into the grotto again and fell into a profound lethargy. During this sleep of death, Eurydice appeared to me. She was floating in a nimbus, pale as a lunar ray, and said to me, 'For my sake you have braved Hell; you have sought me among the dead. Here I am; I come at your call. I do not dwell in the heart of the earth, but the region of Erebus, the place of shadows between earth and the moon. I whirl in this limbo, sorrowing like yourself. If you wish to free me, save Greece by giving her light. Then I myself, finding wings again, shall climb to the stars and you will find me in the light of the gods. Until then I must wander in the troubled and painful sphere . . .' Three times I tried to seize her, three times she vanished from my arms like a phantom. I heard only the sound of a string that is broken. Then a weak voice, like a gentle breath, sad like a farewell kiss, murmured: 'Orpheus!'

"At this voice I awakened. This name, uttered by a soul, had changed my being. I felt the sacred tremor of an overwhelming desire and the power of a superhuman love pass through me. Eurydice alive would have given me the delirium of happiness; Eurydice dead made me find truth. It was with love that I put on the robe of linen, dedicating myself to the Great Initiation and to the ascetic life; it was through love that I entered into magic and sought divine knowledge; it was through love that I crossed the caverns of Samothrace, climbed the walls of the pyramids and entered the tombs of Egypt. I searched death to find life; and beyond life I saw the limbus, the souls, the transparent spheres and the ether of the gods. Earth opened her abysses, the sky, its flaming temples. The priests of Isis and Osiris gave their secrets to me. They had only those gods; I had Eros! Through him I spoke, sang and conquered! Through him I spelled the word of Hermes and the word of Zoroaster; through him I pronounced the word of Jupiter and Apollo!

"But the hour for confirming my mission by my death is come. Once more I must descend into Hell to ascend into Heaven. Listen, dearest child, to my word: You will bear my doctrine to the temple of Delphi and my law to the Council of the Amphyctions. Dionysus is the Sun of the initiates; Apollo will be the Light of Greece; the Amphyctions, guardians of his justice."

The hierophant and his disciple had reached the edge of the valley. Before them spread a clearing, surrounded by great masses of dark forest. Men were encamped at the edge of the forest, sleeping beside dying fires and flickering torches. Orpheus walked calmly into the midst of the sleeping Thracians, who were exhausted from a nocturnal orgy. A sentinel, still keeping watch, asked him his name.

"I am a messenger from Jupiter. Call your leaders!" replied Orpheus.

"A priest of the temple!" This cry of the sentinel spreads like an alarm over the whole camp. The men arm themselves; they call one another, swords shine. Astonished, the leaders surround the pontiff.

"Who are you? What have you come to do?"

"I am a representative of the temple. All of you,—kings,

leaders, warriors of Thrace,—give up fighting with the Sons of Light and recognize the divinity of Jupiter and Apollo! The gods from above speak to you through me. I come as a friend if you listen to me, as a judge if you refuse to hear me."

"Speak!" cried the leaders.

Standing beneath a tall elm tree, Orpheus spoke. He spoke of the good deeds of the gods, of the glory of celestial light, of that pure life which he led up there with his fellow-initiates under the Eye of the great Ouranus, and which he wished to communicate to all men, promising to lessen their strife, to heal their sick and to teach them of the seeds which produce the divine fruits of life: joy, love, beauty. And as he spoke, his serious, gentle voice vibrated like the strings of a lyre and went deeper and deeper into the hearts of the wavering Thracians.

From the heart of the forest the curious Bacchantes, torches in their hands, had also come, attracted by the music of a human voice. Scantily clothed in panther skins, they came to display their brown breasts and superb bodies. In the light of their torches, their eyes shone with vice and cruelty. But, calmed by the voice of Orpheus, they gathered around him or sat at his feet like tamed beasts. Some, seized wth remorse, stared mournfully at the ground; others listened as though enraptured. And the Thracians, deeply moved, murmured among themselves, "A god is speaking; Apollo himself is charming the Bacchantes!"

Meanwhile at the edge of the forest, Aglaonice was watching. The high priestess of Hecate, seeing the Thracians motionless and the Bacchantes controlled by a magic more powerful than hers, sensed the victory of Heaven over Hell, and saw her diabolical power crumbling into the darkness whence it had come, before the speech of the divine charmer. She threw herself before Orpheus violently, screaming,

"A god, you say? Well I say he is Orpheus, a man like yourselves, a magician who is deceiving you, a tyrant who is usurping a crown for himself! A god, you say? The son of Apollo? Him? The priest? The proud pontiff? Throw yourselves upon him! If he is a god, let him defend himself . . . And if I lie, let me be destroyed!"

Aglaonice was followed by a few leaders who were incited by her sorcery and inflamed with her hate. They threw themselves upon the hierophant. Orpheus uttered a great cry and fell, pierced by their swords. He raised his hand to his disciple, and said,

"I die, but the gods live!"

Then he breathed his last. Leaning over his body, the sorceress of Thessalia, whose face now resembled Tisiphone's, gazed with savage joy upon the last breath of the prophet, and prepared to draw an oracle from her victim. But great was the terror of the Thessalians upon seeing his corpse-like head revive in the flickering torchlight. A redness spread over the face of the dead man. His eyes opened wide, and a deep, gentle, terrible gaze fixed itself upon her . . . Meanwhile, a strange voice —the voice of Orpheus—once more came from those quivering lips, distinctly pronouncing the melodious and revengeful syllables,

"Eurydice!"

Before that stare and that voice, the terror-stricken priestess drew back, crying out, "He is not dead! They are going to pursue me forever! Orpheus! Eurydice!" Uttering these words, Aglaonice disappeared as though scourged by a hundred Furies. The bewitched Bacchantes and Thracians, seized with the horror of their crime, fled into the night, uttering cries of distress.

The disciple remained alone beside the body of his master. When a sinister ray of Hecate came to light up the bloodstained linen and pale face of the great initiator, it seemed to him that the valley, river, mountains and deep forests groaned like a great lyre.

Orpheus' body was burned by his priests, and his ashes were carried into the distant sanctuary of Apollo where they were venerated with a reverence given to the god himself. None of the rebels dared ascend to the temple of Kaoukaion. The tradition of Orpheus, his knowledge and his Mysteries were perpetuated there and spread to all the temples of Jupiter and Apollo. The Greek poets said that Apollo had become jealous of Orpheus because he was invoked more often than he. The truth is that when the poets sang of Apollo, the great initiates called upon the soul of Orpheus, savior and master of divination.

Later the Thracians, converted to the religion of Orpheus, related that he had descended into Hell to search for the soul of his wife, and that the Bacchantes, jealous of his eternal love, had torn him to pieces. But the Thracians said that his head, cast into Ebre and carried away by its storm-tossed waves, still calls, "Eurydice, Eurydice!"

Thus the Thracians honored as a prophet the one whom they had killed as a criminal, and who had converted them by his death. Thus the Orphic Word filtered mysteriously into the veins of Hellas by the hidden ways of the sanctuaries of initiation. The gods were harmonized by his voice like a temple chorus of initiates at the sounds of an invisible Lyre—and the soul of Orpheus became the soul of Greece.

PYTHAGORAS

The Mysteries of Delphi

Know yourself—and you will know the universe and the gods.
—Inscription in the Temple of Delphi.

Sleep, dream and ecstasy are the three doors opening upon the Beyond, whence come to us the science of the soul and the art of divination.

Evolution is the law of Life.

Number is the law of the Universe.

Unity is the law of God.

30

Greece in the Sixth Century

THE soul of Orpheus had crossed the stormy sky of nascent Greece like a divine meteor. Once he had disappeared, darkness covered it once again. After a series of revolutions the tyrants of Thrace burned his books, overturned his temples, drove out his disciples. The Greek kings and many cities, more jealous of their frenetic licence than loving that justice which flows from pure doctrines, imitated them. They wished to erase his memory, to destroy his last remains, and this was so well done that a few centuries after his death, a part of Greece doubted that he had ever existed. In vain the initiates preserved his tradition for more than a thousand years; in vain Pythagoras and Plato spoke of him as of a divine man; the sophists and rhetoricians saw in him nothing more than a legend concerning the origin of music. Even today students firmly deny the existence of Orpheus. They base themselves on the fact that neither Homer nor Hesiod mentions him. But the silence of these poets is amply explained by the censorship the local governments had placed upon the memory of the great initiator. The disciples of

Orpheus missed no opportunity to rally all powers under the supreme authority of the temple of Delphi, and did not cease to repeat that it was necessary to submit the differences arising between the various states of Greece to the Council of the Amphictions. This annoyed the demagogues as well as the tyrants. Homer, who probably received his initiation in the sanctuary of Tyre, and whose mythology is the poetic translation of the theology of Sankoniaton,—Homer the Ionian may very well not have known the Dorian Orpheus, whose tradition was held all the more secret since it was more persecuted. As for Hesiod, born near the Parnassus, he should have known Orpheus' name and teaching through the sanctuary of Delphi, but his initiators imposed silence upon him, and with good reason.

Nevertheless, Orpheus lived in his work, he lived in his disciples and even in those who denied him. What is this work? Where must one find this life-soul? Is it in the fierce military oligarchy of Sparta where knowledge was scorned, ignorance built up into a system and brutality required as a complement of courage? Is it in those stern wars of Messenia in which one sees the Spartans pursue a neighboring people to the point of extermination and those Romans of Greece preface the Tarpeian rock and blood-stained laurels of the Capitol by thrusting brave Aristomenes, the defender of his country, over a precipice? Is it in the turbulent democracy of Athens, ever ready to drink of tyranny? Is it in the Praetorian Guard of Pisitratus, or in the dagger of Harmodius and Aristogiton, hidden in a myrtle branch? Is it in the numerous cities of Hellas, of Greater Greece and Asia Minor, of which Athens and Sparta are contrasting types? Is it in all these democracies and tyrannies—envious, jealous, forever ready to tear each other asunder?—No. The soul of Greece is not there. It is in her temples, in her Mysteries and in their initiates. It is in the sanctuary of Jupiter at Olympus, of Juno at Argos, of Ceres at

Eleusis; it reigns over Athens with Minerva, it shines at Delphi with Apollo, who dominates and penetrates all the temples with his light. This is the center of Hellenic life, the head and heart of Greece. It is here that the poets who interpret sublime truths to the people in living images, and the wise men who propagate them in subtle dialectic, will receive instruction. The spirit of Orpheus moves everywhere the heart of immortal Greece throbs. We shall find it in the contests of poetry and athletics, in the games of Delphi and Olympus, important institutions which the successors of the Master invented in order to reconcile and unite the twelve Greek tribes. We are very near it in the Council of the Amphictions, that assembly of initiates, the supreme arbitration court which met at Delphi, manifesting great power of justice and concord, in which Greece found her unity in hours of bravery and abnegation.[53]

But this Greece of Orpheus, her spirit a pure doctrine guarded in the temples, her soul, a plastic religion, her body, a high court of justice located at Delphi,—this Greece began to be threatened in about the seventh century. The commands of Delphi were no longer respected; sacred lands were trespassed upon. This was because the race of great inspired ones had disappeared. The spiritual and moral level had lowered. The priests sold themselves to political power; even the Mysteries began to be corrupted from this time. The general aspect of Greece had changed. The ancient priestly and agricultural royalty was followed here by tyranny pure and simple, there by military aristocracy, elsewhere by anarchical democracy. The temples had become powerless to warn men of impending dissolution. They needed a new helper. A popularization of esoteric teaching had become necessary. In order that the thought of Orpheus could live and expand in all its brilliance, it was necessary that the wisdom of the temples should pass into the ranks of the laity. Therefore, hidden under various disguises it slipped into the heads of civil legislators, into the schools of poets, beneath the porticos of philosophers. In their teaching the latter felt the same requirement that Orpheus had recognized in regard to religion—that of two doctrines: one public, the other secret. These doctrines expounded the same truth in a different degree and under different forms commensurate with the development of the pupils. This evolution gave Greece its three great centuries of artistic creation and intellectual splendor. It allowed Orphic thought, Greece's first impetus and ideal synthesis, to concentrate all its light and to radiate it over the entire world. This took place before Greece's political edifice, undermined by internal dissensions, shook beneath the attacks of Macedonia and finally crumbled under the iron hand of Rome.

The evolution of which we speak had many co-workers. It gave birth to physicists like Thales, legislators like Solon, poets like Pindar, heroes like Epaminondas; but as an official leader it had an initiate of the first order, a sovereign intelligence, creative and disciplined. Pythagoras is the master of secular Greece, as Orpheus is the master of sacerdotal Greece. Pythagoras interprets and continues the religious thought of his predecessor, applying it to the new age. But his interpretation is a creation. For he coordinates the Orphic inspirations into a complete system; he furnishes its scientific proof in his teaching, its moral proof in his institute of education, embracing them in the Pythagorean order, which outlives him.

Although he appears in the broad daylight of history, Pythagoras has remained an almost legendary figure. The main reason for this is the dreadful persecution he experienced in Sicily, and which cost the lives of so many Pythagoreans. Some perished, crushed under the debris of their school which had been set afire, others died of starvation in a temple. The memory and teaching of the Master was perpetuated only by those survivors who were able to flee into Greece. At great pains and expense Plato obtained through Archytas one of Master's manuscripts. Pythagoras, by the way, never wrote his esoteric doctrine except in secret signs and in symbolic form. His real work, like that of all reformers, was effected through his oral teaching. But the essence of his system consists in the *Golden Verses* of Lysis, in the commentary of Hierocles, in fragments by Philolaus and Archytas, as well as in Plato's *Timaeus* which contains Pythagoras' cosmogony. Finally, the writers of antiquity are filled with the spirit of the philosopher of Croton. They have an endless store of anecdotes which depict his wisdom, charm and miraculous power over men. The Neoplatonists of Alexandria, the Gnostics and even the early Church Fathers quote him as an authority. These are valuable testimonies, in which eternally vibrates the powerful wave of enthusiasm that the great personality of Pythagoras knew how to communicate to Greece, and whose last effects are still felt eight centuries after his death.

From a higher point of view, when opened with the keys of comparative esoterism, his doctrine presents a magnificent composite, a solid whole, whose parts are bound by a fundamental concept. In it we find a rational reproduction of the esoteric doctrine of India and Egypt, to which he gave clarity and Hellenic simplicity, adding a more forceful feeling and a more exact idea of human freedom.

At the same time and in various parts of the globe, great reformers were making similar doctrines more generally known. In China, Lao-Tse departed from the esoterism of Fo-Hi; the last Buddha, Sakya-Moni, was preaching on the banks of the Ganges; in Italy, the Etruscan priesthood sent an initiate to Rome. This initiate was King Numa, who, armed with the Sibylline Books, sought to restrain the threatening ambition of the Roman Senate by wise institutions. And it is not by chance that these reformers appear at the same time among such different peoples. Their various missions are united in a common goal. They prove that at certain times a single spiritual current mysteriously passes through all mankind. Where does it come from?—From that divine world which is beyond our sight, but whose seers and prophets are its ambassadors and witnesses.

Pythagoras travelled over the entire ancient world before giving his teachings to Greece. He saw Africa and Asia, Memphis and Babylon, their politics and their initiation. His tempestuous life resembles a boat launched in the midst of a storm; with sails unfurled he pursues his goal without deviating from his path, the picture of calmness and strength in the midst of unleashed elements. His doctrine gives the sensation of a cool night following the stifling heat of a torrid day. It reminds one of the beauty of the firmament, which bit by bit displays its scintillating archipelagos and its ethereal harmonies above the head of the seer.

Let us try to remove Pythagoras' life and work from both the obscurities of legend and the prejudices of the schools.

31

Years of Travel: Samos, Memphis, Babylonia

AT the beginning of the sixth century B.C. Samos was one of the most flourishing islands of Ionia. Its port faced the purple mountains of Asia Minor, from which came all wealth and culture. Behind a broad bay, the city spread itself along the green shore and arose like an amphitheater against the mountainside, at the foot of a promontory crowned with the temple of Neptune. The columns of a magnificent palace overlooked it. There the tyrant Polycrates reigned. Having deprived Samos of its freedoms, he had given it the radiance of the arts and an Asiatic splendor. Courtesans of Lesbos, summoned to Samos by him, invited young men of the city to their festivals where they taught them the most refined voluptuousness, accompanied by music, dancing and feasting. Called by Polycrates, Anacreon was brought to Samos in a trireme with velvet sails and golden masts. And, a silver cup in his hand, before this high court of pleasure the poet had his caressing odes played, perfuming the hearers like a shower of roses.

The good fortune of Polycrates had become proverbial in all

Greece. His friend, the Pharaoh Amasis warned him several times to fear such continuous happiness, and above all not to boast about it. Polycrates answered the Egyptian monarch's warning by throwing his ring into the sea. "I make this sacrifice to the gods," he said. The next day a fisherman brought back to the tyrant the precious ring which he had found in the belly of a fish. When the Pharaoh heard this, he said that he was breaking his friendship with Polycrates because such brazen luck would draw upon him the vengeance of the gods. In any case, Polycrates met a tragic end. One of his satraps lured him into a neighboring province, caused him to be tortured to death and ordered his body fastened to a cross on Mount Mycale. Hence, one day as the blood-red sun set in the west, the Samians could see the body of their tyrant crucified on a promontory facing the island where he had ruled in glory and pleasure.

But let us return to the beginning of Polycrates' reign. On a clear night, a young man was sitting in a grove not far from the temple of Juno, whose Dorian façade was bathed in full moonlight, revealing its mystical majesty. For a long time a scroll of papyrus containing one of Homer's songs laid on the ground at his feet. His meditation, begun at dusk, continued into the silence of the night. The sun had set long ago, but its flaming disk still floated before the gaze of the young dreamer. His thought was wandering far from the visible world.

Pythagoras was the son of a rich ring merchant of Samos, and of a woman named Parthenis. The Pythoness of Delphi, consulted during a trip by the newly-married couple, had promised them "a son who will be useful to all men for all time," and the oracle had sent the husband and wife to Sidon in Phoenicia so that the promised son might be conceived, formed and brought into the world far from the disturbing influences of his homeland. Even before his birth the wondrous child had been fervently dedicated by his parents to the light of Apollo in the moonlight of love. The child was born. When he was one year old, in harmony with the counsel given in advance by the priests of Delphi, his mother brought him to the temple of Adonai in a valley of Lebanon. There the high priest had blessed him, and the family returned to Samos. Parthenis' child was very beautiful, gentle, even-tempered and filled with justice. Intellectual passion alone shone in his eyes, giving a secret power to his deeds. Far from restraining him, his parents had encouraged his early desire for wisdom. He had been able to confer freely with the priests of Samos and with the scholars who were beginning to establish schools in Ionia, where they taught the principles of physics. At eighteen he had studied the lessons of Hermodamas of Samos, at twenty, those of Pherecydus at Syros; he had even conferred with Thales and Anaximander at Miletus. These masters had opened new horizons to him, but none had satisfied him. Among their contradictory teachings he inwardly sought the link, the synthesis, the unity of the Great Whole. Now Parthenis' son had reached one of those crises where the mind, excited by the contradictions in things, concentrates all its faculties in a supreme effort to see through to the goal, to find the road which leads to the sunlight of truth, to the center of life.

On this warm, beautiful night, Parthenis' son looked at the earth, the temple and the starry sky. Demeter, the earth-mother, was there beneath and around him; her nature he wished to fathom. He breathed her powerful emanations, he felt the invincible attraction which bound him as a thinking atom to her breast, like an inseparable part of herself. These wise men whom he had consulted had told him, "Everything comes from her. Nothingness does not come from nothingness. The soul comes from water, or fire, or both. Subtle emanation of the elements, it escapes, only to return. Resign yourself to its fatal law. Your only merit will be to know it and to submit to it."

Then he looked at the firmament and the letters of fire which the constellations form in the unfathomable depths of space. These letters had to have a meaning. For if the infinitely small, the movement of atoms, has its reason for being, would not the infinitely great, the outspread stars, whose grouping represents the body of the universe, also have significance? Indeed, each of these worlds has its own law, and all move together according to number, and in supreme harmony! But who will decipher the alphabet of the stars? The priests of Juno had said to him, "The world of the stars is the heaven of the gods, which was before earth. Your soul comes from there. Pray to the gods that your soul may ascend there once again."

This meditation was interrupted by a voluptuous song which came from a garden on the banks of the Imbrasus. The lascivious voices of the Lesbians languidly mixed with the sounds of the zither; young men responded with Bacchic airs. Suddenly these voices were drowned by piercing, mournful cries coming from the port. These were the rebels whom Polycrates had ordered into a ship, to be sold as slaves in Asia. They were driven with lashes tipped with nails so that they could be tightly crowded into the rowers' galley. Their cries and blasphemies faded into the night. Everything became silent once again.

The young man felt a painful tremor surge up in him, but he repressed it and concentrated his thoughts. The problem was before him, more poignant and sharp than ever. Earth said, *Fate!* The sky said, *Providence!* And mankind, poised between the two, responded, *Folly, Grief, Slavery!* But deep within himself the future initiate heard an invincible voice which answered the chains of earth and the glory of heaven with the cry, *Freedom!* Who then was right—the sages, the priests, the madmen, the unhappy, or himself? All these voices spoke the truth; each was triumphant in its own sphere, but not one revealed to him his reason for being. The three worlds existed, eternal as the heart of Demeter, as the light of the stars and as the human heart. But only one who could find their agreement and the law of their balance would be a true sage; he alone would possess divine knowledge and would be able to help men. In the synthesis of the three worlds was to be found the secret of the cosmos!

Upon pronouncing this word which he had just discovered, Pythagoras stood up. His fascinated gaze fixed itself upon the Dorian façade of the temple. The severe building seemed transfigured beneath the chaste rays of Diana. He thought he saw the ideal image of the world and the solution he was seeking. For the base, columns, architrave and triangular pediment suddenly represented for him the threefold nature of man and universe, of microcosm and macrocosm, crowned with divine unity, which is itself a trinity. *Cosmos,* dominated and penetrated by God, formed

> The holy Tetrad, vast and pure symbol,
> Origin of Nature and model of the gods.

Yes, it was there, hidden in those geometric lines,—the key to the universe, the science of numbers, the ternary law which rules the constitution of beings, that of the septenary which controls their evolution. And in a tremendous vision Pythagoras saw the worlds move according to the rhythm and harmony of the sacred numbers. He saw the equilibrium of earth and heaven, whose balance human freedom holds; he observed the three worlds, the natural, human and divine, supporting each other, determining one another and playing the universal drama through a double movement—a rising and a falling. He divined the spheres of the invisible world enveloping the visible and giving it life unceasingly; he finally perceived the purification and liberation of man from this earth by a threefold initiation. He saw all this, and his life and work in an instantaneous and clear illumination, with that irrefutable certainty of spirit which feels itself in the presence of truth. It was seen as if in a flash of lightning. Now it was a question of proving through reason what his pure intelligence had grasped in the Absolute; in order to do this a lifetime and a herculean effort were needed.

But where could he find the knowledge necessary to bring such an effort to a happy conclusion? Neither the songs of Homer, the sages of Iona nor the temples of Greece sufficed.

The spirit of Pythagoras which suddenly had found wings, began to look into his past, his birth hidden beneath veils of mystery, and into the love of his mother. A memory of his childhood came to him clearly. He recalled that when he was one year old his mother had carried him into a valley of Lebanon, to the temple of Adonai. He saw himself a child again, his arms around Parthenis' neck, in the midst of tremendous mountains and enormous forests, where a river descended in a great waterfall. His mother was standing on a terrace shaded by tall cedars. Before her a majestic priest with a white beard smiled at mother and child while uttering serious words the child did not understand. Later his mother often reminded him of these strange words of the hierophant of Adonai: "O woman of Iona, your son will be great in knowledge, but remember that if the Greeks still possess the wisdom *of the gods,* the science *of God* is to be found only in Egypt." These words came back to him along with the memory of his mother's smile, the handsome face of the old man and the distant roar of the waterfall, dominated by the voice of the priest in a setting as beautiful as the dream of another life. For the first time he guessed the meaning of the oracle. Indeed he had heard men speak of the prodigious knowledge of the Egyptian priests and their awe-inspiring Mysteries, but he thought he could do without them. Now he realized that he needed this wisdom of God in order to penetrate to the very heart of nature, and that he would find it only in the temples of Egypt. And it was gentle Parthenis with her mother-instinct, who had prepared him for this work, had carried him as an offering to the supreme God!

From that moment his decision was made to go to Egypt, there to have himself initiated.

Polycrates boasted that he was the patron of philosophers as well as of poets. He promptly gave Pythagoras a letter of recommendation to Pharaoh Amasis, who in turn presented him to the priests of Memphis. The latter received him unwillingly, and only after he had overcome many difficulties. The Egyptian sages distrusted the Greeks, for they considered them superficial and undependable. Therefore they did everything to discourage this young man from Samos. But with an unshakable patience and courage the novice submitted himself to the delays and the oral tests that were imposed upon him. He knew in advance that he would achieve knowledge only by a complete domination of his entire being. His initiation lasted twenty-two years under the pontificate of the high priest, Sonchis. In the section on Hermes we have experienced the tests, the temptations, the terrors and ecstasies of the initiate of Isis, including the seeming cataleptic death of the adept and his resurrection into the Light of Osiris. Pythagoras went through all these stages, which allowed him to realize, not as empty theory but as something he had experienced, the doctrine of the Word-Light or the Universal Word, and the evolution of mankind through seven planetary cycles. At each step of this ascent the tests became more and more difficult. A hundred times one risked one's life, especially if one wished to reach the manipulation of spiritual forces, the dangerous practice of magic and theurgy.

Like all great men, Pythagoras had faith in his star. Nothing that could lead to knowledge rebuffed him, and fear of death did not stop him, because he saw the life beyond. When the Egyptian priests had recognized in him an extraordinary strength of soul and that impersonal desire for wisdom which is the rarest thing in the world, they revealed to him the treasures of their experience. Now he was able to delve deeply into sacred mathematics, the science of numbers, or the universal principles, which he made the center of his system and formulated in a new way. The severity of Egyptian temple discipline taught him the tremendous power of the human will when wisely exercised and guided, and its infinite applications to the body as well as to the soul. "The science of numbers and the art of the will are the two keys of magic," said the priests of Memphis. "They open all the doors of the universe." It was in Egypt, therefore, that Pythagoras acquired this divine insight which allows one to see the spheres of life and of the sciences in a concentric order, to understand the *involution* of the mind in matter through universal creation, and its *evolution,* or its reascent to unity through this individual creation, which is called the development of consciousness.

Pythagoras had achieved the summit of Egyptian priesthood and perhaps dreamed of returning to Greece, but war came and spilled over into the Nile basin, bringing all its calamities, drawing the initiate of Osiris into a new whirlwind. For a long time the despots of Asia had been plotting the destruction of Egypt. Their attacks which had been repeated for centuries, had failed in face of the wisdom of the Egyptian institutions, before the power of the priesthood and the strength of the Pharaohs. But the ancient kingdom, shelter of the wisdom of Hermes, could not last forever. The son of the conqueror of Babylon, Cambyses, pounced upon Egypt with his vast armies, starving like a cloud of locusts, and put an end to the rule of the Pharaohs. In the eyes of the sages this was a catastrophe for the whole world. Until then, Egypt had shielded Europe against Asia. Its protective influence extended throughout the Mediterranean area by means of the temples of Phoenicia, Greece and Etruria with which the Egyptian priests were in constant contact. Once this contact was destroyed, the Bull would disappear, head lowered, on the shores of Hellas.

Pythagoras saw Cambyses invade Egypt. He observed the Persian despot, heir of the crowned scoundrels of Nineveh and Babylon, sack the temples of Memphis and Thebes and destroy that of Ammon. He saw the Pharaoh Psammetichus led before Cambyses, bound in chains, placed on a mound, around which were assembled the priests, the leading families and the king's court. He saw the daughter of the Pharaoh clothed in rags, followed by all her ladies-in-waiting, similarly dishonored, as well as the royal prince and two thousand young men paraded with bits in their mouths and halters on their necks, later to be beheaded. The Pharaoh Psammetichus scarcely could restrain his sobs at this terrible scene, while the infamous Cambyses, seated on his throne, enjoyed the grief of his fallen rival. For Pythagoras this was a cruel but instructive lesson in science. What a picture of unleashed animal nature in man, culminating in the monster of despotism who treads everything underfoot and by his ugly apotheosis imposes upon humanity the reign of the most implacable destiny!

Cambyses had Pythagoras transported to Babylon along with a part of the Egyptian priesthood, and imprisoned him there. This colossal city which Aristotle compares to a country surrounded with walls, offered a vast field of observation. Ancient Babel, the great prostitute of the Hebrew prophets, after the Persian conquest was more than ever a pandemonium of peoples, languages, cults and religions in the midst of which Asiatic despotism raised its lofty tower. According to Persian traditions, its foundation dated back to the legendary Semiramis.

It is she, they said, who built its monstrous enclosure, some fifty miles in circumference, the Imgum-Bel, its walls where two chariots ran abreast, its terraces, rising one above the other, its mighty palaces with polychrome reliefs, its temples supported by stone elephants and overhung with multi-colored dragons. There the series of despots who had conquered Chaldea, Assyria, Persia, a part of Tartary, Judea, Syria and Asia Minor, had followed one another. There Nebuchadnezzar, the assassin of Magi, had the Jewish people led into captivity. The latter continued to practice their cult in a corner of the vast city, four times larger than London. The Jews even had provided the king a powerful minister, the prophet Daniel.

With Belshazzar, son of Nebuchadnezzar, the walls of old Babel finally crumbled under the avenging blows of Cyrus, and for several centuries Babylon passed under Persian domination. As a result of this series of events, at the time Pythagoras came there, representatives of three different religions rubbed elbows with each other in the high priesthood of Babylon: the ancient Chaldean priests, survivors of the Persian Magi and the elite of the Jewish captivity. The proof that these various priesthoods agreed among themselves in esoteric matters is seen in the role of Daniel who, while constantly affirming the God of Moses, remained prime minister under Nebuchadnezzar, Belshazzar and Cyrus.

Pythagoras had to broaden his horizon still further by studying these doctrines, religions and cults, whose synthesis a few initiates still preserved. In Babylon he was able to increase his knowledge of the Magi, heirs of Zoroaster. If the Egyptian priests alone possessed the universal keys of the holy sciences, the Persian Magi had the reputation of having advanced furthest in the practice of certain arts. They attributed to themselves the manipulation of hidden powers of nature which are called pantomorphic fire and astral light. In their temples, it is said, darkness was created in broad daylight, lamps lighted of themselves, one saw the gods shining and heard the thunder roll. The Magi called that bodiless fire, that generating agent of electricity which they knew how to condense or disperse at will, the celestial lion. The electric currents of the atmosphere, magnetism of earth which they claimed they could aim at men like arrows, they named serpents. They also had made a special study of the suggestive, magnetic and creative power of human speech. They employed formulas, borrowed from the oldest languages of earth, for the evocation of spirits. The following is the psychic reason they themselves gave for this: "Do not change any of the barbaric names of evocation, for they are the pantheistic names of God; they are magnetized by the adorations of multitudes and their power is ineffable." These evocations, practiced in the midst of purifications and prayers were, properly speaking, what was later called *black magic*.

In Babylon, therefore, Pythagoras penetrated the Mysteries of ancient magic. At the same time, in this den of despotism he saw a great spectacle: above the debris of crumbling religions of the Orient, above their decimated and degenerated priesthood, a group of initiates, courageous, united, defend their science, their faith and, as much as they can, justice. Standing before despots as did Daniel in the lion's den, always near being devoured, they charmed and subdued the wild beast of absolute force through their spiritual power, disputing every inch of ground with him.

After his Egyptian and Chaldean initiation, the child of Samos knew much more about physics than his teachers, far more than any Greek, priest or layman, of his time. He knew the eternal principles of the universe and their applications. Nature had opened her depths to him; the crude veils of matter were torn from his eyes to show him the wonderful spheres of nature and of spiritualized mankind. In the temple of Nith-

Isis at Memphis, in that of Bel at Babylon, he had learned many secrets of the history of religions, of the history of continents and races. He had been able to compare the advantages and disadvantages of Jewish monotheism, of Greek polytheism, Hindu trinitarianism and Persian dualism. He knew that all these religions were rays of the one truth, filtered by different degrees of intelligence and intended for various social conditions. He held the key, that is, the synthesis of all these doctrines of esoteric science. His gaze, embracing the past and looking into the future, had to judge the present with extraordinary clarity. His experience showed him mankind threatened by the greatest calamities, by the ignorance of priests, the materialism of scientists and the lack of discipline of democracies. In the midst of universal deterioration he saw Asiatic despotism increase, and from this black cloud a terrible tempest was about to break over defenseless Europe.

Therefore he realized that it was time to return to Greece, in order to accomplish his mission there. It was there that he was to begin his work.

Pythagoras had been confined in Babylon for twelve years. In order to leave, a release from the king of the Persians was necessary. A fellow-Greek, Democedes, the king's physician, interceded in his favor and obtained the philosopher's freedom. Therefore Pythagoras returned to Samos after thirty-four years of absence. He found his country crushed under a satrap of the great king. Schools and temples were closed; poets and scientists had fled like a flock of sparrows before the Persian Caesarism. At least he had the consolation of being present at the death of his first teacher, Hermodamas, and of finding his mother, Parthenis, who alone had not doubted his return. Everyone else had thought that the adventurous son of the jeweler of Samos was dead, but never had she doubted the oracle of Apollo. She realized that beneath his white Egyptian priest's robe, her son was preparing for a high mission. She knew that from the temple of Nith-Isis emerged the beneficent Master, the luminous prophet of whom she had dreamed in the sacred grove of Delphi, and whom the hierophant of Adonai had promised her beneath the cedars of Lebanon.

Now a small ship was carrying this mother and her son on the blue waves of the Cyclades into a new exile. With all their possessions they were fleeing from oppressed and lost Samos. They had set sail for Greece. But it was neither Olympic crowns nor the poet's laurels which tempted the son of Parthenes. His work was more mysterious and greater: to awaken the sleeping soul of the gods in the sanctuaries, to give back power and prestige to the temple of Apollo and finally, to establish somewhere a school of knowledge and life from which would come, not politicians and sophists, but initiated men and women, true mothers and pure heroes!

32

The Temple of Delphi, Apollonian Science, Theory of Divination, The Pythoness Theoclea

FROM the plain of Phocis one traversed the smiling meadows which border the banks of Plistios, to descend between high mountains into a winding valley. At each step the way became narrower and the country more impressive and more desolate. One finally reached a circle of rugged mountains topped with sharp peaks, a veritable vortex for electricity, overhung with frequent storms. Suddenly at the end of the dark gorge, the city of Delphi appeared like an eagle's nest on a rock, surrounded with precipices and overhung by the two crests of Parnassus. From afar one saw gleaming bronze Victories, brass horses, innumerable gold statues placed along the sacred way, arranged like a guard of heroes and gods around the Dorian temple of Phoebus Apollo.

This was the holiest place in Greece. There Pythia prophesied, there the Amphictions met, there all the Greeks had erected chapels around the sanctuary enclosing treasures and offerings. There processions of men, women and children coming from afar, ascended the sacred way to greet the god of light. From time immemorial religion had dedicated Delphi to the veneration of peoples. Its central location in Hellas, its rock, sheltered from surprise attacks and easily defended, had helped. The god was made to strike the imagination; a uniqueness gave him his prestige. In a cavern behind the temple a fissure opened, from which came cold vapors which induced, it was said, inspiration and ecstasy. Plutarch relates that in very ancient times a shepherd, having sat down at the edge of the crevice, began to prophesy. At first he was thought insane, but when his predictions came true, people paid attention to the phenomenon. Priests took possession of the place and dedicated it to the god. From this came the institution of Pythia, whom they had sit over the fissure upon a tripod. The vapors rising from the abyss gave her convulsions, strange attacks and provoked in her that second sight which is experienced by unusual somnambulists. Aeschylus, whose statements carry weight, for he was son of a priest of Eleusis and himself an initiate, tells us in the *Eumenides* through the mouth of Pythia that Delphi first had been dedicated to Earth, then to Themis (Justice), then to Phoebe (mediatory Moon) and finally to Apollo, the solar god. Each of these names represents long periods in the symbolism of the temples and embraces centuries. But the fame of Delphi dates from Apollo. Jupiter, said the poets, desiring to know the center of the earth, caused two eagles to fly simultaneously from the east and the west; they met at Delphi. Where does this prestige come from,—this universal and uncontested authority, which made Apollo the Greek god *par excellence?*

History teaches us nothing about this important point. Question the orators, poets, philosophers; they give only superficial explanations. The real answer to this question remained the secret of the temple. Let us try to fathom it.

According to Orphic thought, Dionysus and Apollo were

two different revelations of the same divinity. Dionysus represented esoteric truth, the heart and interior of things—accessible to the initiates alone. He held the mysteries of life, of past and future incarnations, of the relationships between soul and body, the heaven and earth. Apollo personified the same truth applied to terrestrial life and the social order. Inspirer of poetry, medicine, and law, he represented science through divination, beauty through art, the peace of peoples through justice and the harmony of soul and body through purification. In a word, for the initiate, Dionysus meant nothing less than the evolving divine spirit in the universe, and Apollo his manifestation to earthly man. The priests caused the people to understand this by means of a legend. They told them that in Orpheus' time, Bacchus and Apollo had fought for the tripod of Delphi. Bacchus had willingly yielded it to his brother and had withdrawn to one of the summits of Parnassus where Thebian women celebrated his Mysteries. In reality, the two great sons of Jupiter divided the world empire. One reigned over the mysterious Beyond, the other, over the living.

Therefore we find in Apollo the Solar Word, the Universal Word, the Great Mediator, the Vishnu of the Hindus, the Mithras of the Persians, the Horus of the Egyptians. But in the Greek legend of Apollo, the old ideas of Asiatic esoterism were adorned with a plastic beauty, an incisive splendor, which caused them to penetrate more deeply into human consciousness like the arrows of a god. "White winged serpents, shot from his golden bow," Aeschylus called them.

Apollo bursts forth out of the deep night at Delos; all the goddesses greet his birth. He walks, he seizes his bow and lyre, his arrows whirr through the air, his quiver rattles on his shoulder. The sea throbs, and all the island shines in a flood of flame and gold. He is the epiphany of divine light, who by his august presence creates order, splendor and harmony of which poetry is the marvelous echo. The god goes to Delphi and with his arrows pierces a monstrous serpent which had been laying waste the country. By this deed he makes the land safe and establishes the temple. Picture the victory of this divine light over darkness and evil! In the ancient religions the serpent symbolized both the fateful circle of life and the evil resulting from the latter. Nevertheless, from this endangered and vanquished life comes knowledge. Apollo, destroyer of the serpent, is the symbol of the initiate who pierces nature with science, subdues it to his will and, breaking the cycle of flesh, ascends in splendor of spirit while the broken fragments of human animality writhe in the dust. This is why Apollo is the master of expiations, of purifications of soul and body. Sprinkled with the blood of the monster, he expiated, purified himself in an exile of eight years, under the bitter laurels of the valley of Tempe. Apollo, teacher of men, likes to sojourn among them; he enjoys himself in their cities among male youth, in the contests of poetry and the palestra, but he lives there only temporarily. In autumn he returns to his homeland, to the country of the Hyperboreans. The latter are the mysterious people of luminous, transparent souls who live in an eternal aurora of perfect happiness. His true priests and beloved priestesses are there. He lives with them in an intimate, deep community and when he wishes to make a royal gift to men, from the land of the Hyperboreans he sends one of those great, luminous souls, causing it to incarnate upon earth in order to teach and delight mortals.

Apollo returns to Delphi every spring when peans and hymns are sung. He arrives, visible only to the initiates, in his Hyperborean brightness, drawn in a chariot by melodious swans. He returns to live in the sanctuary where Pythia transmits his oracles, where the wise men and poets listen. Then the nightingales sing, the Fountain of Castalia bubbles with silver wavelets, the living echoes of a blinding light and celestial music penetrate the heart of men and women, even moving through the veins of nature.

In this legend of the Hyperboreans the esoteric essence of the myth of Apollo sheds its brilliant rays. The country of the Hyperboreans is the after-life, the empyrean of victorious souls whose astral auroras lighten the multicolored regions. Apollo himself personifies immaterial and intelligible light, of which the sun is but the physical reflection, and whence flows all truth. The wondrous swans which draw him are the poets, the divine genii, messengers of his great solar soul, leaving in their wake tremors of light and melody. Hyperborean Apollo therefore personifies the descent from heaven to earth, the incarnation of spiritual beauty in flesh and blood, the afflux of transcendent truth through inspiration and divination.

But now we must lift the golden veil from the legends and penetrate into the temple itself. How was divination practiced? Here we touch upon the arcana of Apollonian science and the mysteries of Delphi.

In antiquity a strong tie united divination with the solar cults. The cult of the sun is the golden key to all Mysteries referred to as "magic."

From the beginning of civilization the worship of Aryan man was directed to the sun as the source of light, warmth and life. But when the thought of the wise men rose from phenomenon to cause, they perceived behind this sensitive fire and visible light a non-material fire and an intelligible light. They identified the first with the male principle, with creative spirit, the intellectual essence of the universe, and the second with its female principle, its formative soul, its plastic substance. This intuition traces back to an unknown time. The concept of which I speak is mixed with the oldest mythologies. It flows in the Vedic hymns under the form of *Agni*, the universal fire, which penetrates everything. It unfolds in the religion of Zoroaster, of which the cult of Mithras represents the esoteric part. Mithras is the male fire and Mitra the female light. Zoroaster formally says that by means of the Living Word the Eternal created celestial Light, seed of Ormuzd, principle of material light and material fire. For the initiate of Mithras, the sun is but a crude reflection of this Light. In his hidden grotto, the vault of which is painted with stars, he invokes the Sun of mercy, the Fire of Love, Conqueror of evil, Reconcilor of Ormuzd and Ahriman, Purifier and Mediator who inhabits the soul of the holy prophets. In the crypts of Egypt the initiates look for this same Sun under the name Osiris. When Hermes asks to view the origin of things, first he feels plunged into the ethereal waves of a delightful Light where all living forms move. Then, thrust into the darkness of dense matter, he hears a voice and recognizes the Voice of Light. At the same time a fire bursts forth from the depths; immediately, order and light result from chaos. In the *Book of the Dead* of the Egyptians, souls painfully sail toward this light in Isis' boat. Moses completely adopted this doctrine in *Genesis:* "Elohim said, Let there be light, and there was light." But the creation of this light precedes that of the sun and stars. This means that in the order of the elements and of cosmogony, intelligible Light precedes material light. The Greeks who cast the most abstract ideas into human form and dramatized them, expressed this same teaching in the myth of the Hyperborean Apollo.

As in the great temples of Egypt, the divination practised at Delphi was composed of an art and a science. The art consisted in penetrating the past and future through clairvoyance or prophetic ecstasy; its science consisted in calculating the future according to the laws of universal evolution. Art and science controlled each other. It is known that clairvoyance and prophecy were practised at Delphi through the inter-

mediary of young and old women called the Pythia or Python·
esses, and who played the passive role of somnambulists. The
priests interpreted, translated and arranged their often confusing oracles according to their own points of view. Modern
historians have seen in the institution of Delphi merely the
exploitation of superstition by intelligent charlatanism. But
in addition to the assent by all philosophical antiquity to the
divining science at Delphi, several oracles reported by Herodotus, such as those concerning Croesus and the Battle of Salamis,
speak in its favor. Doubtless this art had its inception, its flowering and its decadence. Charlatanism and corruption eventually became mixed with it—witness King Cleomenes who
bribed the high priestess of Delphi in order to deprive Demara-
tus of his throne. Plutarch wrote a treatise inquiring into the
reason for the extinction of the oracles, and this degeneracy was
regarded by all the ancient world as a great misfortune. During
the preceding era, divination was cultivated with a religious
sincerity and a scientific thoroughness which raised it to the
height of a true priesthood. Above the entrance to the temple
one read the inscription, "Know thyself," as well as, "Let
no one without clean hands come near." These words warned
everyone that earthly passions, lies and hypocrisies were not to
pass over the threshold of the sanctuary, and that within its
portals, divine truth reigned with fearful solemnity.

Pythagoras came to Delphi only after having visited all the
temples of Greece. He had spoken with Epimonides in the
sanctuary of Jupiter Idaean; he had attended the Olympic
Games; he had been present at the Mysteries of Eleusis, where
the hierophant had given up his place to him. Everywhere he
had been received as a teacher. He was awaited at Delphi.
There the divining art had declined, and Pythagoras wished to
restore it to its former profundity, strength and prestige. Therefore he came to Delphi less to consult Apollo than to enlighten

his interpreters, rekindle their enthusiasm and awaken their energies. His deeds for them would act in turn upon the soul of Greece and prepare it for its future.

Fortunately in the temple he found a marvelous instrument which a providential plan seemed to have reserved for him.

Young Theoclea belonged to the school of priestesses of Apollo. She came from one of those families in which the priestly dignity is hereditary. The great impressions of the sanctuary, the ceremonies of the cult, the paeans, the festivals of Pythian and Hyperborean Apollo had nourished her in childhood. One can imagine her as one of those young girls who have an inborn and instinctive aversion for the things which attract others. They do not like Ceres at all, and fear Venus, for the heavy terrestrial atmosphere disturbs them and physical love, dimly seen, seems to them a rape of the soul, a pollution of their undefiled, virginal being. On the other hand, they are strangely sensitive to mysterious currents, to astral influences. When the moon shone in the dark groves of the Fountain of Castalia, Theoclea saw white forms gliding there. In broad daylight she heard voices. When she exposed herself to the rays of the rising sun, their vibration plunged her into a kind of ecstasy in which she heard invisible choirs. Nevertheless, she was completely insensitive to superstitions and to the popular idolatries of the cult. Statues meant nothing to her, and she had a horror of animal sacrifices. She did not speak to anyone of the appearances which disturbed her sleep. She felt instinctively that the priests of Apollo did not possess the supreme Light which she needed. On the other hand, they hoped to be able to convince her to become a Pythoness, but she felt herself drawn by a higher world, whose key she did not possess. Who were these gods who seized her with inspirations and tremors? She wished to know them before surrendering herself to them. For great souls need to see clearly, even in giving themselves to divine powers.

With what deep anticipation, with what mysterious foreboding must Theoclea's soul have been stirred when she saw Pythagoras for the first time, when she heard his eloquent voice resound within the Apollonian sanctuary! She felt the presence of the initiator for whom she was waiting; she recognized her teacher. She wanted to know; through him she would know, and this inner world, this world which she bore within her,—he would make it speak! For his part, the certainty and penetration of his gaze must have recognized in her the living, vibrant soul he was seeking, the one who would become the interpreter of his thought in the temple, who would infuse the latter with a new spirit. From the first glances they exchanged, from the first word spoken, an invisible chain bound the sage of Samos to the young priestess who listened to him silently, drinking in his words with her large, attentive eyes. Someone has said that the poet and the lyre knew each other by the profound vibration which came about when they were in each other's presence. In this manner Pythagoras and Theoclea recognized each other.

At sunrise Pythagoras had long conversations with the priests of Apollo, ordained saints and prophets. He asked that the young priestess be admitted in order that he might initiate her into his secret teaching and prepare her for her task. Therefore she was allowed to attend the lessons which the master gave every day in the sanctuary. At this time Pythagoras was in the prime of life. He wore a white robe folded in Egyptian style; a band of velvet was wrapped around his broad forehead. When he spoke, his slow, serious eyes rested upon his hearer, enveloping him with a warm light. The very air about him seemed to become lighter and completely filled with intelligence.

The conversations between the sage of Samos and the highest

representatives of Greek religion were of the utmost importance. It was not only a question of divination and inspiration,
but of the future of Greece and the destiny of the entire world.
The knowledge, titles and powers he had acquired in the temples of Memphis and Babylon gave him the highest authority.
To those who inspired Hellas he had the right to speak as a
superior and guide. He did this with the eloquence of his
genius, with the enthusiasm of his mission. To enlighten them,
he began by telling of his youth, his battles and his Egyptian
initiation. He spoke to them of Egypt, the mother of Greece,
old as the world, unchangeable as a mummy covered with hieroglyphs in the depths of its pyramids, but possessing in its
tomb the secret of peoples, of languages and of religions. Before
their eyes he unfolded the Mysteries of the great earthly and
heavenly Isis, mother of gods and men; and, passing them
through his trials, he plunged with them into the Light of
Osiris. Next he enabled them to experience the Babylon of the
Chaldean Magi, their secret sciences, and those deep massive
temples where they evoked the living fire in which demons and
gods move.

Listening to Pythagoras, Theoclea experienced surprising
sensations. All that he said engraved itself in her mind in characters of fire. These things seemed both wonderful and familiar
to her. While learning it was as though she actually was remembering. The words of the master enabled her to turn the
pages of the universe like a book. She no longer saw the gods
in their human likenesses, but in their actual natures, as they
formed objects and spirits. With the gods she penetrated,
ascended and descended through space. Sometimes she had
the illusion of no longer feeling the limits of her body, and of
being dispersed into infinity. Thus, little by little her imagination entered the invisible world, and the former impressions of
it which she found in her own soul told her that this world was

real, was the only reality, and that the outer world was only semblance. She felt that soon her inner eyes would open, and that she would see the spiritual world directly.

From these heights the master suddenly led her back to earth by describing the misfortunes of Egypt. After speaking of the greatness of Egyptian wisdom, he told of its drowning beneath the waves of the Persian invasion. He painted the horrors of Cambyses, the pillaged temples, the sacred books destroyed in a holocaust, the priests of Osiris murdered or exiled, the monster of Persian despotism assembling under his iron hand all the old Asiatic barbarism, the wandering half-savage races of central Asia and the borders of India, now waiting only for the opportunity to fall upon Europe. Indeed, this gathering cyclone would break over Greece as surely as lightning must come from a cloud which gathers itself in the sky. Was divided Greece prepared to resist this terrible onslaught? The master was certain that it was not. Peoples do not escape their destinies, and if they do not watch unceasingly, the gods will even hasten the day of reckoning. Had not Egypt, wise nation of Hermes, crumbled after six thousand years of prosperity? Alas! Greece, beautiful Iona, would pass away even more quickly! A time will come when the solar god will abandon this temple, foreigners will overturn its stones and shepherds will lead their herds to graze upon the site of ruined Delphi. . . .

At these sinister prophecies, the face of Theoclea was transformed with terror. She sank to the ground, and, embracing a column with her arms, her eyes staring, sunk in thought, she resembled the genius of Grief weeping over the sepulchre of Greece.

"But," continued Pythagoras, "these are secrets which must be buried in the depths of the temples. The initiate attracts death or repels it at will. By forming a magic chain of wills, the initiates can also prolong the life of peoples. It is for you to postpone the fatal hour. It is for you to cause Greece to shine; it is your task to cause the Word of Apollo to radiate in her. Peoples reflect what their gods do, but the gods reveal themselves only to those who call upon them. Who is Apollo? He is the Word of the One God Who is eternally manifest in the world. Truth is the Soul of God, His Body and His Light. The sages, seers, prophets alone see this; men see only its shadow. The glorified spirits whom we call heroes and demi-gods inhabit this Light by legions, in infinite spheres. This is the true glory of Apollo, Sun of the initiates; without its rays nothing great is accomplished upon earth. As the magnet attracts iron, so by our thoughts, our prayers, our actions, we attract divine inspiration. It is for you to transmit to Greece the Word of Apollo, and Greece will shine with an immortal light!"

Through words like this Pythagoras succeeded in giving the priests of Delphi an awareness of their mission. Theoclea absorbed them with a silent, intense passion. Under the thought and will of the master she became transformed. Standing in the midst of the astonished elders, she undid her black hair, shaking it out as though she felt a fire running through it. Already her eyes, opened wide, transfigured, seemed to contemplate the solar and planetary Genii in their luminous orbits, with their powerful radiations.

One day she fell into a deep, clear sleep. The five prophets surrounded her, but she remained insensible to their voices as well as to their touch. Pythagoras approached her and said, "Arise, and go where my thought sends you! For now you are a Pythoness!"

At the voice of the teacher, a tremor ran through her whole body and lifted her in a long vibration. Her physical eyes were closed; she was seeing with the inner eye.

"Where are you?" asked Pythagoras.

"I am climbing . . . I continue climbing."

"And now?"

"I am bathing in the Light of Orpheus . . ."

"What do you see in the future?"

"Great wars . . . mighty men . . . victories . . . Apollo returns to inhabit his sanctuary, and I shall be his voice! But you, his messenger, Alas! Alas! You are about to leave me . . . and you will carry his Light into Italy!"

With eyes closed the seeress spoke for a long time in her musical, pulsing, rhythmic voice; then, suddenly with a sob, she fell as though dead.

Thus Pythagoras poured his pure teachings into Theoclea's heart and tuned her like a lyre for the breath of the gods. Once exalted to this height of inspiration, she became a torch for him, by which he could fathom his own destiny, penetrate the possible future and move into the shoreless reaches of the Invisible. This living counter-proof of the truths he taught filled the priests with admiration, awakened their enthusiasm and revived their faith. The temple now had an inspired Pythoness, as well as priests initiated in divine wisdom and art. Again Delphi could become a center of life and activity.

Pythagoras remained there for a whole year. Only after instructing the priests in all the secrets of his teaching, and preparing Theoclea for her ministry did he depart for Greater Greece.

33

The Order and the Teaching

THE city of Croton was located on the Gulf of Tarentum, near the Lacinian promontory, facing the open sea. Like Sybaris, it was one of the most flourishing cities of southern Italy. It was renowned for its Dorian constitution, its athletes, victors in the Olympic Games and its doctors, rivals of the Asclepiad. The Sybarites owed their fame to their luxury and indolence. The Crotons perhaps would have been forgotten despite their virtues had they not had the privilege of providing a shelter for the great Pythagorean school of esoteric philosophy, which can be considered the mother of the Platonic School and the ancestor of all idealist schools. However noble the descendants may have been, the ancestor far surpassed them. The Platonic School stemmed from an incomplete initiation; the Stoic School lost the true tradition. The other systems of ancient and modern philosophy are more or less fortunate speculations, while the doctrine of Pythagoras was based on an experimental science and was accompanied by a complete organization of life.

Like the ruins of the ancient city, today the secrets of the Order as well as the teacher's thought are buried deeply underground. Nevertheless, let us try to call them to life once again. For us this will be opportunity to penetrate into the heart of esoteric teaching, the arcanum of religions and philosophies, and to lift a corner of Isis' veil in the light of Greek genius.

For several reasons Pythagoras chose this Dorian colony as the center of his activity. His aim was not only to teach esoteric doctrine to a circle of chosen disciples, but also to apply these principles to the education of youth and to the life of the state. This plan required the establishment of an institute for the initiation of the laity, with the underlying design of slowly transforming the political organization of the cities in the image of Pythagoras' philosophical and religious ideas. It is certain that none of the republics of Hellas or of Peloponnesus would have tolerated this innovation. The philosopher would have been accused of conspiring against the state. The Greek cities of the Gulf of Tarentum, less influenced by demagogues, were more liberal. Pythagoras was not disappointed in his hope of finding a favorable reception for his reforms in the senate of Croton. In addition, his aims extended beyond Greece. Envisioning the evolution of ideas, he foresaw the fall of Hellenism and dreamed of planting the principles of a scientific religion in the human mind. By establishing his school on the Gulf of Tarentum, he spread his esoteric ideas into Italy, and in his doctrine he preserved the purified essence of Oriental wisdom for the peoples of the Occident.

Upon his arrival in Croton, which then inclined toward the pleasure-filled life of neighboring Sybaris, Pythagoras brought about a veritable revolution. Porphyry and Iamblicus depict his first activities there as those of a magician rather than of a philosopher. He assembled the young men at the temple of Apollo, and by his eloquence succeeded in wresting them from debauchery. He called the women to the temple of Juno, and persuaded them to bring their golden robes and their ornaments to that place as trophies of their victory over vanity and luxury. He enveloped the austerity of his teaching in mercy; from his wisdom shone a heart-warming flame. The beauty of his face, the nobility of his person, the charm of his manner and his voice won the people. The women compared him to Jupiter; the young men to the Hyperborean Apollo. He captivated the crowd, who were astonished that at his words they fell in love with virtue and truth.

The senate of Croton or "Council of One Thousand" became concerned about his growing influence. They summoned Pythagoras before them to give an account of his conduct and of the means he used to master people's minds. This was an opportunity for him to explain his ideas on education, and show that, far from threatening the Dorian constitution of Croton, his teaching would only strengthen it. When he had won over the wealthiest citizens and the majority of the senate to his project, he proposed to them the creation of an institute for him and for his students. This brotherhood of lay initiates would lead a communal life in a specially constructed building, but without separating themselves from civil life. Those among them who already were qualified as teachers could instruct in physics as well as the psychic and religious sciences. As for the young men, they would be admitted to the classes of the institute at various levels of initiation according to their intelligence and their willingness, subject to the control of the leader of the Order. But first they had to submit themselves to the rules of communal life and to pass the entire day in the institute under the supervision of their teachers. Those who wished to enter the Order formally would give up their wealth to a curator, with the privilege of taking it back whenever they wished. There would be a section for women in the institute, with parallel initiation, but differentiated and adapted to the duties of their sex.

This project was adopted with enthusiasm by the senate of Croton, and after a few years a building, surrounded with broad porticoes and beautiful gardens, appeared on the outskirts of the city. The Crotons called it the Temple of the Muses, and in reality, at the center of these buildings, near the modest habitation of the master, was a temple dedicated to these divinities.

Thus the Pythagorean institute was born. It became a school of education, an academy of sciences, as well as a small model city under the direction of a great initiate. Through theory and practice, through science and art united, the Pythagoreans slowly attained that science of sciences, that magic harmony of soul and mind with the universe, which they considered the arcanum of philosophy and religion. The Pythagorean school has a supreme interest for us because it was the most remarkable attempt at lay initiation. Anticipated synthesis of Hellenism and Christianity, it grafted the fruit of science onto the tree of life; it knew that inner living attainment of truth which deep faith alone can give. It was an ephemeral attainment, but nevertheless was of major importance.

In order to obtain some impression of it, let us enter the Pythagorean institute with the novice, following his initiation step by step.

THE TEST

The white home of the initiate brothers stood on a hill among cypress and olive trees. From below, passing along the coast, one saw its porticoes, gardens and gymnasium. The Temple of the Muses, with its circular colonnade was larger than the two wings of the building. From the terrace of the outer gardens one overlooked the city with its Prythaneum, its harbor, its great assembly square. In the distance, the gulf extended itself between the sharp coasts like an agate cup, and with its blue line the Ionian Sea marked the limit of the horizon. Sometimes women clothed in various colors could be seen leaving the left wing of the building, passing down the long avenue of cypresses toward the sea. They were going to perform their rites in the temple of Ceres. Often from the right wing, men in white robes could be seen ascending to the temple of Apollo. And it was not the least attraction for the seeking mind of youth to think that the school of the initiates was placed under the protection of those two divinities. Indeed, the great goddess, Ceres, embraced the deep Mysteries of Woman and Earth, and Apollo, the solar god, revealed those of Man and Heaven.

Therefore this little city of the elect shone outside and above the populous city of Croton. Its tranquil serenity appealed to the noble instincts of youth; nothing that went on inside its doors was seen, and it was known that it was not easy to gain admission to its activities. A simple green hedge served as the only barrier to the gardens of Pythagoras' institute, and the entrance door remained open all day long. But a statue of Hermes was placed there, and on its pedestal could be read: *Eskato Babeloi, Go Back, Profane Ones!* Everyone obeyed this commandment of the Mysteries.

Pythagoras was extremely strict when it came to admitting novices, saying, "Every wood is not fit for fashioning a Mercury." The young men who wished to enter the Order had to undergo a period of probation. Presented by their parents or one of the teachers, they were allowed first to enter the Pythagorean gymnasium where the novices entered into games suited to their age. At first glance the young man observed that this gymnasium did not resemble those in the city. Here were no

violent shouts, no noisy groups, neither ridiculous bragging
nor vain display of strength by athletes in embryo, challenging
one another and showing their muscles. Here were groups of
affable, distinguished young men walking two by two beneath
the porticoes or playing in the arena. With kindness and simplicity the newcomer was invited to share in their conversation
as if he was one of them; there was no eyeing him with a suspicious look or greeting him with a malignant smile. In the
arena they practiced running, as well as throwing javelin and
discus. They also carried out make-believe combats in the
form of Dorian dances, but Pythagoras had strictly forbidden
physical combats in his institute, saying that these were superfluous and even dangerous, in that they tended to develop pride
and hatred along with strength and agility. He believed that
men destined to practice the virtues of friendship should not begin by attacking one another and rolling in the sand like wild
beasts, that a real hero knows how to fight courageously, but
without anger, and that hatred makes a man inferior to any
adversary. The newcomer heard these sayings of the teacher
repeated by the novices, who were very proud to be able to communicate their precocious wisdom to him. At the same time
they asked him to express his own opinions and to contradict
theirs freely. Emboldened by these advances, the naive candidate soon showed his true nature. Happy at being listened to
and admired, he made speeches and boasted as much as he
liked. During this time the teachers observed him closely without once reprimanding him. Unknown to him, Pythagoras
came in order to study his gestures and his words. Pythagoras
gave particular attention to the bearing and laughter of the
young men. Laughter, he said, reveals the character in an in-
fallible manner, and no dissimulation can beautify the laugh
of a wicked man. In addition, he had made such a profound

study of human physiognomy that in the latter he could discern the depths of the soul.

Through these detailed observations, the master obtained a precise idea of his future disciples. At the end of a few months the decisive tests came. These were imitations of Egyptian initiation, but were very much milder and had been adapted to the Greek nature, whose sensitivity could not have survived the mortal terrors of the crypts of Memphis and Thebes. The Pythagorean aspirant was made to spend the night on the outskirts of the city in a cavern where it was said there were monsters and phantoms. Those who did not have the strength to bear the dread experiences of loneliness and night, who refused to enter or fled before morning, were considered too weak for initiation and were sent away.

The moral test was more serious. Suddenly, without preparation, one fine morning the hopeful disciple was locked in a dismal, bare cell. He was handed a slate and was coldly ordered to find the meaning of one of the Pythagorean symbols, for example, "What is the meaning of a triangle inscribed in a circle?" or, "Why is the dodecaedron, enclosed in a sphere, the number of the universe?" He spent twelve hours alone in his cell with his slate and his problem, with a pitcher of water and dry bread for food. Afterward he was led into a room before the assembled novices. On this occasion they had orders mercilessly to ridicule the miserable one who, cross and starved, appeared before them like a guilty man. "There," they said, "is the new philosopher! How inspired his countenance looks! He is about to tell us his meditations! Do not conceal from us what you have discovered! You shall go through all the symbols; another month of this, and you will become a great sage!"

Meanwhile the master was observing the attitude and countenance of the young man very attentively. Irritated by his fast, overwhelmed by the sarcastic tauntings, humiliated at his inability to solve an incomprehensible enigma, he had to make a great effort to control himself. Some would cry out in rage; others answered with cynical words; others, beside themselves, broke their slates in fury, pouring curses upon the school, the master, and his students. Pythagoras then appeared and calmly said that, having so poorly withstood the test of vanity, the aspirant was requested not to return to a school about which he held such a bad opinion, where the elementary virtues had to be friendship and respect for the teachers. Ashamed, the rejected candidate went away, sometimes becoming a dreadful enemy of the Order, like the celebrated Cylon who later stirred up the people against the Pythagoreans and brought about the destruction of the Order itself. On the other hand, those who bore the attacks with calmness, who answered the provocations with accurate and spiritual reflections, declaring that they were ready to begin the test again a hundred times over in order to obtain a bit of wisdom, were solemnly admitted to the novitiate, amid the enthusiastic congratulations of their new fellow students.

THE FIRST STEP—PREPARATION

The Novitiate and the Pythagorean Life

Only then did the novitiate, called *preparation (paraskeis)*, begin. It lasted at least two years, and could extend to five. During their instruction, the novices or listeners (*akousikoi*), were placed under a rule of absolute silence. They had no right to make any objection to their instructors, or to discuss their teachings. They had to receive the latter with respect, then to meditate upon them at length within themselves. In order to impress this rule upon the mind of the new listener, he was shown a statue of a woman covered with a long veil, her finger placed upon her lips. She was the *Muse of Silence*.

Pythagoras did not believe that a youth was capable of understanding the beginning and end of things. He thought that to exercise him in dialectic and reasoning before he had been given the meaning of truth, made an empty and a pretentious sophist. Above all he wished to develop in his pupils the archetypal, higher faculty of man—Intuition. And for this reason he did not teach mysterious or difficult things. He proceeded from natural feelings and the first duties of man at his entry into life, and showed their relationship with universal laws. Since he first inculcated in the young men a love for their parents, he enlarged this sentiment by assimilating the idea of father to that of God, the Great Creator of the universe. "Nothing is more venerable," he said, "than the quality of the father. Homer called Jupiter the ruler of the gods, but to show all his greatness, he called him the Father of gods and men." He compared the mother to generous and beneficent nature. As celestial Cybele produces the stars and Demeter produces the fruits and flowers of the fields, so the mother nourishes the child with all joy. Therefore in his father and mother the son should honor the representatives, the earthly representations of these great divinities. He further showed that the love one has for one's country comes from the love one felt for one's mother in childhood. Parents are given to us, not by chance, as man generally believes, but by an antecedent and higher order called Fortune or Necessity. It is *necessary* to honor them, but one ought to *choose* one's friend. The novices were urged to group themselves in twos according to their affinities. The youngest was to seek in the eldest the virtues he himself pursued, and the two companions should inspire each other to the better life. "The friend is another self; one must honor him like a god," said the master. If the Pythagorean rule imposed upon the novice *listener* absolute submission with regard to his teachers, it left him complete freedom in the joy of friendship; it even made friendship the stimulus to all virtues, the poetry of life, the pathway to the ideal.

Individual strength thus was awakened, morality became living and poetic, the rule accepted with love ceased to be a restriction and became the very affirmation of individualism. Pythagoras wished obedience to be an assent. In addition, moral training paved the way for philosophical teaching. For the relationships that were established between social duties and the harmonies of the cosmos caused one to feel the law of correspondences and universal concordances. In this law lies the principle of the Mysteries, of esoteric teaching and of all philosophy. The mind of the pupil thus became accustomed to finding the mark of an invisible order upon visible reality. General maxims, concise formulations opened vistas upon the higher world. Morning and evening *The Golden Verses* sounded in the student's ear, accompanied by the accent of the lyre:

> *Render dedicated worship to the immortal gods;*
> *Keep, then, your faith.*

In analyzing this maxim, it was shown that the gods, seemingly different, were basically the same among all peoples since they corresponded to the same spiritually animate forces active throughout the universe. The sage therefore could honor the gods of his own country, at the same time making of their essence an idea different from that of the common man. Tolerance for all cults, oneness of all peoples, unity of religions in esoteric science—these new ideas were vaguely outlined in the novice's mind like grandiose divinities dimly seen in the splendor of the setting sun. And the Golden Lyre continued its grave teachings:

Revere the memory
Of heroes who are benefactors, of spirits which are demigods!

Behind these lines the novice saw as through a veil the divine Psyche, the human soul, shining. The heavenly road glistened like a stream of light. For in the worship of heroes and demigods the initiate viewed the doctrine of the future life and the mystery of universal evolution. This great secret was not revealed to the novice, but he was being prepared to understand it by hearing about a hierarchy of beings called heroes and demigods who are superior to mankind, and who are its guides and protectors. It was added that since they were intercessors between man and the divine, through them man could succeed by degrees in coming close to the spiritual by practising heroic virtues. "But how can one communicate with these invisible Genii?" "Where does the soul come from?" "Where is it going, and why this dark mystery of death?" The novice did not dare formulate these questions, but they were divined from his expressions. And in reply his teachers would show him fighters on earth, statues in the temple, and glorified souls in the sky, "in the fiery citadel of the gods," which Hercules had reached.

In the heart of the ancient Mysteries, all the gods were reestablished in the One Supreme God. This revelation, together with all its consequences, became the key to the cosmos. For this reason it was reserved entirely to initiation proper. The novice knew nothing about this. He was allowed to see this truth only in part through what was called the power of Magic and Number. For numbers, the master taught, contain the secret of things, and God is universal harmony. The seven sacred modes built on the seven notes of the heptachord correspond to the seven colors of light, to the seven planets and to the seven forms of existence, which are reproduced in all the spheres of material and spiritual life, from the least to the greatest. The melodies of these modes, wisely instilled, should bring the soul into harmony, making it capable of vibrating exactly with the breath of truth.

To this purification of the soul necessarily corresponded that of the body, which was obtained by hygiene and the strict discipline of habits. To conquer one's passions was the first duty of initiation. One who has not made an harmonious entity of his own being, cannot reflect divine harmony. Nevertheless, the ideal of the Pythagorean life had nothing of the ascetic element, since marriage was considered sacred. But chastity was recommended to the novices and moderation to the initiates as a source of power and perfection. "Do not yield to pleasure except when you agree to be untrue to yourself," said the master. He added that pleasure does not exist by itself, and compared it to "the song of the Sirens who, when they are approached, vanish and in their place cause broken bones and bloody flesh on a reef devoured by the waves, while real joy is similar to the concert of the Muses, which leaves a celestial harmony in the soul." Pythagoras believed in the virtues of the female initiate but he greatly mistrusted the uninitiated woman. To a disciple who asked him when he would be allowed to approach a woman, he answered ironically, "When you become tired of your composure."

The Pythagorean day was arranged in the following manner. As soon as the burning sun arose out of the blue waves of the Ionian Sea, gilding the columns of the temple of the Muses above the home of the initiates, the young Pythagoreans sang a hymn to Apollo while executing a Dorian dance of a masculine and sacred nature. After the required ablutions, they walked to the temple in silence. Each awakening is a resurrection which has its flower of innocence. The soul should wrap itself in meditation at the beginning of the day, and remain pure for the morning lesson. In the sacred groves they gathered around the master or his interpreters and the lesson was conducted in the cool shade of the tall trees or in the shadow of the porticoes. At noon a prayer was said to the heroes and benevolent Genii. Esoteric tradition assumed that good spirits prefer to approach the earth with the solar radiation, while evil spirits haunt the shadows and pervade the atmosphere when night comes. The frugal noonday meal generally consisted of bread, honey and olives. The afternoon was dedicated to gymnastic exercises, followed by study, meditation and work on the lesson of the morning. After sunset, prayer was said in a group and they sang a hymn to the cosmogonic gods, to celestial Jupiter, to Minerva Providence and to Diana, protectress of the dead. During this time, styrax, balm or incense was burning on the altar in the open air, and the hymn, blended with the perfume, sweetly ascended in the dusk as the first stars pierced the pale blue sky. The day ended with the evening meal, after which the youngest gave a reading, analyzed by the eldest.

Thus flowed the Pythagorean day, limpid as a stream, clear as a cloudless morning. The year was regulated according to the great astronomical festivals. For example, the return of Hyperborean Apollo and the celebration of the Mysteries of Ceres brought together novices and initiates, men and women of all degrees. The young girls were seen playing ivory lyres; married women in peplos of deep-red and saffron, performed in antiphonal choirs, accompanied by songs with the harmonious movements of the strophe and antistrophe which tragedy later imitated. In the midst of these great festivals where divinity seemed present in the grace of forms and movements, in the incisive melody of the choirs, the novice experienced something like a foretaste of esoteric powers, the omnipotent laws of the universe and the deep, transparent heavens. Marriage and funeral rites had a more intimate but no less solemn character. One unusual ceremony made a special appeal to the imagination. When a novice voluntarily left the institute to resume ordinary life, or when a disciple had betrayed a secret of the teaching, which happened but once, the initiates erected a tomb in the consecrated enclosure, as if he were dead. The master would say, "He is more dead than the dead, since he has returned to evil life; his body walks among men, but his soul is dead; let us mourn for it." And this tomb, erected to a living being, tortured him like his own phantom, like a sinister omen.

THE SECOND STEP—PURIFICATION

The Numbers—Theogony

It was a beautiful day, "a golden day," as the elders said, when Pythagoras received the novice in his home, solemnly accepting him as one of his disciples. Now the novices entered into intimate and direct relationship with the master; they were invited into the inner court of his home, reserved for his faithful students. From this fact we derive the name *esoterics*, those of the inside, opposed to *exoterics*, those of the outside. Real initiation began at this stage.

This revelation consisted of a complete and rational explanation of esoteric doctrine from its beginnings, continued with the mysterious science of numbers, to the final consequences of universal evolution, and dealt with the destinies and supreme goals of the divine Psyche, of the human soul. This science of numbers was known under various names in the temples of Egypt and Asia. Since it provided the key to all doctrine it was carefully concealed from the uninitiated. The numbers, letters and geometric figures, or the human representations which served as signs for this algebra of the secret world were understood only by the initiate. The latter revealed their meaning to the adepts only after they had taken the oath of silence. Pythagoras formulated this science in his book called *Hieros Logos,* The Sacred Word. This work has not come down to us, but the later writings by the Pythagoreans, by Philolaus of Archytas, and by Hierocles, the *Dialogues* of Plato, the treatises of Aristotle, as well as those of Porphyrus and Iamblicus, have made the principles known. If they have remained a closed book for modern philosophers, it is because their meaning and depth cannot be understood except by comparison with the esoteric doctrines of the Orient.

Pythagoras called his disciples mathematicians because his higher teaching began with the study of numbers. But his sacred mathematics or science of principles was both transcendent and more alive than the secular mathematics known to our modern scientists and philosophers. Number was not considered an abstract quantity but an intrinsic and living virtue of the supreme *One,* of God, the Source of universal harmony. The science of *numbers* was that of the living forces of *divine faculties* in action in the world and in man, in macrocosm and microcosm . . . By penetrating these, by distinguishing and explaining their workings, Pythagoras made nothing less than a theogony or a rational theology.

A real theology should provide the principles for all the sciences. It will be the science of God only if it manifests the unity and link between the sciences of nature. It deserves its name only on condition that it constitutes the organ and synthesis of all the others. And this is exactly the role that the science of the Sacred Word played in the Egyptian temples, later formulated and made more exact by Pythagoras under the

name of the science of numbers. It claimed to provide the key
of being, science and life. The adept, guided by the master,
had to begin by contemplating the principles in his own intellect, before following their manifold applications in the vast
cycles of evolution.

A modern poet felt this truth when he made Faust descend
to the Mothers in order to restore life to Helena's phantom.
Faust seizes the magic key, earth crumbles beneath his feet,
dizziness overwhelms him and he plunges into the emptiness
of space. Finally he arrives at the realm of the Mothers who
guard the archetypal forms of the Great All. These Mothers are
Pythagoras' numbers, the divine forces in the world. The poet
has rendered for us the awe of his own thought at this plunge
into the Abyss of the *Unfathomable*. For the ancient initiate, in
whom the direct view of Intelligence slowly awakened like a
new sense, this inner revelation seemed rather to be an ascent
into the great incandescent sun of truth where, in the fullness
of Light he viewed beings and forms projected into the whirlwind of lives by a great outpouring.

He did not reach in a single day that inner possession of
truth in which man sees universal life as reality by means of
the concentration of his faculties. Years of exercise and that
accord of intelligence, so difficult to attain, were necessary. Before using the Creative Word—and how few succeed—it is
necessary to spell the Sacred Word, letter by letter, syllable by
syllable.

Pythagoras was in the habit of teaching in the Temple of the
Muses. At Pythagoras' request, and according to his designs,
the magistrates of Croton had had the temple built very near
his home, in an enclosed garden. Only the disciples of the
second degree entered it with the master. In the interior of this
circular temple could be seen the nine Muses, carved in marble.
Standing in the center, covered with a veil, Hestia watched,

solemn and mysterious. With her left hand she protected the flame of the hearth; with her right she pointed to Heaven. Among the Greeks as well as the Romans, Hestia or Vesta is the guardian of the divine element present in everything. Conscious of the sacred fire, she had her altar in the temple of Delphi, in the Prytaneum of Athens, as well as in the humblest home. In Pythagoras' sanctuary she symbolized the divine, central science of Theogony. Surrounding her statue the esoteric Muses in the circular temple, in addition to their traditional and mythological names, bore the names of the esoteric sciences and sacred arts of which they had custody. *Urania* presided over astronomy and astrology; *Polymnia,* the science of souls in the other life and the art of divination; *Melpomene* with her tragic mask, the science of life and death, of transformations and of rebirths. Together these three higher Muses constituted cosmogony or celestial physics. *Calliope, Clio,* and *Euterpe* presided over the science of man, or psychology, with its corresponding arts, medicine, magic, ethics. The last group, *Terpsichore, Erato,* and *Thalia,* embraced earthly physics, the science of the elements, stones, plants, and animals.

Thus from the very start the organism of the sciences, imitating the organism of the universe, appeared to the disciple in the living circle of the Muses, lighted by the divine flame.

Having led his disciples into this little sanctuary, Pythagoras opened the book of the Word and began his esoteric teaching.

"These Muses," he said, "are only the earthly prototypes of divine powers whose incorporeal, sublime beauty you are about to view within yourselves. Just as they look at the Fire of Hestia from which they emanate and which gives them movement, rhythm, and melody, so you must plunge into the central Fire of the Universe, into divine Spirit, in order to spread out with it in its visible manifestations." Then, with a powerful, sure hand, Pythagoras lifted his disciples from the world of forms and realities; he erased time and space, causing them to descend with him into the *Great Monad,* into the essence of the Uncreated Being.

Pythagoras called this the first One, composed of harmony, the Male Fire which passes through everything, the Spirit which moves by itself, the Indivisible, great non-manifest, whose creative thought the ephemeral worlds make manifest, the Unique, the Eternal, the Unchangeable hidden under the many things which pass away and change. "Essence conceals itself from man," said Philolaus, the Pythagorean. "Man knows only the things of this world, where the finite is combined with the infinite. And how can he know them? Because between him and things is a harmony, a relationship, a common principle, and this principle is given to them by the One who gives them dimension and intelligibility, along with their essence. He is the common measure between object and subject, the reason for things by which the soul shares in the final cause of the One.[54] But how can one approach Imperceptible Being? Has anyone ever seen the Master of Time, the Soul of the Suns, the Source of Intelligence? No, and it is only in becoming one with Him that one fathoms His Essence. He is like an invisible fire placed at the center of the universe, whose living flame moves in all worlds and impels all." He added that the work of initiation was to get closer to the great Being by resembling Him, by making oneself as perfect as possible, by mastering things through intelligence, by thus becoming active like Him, and not passive like them. "Your being is yours; is your soul not a microcosm, a little universe?—But it is filled with storms and discords. Therefore, it is a question of effecting unity in harmony. Then,—only then—will God descend into your consciousness; then will you share His power; then will you make of your will the stone of the hearth, the altar of Hestia, the throne of Jupiter!"

God, indivisible Substance, therefore, has as a number the Unity which contains Infinity; as a name, that of Father, Creator, or Eternal Masculine; as a sign, the Living Fire, the symbol of the Spirit, the essence of Everything. This is the first principle.

But divine faculties are similar to the mystic lotus which the Egyptian initiate, lying in his sepulchre, sees emerging from the blackness of night. At first it is only a brilliant dot, then it opens like a flower, the incandescent center spreading out like a rose of light with a thousand petals.

Pythagoras said that the Great Monad acts as a *creative Dyad*. From the moment God is manifest, He is double; indivisible Essence, divisible Substance, masculine, active, animating and passive feminine principles. Therefore the Dyad represented the union of the Eternal Masculine and Eternal Feminine in God, the two basic, corresponding divine faculties. Orpheus poetically expressed this idea in the line,

Jupiter is the divine Husband and the divine Wife.

All polytheisms, by representing divinity sometimes in the masculine, sometimes in the feminine form, have been aware of this idea intuitively.

This eternal Nature, this great Wife of God, is not only earthly nature but heavenly nature, invisible to our eyes of flesh, the Soul of the world, the Primordial Light,—in turn Maia, Isis, or Cybele who, first vibrating under the divine impulse, contains the essences of all souls, the spiritual archetypes of all beings. Demeter is next, the living earth and all earths, along with the bodies they enclose, into which souls are incarnated. Then she is Woman, companion of Man. In humanity, Woman represents nature; and the perfect image of God is not Man alone, but Man and Woman. Hence their invincible, charming, fateful attraction; hence the intoxication of love, into which the dream of infinite creation plays, as well as the vague feeling that the Eternal Masculine and the Eternal Feminine enjoy a perfect union in the Heart of God. "Honor, therefore, be to Woman, on earth and in Heaven," said Pythagoras, in harmony with all the ancient initiates. "She makes us understand that great Woman, nature. Let her be Her sanctified image and help us to return by degrees to the great Soul of the World who gives birth, preserves and renews,—to the divine Cybele who bears the people of souls in her cloak of light!"

The Monad represents the essence of God, the Dyad, His generative and reproductive faculty. The latter generates the world; it is the visible unfolding of God in space and time. But the real world is threefold. Man is composed of three elements, distinct yet blended into one another: body, soul and spirit. The universe likewise is divided into three concentric spheres: the natural world, the human world and the divine world. *The Triad* or *the threefold law,* therefore, is the essential law of things and the actual key to life. For this law is found at all stages of the ladder of life, from the constitution of the organic cell through the physiological constitution of the animal body, the functioning of the blood system and the cerebro-spinal system, to the hyperphysical constitution of man, universe and God. Thus, as if by enchantment it opens the internal structure of the universe to the astonished mind; it reveals the infinite correspondences of macrocosm and microcosm. It acts like a light which would pass into things in order to make them transparent, and to illuminate the small and large worlds like so many magic lanterns.

Let us understand this law by means of the basic correspondence of man and universe.

Pythagoras stated that the mind of man receives its immortal, invisible and entirely active nature from God. For the mind moves of its own accord. He called the body its mortal, divisible, passive part. He thought that what we call soul is closely linked with the mind, but that it is formed of a third intermediate element which comes from the cosmic fluid. Therefore the soul resembles an etheric body which the mind weaves and constructs. Without this etheric body the material body could not be moved, and would be only an inert, lifeless mass.[55] The soul has a form similar to that of the body, to which it gives life and which it outlives after dissolution or death. Then, according to a metaphor employed by Pythagoras and Plato, it becomes a subtle chariot which carries the spirit toward the divine spheres or lets it fall back into the dark regions of matter, depending upon whether it is more or less good or evil. And the constitution and evolution of man are repeated in widening circles, involving every scale of being and all spheres. Just as the human psyche struggles against the spirit which attracts it and the body which holds it, so humanity evolves between the natural and animal worlds where it is held by earthly roots, and the divine world of pure spirits, its celestial source, toward which it strives to raise itself. And what occurs in mankind takes place on all earths and in all solar systems in ever-varying proportions, in ever new modes. Extend the circle to infinity and, if you can, embrace the limitless worlds with a single concept. What do you find?—Creative thought, astral fluid and worlds in evolution: mind, soul and body of Divinity. Lifting veil after veil, and tapping the qualities of that Divinity itself, you will discover the Triad and Dyad enveloping each other in the dark depths of the Monad like an efflorescence of stars in the abysses of infinity.

From this brief sketch one perceives the major importance Pythagoras attached to the threefold law. It can be said that it forms the cornerstone of esoteric science. All the great religious initiators were aware of it; all spiritual leaders felt it. An oracle of Zoroaster said,

The number Three reigns everywhere in the Universe,
And the Monad is its beginning.

The great accomplishment of Pythagoras is that he formulated the threefold law with the clarity of Greek genius. He made it the center of his theogony and the foundation of the sciences. Already concealed in Plato's exoteric writings, but completely misunderstood by later philosophers, this concept has been fathomed in modern times by only a few rare initiates of the esoteric sciences.[56] Today one can begin to recognize what a broad, solid base the law of universal threefoldness afforded the classification of the sciences, the building of a cosmogony and a psychology.

Just as the universal threefold law is centered in the unity of God, or in the Monad, so human threefoldness is centered in the consciousness of self and in the will, which gathers all the faculties of body, soul and spirit into a living unity. Human and divine threefoldness, summed up in the Monad, constitutes the sacred Tetrad. But man realizes his own unity only in a relative manner. For his will, which acts on all his being, nevertheless cannot act simultaneously and thoroughly in its three organs, that is, in the instinct, in the soul and in the intellect. The universe and God Himself appear to him only one after the other, and are reflected by these three mirrors: 1. Viewed through the instinct and the kaleidoscope of the senses, God is multiple and infinite like His manifestations. Hence polytheism, where the number of gods is not limited. 2. Seen through the rational soul, God is two-fold, that is, mind and matter. Hence the dualism of Zoroaster, of the Manicheans, and of several other religions. 3. Seen through pure intellect He is threefold, that is, spirit, soul and body in all the manifestations of the universe. Hence the trinitarian cults of India (Brahma, Vishnu, Siva) and the Trinity itself of Christianity (Father, Son and Holy Spirit). 4. Conceived through the will which sums up the whole, God is One, and we have the hermetic monotheism of Moses in all its firmness. Here there is no further personification, no further incarnation; we leave the visible universe and return to the Absolute. Alone the Eternal rules over the world, the latter reduced to dust. The diversity of religions therefore stems from the fact that man realizes Divinity only through his own being, which is relative and finite, while at every instant God realizes the unity of the three worlds in the harmony of the universe.

In itself, this last application would prove the somewhat magic virtue of the Tetragram in the order of ideas. Not only would one discover the principles of the sciences, the law of beings and their manner of evolution, but also the reason for the various religions and for their higher unity. It was truly the universal key. Thus one understands the enthusiasm with which Lysis speaks of it in *The Golden Verses,* and one realizes why the Pythagoreans swore by this great symbol:

I swear by the One Who engraved in our hearts
The sacred Tetrad, mighty and pure Symbol,
Source of nature, archetype of the gods.

Pythagoras pursued the teaching of Numbers still further. In each of them he defined a principle, a law, an active force of the universe. But he said that the basic principles are contained in the first four numbers, since in adding or multiplying them one finds all the others. So the infinite variety of beings who make up the universe is produced through the combinations of the three primordial forces: matter, soul and spirit under the creative impetus of divine unity which combines and differentiates them, concentrates and breaks them up. Along with the principal teachers of esoteric science, Pythagoras attached great importance to the number *seven* and the number *ten.* Seven, the compound of three and four, means the union of man and divinity. It is the number of the adepts, of the great initiates, and since it expresses complete fulfillment in everything through seven stages, it represents the law of evolution. The number *ten*, formed by the addition of the first four and which also contains the preceding one, is the perfect number *par excellence,* since it represents all the principles of Divinity evolved and united in a new unity.

Upon completing the teaching of his theogony, Pythagoras showed his disciples the nine Muses, personifying the sciences grouped three by three, presiding at the triple ternary evolved in nine worlds, and with Hestia forming divine Science, Guardian of the Archetypal Fire—the Sacred Decade.

THE THIRD STAGE—PERFECTION

Cosmogony and Psychology—Evolution of the Soul

The disciple had received the principles of science from the master. This first initiation caused the thick scales of matter which had covered the eyes of his mind, to fall. Tearing away the shining veil of mythology, it had snatched him from the visible world and had cast him into limitless spaces, plunging him into the Sun of Intelligence, from which Truth radiates over the three worlds. But the science of numbers was only the preamble to the great initiation. Armed with these principles, it was now a question of descending from the heights of the Absolute into the depths of nature, there to grasp divine thought in the formation of things, and in the evolution of the soul through the worlds. Esoteric cosmogony and psychology were very close to the greatest mysteries of life, as well as to the jealously guarded secrets of the esoteric arts and sciences. Pythagoras preferred to give these lessons at night, free from the profane light of day, on the terraces of the Temple of Ceres, accompanied by the gentle murmuring of the Ionian Sea with its melodious rhythm, beneath the distant phosphorescences of the starry cosmos; or in the crypts of the sanctuary where Egyptian naphtha lamps cast a steady, gentle, clear light. The women initiates attended these nocturnal gatherings. Sometimes priests or priestesses from Delphi or Eleusis came to confirm the teachings of the master either by relating their experiences, or through the clear speech of clairvoyant sleep.

Material and spiritual evolution of the world are two opposite but parallel and concordant movements upon the entire scale of being. One is explained only by the other, and together they explain the world. Material evolution represents the manifestation of God in matter through the activity of the soul of the world. Spiritual evolution represents the development of consciousness in the individual monads and their efforts to rejoin, across the cycle of lives, the divine spirit from which they emanate. To see the universe from the physical point of view or the spiritual point of view is not to consider a different object; it is to look at the world from two opposite viewpoints. From the terrestrial point of view the rational explanation of the world must begin with material evolution, since it is from this aspect that it appears to us. However, by causing us to see the work of universal Mind in matter and by pursuing the development of individual monads, this rational explanation leads to the spiritual point of view, causing us to pass from the outside to the inside of things.

In this way Pythagoras explained the universe as a living being, animated by a great Soul, and permeated with a great Intelligence. The second part of his teaching therefore began with Cosmogony.

If one relies upon the divisions of heaven which we find in the esoteric fragments of the Pythagoreans, this astronomy would be similar to the astronomy of Ptolomy—a motionless earth with the sun, the planets and the entire firmament revolving around it. But the very nature of this astronomy indicates that it is entirely symbolic. At the center of his universe Pythagoras places Fire, of which the sun is but a reflection. And in all the esoterism of the East, Fire is the sign of Spirit, of divine universal Consciousness. Therefore, what our philosophers generally accept as the physics of Pythagoras and Plato is nothing but a figurative description of their secret philosophy, luminous for the initiates, but all the more impenetrable for the common man, since it was made to pass for explanations of simple physical phenomena. Let us therefore regard it as a sort of cosmography of the life of souls, nothing more nor less. The sublunar region designates the sphere where earthly attraction is exerted, and is called *The Circle of Generations*. By this the initiates meant that for us the earth is the region of corporeal life. All the activities which accompany the incarnation and excarnation of souls take place there. The sphere of the six planets and of the sun corresponds to ascending categories of spirits. Olympus, conceived as a revolving sphere, is called *The Heaven of Fixed Things* because it is assimilated within the sphere of perfect souls. This apparently naive astronomy, therefore, conceals a concept of the spiritual universe.

But everything leads us to believe that the ancient initiates, and particularly Pythagoras, had much more accurate ideas of the physical universe than is generally conceived. Aristotle says positively that the Pythagoreans believed in the movement of the earth around the sun. Copernicus affirms that the idea of rotation of the earth upon its axis came to him while reading in Cicero that a certain Hycetas of Syracuse had spoken of the daily movement of the earth. To his disciples of the third degree, Pythagoras taught the dual movement of the earth. Without the exact calculations of modern science, nevertheless he knew, as did the priests of Memphis, that planets coming from the sun revolve around it; that the stars are so many solar systems governed by the same laws as ours, and that each has its appointed place in the vast universe. He also recognized that each solar world forms a little universe, having its correspondence in the spiritual world and its own heaven. But these ideas would have upset the popular mythology of the ancients, and the masses would have labeled them as sacrilege. Therefore they were never entrusted to profane writing, but were taught only under the seal of the deepest secrecy.[57]

Pythagoras said that the visible universe, the sky with all its stars, is but a passing form of the world-soul, of the great Maia, who concentrates scattered matter out of infinite spaces, then dissolves and scatters it in an imponderable, cosmic fluid. Each solar vortex possesses a part of this universal soul, which evolves for millions of centuries with a special force of impulsion and dimension. As for the powers, kingdoms, species and living souls which will appear successively in the stars of this little world, they come from God, they descend from the Father, that is, they emanate from an unchangeable and higher spiritual order as well as from a former material evolution, from an extinct solar system. Some of these invisible powers which are entirely immortal, direct the formation of this world. Others await its unfolding in cosmic sleep or in divine dream in order that they may return to visible generations according to eternal law. Nevertheless, the solar soul and its central fire which the Great Monad activates directly, cultivates matter to a condition of fusion. The planets are the daughters of the sun. Each of them, fashioned by forces of attraction and rotation inherent in matter, is endowed with a semi-conscious soul coming from the solar soul, and has its distinct character, its particular role in evolution. Since each planet is a varied expression of the thought of God and since it plays a special role in the planetary chain, the ancient wise men identified the names of the planets with those of the great gods which represent the divine Faculties in action in the universe.

The four elements, of which the stars and all beings are formed, are progressive states of matter. The first, denser and cruder than all the others, is the most refractory to spirit; the last, being most refined, shows a great affinity for spirit. *Earth* represents the solid state, *water,* the liquid state, *air,* the gaseous state, *fire,* the imponderable state. The fifth element, or the *etheric,* represents a state of matter so subtle and alive that it is no longer atomic, and is endowed with the property of universal penetration. It is the fundamental cosmic fluid, the astral light or the world-soul.

Pythagoras then spoke to his disciples about Egypt and Asia. He knew that earth in fusion was originally surrounded by a gaseous atmosphere which, liquefied by its subsequent cooling, had formed the seas. According to tradition, he summed up this idea metaphorically by saying that the seas were produced by *the tears of Saturn,* the cosmic age.

But now appear the kingdoms, invisible seeds, floating in the ethereal aura of earth. They swirl in its gaseous robe, then are attracted into the depths of the seas and the first emerging continents. The plant and animal worlds, still combined, appear at almost the same time. Esoteric doctrine accepts the transformation of animal species, not only according to the secondary law of *selection* but also according to the primary law of *percussion* of the earth by celestial powers, and of all living beings by intelligible principles and invisible forces. When a new species appears on the globe, it is because a group of souls of a higher type becomes incarnated at a given time in the descendants of the older species, in order to cause it to ascend by remolding and transforming it. Thus esoteric doctrine explains the appearance of man upon the earth. From the point

324

of view of earthly evolution, man is the crown of all anterior species. But this point of view no more explains his entrance upon the scene than it explains the appearance of the first algae or the first crustaceans on the bottom of the seas. All successive creations presuppose, as does each birth, the *percussion* of earth by the invisible powers which create life. The creation of man presupposes the previous reign of a celestial mankind which presides at the blossoming of earthly mankind.

Pythagoras, enlightened by the temples of Egypt, had precise ideas on the great revolutions of the globe. Indian and Egyptian teaching spoke of the existence of the ancient austral continent, called Atlantis by the Greeks, which had produced the red race and a powerful civilization. It attributed the alternating emergence and submersion of continents to the oscillation of the poles, stating that mankind had passed through six floods. Each interdiluvian cycle brings about the dominance of a great human race. In the midst of partial eclipses of civilization and human faculties, a general upward movement takes place.

Therefore, humanity is constituted and races are launched upon their careers through the cataclysms of the globe. On these continents which emerge from the seas, only to disappear again, in the midst of peoples who pass away, and civilizations which crumble,—what is the great, poignant, everlasting mystery? This is the great inner problem of everyone. It is the problem of the soul, which discovers within itself an abyss of darkness and light, which views itself with a mixture of rapture and fear, saying, "I am not of this world, for it does not suffice to explain myself to me. I do not come from earth, and I am going elsewhere.—But where?" This is the mystery of Psyche, which includes all others.

The cosmogony of the visible world, Pythagoras said, leads us to the history of earth, and the latter brings us to the mystery of the human soul. With this we approach the sanctuary of sanctuaries, the arcanum of arcana. Once its consciousness is awakened, in its own eyes the soul becomes the most astonishing of spectacles. But even this consciousness is but the lighted surface of man's being; beneath it lie obscure and unfathomable abysses. In their unknown depths, the divine Psyche views with fascination all the lives and all worlds: past, present, and future, which Eternity unites.

"Know yourself, and you will know the universe of the gods." —This is the secret of the initiate-sages. But in order to pass through this narrow door into the vastness of the invisible universe, let us awaken in us the direct life of the purified soul, and let us arm ourselves with the torch of Intelligence, with the science of principles and sacred numbers.

Pythagoras thus passed from physical to spiritual cosmogony. After the evolution of the earth, he described the evolution of the soul through the worlds. Outside initiation, this doctrine is known as *the transmigration of souls*. No part of esoteric doctrine has been more falsely represented than this. Hence ancient and modern literature know about it only under naive disguises. Whether his prudence or his oaths prevented him from saying all he knew, Plato, who of all the philosophers contributed most to making it popular, gave only fantastic and sometimes extravagant sketches of it. Few people today doubt that for the initiates it must have had a scientific aspect, in order to open infinite perspectives and to give the soul divine consolation. The doctrine of the ascending life of the soul through the series of existences is the common characteristic of esoteric traditions and the crown of spiritual knowledge. In addition, it is of major importance for us, since the man of today rejects equally the abstract, vague immortality of philosophy and the childish heaven of elementary religion. Nevertheless, the dryness and emptiness of materialism shocks him. Unconsciously he strives for the consciousness of an organic immortality, which responds both to the requirements of his reason and to the needs of his soul. One understands, moreover, why the initiates of the ancient religions, knowing these truths, nevertheless kept them so secret. They are of such nature as would startle unprepared minds. They are closely linked to the profound mysteries of spiritual generation and of generation in the flesh, upon which the destinies of future mankind depend.

This important hour of esoteric teaching, therefore, was awaited with a kind of awe. Through Pythagoras' speech, as through a solemn chant, heavy matter seemed to lose its weight, the things of earth became transparent, visible to the mind. Golden and blue spheres, traced with luminous essences, unfolded their orbits into Infinity.

Then the male and female disciples, grouped around the master in a subterranean part of the Temple of Ceres, called the Crypt of Proserpine, listened with sacred rapture to *The Celestial History of Psyche.*

What is the human soul? It is a part of the great Soul of the world, a spark of the divine spirit, an immortal monad. But if its possible future opens the unfathomable splendors of divine consciousness, its mysterious unfolding traces back to the origins of organized matter. In order to become what it is in modern humanity, it was necessary for it to traverse all the kingdoms of nature, every gradation of beings, gradually becoming developed through a series of innumerable existences. The mind which cultivates the worlds and condenses cosmic matter into enormous masses, is manifest in the successive kingdoms of nature in a varied intensity and an ever greater concentration. A blind and indistinct force in the mineral, individualized in the plant, polarized in the sensitivity and instinct of animals,— it tends toward the conscious monad in this slow unfolding, while the simple monad is visible in the lowest animal. The animate and spiritual element exist, therefore, in every kingdom, although only in an infinitesimal degree in the lower kingdoms. Souls which existed in the germ state in the lower kingdoms sojourn there without leaving them for long periods of time, and it is only after great cosmic revolutions that they pass to higher kingdoms by changing planets. All they can accomplish during the period of life on a given planet is to ascend a few stages. Where does the monad begin? This is the same as asking when a cloud was formed, or when a sun shone for the first time. What constitutes the essence of any human being had to evolve during millions of years across a chain of planets and lower kingdoms, all the while preserving throughout these existences an individual principle, which follows it everywhere. This vague but indestructible individuality constitutes the divine seal of the monad in which God wishes to manifest Himself through consciousness.

The higher one ascends through the series of organisms, the more the monad develops the latent principles which are in it. The polarized force becomes sensitive; sensitivity becomes instinct, instinct becomes intelligence. And as the flickering flame of consciousness is lighted, this soul becomes more independent of the body, more capable of leading a free existence. The fluid, non-polarized soul of minerals and vegetables is linked to the elements of the earth. The soul of animals, strongly attracted by earth fire, sojourns there a certain time when it has left its cadaver, then returns to the surface of the globe to be reincarnated in its species without being able to leave the lower layers of air. These latter are inhabited by elementals or animal souls, which have their role in atmospheric life and a great hidden influence on man. The human soul alone comes from heaven and returns there after death. But at what era of its long cosmic existence did the elemental soul become a human soul? Through what incandescent crucible, what ethereal flame did it pass in order to accomplish this? Transformation was not possible in an interplanetary period except through the meeting of human souls already fully formed, which had developed their spiritual principle in elemental souls and had imprinted their divine prototype, like a fiery seal upon plastic substance.

But how many journeys, how many incarnations and how many planetary cycles are yet to be crossed in order for the human soul, thus formed, to become man as we know him? According to the esoteric traditions of India and Egypt, the individuals who comprise modern humanity probably began their human life on other planets, where matter is less dense than on ours. The body of man was then almost vaporous, his incarnations, light and gentle. His faculties of direct spiritual perception must have been very powerful and very subtle in this first human phase; reason and intelligence, on the other hand, were in the embryonic state. In this semi-corporeal, semi-spiritual state, man saw spirits; all was splendor and charm to his eyes, music to his ears. He even heard the harmony of the spheres. He did not think nor reflect; he scarcely wished. He caused himself to live by drinking in sounds, forms and light. Like a dream he floated from life to death, from death to life. This is what the Orphics called *The Heaven of Saturn*. According to Hermes' teaching, it was only as man incarnated on denser and denser planets that he became material. By becoming incarnated in dense matter, mankind lost its spiritual sense, but through man's ever greater struggle with the external world, he developed his reason, intelligence and will. Earth is the last stage of this descent into matter which Moses calls the expulsion from Paradise, and Orpheus describes as the fall into the sublunar circle. From here man can painfully reascend the circles in a series of new existences and regain his spiritual senses by the free exercise of his intellect and his will. Then only, say the disciples of Hermes and Orpheus, does man acquire consciousness and come to possess the divine through his deeds. Then only does man become *the Son of God*. And those who have borne this name on earth, before appearing among us, had to descend the dread spiral and ascend it once again.

What then is humble Psyche like at her origin?—A passing breath, a floating seed, a bird which emigrates from life to life, beaten by the winds. And nevertheless, from shipwreck to shipwreck, across millions of years, the soul has become the daughter of God, and no longer recognizes any other home than Heaven! This is why Greek poetry, with rich, profound, luminous symbolism, compared the soul to a winged insect, now a worm, now a heavenly butterfly. How many times was it a chrysalis, how many times a butterfly? It will never know, but it feels that it always has wings!

Such was the past of the human soul. This explains its present condition and allows us partly to see its future.

What is the divine Psyche's situation in earthly life? If one but thinks about it, one cannot imagine one stranger or more tragic. From the moment it painfully awakens in the dense atmosphere of earth, the soul is entwined in the folds of the body. It does not see, breathe or think except by means of the body, yet it is not the body. As it develops, it feels a flickering light forming within itself, something invisible and incorporeal which it calls its spirit, its consciousness. Indeed, man has the inborn feeling of his threefold nature, since he distinguishes, even though instinctively, between his body and his soul, between his soul and his spirit. But the captive, tormented soul struggles with its two companions as in the grip of a serpent of a thousand coils on the one hand, and an invisible genius who calls to the soul, but whose presence is only felt by the beating of its wings and fleeting lights, on the other. Sometimes the body absorbs the soul to such a degree that the latter lives only by sensations and passions; it grovels in bloody orgies of madness, or in the thick vapor of fleshly pleasures until it is frightened because of the great silence of its invisible companion. Sometimes, attracted by the latter, the soul loses itself in such lofty thoughts that it forgets the existence of the body until the latter reminds it of its presence by a tyrannical demand. Nevertheless, an inner voice tells the soul that the link between it and its invisible companion is insoluble, while death will break the soul's attachment to the body. But, tossed back and forth between the two in its everlasting struggle, the soul vanly seeks for happiness and truth. In vain does the soul seek itself in its passing sensations, in its fleeting thoughts, in the world which changes like a mirage. Finding nothing permanent, tormented, blown like a leaf in the wind, it doubts itself as well as the divine world which reveals itself to the soul through the latter's sorrow and inability to reach it. Human ignorance is inscribed in the contradictions of so-called wise men, and human sorrow is written in the unquenchable longing of the human glance. Finally, whatever the extent of his knowledge, birth and death enclose man between two fateful boundaries. They are two doors of darkness, beyond which he sees nothing. The flame of his life lights up as he enters by the one, and flickers out as he leaves by the other. Is it the same with the soul? If not, what becomes of it?

The answers that the philosophers have given to this profound question are very varied. The reply of the initiates of all ages is fundamentally identical. It is in harmony with the universal sentiment and inner spirit of all religions. However, the latter have expressed this truth only in superstitious or symbolic forms. Esoteric doctrine opens much broader perspectives, and its affirmations are in accord with the laws of universal evolution. Instructed by tradition and by numerous experiences of the psychic life, the initiates have said to man, What moves in you, what you call your soul, is an etheric double of the body which encloses within itself an immortal spirit. The spirit creates and weaves its spiritual body by its own activity. Pythagoras calls the spirit *the subtile chariot of the soul* because it is destined to carry the soul from earth after death. *This spiritual body is the organ of the spirit,* its sensitive covering and its volitive instrument. It aids in the animation of the body, which would remain motionless without it. In the apparitions of the dying or the dead, this *double* becomes visible. But this always presupposes a special inner state on the part of the seer. The subtlety, the power and the perfection of the spiritual body vary according to the quality of the spirit it encloses, and between the substance of souls woven in the astral light but impregnated with imponderable fluids of earth and heaven, there are more numerous nuances, greater differences, than between all terrestrial bodies and all states of ponderable matter. This astral body, though much subtler and more perfect than the earthly body, is not immortal like the monad it contains. It changes, it becomes pure according to the atmospheres it passes through. The spirit molds and perpetually transforms it in its image, but never abandons it. And if spirit slowly discards it, it is while it is being clothed with yet more etheric substances. This Pythagoras taught, but he did not conceive the abstract spiritual entity, the formless monad. Spirit in action in the heights of the heavens as well as on the earth, must have an instrument; this instrument is the living soul, bestial or sublime, dark or radiant, but having a human form—the image of God.

What happens at death? At the beginning of the death agony, the soul generally senses its imminent separation from the body. It again sees all its earthly existence in brief tableaux in rapid succession and startling clarity. But when the exhausted life ceases, the soul becomes troubled and loses consciousness entirely. If it is a holy or pure soul, its spiritual senses are already awakened by the gradual separation from matter. Before dying, in one manner or another, even if only by a looking into its own state, it has the feeling of the presence of another world. At the silent urgings, the distant calls, the dim rays of the Invisible, earth already has lost its solidity, and when the soul finally escapes the cold body, joyful because of its deliverance, it feels itself lifted in a great light toward the spiritual family to which it belongs.

But it is not thus with the ordinary man whose life has been divided between material instincts and higher aspirations. He awakens in a semi-consciousness, as in the torpor of a nightmare. He no longer has arms to stretch or voice to speak with, but he remembers, he suffers, he exists in a limbo of darkness and fear. The only thing he perceives is the presence of his body, from which he is detached, but for which he still feels a very strong attraction. For it is through the body that he lived, and now what is he? He seeks for himself with fright in the frozen fibers of his brain, in the congealed blood of his veins, and no longer finds himself. Is he dead? Is he alive? He would like to see, to cling to something, but he does not see; he grasps nothing. Darkness encloses him; around him, in him, everything is chaos. He sees but one thing, and that thing attracts him and horrifies him. . . . It is the sinister phosphorescence of his own cast-off skin; and the nightmare begins again. . . .

This state can last for months or years. Its length depends upon the strength of the material instincts of the soul. But, good or bad, infernal or heavenly, slowly this soul will become aware of itself and its new condition. Once free from its body, it will escape into the abysses of the earthly atmosphere, whose magnetic streams carry it here and there, and whose wandering forms, more or less similar to itself, the soul begins to perceive like fleeting lights in a thick fog. Then on the part of the still heavy soul begins a severe struggle to ascend into the higher layers of air, to free itself from earthly attraction, to reach the region which is suited to it and which friendly guides alone can reveal in the sky of our planetary system. But before hearing and seeing them, the soul often requires a long period of time. This phase of the life of the soul has been given various names in different religions and mythologies. Moses calls it Horeb; Orpheus, Erebus; Christianity, Purgatory, or "the valley of the shadow of death." The Greek initiates identified it with the cone of shadow which extends to the moon, and which earth forever trails behind it, for this reason calling it "the gulf of Hecate." According to the Orphics and Pythagoreans, in this dark vortex whirl souls which through desperate efforts seek to reach the circle of the moon, while the violence of the winds beats them back to earth by the thousands. Homer and Virgil compare them to whirling leaves, to flocks of birds overwhelmed by the tempest.

The moon played an important role in ancient esoterism. On the moon's surface, turned toward the heavens, the soul was supposed to purify its astral body before continuing its celestial ascension. It was alleged that heroes and geniuses sojourned a while on its surface turned toward earth in order to become clothed in a body appropriate for our world before reincarnating in it. In some degree the ancients attributed to the moon the power of magnetizing the soul for terrestrial incarnation or demagnetizing it in preparation for heaven. Generally speaking, these assertions, to which the initiates attached both a real and a symbolic meaning, meant that the soul must pass through an intermediate state of purification and rid itself of the impurities of earth before continuing its journey.

But how is one to depict the arrival of the pure soul in its own world? Earth has disappeared like a dream. A new sleep, a delightful swoon surrounds it like a caress. It sees only its winged guide carrying it with the swiftness of light into the widths of space. What is to be said of its awakening in the valleys of an ethereal star, without elemental atmosphere, where everything, mountains, flowers, vegetation, is of an exquisite, sensitive, expressive nature? Above all, what is to be said of these luminous forms, men and women, which surround it like a sacred procession, to initiate it into the holy mystery of its new life? Are these gods and goddesses? No, they are souls like itself; and the wonder is that their intimate thought is expressed upon their faces, and that tenderness, love, desire or fear shine through these diaphanous bodies in a spectrum of shining colors. Here, bodies and faces no longer are masks of the soul, but the transparent soul appears in its true form and shines in the full light of its pure truth.

Psyche has found her divine home. For the secret light in which she is bathing, which emanates from herself and which returns to her in the smile of beloved men and women,—this light of happiness is the World-Soul. The soul feels the presence of God! Now there are no more obstacles. Now the soul will love, will know, will live without any limit other than its own wings.

O strange and marvelous happiness! The soul feels joined to all its companions by profound affinities. For in the life of the beyond, those who do not like each other flee one another, and only those who understand each other remain together. The soul will celebrate the divine Mysteries with them in the most beautiful temples, in a more perfect communion. There will be living and ever new poems, of which each soul will be a strophe and in which each one will relive his life in that of the others. Then, ecstatic, the soul will throw itself into the light from above at the call of the envoys, of the winged spirits, of those who are called gods because they have escaped the cycle of rebirths. Led by these sublime intelligences, the soul will attempt to spell the great poem of the Hidden Word, to understand what it can grasp of the symphony of the universe.

The soul will receive the hierarchical teachings of the circles of divine Love; it will strive to behold the Essences which the animating spirits spread through the worlds; it will contemplate the glorified spirits, the living rays of the God of Gods; and it will not be able to bear their blinding splendor, which makes the suns appear pale like dim lamps. And when the soul returns, awed by these dazzling journeys, for it trembles at these immensities, it will hear from afar the call of beloved voices and will fall back upon the golden strands of its star, beneath the pink veil of a gentle sleep, filled with white forms, perfumes and melodies.

Such is the celestial life of the soul which we, dulled by earth, scarcely perceive, but which the initiates divine, the seers live and the law of analogies and universal concordances makes clear. Our crude pictures, our imperfect languages try vainly to translate it, but each living soul feels its essence in its own secret depths. If, in our present state we find it impossible to achieve this, the philosophy of the unseen formulates its psychic conditions for us. The idea of ethereal stars, invisible to us, but forming a part of our solar system and serving as a place of sojourn for happy souls, is often spoken of in the Mysteries and in esoteric tradition. Pythagoras calls it a counterpart of earth, the *antichthon* lighted by the central Fire, that is, by divine Light. At the end of his *Phaedo,* Plato describes this spiritual earth at length, although in a disguised manner. He says that it is as light as air and is surrounded by an ethereal atmosphere.

In the other life, therefore, the soul preserves all its individuality. It retains only the noble memories of its earthly existence and drops the others in that forgetfulness which the poets call Lethe. Freed from its impurities, the human soul feels its consciousness returning. It has passed from the outside of the universe to the inside; with a deep sigh, Cybele-Maia, the world-Soul, has taken it into her breast once again. There Psyche will complete her dream, that dream interrupted at every moment and unceasingly begun again on earth. She will complete it in proportion to her earthly effort and her acquired light, but she will enlarge it a hundredfold. Dashed hopes will flower again in the dawn of her divine life; the dark sunsets of earth will flame forth into shining days. Yes, if man lived but a single hour of ecstasy or abnegation, that single note, taken from the dissonant scale of his earthly life, will be repeated in his other life in wondrous progressions, in aeolian harmonies. The fleeting happiness the charms of music provide, the ecstasies of love, or the raptures of charity are but the separate notes of a symphony which we shall then hear.

Does this mean that the after-life will be only a long dream, a great illusion? What is more real than what the soul feels within it and what it sees fulfilled by its divine communion with other souls? As consistent and transcendent idealists, the initiates have always thought that the only real and durable things of earth are the manifestations of spiritual Beauty, Love and Truth. Since the other life can have no other goal than this Truth, Beauty and Love for those who have made it the aim of their life, they are certain that heaven will be more real than earth.

The celestial life of the soul can last hundreds of thousands of years, according to its rank and its impelling force. But it is the privilege of only the more perfect, the more sublime, those who have gone beyond the circle of generations to prolong it indefinitely. The former have reached not only temporary rest, but immoral activity in truth; they have created their wings. They are inviolable, for they are light; they govern the worlds, for they see beyond. As for the others, they are led by an inflexible law to be born again in order to undergo a new trial and to elevate themselves to a higher degree or to fall still lower if they fail.

Like earthly life, spiritual life has its beginning, its climax and its decline. When this life is exhausted, the soul feels overcome with heaviness, faintness and melancholy. An invincible force again draws it to the struggle and sufferings of earth. This desire is mixed with terrible apprehensions and a tremendous grief at leaving the divine life. But the time has come; the law must be fulfilled. The heaviness increases, a darkening takes place within it. It sees its luminous companions only through a veil, and this veil, growing ever thicker, causes the soul to sense the imminent separation. It hears their sad farewells; the tears of the happy loved ones permeate it like a celestial dew and will leave in its heart the burning thirst for a forgotten happiness. Then, with solemn vows it promises to *remember:* in the world of darkness to remember light, in the world of falsehood to remember truth, in the world of hate to remember love. Only at this price can the soul gain the return and the immortal crown. Now it awakens in a heavy atmosphere. Ethereal star, diaphanous souls, oceans of light,—all have disappeared. Again the soul is on earth, in the vale of birth and death. Nevertheless, it has not yet lost its celestial memory, and its winged guide, still visible to its eyes, points out the woman who will be its mother. The latter carries within her the seed of a child. But this seed will live only if the spirit comes to animate it. Then, during nine months is accomplished the most impenetrable mystery of earthly life, that of incarnation and maternity.

The mysterious fusion takes place slowly, systematically, organ by organ, fiber by fiber. As the soul is plunged into this warm cave which makes a confused sound and which enlarges, as it feels itself taken into the organism, the consciousness of divine life fades and dies away. For between the soul and the light from above are interspersed waves of blood, tissues of flesh, which bind it and fill it with darkness. Already this distant light is no more than a dying flicker. Finally, dreadful pain compresses it, pressing it into a vice, a bloody convulsion tears it from the maternal soul and fixes it within a throbbing body. —The child is born, a pitiful earthly image, and he cries with fright. But the memory of heaven has returned to the secret depths of the unconscious. It will live again only by science or by pain, by love or by death!

The law of incarnation and excarnation emphasizes the real meaning of life and death. It constitutes the main link in the evolution of the soul, allowing us to follow the latter backward and forward to the depths of nature and of divinity. For this law reveals to us the rhythm and measure, the reason and purpose of immortality. Taking the latter out of the abstract or the fantastic, it makes it alive and logical by showing the correspondences between life and death. Earthly birth is a death from the spiritual point of view, and death is a heavenly birth. The alternation between the two lives is necessary for the development of the soul, and each of the two is both the result and explanation of the other. Whoever has fathomed these truths has arrived at the very heart of the Mysteries, at the center of initiation.

But, you will say, what is there to prove to us the continuity of the soul, of the monad and of the spiritual entity throughout all these existences, since it successively loses memory? And what, we reply, proves to you the identity of your self while you are awake and asleep? You awaken each morning from a strange state as inexplicable as death, you revive from this nothingness, only to fall back into it again in the evening. Was it nothingness? No, for you have dreamed, and for you your dreams have been as real as the reality of waking. A change of the psysiological conditions of the brain has modified the relationships of soul and body and has altered your psychic viewpoint. You were the same individual, but you found yourself in another environment and you were leading another existence. With hypnotized persons, somnambulists and clairvoyants, sleep acquires new faculties which to us seem miraculous but are the natural faculties of the soul when it is detached from the body. Once awakened, these clairvoyants no longer remember what they saw, said and did during their sleep. However, in one of their sleeps, they recall perfectly what happened in the preceding sleep and sometimes foretell with mathematical exactness what will happen in the next one. Therefore they have two consciousnesses, two distinctly alternating lives, but each has its rational continuity and revolves around the same individual.

It is therefore in a very deep sense that the ancient initiate poets called sleep *the brother of death*. For a veil of forgetfulness separates sleeping from waking as it does birth from death. As our earthly life is divided into two alternating parts, so in the immensity of its cosmic evolution the soul alternates between incarnation and spiritual life, between earth and heaven. This alternate passage from one plane of the universe to another is no less necessary to the development of the soul than are the alternations of waking and sleeping to the corporeal life of man. We need the waves of Lethe as we pass from one existence to another. In the present, a salutary veil hides past and the future from us. But the forgetfulness is not complete, and light penetrates through the veil. Innate ideas in themselves prove an anterior existence. But there is more; we are born with a world of vague recollections, mysterious impulses and divine feelings. Among children born of gentle, calm parents are sometimes observed eruptions of wild passions which atavism does not suffice to explain, and which come from a preceding existence. Sometimes in the most humble life is to be found unexplained, sublime faithfulness to an emotion, an ideal. Do these not come from the promises and vows of celestial life? For the hidden memory which the soul has preserved is stronger than all earthly reasoning. Depending upon whether the soul becomes attached to this memory or abandons it, does it conquer or succumb. Real faith is that speechless fidelity of the soul to itself. Therefore one perceives that Pythagoras considered corporeal life to be a necessary extension of the will and celestial life to be a spiritual growth and fulfillment.

Lives follow but do not resemble one another, yet with merciless logic they form a sequence. If each of them has its own law and its special destiny, their succession is governed by a general law which can be called *the repercussion of lives*.[58] According to this law, the deeds of one life have their fatal repercussion in the following life. Not only will man be born again with the instincts and faculties he developed in his preceding incarnation, but the nature of his existence itself will be determined in a large measure by the good or evil use he made of his freedom in the preceding life. "There is no word or action which does not have its echo in Eternity," says a proverb. According to esoteric doctrine this proverb is literally applicable from one life to another.

For Pythagoras, the apparent injustices of destiny, the deformities, miseries, strokes of fate,—misfortunes of all kinds—have their explanation in the fact that each existence is the reward or punishment of the one preceding. A criminal life engenders a life of expiation; an imperfect life, a life of trials. A good life leads to a task; a higher life, to a creative mission. Retribution, which is applied with seeming imperfection from the point of view of a single life, is therefore applied with admirable perfection and minute justice in the sequence of lives. In this sequence there can be progression toward spirituality and intelligence as well as regression toward bestiality and gross materialism. As the soul climbs, by degrees it acquires a greater share in the choice of reincarnations. The inferior soul is subject to the latter; the average soul chooses among those offered to it; the superior soul, who imposes a mission upon itself, chooses reincarnation through self-sacrifice. The higher the soul, the more it preserves in its incarnations the clear and unbroken consciousness of the spiritual life which reigns beyond our earthly horizon, surrounding it like a sphere of light and sending its rays into our darkness. Tradition even has it that the initiator of the first order, the divine prophets of humanity, remembered their preceding earthly lives. According to legend, Gautama Buddha, Sakya-Muni, had found in his ecstasies the thread of his past existences, and of Pythagoras it is said that he claimed he owed the remembrance of some of his former lives to a special favor of the gods.

We have said that in the series of repeated earth lives the soul can regress or advance, depending upon whether it surrenders itself to its lower or to its divine nature. In all lives there are struggles to bear, choices to make, decisions to be formed, the consequences of which cannot be determined. But on the ascending path of good, extending through a long series of incarnations, there must be a lifetime, a year, a day, perhaps an hour when the soul, arriving at a full awareness of good and evil, with a final, supreme effort can lift itself to a height from which it will not have to descend again, and where the way to the heights begins. Likewise, on the descending road of evil, there is a point where the soul can still turn back. But once this point is passed, the hardening is definitive. From incarnation to incarnation it will roll at last to the bottom of darkness. It will lose its humanity. Man will become demon, an animal demon, and his indestructible monad will be forced to begin again the painful, dreadful evolution through a long series of ascending kingdoms and innumerable existences. This is the real Hell, in harmony with the law of spiritual evolution, and is this not as terrible and even more logical than that of exoteric religions?

The soul therefore can climb or descend in the course of its series of incarnations. As for earthly mankind, its journey takes place according to the law of an ascending progression, which is a part of the divine order. This truth, which perhaps we may believe to be a recent discovery, actually was known and taught in the ancient Mysteries. "Animals are relatives of man, and man is the relative of the gods," said Pythagoras. He developed philosophically what the symbols of Eleusis also taught: the progression of ascending kingdoms, the striving from the vegetable world to the animal world, from the animal world to the human world, and in humanity the succession of more and more perfect races. This progression is not accomplished in a uniform manner, but in regular and increasing cycles, enclosed one within the other. Each people has its childhood, its maturity, its decline. It is the same with races as a whole: the red race, the black race, the white race who in turn have reigned on the globe. The white race, still in the fullness of youth, has not yet reached its maturity. At its height it will develop a perfected race out of itself through the reestablishment of initiation and through spiritual selection in marriages. Thus races follow one another; thus mankind progresses.

The ancient initiates went much farther in their forecasts than do modern men. They said that a time would come when the great mass of individuals who compose contemporary humanity would pass to another planet in order to begin a new cycle. In the series of cycles which constitute the planetary chain, all mankind will develop those intellectual, spiritual, transcendent principles which the great initiates cultivated in themselves, and thus humanity will come to a more general efflorescence. Needless to say, such a development embraces not only thousands, but millions of years, and it will bring about such changes in the condition of mankind that we cannot even imagine them. In an attempt to characterize them, Plato said that in that future age, the gods really will inhabit the temples of men. It is logical to conclude that in the planetary chain, that is, in the successive evolutions of humanity on other planets, mankind's incarnations become of an ever more ethereal nature, which will bring them unconsciously closer to the purely spiritual state, that eighth sphere which is beyond the circle of generations and by which the ancient initiates indicated the divine state.

What then is the final goal of man and mankind, according to esoteric doctrine? After so many lives, deaths, rebirths, intervals and reawakenings, what is the end of Psyche's labors? The initiates say that the goal will have been attained when the soul will have decisively conquered matter; when, developing all its spiritual faculties, the soul will have found within itself the principle and goal of all. Then, since incarnation will be no longer necessary, the soul will enter the divine state through a complete union with divine intelligence. For Pythagoras, the apotheosis of man was not submersion into unconsciousness but creative activity in supreme consciousness. The soul, having become pure spirit, does not lose its individuality; it terminates it, since it rejoins its archetype in God. It remembers all its anterior existences, which seem to it like so many stepping-stones, necessary in order to reach the stage where it embraces and penetrates the universe. In this state, man is no longer man, as Pythagoras said; he is a demigod. For in all his being he reflects the ineffable Light whose immensity is God. For Pythagoras, knowledge is power; loving means creating; existing means radiating truth and beauty.

Is this boundary definitive? Spiritual Eternity has other measures than solar time; it has its own stages, norms and cycles, and these are entirely beyond human conception. But the law of progressive analogies in the ascending kingdoms of nature allows us to affirm that once spirit has reached this sublime state it can no longer regress. Therefore, even if the visible worlds change and pass away, the invisible world, which is its own reason for being, is immortal.

With these luminous perspectives Pythagoras concluded the story of the divine Psyche. The last word had died away on the lips of the sage, but the meaning of the incommunicable Truth remained suspended in the motionless air of the crypt. Each listener thought he had finished the dream of lives and was awakening in great peace, borne upon the sweet ocean of the one, endless life. The naphtha lamps softly lighted the statue of Persephone, standing there in the form of the Celestial Reaper, causing her symbolic story to come to life in the sacred frescoes of the sanctuary. At times a priestess, entering into a state of ecstasy at the harmonious voice of Pythagoras, seemed in her attitude and in her shining face to incarnate the ineffable beauty of her vision. And the disciples, seized with a religious ecstasy, looked on in silence. But soon, with a calm and certain gesture, the master brought the "inspired" prophetess back to earth. Slowly her features relaxed, she slumped into the arms of her companions and fell into a deep lethargy from which she awakened troubled, sad and exhausted from her journey.

Then they went out from the crypt and entered into the gardens of Ceres, into the freshness of dawn, which began to turn the sea white at the margin of the starry sky.

FOURTH STAGE—EPIPHANY

The Adept—The Woman Initiate—Love and Marriage

With Pythagoras we have reached the summit of ancient initiation. From this summit, earth appears in deep shadow like a dying star. From above, sidereal perspectives open and like a marvelous unity the Epiphany of the Universe unfolds.[59] But the purpose of the teaching was not to absorb man in contemplation or ecstasy. The master had walked with his disciples in the measureless regions of the cosmos; he had plunged with them into the depths of the Invisible. From this awesome journey the true initiates were to return to earth better, stronger and more suited for the tests of life than before.

The initiation of the intelligence was to be followed by that of the will, the most difficult of all. For now it was for the disciple to cause truth to descend into the depths of his being, to apply it in his daily life. To attain this, according to Pythagoras it was necessary to bring together three perfections: to realize truth in the intellect, virtue in the soul and purity in the body. A wise hygiene and temperate continence was to preserve corporeal purity. This was required not as an end, but as a means. All bodily excess leaves a trace, a stain, as it were, in the astral body, the living organism of the soul, and also in the spirit. For the astral body contributes to all the deeds of the physical body, in fact, it effects them since without it the material body is an inert mass. It is necessary, therefore, for the body to be pure in order that the soul also may be pure. Therefore, in the constant light of intelligence the soul must acquire courage, abnegation, devotion and faith—in short, virtue, and make of the latter a second nature which substitutes for the first. Finally, it is necessary for the intellect to attain the wisdom to distinguish good and evil in everything, and to see God in the smallest of beings as well as in the totality of worlds.

At this height man becomes an "adept," and if he is able to summon sufficient energy, he enters into possession of new faculties and powers. The inner senses of the soul open and will radiate into the outer faculties. His bodily forces, penetrated by the effluvia of his astral nature, electrified by his will, acquire a seemingly miraculous power. In certain instances he is able to heal the sick by the laying on of hands, or by his presence alone. Often he reads the thoughts of men at a single glance. Sometimes in the waking state he sees events which are taking place afar off.[60] From a distance, through the concentration of thought and will, he acts upon persons who are attached to him by bonds of personal sympathy, causing his image to appear to them as though his astral body could be transported outside his physical body. Finally, the adept feels himself surrounded and protected by invisible, higher, luminous Beings who lend him their strength and help him in his mission.

Rare are the adepts; rarer still are those who attain this power. Greece knew but three: Orpheus, at the dawn of Hellenism; Pythagoras, at its height; Apollonius of Tyana, in its decline. Orpheus was the great inspired one, the great initiator of Greek religion; Pythagoras, the organizer of esoteric science and the philosophy of the Schools; Apollonius, the Stoic moralist and the popular magician of the period of decadence. But in all three the divine fire shines; their spirits are aflame for the well-being of souls, their undaunted energy is clothed with gentleness and serenity. But one must not come too close to those great, calm countenances. One feels the furnace of ardent but eternally controlled will burning underneath.

Pythagoras represents an adept of the first rank who is most accessible to the modern mind. But he himself could not, nor did he pretend to make perfect adepts of his disciples. A great age always has a great inspirer at its inception. His disciples and their pupils form the magnetic chain which spreads his thought through the world. At the fourth stage of initiation Pythagoras therefore contented himself with teaching his faithful ones the application of his doctrines in life. For "Epiphany," seen from a higher viewpoint, provided a collection of deep and regenerating attitudes toward earthly things.

The origin of good and evil remains an incomprehensible mystery for one who has not taken into account the origin and end of things. A morality which does not consider the supreme destinies of man will be only utilitarian and very imperfect. Moreover, real human freedom does not exist for those who are slaves of their passions, and it rightfully does not exist for those who do not believe in the soul or in God, those for whom life is a lightning bolt between two vacuums. The first live in bondage to the soul, chained by passions; the second, in bondage to the intellect limited to the physical world. This is not true for the religious man, for the true philosopher, and certainly not for the initiate, who recognized truth in the threefoldness of his being.

In order to understand the origin of good and evil, the initiate looks at *the three worlds* with the eye of the spirit. He sees the dark world of matter and animality where ineluctable *Destiny* reigns. He sees the luminous world of the Spirit, which for us is the invisible world, the great hierarchy of freed souls where divine law reigns. These freed souls are *Providence in action.* Between the two he sees mankind rooted in the natural world on the one hand and touching the summits of the divine world on the other. The genius of humanity is Freedom, for from the moment man perceives truth and error, he is free to choose between them. He is at liberty to unite with Providence in fulfilling truth, or to fall under the law of Fate by following falsehood. Evil causes man to descend toward the fatality of matter; Good causes him to climb toward the divine law of Spirit. Man's real destiny is forever to climb higher by his own effort. But in order to do this, he must also be free to descend again.

The scope of freedom widens to the infinitely great as one ascends; it shrinks to the infinitely small as one descends. The higher one climbs, the freer one becomes; the more one enters into the light, the more one acquires strength for good. The more one descends, the more one becomes a slave, because each fall into evil weakens one's understanding of truth and one's capacity for doing good. Therefore, destiny reigns over the past, Freedom, over the future, and Providence, over both. Providence rules over the ever-existing present, which can be called Eternity.[61]

From the combined action of Destiny, Freedom and Providence come innumerable destinies, hells and paradises of souls. Evil, being a lack of accord with divine law, is not the work of God but of man. It has only a relative, illusory, temporal existence. Good, since it is in accord with divine law, has a real, eternal existence. The priests of Delphi and Eleusis, as well as the philosopher- initiates never wished to reveal these profound ideas to the people, for the latter would have understood them only imperfectly and would have abused them. In the Mysteries this doctrine was symbolically represented by the dismemberment of Dionysus, thus hiding what were called "the sufferings of God" beneath an impenetrable veil for the uninitiated.

Another major factor in social and political relationships is the inequality of *human conditions*. The spectacle of evil and pain is something frightening in itself. In addition, the distribution of these two, apparently arbitrary and unjust, is the source of all hatreds, revolts and denials. Here again as in the problem of the origin of good and evil, esoteric wisdom brings into our earthly darkness its sovereign light of peace and hope. As a matter of fact, the diversity of souls, conditions and destinies cannot be justified *except* by the plurality of existences, and by the teaching of reincarnation. If a man is born for the first time into this life, how can one explain the numberless evils which seem to fall upon him? How can one believe that there is eternal justice, when some men are born into a condition which brings misery and humiliation while others are born into good fortune and live happily? However, if it is true that we have lived previous lives, that we shall live still others after death, that over all these existences rules the law of recurrence and repercussion, then the differences of soul, of condition and of destiny are but the effects of former lives and represent the manifold applications of this law. Differences in human conditions stem from an unwise use of freedom in preceding lives, while differences in human intelligence arise from the fact that men go through earth existences in highly varying stages of evolution, extending all the way from the primitive conditions of backward peoples to the angelic states of saints and even to the divine royalty of genius.

In reality, earth resembles a boat, and all of us who inhabit it are travelers who come from far countries and are scattered to all points of the horizon. The teaching of reincarnation gives a reason for existence in line with justice and eternal logic. It explains the cause of the most frightening evil as well as the most desirable happiness. All physical and moral suffering, all happiness and unhappiness, will appear in their manifold aspects as the natural and wise fruits of the instincts and actions, the mistakes and virtues of a long past. For in its hidden depths the soul preserves all that it accumulates in its various earth lives. Lysis expresses this truth under a veil in his *Golden Verses:*

PYTHAGORAS

You will see that the evils which devour men
Are the fruit of their choice; and that these unhappy ones
Seek far from them the good whose source they bear.

Far from weakening the sentiment of fraternity and human solidarity, the teaching of reincarnation can but reinforce it. We owe help, sympathy and charity to all, for all of us are of the same human race, though at various stages of development. All suffering is sacred, for pain is the crucible of souls. All sympathy is divine, for it makes us feel the invisible chain which links all worlds. The virtue of grief is the reason of genius. Indeed, sages and saints, prophets and divine creators shine with a more supernal beauty for those who know that they too have come out of universal evolution. How many lives, how many victories were required for this power which amazes us? From what heavens already traversed does this inborn light of genius come? We do not know. But these lives have been, and these heavens exist. Therefore the conscience of nations is not mistaken, the prophets did not lie when they called men the sons of God, the ambassadors of the Most High. For their mission is willed by eternal Truth; invisible legions protect them, and in them speaks the living Word!

Among men is a diversity which comes from the primitive essence of individuals. Another, as has been said, arises from the degree of spiritual evolution which men have attained. From the latter point of view one recognizes that men can be grouped in four categories, comprising all subdivisions and variations:

1st. For the great majority of men, the will acts mainly in the body. Therefore they can be called *instinctive persons*. Their activity is not only physical, but also includes the exercise and development of their intelligence in this world. Hence they have a genius for commerce and industry.

2nd. At the second stage of human development the will and

351

consciousness reside in the soul, that is, in sensitivity reacted upon by intelligence, which constitutes understanding. These are the *spirited* or *passionate* persons. By temperament they are adapted to be soldiers, artists or poets. The great majority of men of letters and scientists are of this type, for they live in relative ideas, modified by passions or bound by a limited horizon without having risen to the pure idea or universality.

3rd. In a third class of much rarer men the will has acquired the habit of acting principally in the pure intellect. It works to free intelligence from the tyranny of passions and limitations. This gives all their concepts the character of universality. These are the *intellectuals*. These men are the hero-martyrs, the poets of the first rank and above all, the true philosophers and sages, who, according to Pythagoras and Plato, should govern humanity. In these men passion is not extinct, for without passion nothing is done. Passion constitutes the fire and electricity of the moral world. However, among these men the passions have become the servants of intelligence, while in the second category, the intelligence is frequently the servant of the passions.

4th. The highest human ideal is realized by the fourth group of men. To the majestic control of soul and instincts by intelligence, they have added dominion over all their being. Through the mastery and control of all their faculties they exercise the great mastery. They have brought about a unity in the human threefoldness. Thanks to this marvelous concentration of all the powers of life, their will acquires an almost unlimited strength, an all-pervading, creative magic. These men have had various names in history. They are *the archetypal men, the adepts, the great initiates,* the sublime geniuses who transform humanity. They are extremely rare in history; Providence dispenses them upon earth at long intervals of time, like stars in the sky.[62]

It is evident that this last category of human beings is beyond rule or classification. But a constitution of human society which does not take into account the first three categories, which does not provide each of them with its normal life and the necessary means of developing, is merely external and is not organic. It is evident that in a primitive age, which probably dates from Vedic times, the Brahmans of India established the division of society into castes on the threefold principle. But with time this highly just and fruitful division changed into priestly and aristocratic privilege. The principle of vocation and initiation gave way to that of heredity. The closed castes ended by becoming petrified, and the irremediable decadence of India followed.

Under the reigns of all the Pharaohs, Egypt preserved the threefold constitution with its open and mobile castes. The principle of initiation applied to the priesthood, and that of examination to all civil and military functionaries; this arrangement continued for five to six thousand years without changing its form. As for Greece, its volatile temperament caused it to pass rapidly from aristocracy to democracy, from democracy to tyranny. It revolved in this vicious circle like a sick person who goes from fever to lethargy, only to return to fever. Perhaps it needed this stimulus in order to produce its unique work: the translation of the profound but obscure wisdom of the Orient into a clear, universal language, the creation of the Beautiful through art, and the establishment of exoteric, rational science following secret, intuitional initiation. Greece also owed her religious organization and her highest inspirations to this principle of initiation. Socially and politically speaking, it can be said that she always lived in the provisional and in the excessive. In his capacity as an adept, from the heights of initiation, Pathagoras understood the eternal principles which rule society, and pursued the plan of a great re-

353

form according to these truths. We shall see how he and his school were shipwrecked in the storms of democracy.

From the pure summits of his teaching the life of worlds unfolds in harmony with the rhythms of eternity. What a splendid Epiphany! But in the magic rays of the unveiled firmament, earth, humanity and life also reveal their hidden depths to us. One must find the infinitely great in the infinitely small in order to feel the presence of God. This is what the disciples of Pythagoras experienced when, as the crown of his teaching, their master showed them how eternal truth is manifest in the union of man and woman in marriage. They were about to find in the very heart of life the beauty of the sacred numbers which they had heard and viewed in Infinity, and God would shine forth for them out of the great mysteries of the sexes and of love.

Antiquity understood a major truth which the succeeding ages have all too greatly misunderstood. In order to fulfill her functions of wife and mother, woman needs instruction, a special initiation. Hence purely feminine initiation, that is, one entirely reserved for women, existed in India in Vedic times, and the woman was the priestess at the domestic altar. In Egypt this initiation dates back to the Mysteries of Isis. Orpheus organized it in Greece. Until the extermination of paganism it flourished in the Dionysian Mysteries as well as in the temples of Juno, Diana, Minerva and Ceres. It consisted in symbolic rites, ceremonies, nocturnal festivals and in special teaching given by the older priestesses or by the high priest, and dealt with the most intimate things of conjugal life. Advice and rules concerning the relationship between the sexes as well as information on times of the year and of each month favorable to successful conception were given. The greatest importance was placed upon physical and moral hygiene of the woman during pregnancy so that the sacred work, the creation of the child, might be accomplished according to divine laws. In brief, the science of conjugal life and the art of maternity were taught. The latter extended far beyond the birth of the child.

Until seven years of age, the children remained in the gyneceum, which the husband did not enter, under the exclusive care of the mother. The wisdom of antiquity considered the child to be a delicate plant which needs the arm of maternal environment in order not to become stunted. It was believed that the father would deform the child. Therefore in order to cause it to unfold properly the kisses and caresses of the mother were considered necessary. The powerful, enveloping love of woman is needed to defend the soul, frightened by the attacks of external life. Because in full consciousness she fulfilled these lofty functions considered divine by antiquity, woman was really the priestess of the family, the guardian of the sacred fire of life, the Vesta of the hearth. Feminine initiation therefore can be considered the true cause of the beauty of the race, of the power of generation, the continuance of families in ancient Greece and Rome.

By establishing a section for women in his institute, Pythagoras only refined and intensified what had existed before him. Through him, along with the rites and precepts, the woman initiates received the supreme principles of their function. Thus he gave to those who were worthy the consciousness of their role. He revealed to them the transfiguration of love in perfect marriage, in other words, the interpenetration of two souls at the very center of life and truth. In his power, man is the representative of principle and of creative mind. Woman personifies nature in its plastic force, in its marvelous earthly and divine achievements. Therefore, when these two beings succeed in entering into one another completely, into body, soul and spirit, they will form by themselves a miniature of the universe.

But in order to believe in God, woman needs to see Him living in man. For this reason, man must be initiated. Man alone, through his profound knowledge of life and his creative will, can fertilize the feminine soul, thus transforming it through the divine ideal. And the beloved woman transmits this ideal to him, multiplied in her vibrant thoughts, in her subtle sensations, in her profound insights. She transmits to him his image, transfigured by enthusiasm, because she *becomes* his ideal. For *she brings this about* through the power of love in her own soul. Through her his ideal becomes alive and visible; it becomes flesh and blood. Man creates through desire and will; woman physically and spiritually generates through love.

In her role as lover, wife, mother, or inspired one, woman is no less great, and is even more divine than man. For to love is to forget. Woman, forgetting herself, lost in her love, is always sublime. In this forgetfulness she finds her celestial rebirth, her crown of life, the immortal radiation of her being.

Love has reigned as master in literature for two centuries. This is not the purely sensual love which lights up at the beauty of the body, as with the ancient poets; neither is it the tasteless cult of an abstract, conventional ideal, as in the Middle Ages. No, this is love both sensual and psychic which, released in full freedom and in complete individual fantasy, gives itself unbounded expression.

Frequently the two sexes make war on one another, even in love. This takes the form of a revolt of woman against the egotism and brutality of man, the disdain of man for woman's infidelity. Vanity, expressing itself in cries of flesh, and powerless rage of the victims of pleasure, makes them slaves of debauchery. Here, profound passions and attractions become all the more powerful when they are bettered by the worldly conventions of social institutions. Hence those loves, filled with tempest, moral collapse and tragic catastrophe, around which the modern novel and drama revolve almost exclusively.

Weary, finding God neither in science nor in religion, man seeks Him desperately in woman. And he does well, but it is only through the initiation into the great truths that he will find God in her, and she will find God in him. Between these souls who know neither each other nor themselves, who sometimes leave one another with curses, there is a deep thirst to penetrate one another and to find in this fusion impossible happiness. In spite of the aberrations and outbursts which result, this desperate search is necessary; it comes from a *divine unconsciousness*. It will be a vital point in the rebuilding of the future. For when man and woman have found each other through deep love and initiation, their union will be a radiating and creative power *par excellence*.

Psychic love, the love-passion of the soul, has entered literature comparatively recently, and through it, universal consciousness. But it has its origin in ancient initiation. If Greek literature scarcely lets the existence of psychic love be suspected, this is due to the fact that it was a profound secret of the Mysteries. Nevertheless, religious and philosophical tradition has preserved the trace of the initiate woman. Behind official poetry and philosophy a few female forms appear, half-veiled but luminous. We already know the Pythoness Theoclea who inspired Pythagoras; later will come the priestess Corinne, the often successful rival of Pindar, himself the most initiated of the Greek lyricists; finally, the mysterious Diotime appears in Plato's *Banquet* to give the supreme revelation of love.

Beside these exceptional roles, the Greek woman exercised her function as a veritable priestess in the home and in the gyneceum. Those heroes, artists and poets whose songs, works in marble and sublime deeds we admire, were rightly her own creation. It was she who conceived them in the mystery of love, who molded them in her womb with the desire for beauty, who caused them to unfold by nestling them under her maternal wings. In addition, for a man and a woman who are truly initiated, the creation of the child has an infinitely more beautiful meaning, a greater import than otherwise. When father and mother know that the soul of the child exists before its earthly birth, conception becomes a sacred act, the call of a soul to incarnation. Between the incarnated soul and the mother is almost always a great degree of similarity. As evil, perverse women attract demonic spirits, tender mothers attract divine spirits.

Is this invisible soul which one awaits and which will come and go so mysteriously and so certainly, not a thing divine? Its birth, its imprisonment in flesh, will be a painful thing, for between it and the heaven it has left behind, a crude veil is interposed. If it ceases to remember, it will suffer no less! And sacred and divine is the task of the mother, who must create for it a new home, must make its prison livable, its trial easier to bear.

Thus, the teaching of Pythagoras which had begun in the depths of the Absolute with the divine Trinity, ended in the very center of life with the human trinity. In the father, mother and child, the initiate now knew how to recognize Spirit, Soul and Heart of the living Universe. For him this last initiation constituted the foundation of a social work conceived in all the sublimity and beauty of the ideal,—a creation to which each initiate was to bring a building-stone.

34

The Family of Pythagoras —
The School and its Destiny

AMONG the women who followed the teaching of the master was a young girl of great beauty. Her father, a Croton, was named Brontinos; her own name was Theano. At that time Pythagoras was nearly sixty, but great self-mastery of passions and a pure life entirely dedicated to his mission had preserved his manly strength. Youthfulness of soul, that immortal flame which the great initiate draws from his spiritual life and which he nourishes with the hidden forces of nature, shone in him. The Greek Magus was not in his decline, but at the summit of his power. Theano was attracted to Pythagoras by the almost supernatural radiance which emanated from his being. Serious and reserved, she had sought from the master an explanation concerning those Mysteries which she loved without understanding them. But when in the light of truth, in the gentle warmth which slowly enveloped her, she felt her soul open within her like a mystical rose of a thousand petals, when she felt that this unfolding came from him and from his speech, she was drawn to the master with a boundless rapture and a passionate love.

Pythagoras had not sought to attract her. His affection belonged to all his disciples. He was dreaming only of his school, of Greece, of the future of the world. Like many great adepts, he had given up the love of woman in order to devote himself fully to his work. The magic of his will, the spiritual possession of so many souls which he had guided and who remained attached to him as to an adored father, the mystical incense of all these unexpressed loves and that exquisite perfume of human sympathy which united the Pythagorean brothers,—for him, all of this took the place of pleasure, happiness and love. But one day when he was alone, meditating on the future of his school in the crypt of Proserpine, he saw coming to him that beautiful and serious virgin to whom he had never spoken in private. She knelt before him, and without lifting her head, she begged the master to free her from an impossible and unhappy love which was consuming her body and devouring her soul. Pythagoras asked the name of the one whom she loved. After long hesitation, Theano confessed that it was he himself, but at the same time she said that she would submit to his will. Pythagoras said nothing. Encouraged by his silence, she lifted her head and looked toward him pleadingly, offering him the essence of her life and the perfume of her soul.

The sage was disturbed; he knew how to conquer his senses, he had subdued his imagination, but the light of this soul had penetrated him. In this virgin, matured by passion, transfigured by absolute devotion, he had found his life-companion and had glimpsed a more complete fulfillment of his work. Pythagoras raised the young girl to her feet and drew her to him.

In the master's eyes Theano could read that their destinies were joined forever.

PYTHAGORAS

By his marriage to Theano, Pythagoras placed *the seal of fulfillment* upon his work. The union, the fusion of two lives was complete. One day when the wife of the master was asked how much time is necessary for a woman to become pure after having had relationship with a man, she answered, "If it is with her husband, she *is* pure immediately; if it is with another, she *never* is pure."

It is not marriage which sanctifies love; it is love which justifies marriage. Theano entered so completely into the thought of her husband that after his death she served as the center of the Pythagorean Order, and a Greek author quotes as an authority her opinion on the doctrine of numbers. She gave Pythagoras two sons, Arimnestus and Telaugus, and one daughter, Damo. Telaugus later became the tutor of Empedocles and transmitted to him the secrets of the teaching.

Pythagoras' was a model family. His house was called the temple of Ceres, and his court, the temple of the Muses. In the family and religious festivals the mother led the chorus of women, and Damo, the chorus of young girls. Damo was worthy of her father and mother in every way. Pythagoras had entrusted certain writings to her with the express prohibition against communicating them to anyone outside the family. After the dispersal of the Pythagoreans, Damo fell into extreme poverty. She was offered a large sum for the valuable manuscript, but faithful to the wish of her father, she always refused to surrender it.

Pythagoras lived in Croton for thirty years. At the end of twenty years this extraordinary man had acquired such power that those who called him a demigod did not exaggerate. His influence was something tremendous; never has any philosopher exercised anything equal to it. It extended not only to the school at Croton and to its branches in the other cities of the Italian coast, but also to the political life of all those little states. Pythagoras was a reformer in every sense of the word. Croton, an Achaean colony, had an aristocratic constitution. *The Council of One Thousand,* composed of representatives of great families, exercised the legislative and supervised the executive power. Popular assemblies existed, but their activities were restricted. Pythagoras wanted the state to be an order and a harmony and liked oligarchic restraint no better than the chaos of demagoguery. Accepting the Dorian constitution as it was, he simply tried to introduce a new method of activity into it. His courageous plan was to establish over and above the political authority a scientific power having a deliberative and consultative voice in vital questions. This scientific power was to be the keystone, the supreme regulator of the state. Over the Council of One Thousand he organized *The Council of Three Hundred,* chosen by the first, but recruited from among the initiates alone. Their number was sufficient for this. Porphyrus relates that two thousand citizens of Croton gave up their customary life and assembled themselves together to live a communal life along with their wives and children, after having given over their property to the community. In control of the state Pythagoras therefore wanted a scientific government, less secret, but as highly placed as the Egyptian priesthood. What he effected for a moment remained the dream of all the initiates who participated in political life. He introduced the principle of initiation and examination into the government of the state and reconciled in this higher synthesis the elective or democratic principle with a government formed on the basis of intelligence and virtue. Hence the Council of Three Hundred formed a kind of political, scientific and religious order, whose recognized leader was Pythagoras. By a solemn and awesome vow they pledged him secrecy as absolute as that of the Mysteries. These societies or *Hetaries* spread out from Croton, where the parent society was formed, into almost all the cities of Greater Greece, where they exercised a great political influence. The Pythagorean Order had as its goal to become the head of the state in all of southern Italy. Branches existed in Tarente, Heraclea, Metapontus, Regium, Himere, Catane, Agrigente, Sybaris and, according to Aristoxenus, even among the Etruscans. As for the influence of Pythagoras on the government of these great, rich cities, one cannot imagine one higher, more liberal, or more peaceful. Everywhere he appeared he reestablished order, justice and concord. Summoned before a tyrant of Sicily, by his eloquence alone he persuaded the latter to give up ill-acquired riches and restore rights he had stolen. Cities that were in bondage to one another, he set free. So beneficent were Pythagoras' deeds that everywhere he went people said, "He has not come to teach, but to heal!"

The sovereign influence of a great spirit, a great character, that magic of the soul and of the intellect, stirs up terrible jealousies and violent hatreds, just because it is invulnerable. Pythagoras' power lasted for a quarter of a century. The indefatigable adept had attained the age of ninety when reaction came. The spark came from Sybaris, the rival of Croton. An uprising took place there, and the aristocratic party was defeated. Five hundred exiles asked the Crotons for asylum, but the Sybarites demanded their extradition. Fearing the anger of an enemy city, the magistrates of Croton were about to give way to their demand when Pythagoras intervened. Upon his entreaties, the Crotons refused to surrender the unfortunate fugitives to their implacable adversaries. At this refusal, Sybaris declared war on Croton, but the army of the Crotons, led by the famous athlete Milon, a disciple of Pythagoras, completely defeated the Sybarites. The fall of Sybaris followed. The city was conquered, sacked, utterly destroyed, and was turned into a wilderness. It is impossible to claim that Pythagoras approved such reprisals, for they were contrary to his principles and those of all initiates. But neither he nor Milon could bridle the uncontrolled passions of a victorious army, aroused by ancient jealousies and stimulated by an infamous attack.

All vengeance, whether of individuals or of peoples, brings in return a recoil of the passions thus unleashed. The nemesis of the latter was fearful; the consequences fell upon Pythagoras and on his entire Order. After the sack of Sybaris, the people demanded the division of lands. Not satisfied with this, the democratic party proposed a change in the constitution which removed the privileges of the Council of One Thousand and suppressed the Council of Three Hundred, allowing only a single authority and demanding universal suffrage. Naturally the Pythagoreans who were part of the Council of One Thousand were opposed to a reform contrary to their principles, and one which attacked the patient work of the master at its roots. Already the Pythagoreans were the object of that blind hatred which mystery and superiority always stimulate in the mob. Their political attitude brought the fury of demagoguery upon them, and a personal hatred against the master caused the final explosion.

A certain Cylon had once presented himself for admission into the school. Pythagoras, who was very strict in admitting disciples, rejected him because of his violent, imperious nature. This rejected candidate became a bitter opponent. When public opinion began to turn against Pythagoras, he organized a large body of people in opposition to the Order of the Pythagoreans. Cylon succeeded in gathering around him the principal leaders of the people, and began to plot a revolution which was to begin with the expulsion of the Pythagoreans.

Before a surging mob, Cylon climbs to the rostrum and reads extracts stolen from the secret book of Pythagoras, titled *The Holy Word, Hieros Logos*. The teachings are distorted, dishonored. A few orators try to defend the brothers of silence who respect even animals, but the speakers are received with bursts of laughter. Cylon mounts and remounts the tribunal. He claims that the religious catechism of the Pythagoreans attacks freedom. "And that is saying little," adds the tribune. "Who is this teacher, this so-called demigod, who is blindly obeyed and who has only one word for the brothers, 'the master said so!'? What creates this indissoluble friendship uniting all the members of the Pythagorean *hetaries,* if not disdain and scorn for the people? Always they have the words of Homer on their lips, that the prince must be the shepherd of his people. For them, therefore, the people are but a stupid mob! Yes, the very existence of the Order is a permanent conspiracy against popular rights! As long as he is not destroyed, there will be no freedom in Croton!"

One of the members of the popular assembly, moved by feelings of loyalty, cried out, "At least let Pythagoras and the Pythagoreans come and justify themselves on our rostrum before condemning them!" But Cylon answered haughtily, "Haven't these Pythagoreans robbed you of the right to judge and decide on public affairs? What right have they to be heard here today? Did they ask you before they stripped you of the right to exercise justice? Well then, now it's your turn! Strike without hearing!" A thunder of applause greeted these words, and the mob became more and more excited.

One evening when the forty leading members of the Order were assembled at Milon's home, the tribune led an attack upon them. The house was surrounded. The Pythagoreans, together with the master, barricaded the doors. The furious crowd set fire to the house, and soon the building was a mass of flames. Thirty-eight Pythagoreans, the chief disciples of the master, the flower of the Order, along with Pythagoras himself, perished. Some were destroyed by the fire, others were put to death by the people.[63] Only Archippus and Lysis escaped destruction.

Thus died that great sage, that divine man who had tried to introduce wisdom into the government of men. The murder of Pythagoras was the signal for a general uprising in Croton and all along the Gulf of Tarento. The cities of Italy drove out the unfortunate disciples of the master. The Order was dispersed but its remnants spread into Sicily and Greece, everywhere sowing the word of the master. For example, Lysis became Epaminondas' teacher.

After new revolutions the Pythagoreans were able to return to Italy on the condition that they would no longer form a political body. The spirit of brotherhood did not cease to unite them; they considered themselves members of one and the same family. One of them, poor and sick, was received by an innkeeper. Before dying, the disciple traced a few mysterious signs on the door of the house, saying to his host, "Rest assured, one of my brothers will pay my debt." A year later, a stranger passing this same inn saw the signs and said to the host, "I am a Pythagorean; one of my brothers died here; tell me what I owe you for him." The Order itself survived for two hundred and fifty years. As for the ideas and traditions of the master, these live even today.

The regenerating influence of Pythagoras on Greece was tremendous. It was exerted mysteriously but surely through the temple where he had worked. We have seen how at Delphi it gave a new power to divinatory science, strengthened the authority of the priests and formed a model Pythoness with its art. Thanks to this inner reform which awakened enthusiasm in the very heart of the sanctuaries and in the soul of the initiates, Delphi became more than ever the moral center of Greece. This was clearly evident during the Median wars. Thirty years had hardly elapsed since Pythagoras' death when the Asiatic cyclone, foretold by the sage of Samos, burst upon the coast of Greece.

In this epic struggle of Europe against barbaric Asia, Greece, representative of freedom and civilization, has behind her the science and genius of Apollo. It is he whose patriotic and religious inspiration stills the growing rivalry between Sparta and Athens. It is he who inspires the Miltiades and Themistocles. At Marathon the enthusiasm is such that the Athenians think they see two shining warriors fighting in their ranks. Some recognize Theseus and Echetos, others Castor and Pollux.

When the invasion of Xerxes, ten times more formidable than that of Darius, overflows Thermopylae and submerges Hellas, from her tripod Pythia indicates salvation to the ambassadors from Athens and helps Themistocles conquer the ships of Salaminus. The pages of Herodotus tremble with her gasping prophecy: "Abandon the houses and high hills if the city is built in a circle . . . the fire and the fearful . . . Mars, mounted on a Syrian chariot, will destroy your towers . . . the temples topple, from their walls drips a cold sweat, from their tops flows black blood. . . . Leave my sanctuary! Let a wooden wall be for you an impregnable rampart. . . . Flee! Turn your back on the numberless horsemen! O divine Salaminus! How disastrous you will be for the sons of women!"[64]

In Aeschylus' account the battle begins with a cry which resembles a hymn of praise to Apollo: "Soon the day on white chargers, spread its shining light over the world. At that moment an immense clamor, modulated like a solemn chant, arises from the ranks of the Greeks. The echoes of the island respond with a thousand deafening voices." Need one be surprised that, drunk with the wine of victory at the battle of Mycale, the Greeks, facing conquered Asia, chose as their rallying cry, "Hebe, eternal youth?" Indeed, the breath of Apollo broods over these amazing Median wars. It is a religious enthusiasm which works miracles, carries away the living and

367

the dead, lights up trophies and decorates the tomb. All the temples have been burned, but that of Delphi has remained standing. The Persian army has arrived to destroy the sacred city. Everybody trembles. But the solar god says through the voice of the pontiff, "I shall defend myself!"

By order of the temple, the city is emptied; the inhabitants take refuge in the grottos of Parnassus; only the priests remain on the steps of the sanctuary, with the sacred guard. The Persian army enters the city, now silent as a tomb; only the statues watch the invaders pass. A black cloud gathers at the mouth of the gorge; thunder rolls and lightning falls upon the Persians. Two enormous rocks fall from the summit of Parnassus. Tumbling down, they crush many of the invaders.[65] At the same time cries come from the temple of Minerva and flames arise from the earth beneath the tread of the enemy. At these wonders, the frightened barbarians draw back; their army flees. Indeed, the god has defended himself!

Would these marvels really have happened, would these victories—so famous in human history—really have taken place if thirty years earlier Pythagoras had not appeared in the Delphic sanctuary to light the sacred fire once again? It is doubtful.

Something more should be said about the teacher's influence upon philosophy. Before him there had been moral philosophers on the one hand, moralists on the other. Pythagoras united morality, science and religion in his vast synthesis. This synthesis is nothing other than the esoteric doctrine, whose full light we have tried to discover in the depths of Pythagorean initiation. The philosopher of Croton was not the inventor, but was the enlightened organizer of these primordial truths in the scientific order of things. Therefore his system has been chosen as the most favorable background for a complete outline of the doctrine of the Mysteries.

Those readers who have followed the master with us will

have understood that at the heart of this doctrine shines the sun of the one Truth. Its scattered rays are found in philosophies and religions, but their center is here. What is needed to reach this Truth? Observation and reason are not enough. Above all, one must have *intuition*.

Pythagoras was an adept, an initiate of the first rank. He possessed a direct view of the spirit, the key of secret sciences and the way to the spiritual world. Therefore he drew from the original source of Truth. To these transcendent faculties of the intellectual and spiritualized soul he linked detailed observation of physical nature and the masterly classification of ideas through his keen reason. As a result, none was better equipped to build the edifice of the science of the cosmos.

PLATO

The Mysteries of Eleusis

Men have called Love Eros because he has wings; the gods called him Pleros, for he has the power of giving wings.
—Plato, *The Banquet*

In heaven, learning is seeing; on earth, it is remembering. Happy is he who has gone through the Mysteries; he knows the source and end of life.

—Pindar

35

The Youth of Plato and
The Death of Socrates

SINCE we have attempted to make the greatest of the initiates of Greece live again in Pythagoras, and through him to examine the primordial and universal basis of religious and philosophic truth, it would be possible to omit mentioning Plato, who simply gave the truth a more imaginative and popular form. However, for this very reason we shall pause before the noble figure of the Athenian philosopher.

There is a basic doctrine and synthesis of religions and philosophies. It is developed and deepened in the course of ages, but the foundation and heart remain the same. We have presented its main aspects, and is this not sufficient? No. It still remains for us to show the providential reason for its diverse forms, according to races and times. It is necessary to re-establish the chain of the Great Initiates, who were the real initiators of mankind. The strength of each of them will then be multiplied by that of all the others, and the unity of truth will appear in the very diversity of its expression.

Like everything living, Greece had her aurora, her noontime and her sunset. This follows the law of days, men, peoples, earths, heavens. Orpheus is the initiate of the dawn; Pythagoras, that of noontime; Plato, that of the sunset of Hellas, a sunset of glowing red, which in turn becomes the pink of a new dawn, the aurora of mankind. Plato follows Pythagoras, as in the Mysteries of Eleusis the torchbearer followed the hierophant. With him once again we shall enter by a new road, through the avenues of the sanctuary to the very heart of the temple, to the contemplation of the great arcanum.

Before traveling to Eleusis, however, let us listen to our guide, to the divine Plato. Let him cause us to see his native skies; let him tell us the story of his soul and lead us to his beloved master.

He was born in Athens, the city of the Beautiful and of humanity. Attica, exposed to all winds, sails like a ship in the Aegean Sea, and like a queen rules the islands, those white sirens lying on the deep blue of the waves. He grew up at the foot of the Acropolis under the eye of Pallas Athena, on that wide plain bordered by purple mountains and enveloped with a luminous blue, between the Pentelicus with its marble sides, the Hymette, crowned with scented pines where bees hum, and the quiet Bay of Eleusis.

Somewhat somber and troubled was the political horizon during Plato's childhood and youth. He passed his childhood during the dreadful Peloponnesian War, that fratricidal battle between Sparta and Athens which paved the way for the dissolution of Greece. The great days of the Medic wars had passed; the time of Marathon and Salamis had gone. The year of Plato's birth, 429 B.C., is that of the death of Pericles, the greatest statesman of Greece, as honest as Aristides, as clever as Themistocles, the most perfect representative of Hellenic civilization, the tamer of that turbulent democracy, the burning patriot who knew how to preserve the calm of a demi-god in the midst of general revolts. Plato's mother doubtless told her son about a scene she must have witnessed two years after the birth of the future philosopher. The Spartans had invaded Attica; Athens, its national existence already threatened, had fought through an entire winter, and Pericles was the soul of its defense. In that dark year an impressive ceremony took place in the Ceramicus. The coffins of warriors who had died for the country were placed on funeral chariots and the people were called together before the monumental tomb which was destined to unite them. This mausoleum seemed a magnificent and sinister symbol of the grave Greece was digging for herself by her criminal fighting. It was then that Pericles uttered the most beautiful speech that has been preserved from antiquity. Thucydides transcribed it on tablets of brass, and this address shines there like a shield on the pediment of a temple. "The tomb of heroes is the whole universe, not columns covered with insipid inscriptions."—Does not the consciousness of Greece and her immortality breathe in this saying?

But with Pericles dead, what remained of the Greece who had lived in her men of action? Inside Athens were the discords of a demagoguery at bay; outside, the Lacedaemonian invasion ever at the gates, war on land and sea and the king of Persia's gold circulating like a corrupting poison in the hands of tribunes and magistrates. Alcibiades had replaced Pericles in the public favor. From a deceitful youth of Athens, this individual had become the man of the hour. Adventurer, politician, intrigant, charmer, he led his country to its ruin while he laughed. Plato had observed him well, for later he gave an excellent psychological study of this personality. He compares the mad lust for power which filled Alcibiades' soul with a great winged hornet "around whom the passions, crowned with flowers, perfumed with essences, intoxicated with wine and all the free pleasures which follow, come to buzz, goading him, elevating him and finally arming him with the fire of personal ambition. Then this tyrant of the soul, raging in madness, acts. If in himself he discovers thoughts and honest sentiments which can still evoke shame, he pursues and kills them. As a result he purges the soul of all temperance, filling it with the fury he has created."

The sky over Athens therefore was rather dark during Plato's youth. When he was twenty-five he took part in the capture of Athens by the Spartans, following the disastrous naval battle of Aigos Potamos. Then he saw the entrance of Lysander into his native city, which meant the end of Athenian independence. He saw the great walls, constructed by Themistocles, demolished to the sound of festive music and the triumphant enemy literally dance upon the ruins of the country. Then came the Thirty Tyrants and their proscriptions.

These spectacles saddened Plato's youthful soul, but they could not trouble it, for that soul was as gentle, as limpid, as open as the canopy of heaven above the Acropolis. Plato was a tall young man with broad shoulders; he was serious, meditative, almost always silent. However, when he opened his mouth an exquisite sensitivity, a charming gentleness streamed with his words. In him was nothing striking or excessive. His many capabilities were disguised, blended into the higher harmony of his being. A winged grace, a natural modesty hid the serious side of his mind; an almost feminine tenderness veiled the firmness of his character. In him, virtue was clothed with a smile and pleasure with an innocent purity. However, the dominant, extraordinary, unique characteristic of this soul was that in being born, it seemed to have made a mysterious pact with Eternity. Indeed, only the eternal seemed to live in the depths of his great eyes; other things pass away quickly like vain appearances in a deep mirror. Behind the visible, changing, imperfect forms of the world and its beings, the invisible, perfect, eternally radiant forms of these same beings, seen by the mind, and which are their everlasting achetypes, appeared to him. This is why the young Plato, without having formulated his doctrine, not even knowing that one day he would be a philosopher, was already aware of the divine reality of the Ideal and of its omnipresence. This is why upon seeing the processions of women, the funeral chariots, the armies, the festivals and mourning, his gaze seemed to see something else, and to say, "Why are they weeping? Why are they shouting with joy? They think they exist, yet they do not exist. Why can I not attach myself to what is born and to what dies? Why can I love only the Invisible which never is born, never dies, but remains forever?"

Love and harmony are the core of Plato's soul, but what harmony and what love?—The love of that everlasting Beauty and Harmony which embrace the universe. The greater and deeper the soul, the longer the time required for it to know itself.

Plato's first enthusiasm was expressed in the arts. He was of fair and noble birth; his father claimed descent from King Codrus, his mother from Solon. His youth was that of a rich Athenian surrounded by the luxuries and seductions of an era of decadence. He enjoyed these without excess but without prudishness, living the life of his peers, enjoying a fine inheritance, surrounded and entertained by his many friends. So well has he described the passion of love in all its phases in his *Phedre* that it is impossible that he did not experience its transports and cruel disillusions. A single line, as passionate as a line from Sappho, as bright as a starry night on the sea of the Cyclades, has come down to us: "Would I were the heaven, thus to be all eyes, so that I might look at you!"

In his search for supreme Beauty through all the modes and forms of beauty, he studied painting, music and poetry. The latter clearly seemed to meet all his needs. It ended by determining his desires. Plato had a marvelous facility for all styles of poetry. With equal intensity he enjoyed amorous and dithyrambic poetry, the epic, the tragedy and even comedy with its finest Attic wit. What then did he lack in order to become another Sophocles, thus to rescue the theatre of Athens from its near decadence? This ambition tempted him; his friends were engaged in it. At twenty-seven he had composed several tragedies and was about to present one in a contest.

It was at this time that Plato met Socrates, who used to converse with young men in the gardens of the Academy. He spoke about the Just and the Unjust, about the Beautiful, the Good and the True. The poet listened to the philosopher, returning the next day and the following days. At the end of a few weeks, a complete revolution had taken place within him. The happy young man, the poet filled with illusions, no longer recognized himself. The course of his thoughts, the goal of his life had changed. Another Plato had been born in him at the word of the one who called himself "an *accoucheur* of souls." What had taken place? By what sorcery had this reasoner with the face of a satyr torn the handsome, genial Plato from luxury, pleasure and poetry in order to convert him to the great renunciation that is wisdom?

A very simple man, but a great oddity was this good Socrates. Son of a sculptor, he had carved the three Graces during his adolescence. Then he threw down the chisel, saying that he would rather carve his own soul than blocks of marble. From that moment he dedicated his life to the search for wisdom. He was seen in the gymnasia, on the public square, at the theater, chatting with young men, artists, philosophers and asking each of them to prove what he had affirmed.

For several years the Sophists had fought among themselves in the city of Athens like a cloud of grasshoppers. The Sophist is the counterfeit and living negation of the philosopher, as the demagogue is the counterfeit of the statesman, the hypocrite the counterfeit of the priest, the black magician the infernal counterfeit of the true initiate. The Greek type of Sophist is more subtle, more reasoning, more corrosive than the others, but the type itself is to be found in all decadent civilizations. The Sophists increased as fatally as the worms in a decomposing corpse. Whether they are called atheists, nihilists or pessimists, the Sophists of all centuries resemble one another. They forever deny God and the soul, that is, the supreme Truth and Life. Those of Socrates' time, like Gorgias, Prodicus and Protagoras, said that there is no difference between truth and falsehood. They were confident that they could prove any idea whatsoever, and also its opposite, stating that there is no justice other than force, no truth except the individual's opinion. With this, satisfied with themselves, setting high fees for their lessons, they incited young men to debauchery, intrigue and tyranny.

Socrates approached the Sophists with his insinuating gentleness, his subtle good nature, like an ignorant man who wishes to be taught. His eye shone with fire and benevolence. Then, from question to question, he forced them to say the opposite of what they had first claimed and to confess candidly that they did not even know what they were talking about. Socrates then showed that the Sophists, who pretended to possess universal knowledge, knew neither the cause nor the principle of anything. Having thus reduced them to silence, he did not glory in his victory, but, smiling, thanked his adversaries for having taught him by their answers, adding that to know that one knows nothing is the beginning of real wisdom.

What did Socrates himself believe and teach? He did not deny the gods; he rendered them the same worship as did his fellow citizens, but he said that their nature was impenetrable and confessed that he understood nothing of the physics or metaphysics which were taught in the Schools. The important thing, he said, is to believe in the Just and True and apply it in one's life. His discussions carried great weight for he himself furnished the example, since he was an irreproachable citizen, an intrepid soldier, honest judge, faithful and impartial friend, the absolute master of all his passions.

Thus the tactics of moral education change according to time and place. In the circle of his initiate disciples, Pythagoras derived morality from the heights of cosmogony. In Athens, on the public square, among men like Cleon and the Gorgias, Socrates spoke of the innate sense of the Just and True in order to rebuild the world and the weakened social state. And both Pythagoras and Socrates, the one in the descending order of principles, the other in the ascending order, affirmed the same truth. Pythagoras represents the principles and method of the highest initiation; Socrates announces the age of open science. In order not to forsake his role as a public exponent, Socrates refused to have himself initiated into the Mysteries of Eleusis; on the other hand, he understood and believed in the total and supreme Truth which the great Mysteries taught. When he spoke of them, the expression of the good, spirited Socrates changed like an inspired faun, possessed by a god. His eyes lighted up, color passed over his face and from his lips fell one of those simple, luminous statements which reveal the very foundations of things.

Why was Plato so irresistibly charmed and captivated by this man? In seeing him, Plato understood the superiority of the Good over the Beautiful. For the Beautiful accomplishes the True only in the mirage of art, while the Good is brought about in the depths of souls. Rare and powerful is this charm, for the senses have no share in it. The sight of a truly just man made the shimmering splendors of visible art fade in Plato's soul, finally to disappear in presence of a diviner dream.

This man showed him the inferiority of that beauty and glory he had believed in until then, when compared with the beauty and glory of the active soul, which forever attracts other souls to the same Truth. On the other hand, the pomp of art merely succeeds in reflecting for an instant a deceptive truth, under a disguise. This shining, eternal Beauty, "the splendor of the True," killed the changing, deceptive beauty in Plato's soul. Thus, abandoning and forgetting all he had loved previously, Plato gave himself to Socrates in the flower of his youth, with all the poetry of his soul. This great victory of Truth over Beauty had incalculable consequences for the history of the human spirit.

Meanwhile, Plato's friends were waiting for him to make his debut in poetry on the tragic stage. He invited them to his house for a great celebration, and all were astonished that he wanted to give this festival at that time, for it was customary to give it only after having won the prize, and when the winning tragedy had been played. But none refused an invitation to the home of a son of a rich nobleman, where the Muses and Graces met in the company of Eros. For a long time his house had been a rendezvous for the elegant youth of Athens.

Plato spent a fortune on the banquet. The table was set in the garden. Young men with torches lighted the way for the guests. The three most beautiful *hetaerae* of Athens attended. The banquet continued all night. Hymns to Love and Bacchus were sung. The flute players danced their most voluptuous dances. At last, Plato himself was asked to recite one of his dithyrambics. Smiling, he arose and said, "This banquet is the last I shall give. Beginning today I renounce the pleasures of life in order to dedicate myself to wisdom, and to follow the teachings of Socrates. Know then: I even renounce poetry, for

I have recognized its inability to express the Truth I seek. No longer will I write verses, and in your presence I am about to burn all those I have composed."

A loud cry of amazement and protest arose from the table, around which the guests, wearing crowns of roses, were lying upon sumptuous couches. These faces, red with wine, gaiety and light table talk, expressed surprise and indignation. Among the gentlemen and Sophists were laughs of incredulity and scorn. They considered Plato's project folly and sacrilege; they challenged him to take back what he had said. But Plato confirmed his decision with a calmness and assurance which would tolerate no turning back. He concluded by saying, "I thank all those who have wished to take part in this farewell celebration, but I shall keep near me only those who wish to share my new life. From now on Socrates' friends will be my only friends."

His words passed like a cold breath over a field of flowers. To happy faces they suddenly brought the sad, troubled look of people in a funeral procession. The courtesans arose and had themselves carried away on their litters, casting hateful glances at the master of the house. The Sophists disappeared with ironic and sportive words: "Farewell, Plato! Be happy! You will come back to us. Farewell! Farewell!" Two serious young men remained with him. He took these faithful friends by the hand, and leaving the half-empty jugs of wine, the roses, the lyres and flutes overturned, the full cups, Plato led them into the inner court of the house. There they saw piled up on a small altar a pyramid of papyrus scrolls. These were Plato's poetic works. Taking a torch, the smiling poet set fire to the pile, saying, "Vulcan, come here! Plato needs you!"

When the flames finally had flickered out, the friends with tears in their eyes, silently said farewell to their future teacher. But Plato, remaining alone, did not weep. A peace, a wonderful serenity filled his whole being. He thought of Socrates whom he was going to see. The light of dawn touched the terraces of the houses, the columns and pediments of the temples; soon the first ray of the sun made Minerva's helmet glisten on the top of the Acropolis. . . .

36

The Initiation of Plato
and the Birth of Platonic Philosophy

THREE years after Plato had become Socrates' pupil, the latter was condemned to death by the Areopagus, and died, surrounded by his disciples, after drinking the hemlock.

Few historical events have been as frequently described as this. However, few happenings have occurred whose causes and significance are so little understood. Today it is believed that the Areopagus was right to condemn Socrates as an enemy of the state religion because in denying the gods, he was attacking the foundation of the Athenian republic. We shall show that this assertion contains two major errors. Let us first recall what Victor Cousin wrote at the beginning of *The Apology of Socrates* in his beautiful translation of Plato's works: "Anytus, it must be said, was a comméndable citizen; the Areopagus, an equitable and temperate tribunal; and, if anything is to be wondered at, it is that Socrates was not accused long before, and that he was not condemned by a larger majority." The philosopher, a Minister of Public Education, did not see that if he was right they should have condemned both philosophy and religion in order to glorify only the politics of lying, violence and absolutism. For if philosophy inevitably destroys the foundations of the social state, it is merely a pompous folly, and if religion can exist only by suppressing the search for truth, it is but a sinister tyranny. Let us try to be fairer to Greek religion and to Greek philosophy.

There is a vital and significant fact which has escaped the attention of most modern historians and philosophers. Persecutions in Greece, which were very rarely aimed toward philosophers, never originated in the temples, but always arose among those engaged in politics. Greek civilization did not know that struggle between priests and philosophers which has played such a great role in our civilization since the destruction of Christian esoterism in the second century of our era. Without interference Thales could teach that the world comes from water, Heraclitus, that it comes from fire; Anaxagoras could say that the sun is a mass of incandescent fire; Democritus could claim that all comes from atoms. No temple was disturbed, for in their sanctuaries all this was known, and more besides. It was also realized that the so-called philosophers who denied the gods could not eradicate them from the national consciousness, and that true philosophers believed in them in the manner of initiates, seeing in them the symbols of the great ranks of the spiritual Hierarchies, of the Divine that penetrates nature, of the Invisible that governs the visible. Esoteric doctrine therefore served as the link between true philosophy and true religion. This is the deep, primordial and final fact which explains their hidden significance in Hellenic civilization.

Who, therefore, accused Socrates? The priests of Eleusis, who had cursed the authors of the Peloponnesian War, shaking the dust from their robes toward the Occident, uttered no word against him. As for the temple of Delphi, it gave him the most beautiful tribute that can be paid to any man. Pythia, asked what Apollo thought of Socrates, answered, "There is no man more free, more just, more intelligent." The two inditements leveled against Socrates: of corrupting youth and of not believing in the gods, were therefore, only pretexts. With regard to the second accusation, Socrates victoriously answered his judges, "I believe in my personal spirit. Therefore I have all the more reason to believe in the gods, who are the spirits of the universe!" Then why this implacable hatred against the sage? He had fought injustice, unmasked hypocrisy, shown the falseness of so many vain pretentions. Men pardon all the vices and all the atheisms, but they do not pardon those who expose them. This is why the real atheists who were sitting in the Areopagus caused the death of the just and innocent, by accusing him of the crime they themselves had committed. In his admirable defense, recorded by Plato, Socrates himself explains this with perfect simplicity, "These are my fruitless searches for wise men among the Athenians who have aroused so much dangerous hostility against me. Hence all the calumnies spread on my account. Intriguers, active and numerous, speaking about me according to a concerted plan and with a very appealing eloquence, for a long time have filled your ears with the most perfidious rumors, ceaselessly pursuing their system of calumny. Today they have won from me Melitus, Anytus and Lycon. Melitus represents the poets; Anytus, the politicians and artists; Lycon, the orators." A tragic poet without talent, a wicked, fanatical man of wealth, a brazen-faced demagogue succeeded in having the best of men condemned to death. But that death made him immortal. Proudly he could say to his judges, "I believe more firmly in the gods than do any of my accusers. It is time for us to leave each other, I to die, and you to live. Which of us has the better part? No one knows but God."

Far from attacking true religion and its national symbols,

Socrates had done everything possible to strengthen them. He would have been the greatest support of his country, if his country had known how to understand him. Like Jesus, he died forgiving his executioners, and became the model of martyred sages for all mankind. For Socrates represents the definitive appearing of individual initiation and open science.

The serene picture of Socrates dying for truth, spending his last hour discussing the immortality of the soul with his pupils, imprinted this most beautiful of spectacles and holiest of Mysteries upon Plato's heart. This was his first, his great initiation. Later he was to study physics, metaphysics and many other sciences, but always he remained Socrates' pupil. He willed us his living image by putting into the mouth of his teacher the treasures of his own thought. This flower of modesty makes him the ideal of the disciple, his fire of ecstasy makes him the poet of philosophers. Regardless of the fact that we know he did not establish his school until he was fifty, and that he lived to be eighty, we can imagine him only as young. For eternal youth is the inheritance of souls who unite divine honesty with depth of thought.

Plato had received from Socrates the great impetus, the active male principle of his life, his faith in justice and truth. He owed the science and substance of his ideas to his initiation into the Mysteries. His genius consists in the new form—at once poetic and dialectic—which he knew how to give them. He did not take this initiation from Eleusis only. He sought it in all the accessible sources of the ancient world. After Socrates' death, Plato began to travel. He studied with several philosophers of Asia Minor. From there he went to Egypt to establish a relationship with its priests, going through the initiation of Isis. Unlike Pythagoras, he did not reach the higher stage where one becomes an adept, where one acquires the effective, direct view of divine Truth and supernatural powers. He stopped at the third stage, which confers perfect intellectual clarity and dominion of intelligence over soul and body. Then he went to southern Italy to talk with the Pythagoreans, knowing full well that Pythagoras had been the greatest of Greek sages. He purchased one of the master's manuscripts at a high price. Thus having dipped into the esoteric tradition of Pythagoras at its very source, he borrowed the main ideas and framework of his system from that philosopher.

Returning to Athens, Plato established his school which has become famous under the name of the Academy. In order to continue Socrates' work, it was necessary to propagate truth. But Plato could not teach the things publicly which the Pythagoreans covered with a threefold veil. The vows, prudence and his goal itself prevented him from doing so. It is really esoteric doctrine which we find in his *Dialogues,* but disguised, altered, charged with a rational dialectic like something foreign, concealed in legend, myth, parable. The esoteric teaching is no longer presented in Plato with the impressive totality Pythagoras gave it, and which we have tried to reconstruct, an edifice established on a firm foundation—all parts of which are strongly cemented, but in analytic fragments. Plato, like Socrates, bases himself on the ground of the young men of Athens, on the worldly attitude of the rhetoricians and Sophists. He fights them with their own weapons. But his genius is always present; at every point he breaks the network of their dialectic to rise like an eagle in a bold flight into the sublime truths which are his home, his native atmosphere. These dialogues have an incisive, singular charm; in addition to the ecstasy of Delphi and Eleusis, here one enjoys marvelous clarity, Attic wit, the malice of the good-natured Socrates, the fine, winged irony of the sage.

Nothing is easier than to discover the different points of esoteric doctrine in Plato and at the same time to observe where he found them. The doctrine of the archetypes of things, expounded in *Phedre* is a corollary of Pythagoras' doctrine of *Sacred Numbers*. The *Timeus* gives a very confusing explanation of esoteric cosmogony. As for the doctrine of the soul, its migrations and its evolutions, this is to be found in all the works of Plato, but nowhere is it more clearly expressed than in the *Banquet,* in *Phaedo,* and in *The Legend of Er,* placed at the end of that dialogue. We see Psyche beneath a veil, but how beautiful and appealing she is in her exquisite form and divine grace!

We have seen that the key to the cosmos, the secret of its constitution, is found in the principle of *the three worlds* reflected by the microcosm and macrocosm in the human and divine ternary. Pythagoras masterfully formulated and summed up this doctrine in the symbol of *the sacred Tetrad.* This doctrine of the eternally living Word constituted the great arcanum, the source of magic, the shining temple of the initiate, his invincible citadel far above the ocean of things. Plato neither could nor wished to reveal this mystery in his public teaching. In the first place the oath of the Mysteries kept him silent. In addition, all would not have understood; the common man would have unworthily profaned this theogonic mystery, which embraces the generation of the worlds. In order to fight the corruption of custom and the unleashing of political passions, something different was necessary. The door to the Beyond was about to close, and with it the great initiation, the door to which opens fully only to the great prophets, to the very rare, true initiates.

Plato replaced the doctrine of the three worlds with three concepts which, in the absence of organized initiation, remained for two thousand years as three roads leading to the supreme goal. These three concepts refer equally to the human world and the divine world; they have the advantage of uniting them, although in a somewhat abstract manner. Here Plato's creative genius is seen. He threw great light upon the world by placing the ideas of the True, the Beautiful and the Good on the same level. Clarifying them one by one, he proved that they are three rays from the same Source which, when united constitute this Source Itself, that is, God.

In seeking the Good, that is, the just, the soul becomes purified; it prepares itself to know truth. This is the first, indispensable condition of the soul's development. By following and enlarging the idea of the Beautiful, it attains the intellectual Beautiful, that intelligible light, that mother of things, that animator of forms, that substance and instrument of God. By plunging itself into the World-Soul, the human soul feels an expansiveness. By pursuing the idea of the True, it attains pure Essence, the principles contained in pure Spirit. It recognizes its immortality by the identity of its principle with the divine Principle. Thus perfection is attained; this is the Epiphany of the soul.

By opening these broad paths to the human spirit, Plato defined and created, outside the narrow systems of particular religions *the category of the Ideal,* which was to replace *organic initiation* for centuries down to our own day. He marked out the three paths which lead to God like the sacred way from Athens to Eleusis by way of the Gate of Ceramicus. Having entered the temple with Hermes, Orpheus and Pythagoras, we are well able to judge the solidity and rightness of the broad roads built by Plato, the divine engineer. Knowledge of initiation gives the justification and reason for the being of Idealism.

Idealism is a bold affirmation of the divine truths by the soul, which in its solitude questions itself and judges celestial realities by its own intimate faculties and its inner voices. *Initiation* is the penetration of these same truths by the experience of the soul, by direct vision of the spirit, by inner awakening. At the highest stage it is the communication of the soul with the divine world.

The Ideal is an ethic, a poetry, a philosophy; *Initiation* is an action, a vision and a sublime presence of truth. The Ideal is the dream and the longing for the divine homeland; Initiation, the temple of the elect, is the clear remembering and even the possessing of it.

In creating the category of the Ideal, the initiate Plato created a refuge and opened the way of salvation to millions of souls who cannot attain direct initiation in this life, but painfully strive for truth. Thus Plato made philosophy the foyer to a future sanctuary by inviting into it all men of good will. The idealism of his many pagan or Christian sons appears like the preliminary as it were, to the great initiation.

This explains the immense popularity and radiant power of Platonic ideas. This power lies in their esoteric basis. This is why the Academy of Athens, founded by Plato, lasted for centuries and extended into the great Alexandrian School. This is why the first Church Fathers paid homage to Plato; this is why St. Augustine took two-thirds of his theology from him.

Two thousand years had passed since Socrates' disciple had breathed his last sigh in the shadow of the Acropolis. Christianity, the barbaric invasions, the Middle Ages, had passed over the world. But antiquity was born again out of its own ashes. In Florence the Medici wished to establish an Academy, and invited a Greek scientist, exiled from Constantinople, to organize it. What name did Marsilio Ficino give it? He called it *The Platonic Academy*. Today, after so many philosophical systems, built one upon another, have crumbled into dust, today, when science has searched for the ultimate transformations of matter, finding itself before the unexplained and invisible, still today, Plato comes to us. Forever simple and modest, but shining with eternal youth, he holds out the sacred branch of the Mysteries to us, the branch of myrtle and cypress, with the narcissus, *the flower of the soul,* promising a divine renaissance in a new Eleusis.

37

The Mysteries of Eleusis

THE Mysteries of Eleusis were the object of special veneration in Greek and Latin antiquity. The very authors who
ridiculed the mythological fables did not dare touch the cult
of the "great goddesses." Their reign, quieter than that of the
Olympians, proved itself more certain and more effective. At a
very early time, a Greek colony coming from Egypt had brought
into the quiet Bay of Eleusis the cult of the great Isis under the
name of Demeter, the universal Mother. Since then, Eleusis had
continued to be a center of initiation.

Demeter and her daughter Persephone presided over the
minor and major Mysteries, hence the prestige they attained.

In Ceres the people worshipped the Earth Mother and goddess of agriculture; the initiates saw in her the celestial Light-
Mother of souls and divine Intelligence, Mother of the cosmogonic gods. Her cult was officiated over by priests belonging
to the most ancient sacerdotal family of Attica. They called
themselves the sons of the moon, that is, those born to be
mediators between earth and heaven, coming out of the

sphere where the bridge is thrown between the two regions through which souls descend and ascend. From the beginning their function had been "to extol in this abyss of miseries, the pleasures of the heavenly dwelling and to teach the means of finding the path again." Hence their name, Eumolpides, or "singers of gracious melodies," gentle regenerators of men. The priests of Eleusis always taught the great esoteric doctrine which came to them from Egypt, but in the course of ages they clothed it in all the charm of a plastic, captivating mythology. By means of a subtle and profound art, these charmers knew how to use earthly passions to express celestial ideas. They put to good use the appeal of the senses, the pomp of ceremonies, the seductions of art, in order to lead the soul into a better life, and the intelligence to the understanding of divine truths. Nowhere did the Mysteries appear in such human, living, colorful form.

The myth of Ceres and her daughter, Proserpine, form the heart of the cult of Eleusis. Like a shining procession, all Eleusian initiation revolves and develops around this luminous center. And, in its esoteric sense, this myth is the symbolic representation of the story of the soul, of its descent into matter, of its sufferings in the darkness of forgetfulness, then of its reascent, its return to divine life. In other words, it is the drama of the Fall and Redemption in its Hellenic form.

For the cultivated and initiated Athenian of Plato's time the Mysteries of Eleusis offered the explanatory complement, the radiant counterpart to the performance of tragedies in Athens. There in the Theatre of Bacchus, before the public audience, the terrible incantations of Melpomene evoked earthly man, blinded by his passions, pursued by the Nemesis of his crimes, crushed by an implacable and often incomprehensible Destiny. There also were heard the Promethean struggles, the curses of the Erynnies, the despairing cries of Oedipus and the Furies of Orestes. There gloomy Terror and lamentable Pity reigned.

At Eleusis, on the other hand, in the sanctuary of Ceres, everything was bright. The vision widened for those initiates who had become seers. For each soul the story of Psyche-Persephone was a surprising revelation. Life was explained as an expiation or a test. Above and beyond his earthly present, man discovered the starry regions of a divine past and future. After the agonies of death came the hopes, the liberations, the Elysian joys. Through the portals of the open temple came the songs of the happy, the all-encompassing light of a glorious Beyond.

Thus the Mysteries, in comparison with Tragedy, were the divine drama of the soul, completing and explaining the earthly drama of man.

The Lesser Mysteries were celebrated in the month of February at Agrae, a town near Eleusis. The aspirants who had taken a preliminary examination and provided proof of their birth, education and respectability, were received at the entrance of the enclosure by the priest of Eleusis called the *hieroceryx,* or sacred herald, resembling Hermes, and like him wearing the petasus and carrying the caduceus. He was the guide, the mediator, the interpreter of the Mysteries. He led the aspirants to a small temple with Ionic columns, dedicated to *Kore,* the great Virgin, Persephone. The gracious sanctuary of the goddess was hidden at the end of a quiet valley in the midst of a sacred grove, surrounded by yews and white poplars. Then the priestesses of Proserpine, the hierophants, left the temple, wearing immaculate peplos, with bare arms, and crowned with narcissus wreaths. They formed a line at the top of the steps, and began a solemn chant in the Dorian mode. Accompanying their words with broad gestures, they intoned,

"O, neophytes of the Mysteries, here you stand at the threshold of Proserpine! What you are about to see will surprise you.

You will learn that your present life is but a tapestry of false, confused dreams. The sleep which throws around you a mantle of darkness, bears your dreams and your days on its stream like floating debris, which disappears from sight. But there beyond, a world of eternal Light spreads itself! May Proserpine be kind to you, and teach you to cross the river of darkness, to penetrate the celestial Demeter!"

Then the prophantid or prophetess who led the chorus, descended three steps and spoke this curse in a solemn voice, with a look of dread: "But woe to those who may have come here to desecrate the Mysteries!—For the goddess will pursue these perverse hearts through their entire lifetime, and in the kingdom of the Shades she will not release her prey!"

Then several days were spent in ablutions, fasts, prayers and instruction.

On the evening of the last day, the neophytes met in the most secret part of the sacred grove to attend the *Rape of Persephone*. The scene was played in the open air by the priestesses of the temple. This custom was derived from very early times, and the basis of this performance, the dominant idea always remained the same, although the form varied greatly in the course of the ages. From Plato's time, thanks to the then recent development of tragedy, the former hieratic severity gave place to a more humane and refined taste and to a more passionate rendition. Directed by the hierophant, the anonymous poets of Eleusis had made of this scene a little drama which was approximately as follows:

(The neophytes arrive by twos, entering a clearing. At the side one sees rocks and a grotto surrounded by a wood of myrtle and a few poplar trees. In the foreground is a meadow, where Nymphs are lying beside a stream. At the back of the grotto one perceives Persephone seated. Naked to the waist like a Psyche,

her light, graceful breasts chastely emerge from delicate gauze which falls about her like a vapor of blue. She seems to be happy, unaware of her beauty, and is embroidering a long veil of multicolored threads. Demeter, her mother, is standing near her, wearing the kalathos, her scepter in her hand.)

HERMES (*The herald of the Mysteries, to the spectators*): Demeter gives us two excellent things: fruit, so that we do not live like beasts, and initiation, which gives a gentler hope to those who take part in it, both for the end of this life and for all eternity. Listen carefully to the words you are about to hear, to the things you are about to see!

DEMETER (*In a serious voice*): Beloved daughter of the gods, remain in this grotto until my return, and embroider my veil. Heaven is your homeland; the universe is yours. You see the gods; they come at your call. But do not listen to the voice of the wily Eros, with his soft glances, his treacherous counsels. Do not leave the grotto, and never pick the seductive flowers of earth; their deadly perfume will cause you to lose the light of heaven, and even the memory of it! Weave my veil and live happily with the nymphs, your companions, until my return. Then, on my chariot of fire drawn by serpents, I will bear you once again into the splendors of ether, beyond the Milky Way!

PERSEPHONE: Yes, august and fearful mother. By this light which surrounds you and which is dear to me, I promise. May the gods punish me if I do not keep my word! (*Exit, Demeter*)

THE CHORUS OF NYMPHS: O Persephone! O Virgin, O chaste Bride of Heaven, who embroiders the face of the gods in your veil, may you never know the vain illusions, the innumerable misfortunes of earth! Eternal Truth smiles upon you! Your heavenly husband, Dionysus, is waiting for you in the Empyrean. Sometimes he appears to you in the form of the distant sun; his rays kiss you, he breathes your breath, you drink his light . . . You possess each other . . . O Virgin, who then is happier than you?

PERSEPHONE: On this veil of blue with endless folds, I embroider the numberless faces of beings and forms with my ivory needle. I have completed the history of the gods; I have embroidered frightful Chaos with his hundred heads and thousand arms. From him mortals are supposed to come. Who then causes them to be born? The Father of the gods told me that it is Eros. But I have never seen him; I do not know his face. Who then will paint his countenance for me?

THE NYMPHS: Do not think of that! Why this vain question?

PERSEPHONE (*Arising and throwing aside her veil*): Eros, the oldest and the youngest of the gods, inexhaustible source of joys and tears! Thus they spoke of you to me. Terrible god, quite unknown, alone of all the Immortals invisible, the only desirable one, mysterious Eros! What ecstasy, what trembling overcomes me at your name!

THE CHORUS: Do not seek to know more! Dangerous questions have destroyed men and even gods!

PERSEPHONE (*Gazing into the Abyss, her eyes filled with fear*): Is it a memory? Is it a dreadful foreboding? Chaos . . . Man . . . The Abyss of generations, the cry of births, the furious tumult of hate and war . . . the gulf of Death! I hear, I see all this, and this Abyss draws me, overwhelms me! I must descend! Eros with his burning torch makes me descend! I am about to die! Away from me, terrible dream! (*She covers her face with her hands, and sobs.*)

THE CHORUS: O divine Virgin, it is as yet but a dream. Nevertheless it will take form, it will become fateful reality and your heaven will disappear like an empty dream if you yield to your guilty desire! Obey this warning! Take up your needle; weave your veil! Forget the cunning, impudent, criminal Eros!

PERSEPHONE (*Takes her hands from her face, which has changed expression; she smiles through her tears*): Fool that you are! Insensate that I was! I remember now; I heard it said in the Olympian Mysteries: Eros is the handsomest of gods; on winged chariot he presides at the evolutions of the Immortals, at the blending of archetypal essences. He it is who leads bold men, the heroes, from the depths of Chaos to the heights of ether. He knows all. Like the Fire-principle, he transcends all worlds; he holds the keys of earth and heaven! I wish to see him!

THE CHORUS: Rash one, Stop!

EROS (*Emerging from the grove in the form of a winged youth*): You called me, Persephone? Here I am!

PERSEPHONE (*Sitting down*): They called you cunning, but your face is innocence itself! They said you were all-powerful, and you seem a frail child. They say you are a traitor, but the more I look at your eyes, the more my heart opens, the more I put confidence in you, lovely playful youth!—They said you were wise and clever. Can you help me to embroider this veil?

EROS: Willingly! Here I am near you, at your feet! What a marvelous veil! It seems dipped in the blue of your eyes. What admirable forms your hand has embroidered—less beautiful, however, than the divine embroiderer, who has never seen herself in a mirror! (*He smiles mischievously.*)

PERSEPHONE: See myself! Would that be possible? (*She blushes*) But do you recognize these faces?

EROS: Yes, I know them!—The story of the gods. But why do you stop with Chaos? It is there that the fight begins! Will you not weave the War of the Titans, the birth of men and their loves?

PERSEPHONE: My knowledge stops here, my memory fails. Will you not help me embroider the rest?

EROS: (*Throwing her an ardent glance*) Yes, Persephone, but on one condition. First you must come and pick a flower with me on the meadow; the most beautiful flower of all!

PERSEPHONE (*Seriously*): My august, wise mother forbade me. "Do not listen to the voice of Eros," she told me, "Do not pick the flowers of the meadow. Otherwise you will be the most miserable of Immortals!"

EROS: I understand. Your mother does not want you to know the secrets of earth and hell. If you smelled the flowers of the meadow, the secrets would be revealed to you!

PERSEPHONE: Do you know them?

EROS: All of them. And, you see, I am only the younger and more agile for it! O daughter of the gods, the Abyss has terrors and tremors that heaven does not know! He does not understand heaven who has not traversed earth and hell!

PERSEPHONE: Can you make me understand them?

EROS: Yes, Look! (*He touches the earth with the point of his bow; a large narcissus springs up.*)

PERSEPHONE: O, what a lovely flower! It makes my heart tremble; a divine recollection surges up in me! Sometimes, sleeping on my beloved star which an everlasting sunset gilds, upon awakening, on the deep red of the horizon I have seen a star of silver floating in the pearly depth of the pale green sky. It seemed to me that it was the torch of the immortal bridegroom, the promise of the gods, of divine Dionysus. But the

star kept descending . . . and the torch died out in the distance
. . . This marvelous flower resembles that star.

EROS: I who transform and unite everything, I who make the
small in the image of the great, from the depth of the mirror
of heaven, I who mix heaven and hell on earth, who create all
forms in the deep ocean, have brought your star to life again
from the Abyss, in the form of a flower so that you can touch it,
pick it, smell it!

THE CHORUS: Take care that this magic is not a trap!

PERSEPHONE: What do you call this flower?

EROS: Men call it Narcissus; I call it Desire. See how it looks
at you, how it turns to you! Its white petals tremble as if they
were alive. From its golden heart comes a perfume, filling all
the air with pleasure. As soon as you bring this magic flower
close to your eyes, in a great and marvelous tableau you will
see the monsters of the Abyss, the earth-depths and the heart of
men. Nothing will be hidden from you.

PERSEPHONE: O wonderful flower! My heart is beating with
your intoxicating perfume! My fingers burn from touching
you! I want to breathe your aroma, to press you to my lips, to
place you upon my heart, even if I must die for it!

(*The earth opens beside her. Out of a gaping, dark crevice
one sees Pluto on a chariot drawn by two black horses, slowly
arising. He seizes Persephone at the moment she picks the
flower, pulling her violently to him. She struggles vainly in
his arms, screaming loudly. Immediately the chariot sinks
and disappears. Its rumbling dies in the distance, like subterranean thunder. Moaning, the Nymphs dart about the
grove. Eros flees with a burst of laughter.*)

THE VOICE OF PERSEPHONE (underground): My Mother! Help! Mother!

HERMES: O Neophytes of the Mysteries, whose life is still clouded by the fumes of evil life, this is your story. Remember and meditate upon this saying of Empedocles: "Generation is a terrible destruction, which causes the living to pass among the dead. Once you lived the true life, and then, drawn by magic, you fell into the earthly Abyss, subjugated by the body. Your present is but a fatal dream; only the past and future really exist. Learn to remember; learn to forsee."

During this scene, night has fallen. Mournful torches are lighted between the black cypresses beside the little temple, and the spectators move away in silence, followed by the pleading chants of the priestesses, calling: "Persephone! Persephone!"— *The Lesser Mysteries* have ended. The neophytes have become *mystics, the veiled ones.* They will return to their customary occupations, but the great *veil of the Mysteries* has been spread over their eyes. Between them and the external world, a cloud has been introduced. At the same time, an inner eye has opened within them, by which they dimly see another world, filled with attractive forms which move in depths of alternating light and darkness.

The Great Mysteries which followed the *Lesser Mysteries,* and which were also called the *Sacred Orgies,* were celebrated at Eleusis only every five years, in the month of September.

These festivals, all of them symbolic, lasted nine days. On the eighth, the insignia of initiation were distributed to the mystics: the thyrsis and a basket called a cistus, surrounded with branches of ivy. The latter contained mysterious objects. To understand the latter would give one the secret of life. But the basket was carefully sealed. One was not permitted to open it until the end of the initiation and then only in the presence of the hierophant.

Then they were filled with exultant joy; torches were waved, and were passed from one to another; shouts of joy were heard. On that day a procession bore from Athens to Eleusis the statue of Dionysus, which was called Iacchos, crowned with myrtle. His coming to Eleusis announced the great rebirth, for he represented the divine spirit permeating everything, the regenerator of souls, the mediator between earth and heaven.

Then they entered the temple by the mystic door in order to spend the sacred night, the night of initiation there.

They entered first beneath a vast portico in the outer enclosure. There the herald with terrible threats and the cry *Eskato Bebeloi, Go Back, Profane Ones,* dispersed the intruders who sometimes succeeded in slipping into the enclosure unobserved. He made the latter swear, under penalty of death to reveal nothing of what they were about to see, adding, "Here you stand at the subterranean threshold of Persephone. In order to understand the future life and your present condition, it is necessary that you traverse the kingdom of death; this is the test of the initiates. You must know how to brave the darkness in order to enjoy the light!" Then they dressed themselves in the faun's skin, the picture of the laceration and tearing of the soul, as it plunged into corporeal life. After this they extinguished the torches and lamps and entered the subterranean labyrinth.

At first the mystics groped in the darkness. Soon they heard noises, groans and dreadful voices. Lightning flashes, accompanied by thunder, split the darkness. By this light frightful visions could be seen: sometimes a monster, a chimera or a dragon; sometimes a man, torn by the claws of a sphinx; sometimes a human larva. These appearances were so sudden that there was no time to distinguish the means which produced them, while the total obscurity which followed, redoubled the horror. Plutarch compares the terror caused by these visions, to the state of a man on his death bed.

The strangest scene, bordering upon real magic, took place in a crypt where a Phrygian priest, dressed in a flowing Asiatic robe with red and black vertical stripes, was standing before a copper brazier, which dimly lighted the room by its fitful light. With a gesture which tolerated no denial, he forced the arrivals to sit down at the entrance, throwing into the fire large handfuls of narcotic perfumes. Immediately the room was filled with thick, swirling smoke, and soon one could see a confused array of changing animal and human forms. At times long serpents stretched themselves out, only to become sirens, finally to roll themselves up endlessly; at other times busts of voluptuously poised Nymphs with outstretched arms changed into bats. Charming heads of youths were transformed into muzzles of dogs. And all these monsters, beautiful and ugly in turn, fluid, airy, deceiving, unreal, vanishing as quickly as they appeared, turned, glistened, intoxicated, surrounded the fascinated visitors as though to block their way. At times the priest of Cybele raised his short staff amidst the vapors, and the outpouring of his will seemed to impress a whirling movement and a disturbing vitality upon the multiformed circles. "Come," said the Phrygian. The neophytes arose and entered the circle. Then the majority of them felt gently touched by something, others were grasped quickly by invisible hands and thrown to the ground. Some withdrew in fright and returned the way they had come. The more courageous passed only after several attempts, but a truly firm determination made a quick end to the sorcery.[66]

Then they reach a large circular room, poorly lighted by a few torches. In the center is a single column, a bronze tree, whose metallic foliage spreads over the whole ceiling.[67] In this foliage are seen chimera, gorgons, harpies, owls, sphinxes and

404

vampires—images of all earthly evils, of all the demons which fasten upon man. These monsters, reproduced in shining metals, are entwined in the branches, apparently awaiting their prey. Beneath the tree on a magnificent throne sits Pluto-Aidoneus, wearing a cloak of velvet. He is seated on a fawn-skin, his hand holds the trident, his countenance reveals anxiety. Beside the King of the Underworld, who never smiles, is his wife, the tall, slender Persephone. The neophytes recognize in her the features of the hierophant who has already played the role of the goddess in the Lesser Mysteries. She is still beautiful, more beautiful, perhaps, in her sorrow, but how changed she is in her robe of mourning, strewn with silver tears, wearing her crown of gold! She is no longer the Virgin of the Grotto; now she knows the life of the depths, and she suffers. She reigns over the lower powers, she is sovereign among the dead, but is an alien to her own kingdom. A wan smile lights her face, darkened by the shadow of hell. In that smile is the knowledge of Good and Evil, the inexpressible charm of experienced, silent pain! Suffering teaches pity. With a look of compassion she welcomes the neophytes, who kneel and place crowns of narcissus at her feet. Then in her eyes shines a dying flame, a lost hope, a distant remembrance of heaven!

Suddenly at the end of an ascending gallery, torches shine and, like a trumpet blast, a voice exclaims, "Enter, neophytes! Iacchos has returned! Demeter awaits her daughter! *Evohe!*" The sonorous echoes from underground repeat this cry. Persephone rises from her throne as though suddenly awakened from a long sleep, filled with an electrifying thought: "Light! Mother! Iacchos!" She tries to move forward, but Aidonee holds her back by the hem of her robe. She falls back upon her throne as if dead. Then the torches are suddenly extinguished, and a voice shouts, "To die is to be born again!" But the neophytes hasten through the gallery of heroes and demigods toward the opening of the tunnel where Hermes and the torch-bearer await them. Their fawn's skin is taken off, they are sprinkled with lustral water, are clothed in fresh linen and are led into the splendidly lighted temple where the hierophant—the High Priest of Eleusis, the majestic elder, clothed in velvet, receives them.

This is how Porphyrus described the highest initiation of Eleusis:

"Crowned with myrtle, along with the other initiates we enter the entrance hall of the temple, still blind, but the hierophant who is within will soon open our eyes. But first, for nothing is to be done in haste, let us wash in the holy water. We are led before the hierophant. From a book of stone, he reads to us things which we must not divulge, under penalty of death. Let us say only that they are in harmony with the place and circumstance. You would laugh, perhaps, if you heard them outside the temple, but here you have no desire to laugh as you listen to the words of the elder (for he is always old) and as you look at the exposed symbols.[68] And you are far from laughing when, by her special language and signs, by vivid sparkling of light and clouds piled upon clouds, Demeter confirms everything that we have seen and heard from her holy priest. Then, finally, the light of a serene wonder fills the temple; we see the pure Elysian fields; we hear the chorus of the blessed ones. Now it is not merely through an external appearance or through a philosophical interpretation, but in fact and in reality that the hierophant becomes the creator and the revelator of all things; the sun is but his torchbearer, the moon, his helper at the altar, and Hermes, his mystical messenger. But the last word has been uttered: *Knox Om Pax*.[69]

The ritual has been consummated, and we are seers forever."

What then did the great hierophant say? What were the sacred words, what was that supreme revelation?

The initiates learned that the divine Persephone whom they had seen in the midst of the terrors and tortures of hell, was the human soul, bound to matter in this life or subjected, in the next, to illusions and ever greater torments if it lived a slave to its passions. The soul's earthly life is an expiation or a test of preceding existences. But the soul can be purified by discipline; it can remember and have forebodings through the combined effort of intuition, reason and will, and can share beforehand in the great truths of which it must take full and complete possession in the vast Beyond. Then only will Persephone again become the pure, luminous, ineffable Virgin, the dispenser of love and joy. As for her mother Ceres, in the Mysteries she was the symbol of the divine Intelligence and the spiritual principle of man, to which the soul must reunite itself if it is to attain its perfection.

If one is to believe Plato, Iamblicus, Proclus and all the Alexandrian philosophers, within the temple the elite of the initiates experienced visions of an ecstatic and marvelous nature.

I have quoted the testimony of Porphyrus. Here is that of Proclus: "In all the initiations and Mysteries, the gods (here this word means all orders of spirits) manifest themselves in many forms, assuming a great variety of guises; sometimes they appear in a formless light, again in quite different form." This is the passage from Apuleus: "I approached the confines of death, and having reached the threshold of Proserpine, I returned, having been carried across all the elements (the elemental spirits of earth, water, air and fire). In the depths of midnight I saw the sun shining with a glorious light, and at the same time I saw the lower gods and the higher gods.

Drawing near to these divinities, I paid them the tribute of devout adoration."

However vague these testimonies may be, they seem to refer to esoteric phenomena. According to the doctrine of the Mysteries, the ecstatic visions of the temple were produced in the purest of elements, in spiritual light akin to celestial Isis. The oracles of Zoroaster call it 'nature speaking through herself,' that is, an element by means of which the Magus gives a visible, instantaneous expression to thought, and which serves as both body and clothing for souls, which in reality are the most beautiful thoughts of God. This is why the hierophant, if he was able to produce this phenomenon of bringing the initiates into contact with the souls of heroes and gods (Angels and Archangels), was likened at that moment to the Creator, to the Demiurge, the torch bearer, or to the Sun, that is, to supersensible Light, and Hermes, to the divine Word, which is his interpreter. Whatever value these visions may have had, antiquity is unanimous in describing the happy exaltation which the highest revelations of Eleusis produced. A new happiness, a superhuman peace descended into the heart of the initiates. Life seemed conquered, the soul delivered, the fearful cycle of existences fulfilled. With clear joy and an ineffable certainty everyone again found themselves in the pure ether of the universal Soul.

We have just relived the drama of Eleusis in its intimate, hidden meaning. I have indicated the main thread which guides one through this labyrinth; I have shown the great unity dominating its richness and complexity. With a wise and sovereign harmony, the various ceremonies were linked to the divine drama which formed the ideal center, the luminous focal point of these religious festivals. Thus the initiates gradually were identified with the action. At first only simple spectators, later they became actors, and finally they recognized that the drama of Persephone really took place within themselves. And what surprise, what joy they experienced in this discovery! If they suffered, if they fought with her in this present life, like her they had the hope of again finding divine felicity, the light of the great Intelligence. The words of the hierophant, the scenes and revelations of the temple, gave them a foretaste of what was to come.

It seems unnecessary to say that each one understood these things according to his degree of education and his intellectual capacity. For as Plato says (and this is true for all time) many people carry the thyrsus and rod, but are little inspired. After the age of Alexander, the Eleusians were affected in a certain measure by pagan decadence, but their exalted foundation remained, saving them from the decay which struck other temples. Through the depth of their sacred doctrine, as well as through the splendor of their presentation, the Mysteries stood their ground for three centuries in the face of a rising Christianity. Then they joined the elite company, who, without denying that Jesus was a revelation of an heroic and divine nature, did not wish to forget, as the Church of that time already was forgetting, the old science and the sacred doctrine. An edict of Theodosius was required, forbidding the ceremonies of the temple of Eleusis, in order to put an end to this august cult, in which the magic of Greek art had delighted in incorporating the highest doctrines of Orpheus, of Pythagoras and of Plato.

Today the refuge of ancient Demeter has disappeared without a trace beside the silent Bay of Eleusis, and only the butterfly, Psyche's insect, crossing the blue gulf on spring days remembers that here the great exile, the human soul, once evoked the gods, and that here it recognized its eternal home.

JESUS

The Mission of Christ

Think not that I am come to destroy the law or the prophets: I am not come to destroy, but to fulfill.

—Matthew 5:17

The Light was in the world, and the World was made by it, and the world knew it not.

—John 1:10

For as the lightning cometh out of the east and shineth even unto the west, so shall also the coming of the Son of Man be.

—Matthew 24:27

38

The Condition of the World at the Birth of Jesus

T HE world's destiny grew critical; the darkened sky was filled with sinister portents.

Despite the efforts of the initiates, in Asia, Africa and Europe polytheism had ended with the collapse of civilization. This does not exclude the sublime cosmogony of Orpheus, so splendidly extolled but already weakened in the time of Homer. One can lay the blame on the difficulty human nature has in maintaining itself at a high spiritual level. For the great spirits of antiquity, the gods were merely a poetic expression of the hierarchical forces of nature, a speaking image of its internal organism. As symbols of cosmic and animate forces these gods continue to live in the consciousness of mankind. In the thinking of the initiates, this diversity of gods or of forces was superseded and penetrated by the Supreme God or pure Spirit. The chief goal of the sanctuaries of Memphis, Delphi and Eleusis had been to teach this unity of God, along with the moral discipline attached to it. But the disciples of Orpheus, Pythagoras and Plato failed in face of the egotism of the politicians, the meanness of the Sophists and the passions of the crowd.

The social and political disintegration of Greece was the result of her religious, moral and intellectual deterioration. Apollo, the solar Word, the manifestation of the supreme God and of the supraterrestrial world through beauty, justice and divination, grows silent. There are no more oracles, no more inspired men, no more real poets: Minerva, Wisdom and Providence, veils herself before her people who are changing into satyrs, profaning the Mysteries, insulting the sages and gods in the theatre of Bacchus, by means of Aristophanic farces. The Mysteries themselves are corrupted, for sycophants and courtesans are admitted to the festivals of Eleusis. When the soul becomes clouded, religion becomes idolatrous; when thought becomes materialistic, philosophy falls into skepticism. Thus we see Lucian, a poor microbe born from the corpse of paganism, ridiculing the myths after Carneades misunderstood their scientific origin.

Superstitious in religion, agnostic in philosophy, selfish and divided in politics, drunk with anarchy and fatally sworn to tyranny; this is what had become of this divine Greece which transmitted the science of Egypt and the Mysteries of Asia to us in forms of immortal beauty.

If anyone understood what was lacking in the ancient world, if anyone tried to raise it again by an effort of heroism and genius, it was Alexander the Great. This legendary conqueror, like his father, Philip, initiated into the Mysteries of Samothrace, revealed himself much more as the spiritual son of Orpheus than the disciple of Aristotle. Doubtless this Achilles of Macedonia who set out with a handful of Greeks, crossing

Asia to India, dreamed of a universal empire, but not through the oppression of peoples or through crushing religion and free science, as did the Caesars. His great idea was the reconciliation of Asia and Europe through a synthesis of religions, based upon a scientific authority. Thus motivated, he paid homage to the science of Aristotle as well as to Minerva of Athens, Jehovah of Jerusalem, Osiris of Egypt and Brahma of the Hindus. As a true initiate he recognized the same Divinity and the same Wisdom beneath all these symbols. This was the broad view, the superb divination of this new Dionysus! The sword of Alexander was the last lightning-flash of the Greece of Orpheus. It illumined both Orient and Occident. Philip's son died, intoxicated by his victory and his dream, leaving the remnants of his empire to rapacious generals. But his thought did not die with him. He had founded Alexandria, where Oriental philosophy, Judaism and Hellenism were ultimately to blend in the crucible of Egyptian esoterism, awaiting the word of the Resurrection of Christ.[70] As the star-twins of Greece, Apollo and Minerva, faded on the horizon, men saw a threatening sign ascending into the stormy sky: the Roman She-Wolf.

What is Rome's origin? The conjuration of a greedy oligarchy in the name of brute force; the oppression of human intellect, of religion, science and art through deified political power; in other words, the opposite of the truth, according to which a government draws its power only from the supreme principles of science, justice and economy. All Roman history is but the outgrowth of this pact of iniquity by which the Roman senators declared war first on Italy, then on the human race. They chose their symbol well! The brass She-Wolf, raising her wild hair and moving her hyena-head on the Capitoline, is the reflection of this government, the demon which will possess the Roman soul to the very last.

In Greece, at least, men always respected the sanctuaries of

Delphi and Eleusis. In Rome they suppressed science and art from the beginning. The efforts of the sage Numa, an Etruscan initiate, failed before the limitless ambition of the Roman senators. To Rome he brought the Sibylline Books, containing a part of the science of Hermes. He created arbitrating judges, elected by the people; he distributed lands to the latter; he erected a temple to Good Faith and Janus, a hierogram which means universality of law; he submitted the right of war to the Fecials. King Numa, whose memory the people did not cease to cherish, and whom they considered to have been inspired by a divine genius, seems therefore to be a historical intervention of sacred science in government. King Numa does not represent Roman genius, but the genius of Etruscan initiation, which followed the same principles as the Schools of Memphis and Delphi.

After Numa, the Roman Senate burned the Sibylline Books, destroyed the authority of the flamens, demolished the judicial institutions and returned to a system where religion was merely an instrument of political domination. Rome became the hydra which swallowed up peoples as well as their gods. Slowly the nations of the earth were subjugated and plundered. The Mamertine Prison was filled with kings from North and South. Wanting no priests other than slaves and charlatans, Rome assassinates the last guardians of esoteric tradition in Gaul, Egypt, Judea and Persia. She pretends to worship the gods, but worships only her She-Wolf. And now in a bloody dawn appears the last son of that wolf, epitomizing the genius of Rome: *Caesar!* Rome has absorbed all peoples; Caesar, her incarnation, devours all powers. Caesar not only dreams of being Emperor of Nations; uniting the tiara and the diadem in his crown, he has himself named *Pontifex Maximus*. After the Battle of Thapsus he is deified as a hero; after Munda, he is declared a god; finally, his statue is placed in the temple of

416

Quirinus and a school of curates is established, bearing his name: *the Julian priests*. As an example of supreme irony and supreme logic of events, this same Caesar who makes himself god, denies the immortality of the soul in presence of the Senate. Is it possible to say more clearly that there is no longer any god except Caesar?

With the Caesars in control, Rome, heiress of Babylon, lifts her hand over the whole world.—Meanwhile, what has become of the Roman State? It has destroyed all collective life outside the Capital. Dictatorship by the military is established in Italy, extortions by governors and publicans in the provinces. —Conquering Rome settles like a vampire upon the corpse of ancient societies.

Now the Roman orgies can parade openly with their bacchanale of vice, their procession of crimes. They begin with the voluptuous meeting of Mark Antony and Cleopatra; they will end with Messalina's outbursts and Nero's madness. They begin with a lascivious, public caricature of the Mysteries; they will end in the Roman Circus, where wild beasts fall upon naked virgins, martyrs of their faith, to the applause of twenty thousand spectators.

Nevertheless, among the peoples conquered by Rome were those who were called the people of God, and whose genius was the opposite of Roman genius. How does it happen that Israel, worn out by internal struggle, crushed by three hundred years of slavery, had preserved their faith undaunted? Why did these conquered people rise up in the face of Greek decadence and Roman orgies like a prophet, head covered with sackcloth and ashes, eyes flashing in terrible anger? How did they dare predict the fall of the masters who had their feet on their neck, and speak of a yet unknown, final triumph, at a time when they too were approaching final ruin? It is because a great idea lived in Israel. This idea had been inculcated by Moses. Under

Joshua, the Twelve Tribes had raised a memorial stone with the inscription, "This is a covenant between us and Jehovah, who is the only God."

In the chapters on Moses we have seen how and why the lawmaker of Israel made monotheism the cornerstone of his science, of his social law and of a universal religious idea. He had had the genius to understand that the future of mankind depended upon the victory of this idea. In order to preserve it, he had written a hieroglyphic book, built a golden Ark, raised a people out of the nomadic dust of the desert. Moses caused the fire of heaven to flash, the thunder to roar over these witnesses of the spiritual idea. Against them were pitted not only the Moabites, the Philistines, the Amalakites and all the peoples of Palestine, but also the passions and weaknesses of the Jewish people themselves. The book ceased to be understood by the priesthood, the Ark was captured by enemies, and again and again the people almost forgot their mission. Why then, in spite of everything, did they remain faithful? Why did Moses' idea remain engraved in letters of fire upon the brow and heart of Israel? To whom is this singular perseverance due—this magnificent fidelity in the midst of the vicissitudes of a turbulent history filled with catastrophes, the fidelity which gives Israel its unique physiognomy among nations? One can answer, To the prophets, and to the institution of prophecy. By oral tradition, this dates back to Moses.

The Hebrews had prophets in all periods of their history, even until the time of their dispersal, but the institution of prophecy appears in an organic form for the first time in the period of Samuel. It was Samuel who founded those brotherhoods of *Nebiim,* those schools of prophets, in the face of a rising royalty and an already degenerate priesthood. He made the schools the strict guardians of esoteric tradition and of the universal religious thought of Moses, as opposed to the kings, in whom the political idea and nationalism were to predominate. In effect, in these brotherhoods were preserved the remains of Moses' science, the sacred music with its modes and powers, occult therapy and, finally, the art of divination which the great prophets handled with great ability and outstanding reverence.

Divination existed in the most varied forms among all peoples of ancient times. But in Israel prophecy was an unfolding, an elevation, an authority in which monotheism preserved the human soul. Prophecy, represented by the theologians of the earth as direct communication with a personal God, denied by naturalistic philosophy as pure superstition, is in reality but the higher manifestation of the universal laws of the spirit. "The general truths which govern the world," says Ewald in his fine book on the prophets, "in other words, *the thoughts of God,* are unchangeable and unassailable, entirely independent of the fluctuations of things, of the will and the actions of men. Man is originally intended to share in them, to understand them and to translate them freely into actions. Thus he reaches his own real destination. But in order for the Word of the Spirit to penetrate the flesh of man, man must first be shaken to his depths by the great upheavals of history. Then eternal Truth bursts forth like a stream of light. This is why it is so often said in the Old Testament that '*Jehovah is the one living God.*' When man hears the divine call, a new life builds up within him; he no longer feels alone, but finds himself in communion with God and with all Truth. Now he is prepared to move from one truth to another, infinitely. In this new life his thought is identified with the universal Will. He has a clear view of the present and a complete faith in the ultimate victory of the divine idea. The man who experiences this is a prophet, that is, he feels irresistibly compelled to show himself to others as God's representative. *His thought becomes vision,* and that higher Power which makes Truth well up in his soul, sometimes by breaking it, constitutes the prophetic element. *The prophetic manifestations in history have been the thunderbolts and lightnings of Truth."*

From this stream those giants, Elias, Isaiah, Ezekiel and Jeremiah drew their strength. In the depth of their caves or in kings' palaces, they were truly the sentinels of the Lord and, as Elisha says of his master, Elijah, "The chariots and horsemen of Israel." Often with perfect accuracy they foretell the death of kings, the fall of kingdoms and the punishments of Israel. Again, they are mistaken. Although lighted from the sun of divine Truth, in their hands the prophetic torch frequently flickers and grows dark at the breath of national passions. But never do they blunder in regard to moral truths, the true mission of Israel, or the ultimate triumph of justice among men. As true initiates they preach contempt for external cult, the abolition of bloody sacrifices, purification of the soul and charity. Their insight is particularly admirable in what concerns the ultimate victory of monotheism, its liberating and peacemaking role for all people.

The most terrible misfortunes which can strike a nation, including foreign invasion and mass deportation to Babylon, were unable to shake that faith. Listen to Isaiah during Sennacherib's invasion: "Rejoice ye with Jerusalem, and be glad with her, all ye that love her: all ye that mourn for her, rejoice with her with a great joy. For thus saith the Lord: Behold I shall extend peace to her like a river, and the glory of the Gentiles like a flowing stream: then shall ye suck and shall be borne upon her sides, and dandled upon her knees. As one whom his mother comforteth, so shall I comfort you; and ye shall be comforted in Jerusalem. For I know their works and their thoughts; it shall come to pass that I will gather all nations and all tongues; and they shall come and shall behold my glory."

Only today, before the tomb of Christ, is this vision beginning to be fulfilled; but who can deny its prophetic truth when one considers Israel's role in the history of mankind?

No less unshakable than this faith in the future glory of Jerusalem, in its moral grandeur and its religious universality, is the faith of the prophets in a Savior or Messiah. All speak about him. Again, the incomparable Isaiah is the one who sees him most clearly, who describes him with most power in his bold language: "And there shall come forth a rod out of the stem of Jesse, and a Branch shall grow out of his roots: And the spirit of the Lord shall rest upon him, the spirit of wisdom and understanding, the spirit of counsel and might, the spirit of knowledge and of the fear of the Lord. . . . But with righteousness shall he judge the poor, and reprove with equity for the meek of the earth: and he shall smite the earth with the rod of his mouth, and with the breath of his lips shall he slay the wicked." At this vision, the despairing soul of the prophet is calmed, lighting up like a cloudy sky at the tremor of a celestial harp, and all the storms vanish. For now it is truly the picture of the Galilean which is traced before his inner eye: "He shall grow up before him as a tender plant, and as a root out of a dry ground: he hath no form nor comeliness. . . . He is despised and rejected of men; a man of sorrows. . . . Surely he hath borne our griefs, and carried our sorrows: yet we did esteem him stricken, smitten of God, and afflicted. But he was wounded for our transgressions, he was bruised for our iniquities: the chastisement of our peace was upon him; and with his stripes we are healed. . . . He was oppressed, and he was afflicted, yet he opened not his mouth: he is brought as a lamb to the slaughter, and as a sheep before her shearers is dumb, so he openeth not his mouth."

For eight centuries, above dissensions and national misfortunes, the thundering word of the prophets caused the idea and the image of the Messiah to be present, sometimes as a terrible avenger, sometimes as an angel of mercy. Born under Assyrian tyranny, amidst the exile of Babylon, unfolded under Persian domination, the Messianic idea continued to grow during the reign of the Seleucides and Maccabees. When the Roman domination and the reign of Herod came, the Messiah was living in the consciousness of all. If the great prophets had seen him as a just man and a martyr, a true son of God, the people—faithful to the Judaic idea—imagined him as a David, a Solomon or a new Maccabeus. But whoever this restorer of Israel's glory was to be, everyone believed in him, waited for him, called upon him. Such is the power of prophetic activity.

Thus, just as Roman history ended fatally with Caesar by way of destiny's instinctive path and infernal logic, so Israel's history led freely to Christ by way of the conscious path and the divine logic of Providence, manifested in its visible representatives, the prophets. Evil is fatally condemned to contradict itself and to destroy itself because it is false; but the Good, despite all obstacles, engenders light and harmony in the succession of the ages because it is the fecundity of Truth. From its triumph Rome had only Caesarism; from its decline, Israel gave birth to the Messiah, lending truth to that beautiful saying of a modern poet, "Out of its own shipwreck, hope creates the thing contemplated."

A faint expectancy hung over the peoples of the earth. In the excess of their evils, all humanity had a foreboding of a Saviour. For centuries all mythologies had dreamed of a divine child. Temples spoke of him mysteriously; astrologers calculated his coming; in their delirium the Sibyls had screamed of the fall of the pagan gods. The initiates had announced that one day the world would be ruled by one of their own, by a son of God. The earth waited for a spiritual king who would be understood by children, by the humble and the poor.

The great Aeschylus, son of a priest of Eleusis, was almost

murdered by the Athenians because through the mouth of his Prometheus he dared say in the public theatre that the reign of Jupiter-Fate would end. Four centuries later, in the shadow of the throne of Augustus, gentle Virgil announces a new age, and dreams of a marvelous child: "That last Age, predicted by the Cumaean Sibyl, has come. The great order of centuries past is beginning again; already from the heavenly heights a new race descends. Deign, chaste Lucina, to protect this Child, whose birth is to banish the Age of Iron and to restore the Golden Age to the world; already your brother Apollo reigns. . . . See the world in balance, see earth and seas in their immensity, the sky and its deep vault, all nature trembling with the hope of the Age to come."

Where will this child be born? From what divine world will this soul come? By what lightning-flash of love will he descend to earth? By what wondrous purity, by what superhuman energy will he remember the heaven he has left behind? By what still more tremendous effort will he know how to arise once more from the depths of earthly consciousness, leading humanity in his train?

No one would have dared admit it, but everyone awaited him. Herod the Great, Idumean usurper and protégé of Caesar Augustus, was dying in his palace in Jericho after a luxurious and bloody reign, which had covered Judea with marvelous buildings and human hecatombs. Stricken with a frightful malady, a decomposition of the blood, he was breathing his last, hated by all, eaten by fury and remorse, haunted by the specters of his innumerable victims among whom was his innocent wife,—the noble Miriam, descended from the Maccabees, as well as three of his own sons. The seven women of his harem had fled before the royal phantom which, still living, already smelled of the sepulchre. Even his bodyguard had abandoned him. Impassive, watching beside the dying, was his sister Salome, his evil genius, the instigator of his blackest crimes. Diadem upon her brow, her breast shimmering with precious jewels, haughtily she watched, awaiting the last breath of the king so she could seize the royal power.

Thus died the last king of the Jews. At that very moment, the future spiritual king of humanity had just been born. Silently, in profound humility and obscurity, the few initiates of Israel prepared for his reign.

39

Mary — Jesus' Early Development

JEHOSHOUA, whom we call Jesus, from his Hellenized name, *Iesous*, was probably born in Nazareth. It was certainly in this out-of-the-way corner of Galilee that his childhood was spent and the first, the greatest of Christian Mysteries was realized: the unfolding of the soul of Christ. Jesus was son of Myriam, whom we call Mary, the wife of the carpenter, Joseph. She was a Galilean woman of noble birth, and was related to the Essenes.

Legend has embroidered a tapestry of wonders around the birth of Jesus. If legend harbors many a superstition, sometimes it also encloses little-known spiritual truths, because the latter are beyond common perception. One fact seems to stand out in the legendary story of Mary—that Jesus was a child dedicated to a prophetic mission by the wish of his mother before his birth. The same is reported concerning several heroes and prophets of the Old Testament. These sons, dedicated to God by their mothers, were called *Nazarenes*. In this light, it is interesting to read again the stories of Samson and of Samuel.

An angel announces to Samson's mother that she is about to become pregnant, that she will give birth to a son, that his hair will not be cut, "for the child shall be a Nazarite unto God from the womb: and he shall begin to deliver Israel out of the hand of the Philistines." Samuel's mother herself asked God for her son. "Hannah, the wife of Elkanah, was sterile . . . And she vowed a vow and said, O Lord of hosts, if thou wilt indeed . . . give thy handmaid a male child, then I will give him to the Lord all the days of his life, and there shall no razor come upon his head . . . *Then Elkanah knew his wife* . . . Sometime later, after Hannah had conceived, she bore a child and named him Samuel because, she said, I have asked him of the Lord." According to early Semitic roots, SAM-U-EL means *The Inner Splendor of God*. The mother, illumined by the one she was conceiving, considered him *"the ethereal essence of the Lord."*

These passages are extremely important because they cause us to penetrate the constant and living esoteric tradition of Israel, reaching by this means into the true meaning of the Christian legend. Elkanah, the husband, is really Samuel's earthly father according to the flesh, but the Lord is his heavenly Father according to the Spirit. Here the figurative language of Judaic monotheism conceals the doctrine of the prior existence of the soul. The initiate woman makes an appeal to a higher soul in order to receive it into her womb, and to bring a prophet into the world. This doctrine, quite concealed among the Jews and completely absent from their official worship, was a part of the secret tradition of the initiates. It appears in the prophets. Jeremiah affirms it in these terms: "Then the word of the Lord came unto me saying, Before I formed thee in the belly, I knew thee; before thou camest forth out of the womb, I sanctified thee, and I ordained thee a prophet unto the nations." Jesus will say the same thing to the scandalized

Pharisees: "Verily, verily I say unto you: Before Abraham was, I am."

How much of all this can one relate to Mary, the mother of Jesus? It seems that in the early Christian communities, Jesus was considered a son of Joseph and Mary, since Matthew gives us the genealogical tree of Joseph in order to prove that Jesus descends from David. Thus, like a few Gnostic sects they saw in Jesus a son given by the Lord in the same sense as was Samuel. Later, wishing to show Jesus' supernatural origin, legend wove its gold and blue veil: the story of Joseph and Mary, the Annunciation and even Mary's infancy in the temple.

If we try to disengage the esoteric meaning from Jewish tradition and Christian legend, we shall say that providential action, or, more plainly speaking, the influx of the spiritual world which contributes to the birth of each man, whoever he may be, is more powerful and more visible at the birth of men of genius, whose appearance is in no way explained by the single law of physical atavism. This influx reaches its greatest intensity in the instance of one of those divine prophets, destined to change the face of the world. The soul chosen for a divine mission comes from a divine world; it comes freely, consciously, but in order that it can enter the scene of earthly life, a chosen vessel is necessary. This latter is the call of a mother from among the elite. She is one who by her moral bearing, by means of the desire of her soul and the purity of her life, senses, attracts, incarnates in her blood and in her flesh the soul of the Redeemer, destined to become a son of God in the eyes of men. This is the profound truth that the ancient idea of the Virgin Mother concealed. Hindu genius had already expressed it in the legend of Krishna. The Gospels of Matthew and Luke rendered it with simplicity and highly admirable poetry.

"For the soul which comes from heaven, birth is a death,"

Empedocles said, five hundred years before Christ. However sublime a spirit may be, once buried in flesh it temporarily loses the remembrance of its entire past; once taken into the activities of corporeal life, the development of its earthly consciousness is subjected to the laws of the world where it is incarnated. It comes under the power of the elements. The higher its origin, the greater will be its effort to regain its dormant powers, its celestial qualities, and to become aware of its mission.

Intense and sensitive souls need silence and peace in order to blossom. Jesus grew up in the calm of Galilee. His first impressions were sweet, austere and calm. His valley birthplace resembled a bit of heaven fallen upon the side of the mountain. The town of Nazareth has hardly changed in the course of centuries. Its houses, rising in rows beneath the rock, according to the reports of travelers, resemble white cubes scattered in a forest of pomegranate trees, fig trees and vineyards, over which fly great flocks of doves.

Around this refuge of coolness and green blows the sharp air of the mountains; from the heights is seen the open, clear horizon of Galilee. To this impressive landscape add the serious home life of a devout, patriarchal family. The power of Jewish education rested from earliest times in the unity of the Law and of the Faith, as well as in the strong family organization, dominated by national and religious ideals. For the child, the paternal household was a sort of temple. Instead of the frescoed laughing fauns and nymphs which decorated the atria of Greek houses, such as could be seen at Sephoris and Tiberias, in the Jewish houses one saw only passages from the Law and the prophets, whose severe texts were inscribed over the doors and on the walls in Chaldean letters. But the union of the father and mother in the love of their children warmed and illumined the bareness of this interior with a completely spiritual life. In such a home Jesus received his early training; there, from the oral teaching of the father and mother he first learned to understand the Scriptures.

From his early years, the long, strange destiny of the people of God unfolded before his eyes in the periodic Festivals which were celebrated in the family by reading, singing and praying. At the Feast of Tabernacles, a hut of myrtle and olive branches was raised in the courtyard or on the roof of the house as a reminder of the time of the nomadic Patriarchs. They lighted the seven-branched candlestick, unrolled the scrolls of papyrus and read the sacred stories. For the child's soul the Lord was present not only in the starry heavens but also in the candlestick which reflected His Glory, in the speech of the father, as well as in the silent love of the mother. Thus the great days of Israel cradled the childhood of Jesus—days of joy and mourning, of triumph and exile, of afflictions without number and of eternal hope. In face of the burning, penetrating questions of the child, the father was silent. But the mother, raising her large eyes with their gaze like that of a Syrian dreamer, meeting the questioning look of her son, would say, "The word of God lives only in His prophets. One day the Essene sages, the hermits of Mount Carmel and of the Dead Sea will answer you."

One also pictures the child Jesus mixing with his companions and exercising over them that singular prestige which precocious intelligence gives, along with his feeling for justice and active sympathy. We follow him to the synagogue where he hears the Scribes and Pharisees debate, where he himself is to use his dialectical power. We see him repelled by the dryness of these teachers of the Law who tortured the letter to the point of doing away with the Spirit. We also see him observing the pagan life, divining it and compassing it with a glance as he visits wealthy Sephoris, the capital of Galilee, home of Antipas,

dominated by its acropolis and guarded by Herod's mercenaries: Gauls, Thracians, foreigners from many countries.

Perhaps on one of these trips, so frequent in Jewish families,
he visited one of the Phoenician cities, veritable human ant-
hills, swarming at the edge of the sea. From afar he would have
seen the low, thick-columned temples surrounded with dark
bushes, from which came the chanting of the priestesses of
Astarte, accompanied by mournful flutes. Their cry of pleasure,
sharp like pain, awakened in his astonished heart a long tremor
of anguish and pity. Then, with a feeling of deliverance, Mary's
son returned to his beloved mountains. He climbed over the
hill of Nazareth and looked upon the vast horizon of Galilee
and Samaria. He saw Carmel, Gilboa, Tabor, the Sichem
Mountains, ancient witnesses of the patriarchs and prophets.
"The high places" unfolded in a circle; they stood out against
the vastness of the sky like great altars awaiting fire and incense.—Were they waiting for someone?

Yet, however powerful the impressions of the surrounding
world on Jesus' soul may have been, they all paled before the
sovereign truth of his inner world. This truth opened within
him like a luminous flower emerging from a dark stream. It
resembled the increasing clarity which was developing within
him when he was alone, and which he welcomed. Then men and
objects, near or far, seemed transparent in their secret essence.
He read thoughts and beheld souls. Then, in memory, as
though through a thin veil, divinely beautiful, radiant beings
were hovering over him or were assembled in the worship of a
blinding Light.

Marvelous visions haunted his sleep or stood between himself and reality through a virtual dividing of his consciousness.
At the climax of these ecstasies which bore him from region to
region in other worlds, he sometimes felt drawn by a dazzling
Light, then immersed in an incandescent sun. He retained an

ineffable tenderness and an extraordinary strength from these experiences. He felt reconciled with all beings, in harmony with the universe. What then was that mysterious Light which burst forth from within himself and carried him off to the most distant spaces, that Light which first touched him from his mother's large eyes and now united him with all souls by secret ties? Was this not the Source of souls and worlds?

He called it his Heavenly Father.

This primal feeling of unity with God in the light of love— this is Jesus' first great revelation. An inner voice told him to seal it deep within himself, but it was to illumine his entire life. It gave him invincible certainty. It made him gentle and indomitable. Of his thought it made a diamond shield; of his word, a sword of light.

This profoundly secret, mystical life was united in the adolescent with complete clarity in regard to the things of external life. Luke describes him for us at the age of twelve, "growing in strength, in grace and in wisdom." Religious consciousness was the innate thing in Jesus—absolutely independent of the external world. His prophetic and Messianic consciousness could not be awakened except by a shock from outside, by the life of his time and finally by a special initiation and a long inner unfoldment. Traces of this are found in the Gospels and elsewhere.

The first great crisis came to Jesus on that first journey to Jerusalem with his parents, of which Luke has spoken. That city, the pride of Israel, had become the center of Jewish aspirations. Its misfortunes had only served to excite men's minds. One could say that the more the tombs multiplied there, the more hope was exalted. Under the Seleucides, under the Maccabees, first by Pompey, finally by Herod, Jerusalem had suffered dreadful sieges. Blood had flowed like rivers; the Roman legions had slaughtered the people in the streets; mass crucifixions had polluted the hills with infernal scenes. After so many horrors, after the humiliation of the Roman occupation, after decimating the Sanhedrin and reducing the pontiff to the status of a trembling slave, Herod, as though in irony, had rebuilt the Temple more magnificently than that of Solomon. Nevertheless, Jerusalem remained the Holy City. Had not Isaiah, Jesus' favorite author, called it "the bride, before whom all peoples shall kneel?" He had said, "Thou shalt call thy walls Salvation; and thy gates Praise, and the nations shall come to the splendor which shall arise over you." To see Jerusalem and the Temple of Jehovah was the dream of all Jews, especially since Judea had become a Roman province. Pilgrims came there from Perea, Galilee, Alexandria and Babylon. On the way, in the desert, under the palms, beside wells, psalms were sung; the travelers longed for the Temple of the Lord, they looked eagerly for Mount Zion.

A strange feeling of oppression must have come over Jesus' soul when on his first journey he saw Jerusalem with its impressive walls, sitting upon the mountain like a dark fortress, when he saw the Roman amphitheater of Herod beside its gates, the Tower of Antonia overlooking the Temple, Roman legionnaires, spear in hand, watching from above. He climbed the steps of the Temple. He admired the splendor of the marble porticoes where the Pharisees paraded in sumptuous garments. He crossed the Court of the Gentiles, the Court of the Women. With the crowd of Israelites he came near the Gate of Nicanor and the balustrade three cubits long, behind which one could see priests in their robes of purple and deep red, shining with gold and precious stones, officiating before the sanctuary, sacrificing goats and bulls and sprinkling the people with the blood while pronouncing a benediction. This did not resemble the temple of his dreams nor the heaven of his heart.

Then he went down into the more populous sections of the

432

city. There he saw beggars pale from hunger, anguished faces reflecting the last civil wars, tortures and crucifixions. Leaving by one of the gates of the city, he wandered in those rocky valleys, in those dark ravines where quarries, pools and kings' tombs are found, forming a kind of sepulchral belt around Jerusalem. There he saw insane men coming out of caves, uttering blasphemies against the living and the dead. Then, descending by a broad stairway to the pool of Siloam, as deep as a well, he saw beside the yellowish water, lepers, paralytics, the wretched, covered with all kinds of sores. An irresistible impulse forced him to look directly into their eyes, to drink in all their pain. Some asked him for help, others were wan and hopeless; others, stupefied, seemed to suffer no longer.—But how much time had been required for them to become like this?

Then Jesus asked himself, What good is this Temple, these priests, these hymns, these sacrifices, since they cannot remedy all these sorrows? And suddenly, like a stream swollen by endless tears, he felt the sorrows of these souls, of this city, of these people, of all mankind, flow into his heart. He understood that no longer could he experience a happiness which he could not share with others. These looks, these despairing stares, were never to leave his memory. That melancholy bride, Human Suffering, walked beside him, saying to him, 'I will never leave you!'

He went away, filled with sadness and anguish. When once again he saw the luminous peaks of Galilee, a profound cry came from his heart: 'Heavenly Father! . . . I want to know! I want to heal! I want to save!'

40

The Essenes — John the Baptist — the Temptation

He could learn what he wished to know only from the Essenes.

The Gospels have maintained an absolute silence about Jesus' deeds and travels before his meeting with John the Baptist, when, as they relate, he assumed his ministry. Immediately afterward he appears in Galilee with a teaching which has been formulated with the assurance of a prophet and the consciousness of the Messiah. But it is evident that this bold and premeditated beginning was preceded by a long development and a virtual initiation. It is no less certain that this initiation must have taken place in the only association which then preserved in Israel the real traditions of the prophets, together with their way of living. This cannot be doubted by those who, raising themselves above the superstition of the letter and the mechanical mania for the written document, have the courage to discover the connection between things. This is apparent, not only from inner relationships between the teaching of Jesus and that of the Essenes, but also from the very silence Christ and his disciples maintained concerning this sect. Why does one who attacks all the religious groups of his time with unprecedented freedom, never name the Essenes? Why do the Apostles and writers of the Gospels not speak of them? Evidently because they consider the Essenes as their own group, because they are united with them by the vow of the Mysteries and because the sect was linked with the Christians.

In Jesus' time the Order of the Essenes constituted the last remnants of those brotherhoods of prophets organized by Samuel. The despotism of the masters of Palestine, along with the jealousy of an ambitious and servile priesthood had pushed them into retreat and silence. They no longer fought as did their predecessors; they were content with preserving tradition. They had two main centers: one in Egypt beside Lake Maoris, the other in Palestine at Engaddi, beside the Dead Sea. The name "Essenes" which they had given themselves, came from the Syrian word, *Asaya,* meaning physicians, in Greek, *therapeutes,* for their sole avowed ministry, so far as the public was concerned, was that of healing physical and moral maladies. "They studied very carefully," said Josephus, "certain writings on medicine which dealt with the secret properties of plants and minerals." Some possessed the gift of prophecy like Menahim, who had predicted to Herod that he would reign. "They serve God," said Philo, "with a great piety, not by offering Him victims, but in sanctifying their spirit. They flee from cities and apply themselves to the arts of peace. There is not one slave among them; they are all free and work for one another."

The rules of the Order were strict. In order to enter, a novitiate of one year was required. If one had given satisfactory proof of temperance, he was admitted to the ablutions but without entering into relationship with the masters of the Order. Two more years of trial were required before one was received into the Brotherhood. The members swore "by terrible oaths" to observe the duties of the Order and to betray none of its secrets. Then only did they take part in the communal meals, which were celebrated with great solemnity, forming the intimate cult of the Essenes. The garments they wore at these meals they considered sacred, removing them before returning to work. These fraternal love feasts, the primitive form of the Supper instituted by Jesus, began and ended with prayer.

On these occasions the original interpretation of the sacred books of Moses and the prophets was given, but in the explanation of the texts as well as in initiation there were three meanings and three stages. All this resembled the organization of the Pythagoreans,[71] but it is certain that it also existed in about the same form among the ancient prophets, for it is found in all places of initiation. In addition, the Essenes taught the basic ideas of the Orphic and Pythagorean doctrine, including that of the pre-existence of the soul, the consequence of and reason for its immortality. "The soul," as Josephus reported, "descending from the most subtle ether and drawn into the body by a certain natural charm, lives there as in a prison; freed from the bonds of the body as from a long servitude, it flies away with joy."

Among the Essenes the brothers themselves lived in remote places under a community of property and in a state of celibacy, tilling the soil and sometimes educating the children of outsiders. As for the married Essenes, they constituted a sort of Third Order, affiliated with and subject to the other. Silent gentle and serious, they were seen here and there practising the arts of peace. Weavers, carpenters, vine growers or gardeners, they never were weapons makers or merchants. Spread in little groups throughout Palestine, in Egypt, even as far as Mount Horeb, they were dedicated to most generous hospitality. Thus we shall see Jesus and his disciples travel from city to city, from province to province, always certain of finding shelter. "The Essenes," said Josephus, "were of an exemplary morality; they strove to repress all passion and all emotion of anger; they were always kind, peaceful and of the highest good faith in their relations. Their word had more weight than an oath; they considered the oath superfluous in ordinary life. Rather than violate the least religious precept they bore the most cruel tortures with an admirable strength of soul and with a smile on their lips."

Indifferent to the external pomp of the cult in Jerusalem, repelled by the hardness of the Saducees, by the pride of the Pharisees, by the pedantry and dryness of the synagogue, Jesus was drawn to the Essenes by a natural affinity.[72] Joseph's premature death left Mary's son, now a man, entirely free. His brothers could continue their father's trade and maintain the home. His mother allowed him leave in secret for Engaddi. Welcomed as a brother, greeted as one of the elect, he must have rapidly acquired an invincible ascendancy over the masters themselves by means of his superior faculties, his ardent charity and that divine element which pervaded all his being. But from them he received what the Essenes alone could give him: the esoteric tradition of the prophets, and through this, his own historical and religious orientation.

He understood the abyss which separated the official Jewish doctrine from the ancient wisdom of the initiates, the true mother of religions, forever persecuted by Satan, that is, the spirit of Evil, the spirit of egotism, hatred and negation joined with absolute political power and priestly imposture. He learned that under the seal of its symbolism, *Genesis* contained a theogony and a cosmogony as far removed from its literal meaning as the deepest science from the most childish fable. He contemplated the Days of the Elohim, of eternal creation through the emanation of the elements and the formation of the worlds, the origin of souls and their return to God by progressive existences, or *The Generations of Adam*. He was struck by the greatness of the thought of Moses, who desired to pave the way for the religious unity of nations by creating the cult of the One God and by incarnating this idea in a people.

They then communicated to him the doctrine of the Divine Word, already taught by Krishna in India, by the priests of Osiris in Egypt, by Orpheus and Pythagoras in Greece and known among the prophets under the name *the Mystery of the Son of Man and of the Son of God*. According to this teaching, the highest manifestation of God is man, who by virtue of his constitution, his form, his organs and his intellect is the image of the Universal Being, possessing His faculties. But, in the earthly evolution of mankind, God is dispersed as it were, broken up and mutilated in the multiplicity of men and of human imperfection. He suffers, he seeks himself, nevertheless, he is the Son of Man, the perfect Man. The Man symbol, deepest thought of God, remains hidden in the infinite abyss of His desire and His power. However, at certain periods when it is a question of saving humanity from an abyss, of bringing mankind together in order to lift them higher, a chosen one becomes identified with Divinity, draws It to him through strength, wisdom and love and in turn, manifests It to men. Then the Divine, through the power and the breath of the Spirit, is completely present in him; *the Son of Man* becomes *the Son of God* and His living Word. In other ages and among other peoples there had already been Sons of God, but since Moses none had been raised in Israel. All the prophets waited for his Messiah. The seers even said that this time he would be called *the Son of Woman*, of celestial Isis, of the divine

Light, who is the Bride of God, because in him the light of Love would shine with a brilliance as yet unknown to earth.

These hidden things which the patriarch of the Essenes unveiled to the young Galilean on the arid shores of the Dead Sea in the solitude of Engaddi, seemed both marvelous and familiar to him. With great emotion he heard the leader of the Order explain these words which are still read today in the Book of Enoch: "From the beginning, the Son of Man was in the Mysteries. The Most High kept him in His presence, and *manifested him to His elect* . . . But the kings will be frightened and will bow their faces to earth, and fear will seize them when they shall see the *Son of Woman* sitting on the throne of his glory. Then the Elect will call all the forces of heaven, all the saints from on high, and the power of God. Then the Cherubim, the Seraphim, the Ophanim, all the angels of *Power,* all the angels of the *Lord,* that is, of the Elect and of the other *Power,* who serve on earth and above the waters, will lift up their voices."[73]

At these revelations, the words of the prophets, read and meditated upon a hundred times, flamed in the Nazarene's eyes with new, deep and terrible light like flashes of lightning in the night sky. Who then was this Chosen One, and when would he come to Israel?

Jesus spent several years with the Essenes. He submitted himself to their discipline, he studied the secrets of nature and practiced esoteric healing with them. He completely blunted his senses in order to develop his spirit. Not a single day passed without his meditating on the destinies of mankind and in questioning himself. It was a memorable night for the Order of the Essenes and for its new adept when he received, in deepest secret, the higher initiation at the fourth stage, the one granted only in the special case of a prophetic mission, desired by the brother and approved by the Elders. They met in a grotto carved inside a mountain, a vast room containing an altar and seats of stone. The leader of the Order was there with a few Elders. At times two or three Essene women, initiate prophetesses, were admitted to the mysterious ceremony. Bearing torches and palms, they greeted the new initiate, who was clothed in white linen, as "Bridegroom and King," whom they had foretold and whom they now saw for the first time. Then the head of the Order, ordinarily a man of one hundred years (Josephus says that the Essenes lived to a very advanced age), presented *the golden chalice* to him, the symbol of supreme initiation, which held *the wine of the Lord's vineyard,* symbol of divine inspiration. Some said that Moses had drunk from it with the Seventy. Others believed that it dated back to Abraham, who received from Melchizedek this same initiation with the elements of bread and wine. The Elder presented the cup only to that man in whom he had recognized with certainty signs of a prophetic mission. But nobody could define this mission for him; he had to discover it for himself. For this is the law of the initiates: Nothing from the outside; all from within. Henceforth he was free, the master of his actions, liberated from the Order, himself a hierophant, left to the breath of the Spirit, which could cast him into the abyss or bear him to the summits beyond the region of torment and earthly passions.

When the Nazarene took the cup after the songs, prayers and sacramental words of the Elder, a faint ray of dawn, slipping through a crevice in the mountain, gently touched the torches and the long white garments of the young Essene women. The latter trembled when the light fell upon the pale Galilean, for a great sadness appeared upon his beautiful face. Did his wandering gaze rest upon the sick of Siloam? Did he already see his path leading into the depths of that ever present suffering?

Now at this time John the Baptist was preaching beside the Jordan. He was not an Essene, but was a prophet of the people, a member of the strong race of Judah. Driven into the desert by a fierce piety, he had led the most ascetic life in prayers, fasts and macerations. Over his bare skin, tanned by the sun, he wore a garment of camel's skin as a sign of the penance he wished to impose upon himself and his people. For he deeply felt the distress of Israel and awaited the deliverance. In line with the Judaic idea he imagined that the Messiah would come soon as an avenger and a judge; that, as a new Maccabeus, he would organize the people, drive out the Romans, punish the guilty, enter Jerusalem in triumph and reestablish the kingdom of Israel in peace and justice. John announced to the multitudes the imminent arrival of this Messiah; he added that it was necessary to prepare oneself by repentance of the heart. Borrowing the custom of ablutions from the Essenes, transforming it in his own way, he had conceived of baptism in the Jordan as a visible symbol, an external fulfillment of the inner purification he required.

This new ceremony, this vehement preaching before immense crowds in the desert, which bordered the waters of Jordan between the rugged mountains of Judea and Perea, gripped imaginations, drew multitudes. It recalled the glorious days of the ancient prophets; it gave the people what they did not find in the Temple: the inner appeal, and, after the terrors of repentance, a dim but mighty hope. From all parts of Palestine they came to hear the saint of the desert, who announced the Messiah. Large groups, drawn by his voice, remained camped for weeks so they could hear him each day. They did not want to go away, for they were waiting for the Messiah to appear. Many asked to take up arms under his command, to begin the holy war again.

Herod Antipas and the priests of Jerusalem were becoming troubled by this movement. Besides, the signs of the time were serious. Tiberius, seventy-four years of age, was ending his life surrounded by the debaucheries of Capri; Pontius Pilate redoubled his violence against the Jews. In Egypt, the priests had announced that the Phoenix was about to be reborn from its own ashes.

Inwardly aware that his prophetic calling was increasing, but still groping his way, Jesus also came to the desert of Jordan, accompanied by a few Essene brothers, who already were following him as a teacher. He wanted to see the Baptist, to hear him and to submit himself to public baptism. He wanted to enter upon his tasks by way of an act of humility and reverence for the prophet who dared lift his voice against the rulers of the day and to awaken the soul of Israel from its sleep.

He saw the rude ascetic, shaggy and hairy with his visionary leonine head, standing in a wooden pulpit under a rustic tabernacle covered with branches and goatskins. Around him, among the sparse bushes of the desert, was an immense crowd, a whole encampment: tax collectors, Herod's soldiers, Samaritans, Levites from Jerusalem, Idumeans with their herds of sheep. Even Arabs had stopped there with their camels, tents and caravans at "the voice which cried in the wilderness." And that thundering voice rolled over the multitude: "Repent, prepare the way of the Lord; clear his paths!" He called the Pharisees and Sadducees "a generation of vipers." He added that "the axe is already at the root of the trees," and about the Messiah, he said, "I baptize you only with water, but he will baptize you with fire!"

Then toward sunset, Jesus saw these masses of people pressing toward a cove on the banks of the Jordan, and Herod's mercenaries and brigands bent their rough backs beneath the water which the Baptist poured over them. Jesus went nearer. John did not know Jesus; he had heard nothing of him, but he recognized the Essene by his linen robe. He saw him, lost in the crowd, descend into the water to the waist, humbly bending himself to receive the baptism. When the neophyte stood up again, the fearful eyes of the wild preacher and the gaze of the Galilean met. The man of the desert trembled under this ray of wondrous sweetness, and the words escaped him involuntarily, "Are you the Messiah?" The mysterious Essene answered nothing, but bowing his thoughtful head and crossing his hands upon his breast, he asked the Baptist for his benediction. John knew that silence was the law of the Essene novices. Solemnly he raised his two hands; then with his companions the Nazarene disappeared among the reeds beside the river.

The Baptist watched him depart with a mixture of doubt, secret joy and profound melancholy. What were his own knowledge and his prophetic hope before the light he had seen in the eyes of the Unknown, a light which seemed to light up all his being? If this young, handsome Galilean was the Messiah, he had seen the joy of his days! But his own task was finished, his voice was about to be silent. From that day on he began to preach with a deeper and more emotional fervor on the sad theme, "It is necessary that he grow and that I diminish." He began to feel the lassitude and sadness of old lions who are weary with roaring and lie down in silence, awaiting death. . . .

Was he the Messiah? The Baptist's question also resounded in Jesus' soul. Since the unfolding of his consciousness, he had found God in himself and the certainty of the kingdom of heaven in the radiant beauty of his visions. Then human suffering had thrust into his heart its terrible cry of anguish. The Essene sages had taught him the secret of religions, the science of the Mysteries; they had shown him the spiritual decay of mankind, its expectation of a Saviour. But how could he find the strength to save mankind from the abyss?—Here the direct call of John the Baptist fell into the silence of his meditation like the lightning of Sinai.—Was he the Messiah?

Jesus could answer this question only by withdrawing into the deepest part of his being. Hence that retreat, that fast of forty days, which Matthew sums up in the form of a symbolic legend. In reality, in Jesus' life *The Temptation* represents that great crisis, that sovereign vision of Truth which all prophets and all religious initiates must experience before beginning their work.

Above Engaddi where the Essenes cultivated sesame and grapes, a steep path led to a grotto opening in the face of the mountain. It was entered between two Doric columns carved in the rock, similar to those of the retreat of the Apostles in the Valley of Jehosaphat. There one remained suspended over the deep abyss as though in an eagle's nest. At the end of a gorge below, one could see vineyards and human dwellings; in the distance was the Dead Sea, motionless and grey, while further away rose the desolate Mountains of Moab. The Essenes had obtained this retreat for their members who wished to submit themselves to the trial of solitude. Here were found several scrolls of the prophets, strengthening aromatics, dry figs and a little stream of water, the only food of the ascetic in meditation. Here Jesus came.

First he reviewed in his mind all of mankind's past. He weighed the gravity of the present moment. Rome was dominant, and with her what the Persian Magi had called the reign of Ahriman, and the prophets, the reign of Satan, the sign of the Beast, the apotheosis of evil. Darkness was coming over humanity, the somber soul of the earth. From Moses the people of Israel had received the royal and priestly mission of representing the male religion of the Father, the pure Spirit, and of teaching it to the other nations, thus bringing about its triumph. Had Israel's kings and priests fulfilled this mission? The prophets who alone had had an awareness of it, answered with a single voice, No! Israel was dying in the grip of Rome. Was it necessary for the hundredth time to risk such an uprising as the Pharisees still wished, a restoration of the temporal royalty of

444

Israel by force? Should he declare himself the son of David, crying out with Isaiah, "I will crush the people in my anger, and I will make them drunk in my indignation, and I shall overturn their power on the earth?" Should he be a new Maccabeus and have himself named pontiff-king? Jesus could attempt this. He had seen the crowds ready to rise up at the voice of John the Baptist, and the strength which he felt within himself was even greater still! But did might make right? Would the sword put an end to the reign of the sword? Would that not be merely providing new recruits for the powers of darkness, lurking in the shadows, waiting for their prey?

Was it not necessary rather to make accessible to all, that Truth which until then had remained the privilege of a few sanctuaries and rare initiates, to open hearts to it, while waiting for it to enter the understanding through inner revelation and wisdom? In other words, should he not preach the kingdom of heaven to the simple, to substitute for the reign of law that of grace, thus thoroughly transforming mankind while regenerating human souls?

But whose would be the victory? Satan's or God's? Would it be that of the spirit of evil who reigns with the tremendous powers of earth, or of the divine Spirit who reigns in the invisible, heavenly regions and sleeps in the heart of men like a spark within the people? What would be the future of the prophet who would dare to tear the veil from the Temple, to show the emptiness of the sanctuary, to brave both Herod and Caesar?

Nevertheless, it was necessary! The inner voice did not say to him as to Isaiah, "Take a great roll and write in it with a pen of man!" The voice of the Lord cried to him, "Rise up, and speak!" It was a question of finding the living word, the faith which moves mountains, the strength which breaks down strongholds.

Jesus began to pray with fervor. Then, an anxiety, an increasing disturbance overcame him. He had the feeling of losing the marvelous felicity which previously had been his, and of sinking into a dark abyss. A black cloud, filled with shadows of all kinds, enveloped him. He distinguished the faces of his brothers, of his Essene teachers, of his mother. The shadows spoke to him, one after the other: "Fool who desires the impossible!— You do not know what is in store for you! Give it up!" The invincible inner voice answered, "I must!" Thus he fought for a series of days and nights, sometimes standing, sometimes kneeling, sometimes prostrate on the ground. And deeper became the abyss into which he descended, thicker became the cloud around him. He had the sensation of approaching something terrible and indescribable.

At last he entered the state of clear ecstasy to which he was accustomed, in which the deepest part of the consciousness awakens, enters into communication with the living Spirit of things, projecting the images of the past and future upon the diaphanous fabric of a dream. He closes his eyes; the external world disappears. The seer contemplates Truth by the light which floods his being, making of his intelligence a glowing furnace.

Thunder rolls; the foundations of the mountain tremble. A whirlwind from the depths carries the seer away to the top of the Temple of Jerusalem. Rooftops and minarets shine below him like a forest of gold and silver. Hymns arise from the Holy of Holies. Clouds of incense ascend from all the altars, whirling around Jesus' feet. People in festival robes fill the porticoes; beautiful women sing hymns of ardent devotion for him. Trumpets sound, and a hundred thousand voices cry, "Glory to the Messiah!—To the King of Israel!" "You will be that king if you will worship me," says a voice from below. "Who are you?" asks Jesus.

Again the wind carries him away through space to the summit of a mountain. At his feet are the kingdoms of earth, spread out in their golden light. "I am the king of spirits and the prince of earth," says the voice from below.

"I know who you are," cries Jesus. "Your forms are innumerable; your name is Satan! Appear in your earthly form!" The form of a crowned monarch appears, sitting upon a cloud. A dim aureole surrounds his imperial head. The dark figure is outlined against a blood-red cloud; his face is pale, his gaze is like steel. He says, "I am Caesar. Only bow, and I will give you these kingdoms." Jesus says to him, "Get behind me tempter! It is written, You shall worship only the Lord your God." At once the vision fades.

Finding himself alone in the cave of Engaddi, Jesus asks, "By what sign shall I conquer the powers of the earth?" "By the sign of the Son of Man," answers a voice from above. "Show me this sign," says Jesus . . .

A shining constellation appeared upon the horizon. It consisted of four stars in the form of a cross. The Galilean recognized the sign of the ancient initiations, familiar to Egypt and preserved by the Essenes. In the dawn of the world, the sons of Japhet had worshipped it as the sign of earthly and heavenly Fire, the sign of Life with all its joys, of Love with all its marvels. Later the Egyptian initiates had seen in it the symbol of the great Mystery, the Trinity dominated by Unity, the image of sacrifice of the Ineffable Being Who is broken in order to reveal Himself in the cosmos. Symbol of life, death and resurrection, it covered innumerable tombs and temples . . . The splendid cross grew larger, coming nearer as though drawn by the heart of the seer. The four living stars flamed into suns of power and glory. "This is the magic sign of Life and Immortality," said the heavenly voice. "Men once possessed it, but they lost it. Do you wish to give it back to them?" "I do," answered Jesus. "Then look! This is your destiny!"

Abruptly the four stars were extinguished. Night fell. A subterranean rumbling shook the heights, and from the bottom of the Dead Sea came a dark mountain, surmounted by a black cross. A dying man was nailed upon it. A demon-ridden people swarmed over the mountain, shouting with an infernal mockery, "If you are the Messiah, save yourself!" The seer opened his eyes wide, then he fell backward, dripping with a cold sweat. For this crucified man was himself . . . He understood. In order to conquer, it was necessary to become identified with this frightful double, evoked by himself and placed before him like a sinister interrogation. Suspended in uncertainty as in the emptiness of infinite space, Jesus felt the tortures of the crucified one, the insults of men and the deep silence of heaven, all at the same time. "You can accept or reject it," said the angelic voice.

The vision trembled, and the phantom cross with its tortured victim began to dim, when suddenly Jesus saw near him the sick people of the pool of Siloam, and behind them came a whole host of despairing souls, murmuring with lifted hands, "Without you we are lost! Save us, you who know how to love!" Then the Galilean slowly arose, and opening his arms with fullest love, cried out, "Give me the cross!—And let the world be saved!"

Immediately Jesus felt a great tearing in all his limbs, and he uttered a terrible cry . . . At the same time, the black mountain crumbled, the cross was swallowed up; a soft light, a divine happiness, flooded the seer, and in the azure heights a triumphant voice was heard saying, "Satan is no longer master! Death is conquered! Glory to the Son of Man! Glory to the Son of God!"

When Jesus awakened from this vision, nothing around him

had changed. The rising sun gilded the walls of the grotto of Engaddi, a warm dew like tears of angelic love moistened his aching feet and floating mists arose from the Dead Sea. But he was no longer the same. A definitive event had taken place in the unfathomable abyss of his consciousness. He had solved the riddle of his life; he had won the peace, and great certainty had ent 1 into him. A new and radiant consciousness had come forth at the breaking of his earthly being, which he had trodden under his feet and thrown into the abyss. He knew that he had become the Messiah by an irrevocable act of his will.

Shortly afterward he descended to the village of the Essenes. There he learned that John the Baptist had just been seized by Antipas and was imprisoned in the citadel of Makerous. Far from becoming frightened at this event, he saw in it a sign that the time was ripe, that now it was necessary for him to act. Therefore he announced to the Essenes that he was about to preach in Galilee "the Gospel of the Kingdom of Heaven." This meant that he was about to place the great Mysteries within the reach of the simple, to interpret for them the teaching of the initiates. Such courage had not been seen since the time that Sakya Muni, the last Buddha, moved by tremendous pity, had preached on the banks of the Ganges. The same sublime compassion for humanity moved Jesus. But to this he added an inner light, a power of love, a greatness of faith and a strength of action which were his alone. From the abyss of death, which he had fathomed and had tasted in advance, he brought to his brothers hope and life.

41

Jesus' Public Life — His Esoteric Teaching — The Miracles

I HAVE tried to illumine with its own light that part of Jesus' life which the Gospels have left in obscurity or hidden beneath the veil of legend. I have told by what initiation, by what development of soul and spirit the great Nazarene arrived at the Messianic consciousness. In other words, I have tried to reconstruct the inner genesis of the Christ. Once this genesis is recognized, the rest of my task will be easier.

Jesus' public life has been related by the Gospels. In these accounts are divergences, contradictions and additions. Legend, concealing or exaggerating certain Mysteries, still reappears here and there, but from the totality appears such a unity of thought and action, a character so powerful and so unique that invincibly we feel ourselves in the presence of reality, of life. There is no question of reconstructing those inimitable accounts which, in their childish simplicity or their symbolic beauty tell more than all commentaries. But today it is important to clarify Jesus' connection with esoteric traditions and truths, to show the meaning and transcendent significance of his dual teaching.

Of what great news was he the bearer,—the already famous Essene who came from the shores of the Dead Sea to his Galilean homeland, there to preach the Gospel of the Kingdom? How was he to change the face of the world? The thinking of the prophets had reached a climax in him. Richly endowed in his being, he came to share with men this Kingdom of Heaven which he had conquered in his meditations and his struggles, in his infinite pain and boundless joy. He came to tear away the veil that the ancient religion of Moses had cast over the afterlife. He came to say: "Believe, love, act, and may hope be the soul of your actions. Beyond this earth is a world of souls, a more perfect life. I know it; I come from there, and I will lead you to it. But it is not enough to aspire to it. In order to reach it, one must begin by bringing it about here below, first within yourselves, then in mankind. With what?—With love, with active charity."

The young prophet came to Galilee. He did not say that he was the Messiah, but he discussed the Law and prophets in the synagogues. He preached on the shore of the Sea of Galilee in fishermen's boats, beside the green oases which abounded near Capernaum, Bethsaida and Korazim. He healed the sick by the laying on of hands, with a look, or a command, and often by his presence alone. Crowds followed him; already many disciples were attached to him. He recruited them from among the men of the people: fishermen, tax collectors. For he wanted upright, unspoiled natures, ardent and believing, and he irresistibly won them over.

In his choice of men he was led by that gift of spiritual insight which in all epochs has been the special possession of men of action, but especially of religious initiators. A look sufficed for him to fathom a soul. He needed no other test, and when he said, "Follow me," they followed him. With a gesture he called to him the shy, the hesitant, saying, "Come to me, all you who are heavy laden, I will give you rest. My yoke is easy, and my burden is light." He discerned the most secret thoughts of men who, troubled and disturbed, recognized their Master. Sometimes in a man's apparent unbelief he recognized uprightness. Nathaniel having asked, "Can anything good come out of Nazareth?" Jesus replied, "There is a true Israelite, in whom there is no guile!" He required neither oath nor profession of faith from his disciples, but only that they love him and that they believe in him. He put the community of property into practice, not as an absolute rule, but as a principle of brotherhood among his own.

In his little group Jesus thus was beginning to bring about the Kingdom of Heaven that he wished to establish on earth. The Sermon on the Mount offers us a picture of that Kingdom already formed in embryo, with a resumé of Jesus' public teachings. The Master is sitting on the top of the hill; the future initiates are gathered at his feet; down below, the assembled people avidly receive the words which fall from his mouth. What is the new doctor announcing? Fast? Mortification? Public penance? No. He says, "Blessed are the poor in spirit, for theirs is the kingdom of heaven! Blessed are they that mourn, for they shall be comforted." Then in ascending order he unfolds the four sorrowful virtues: the marvelous power of humility, compassion for others, inner goodness of heart, hunger and thirst for righteousness. Then the active, triumphant virtues appear in radiance: mercy, purity of heart, loving-kindness and, finally, martyrdom for righteousness. "Blessed are the pure in heart, for they shall see God!" Like the sound of a golden bell, before the inner eye of the hearers this saying reveals a part of heaven, radiant with stars above the head of the Master. They see the humble virtues, no longer like poor, thin women in the grey robes of penitents, but transformed into beatitudes, into virgins of light, whose radiance dims the splendor of the lilies and the glory of Solomon himself. The gentle motion of their palm branches spreads the perfume of the heavenly kingdom over these transformed hearts.

The wonder is that this kingdom does not unfold itself in the distant expanses of heaven, but within those who are listening to this teaching. The latter exchange astonished glances. These poor in spirit have suddenly become so rich! More powerful than Moses, the magician of the soul has struck their hearts; an immortal stream gushes forth. His popular teaching is contained in the words, "The Kingdom of Heaven is within you!" Now that he explains to them the means necessary for attaining this unknown happiness, they are no longer surprised at the extraordinary things he asks of them: to root out even the desire for evil, to forgive trespasses, to love one's enemies. So powerful is the river of love which overflows from his heart that he draws them to himself.

In his presence, everything seems easy to them. They are struck by the great newness and extraordinary boldness of his teaching. The Galilean prophet places the inner life of the soul above all external piety, the invisible above the visible, the Kingdom of Heaven above all earthly possessions. He orders them to choose between God and Mammon. Finally, in summing up his teaching, he says, "Love your neighbor as yourself, and be perfect, as your Heavenly Father is perfect."

Thus he set forth all the depth of morality and science in popular form. For the supreme goal of initiation is to reproduce divine perfection in the perfection of the soul, and the secret of knowledge resides in the chain of similarities and relationships which link ever more closely the specific to the universal, the finite to the infinite.

Since this was the public and purely moral teaching of Jesus, it is clear that along with it he gave his disciples a secret teaching which explained the first, revealing its inner meaning, penetrating to the depths of the spiritual truths which he had gained from the esoteric tradition of the Essenes and from his own experience. Since this esoteric tradition was violently stifled by the Church after the second century, the majority of theologians no longer knew the true significance of Christ's words, with their sometimes double and triple meanings, and saw in them only the basic or literal meaning. For those who have penetrated deeply into the teaching of the Mysteries of India, Egypt and Greece, the esoteric thought of Christ animates not only his least important words, but all his deeds as well. Already visible in the three synoptic Gospels, it stands out clearly in the Gospel of John. The following example relates to a basic point of his teaching:

Jesus is on the way to Jerusalem. He is not yet preaching in the Temple, but he heals the sick and teaches among his friends. His work of love must prepare the ground where good seed will fall. Nicodemus, the educated Pharisee, had heard of the new prophet. Filled with curiosity, but not wishing to jeopardize his position with his friends, he requests a secret interview with the Galilean, which Jesus grants. Nicodemus arrives at Jesus' home at night, and says to him, "Master! We know that you are a wise man come from God; for no one could work these miracles that you work if God is not with him." Jesus answers, "In very truth I say to you that if a man is not *born again,* he cannot see the kingdom of God." Nicodemus asks if it is possible for a man to return to his mother's womb and be born a second time. Jesus replies, "Indeed, I tell you that if a man is not *born of water and of the spirit,* he cannot enter the Kingdom of God."

In this evidently symbolic form, Jesus sums up the ancient doctrine of regeneration, already known in the Mysteries of

Egypt. To be born again with fire and spirit, and to be baptized with water and fire, marks two degrees of initiation, two stages of internal and spiritual development in man. Here water represents truth perceived by the intellect, that is, in a general, abstract manner. It purifies the soul and develops its spiritual seed.

Rebirth in the spirit, or baptism by heavenly fire, means the assimilation of this truth by the will so that it becomes blood and life, the soul of all actions. The result is a complete victory of spirit over matter, the absolute mastery of the spiritualized soul over the body, now transformed into a docile instrument, a mastery which awakens the soul's sleeping faculties, opens its inner significance, gives it an intuitive view of truth and of the direct effect of one soul upon another. This condition is equivalent to that heavenly state which Christ called the Kingdom of God. The baptism with water, or intellectual initiation, therefore, is a beginning of rebirth; the baptism with the spirit is a total rebirth, a transformation of the soul by the fire of intelligence and will, and, subsequently, in a certain measure, of the elements of the body. In a word, it is a radical regeneration, hence the exceptional powers it gives to man.

This is the earthly meaning of the conversation between Nicodemus and Jesus. It has a second meaning, which can be called the esoteric doctrine of the constitution of man. According to this teaching, man is threefold, consisting of body, soul and spirit. He has an immortal and indivisible part, the spirit; a perishable and divisible part, the body. The soul which links them, shares in the nature of each. As a living organism, it possesses an etheric fluidic body, similar to the material body which, without this invisible double, would have neither life, movement nor unity. Depending upon whether man obeys the promptings of the spirit or the excitations of the body, whether by choice he attaches himself to the one or the other, the fluidic

body etherealizes or densifies, unifies or disintegrates. Therefore after physical death the majority of men must undergo a
second death, that of the soul, which consists in ridding themselves of the impure elements of their astral body, sometimes
even in experiencing its slow decomposition, while the completely regenerated man, having formed his spiritual body
here upon earth, possesses his heaven within himself entering
that region into which his affinity draws him.—And water, in
ancient esoterism, symbolized infinitely transformable, fluidic
matter, as fire symbolized the one Spirit. In speaking of rebirth
by water and spirit, Christ refers to the double transformation
of his spiritual being and his fluidic sheath which awaits man
after his death, and without which he cannot enter the kingdom
of glorified souls and pure spirits. "What is born of flesh is flesh
(i.e., bound and perishable) and what is born of the spirit is
spirit (i.e., free and immortal). The wind blows where it
wishes, and you hear its breath, but you do not know where it
comes from nor where it goes. So it is with every man who is
born of the spirit."

Thus speaks Jesus before Nicodemus in the night-silence of
Jerusalem. A small lamp, placed between them, barely lights
the faces of the two men, and is faintly reflected on the ceiling
of the high room. But in the darkness the eyes of the Galilean
teacher shine with a mysterious glow. How can one not believe
in the soul when one looks into those eyes, sometimes gentle,
sometimes flashing fire? The Pharisee teacher has seen his wisdom of the letter crumble, but dimly he sees a new world. He
has seen the light of the spirit in the eyes of the prophet, whose
long, blond hair falls upon his shoulders. He has been attracted
by the powerful warmth emanating from his being. He has
seen three tiny white flames appear and disappear like a magnetic aureole around Jesus' head. Then he thinks he feels the
breath of the Spirit pass over his heart. Deeply impressed, the

silent Nicodemus steals away to his home in the dark night. He will continue to live among the Pharisees, but in his secret heart he will remain faithful to Jesus.

Let us note a major point of this teaching. According to materialistic concepts the soul is an ephemeral and accidental result of the forces of the body. In the usual spiritual teaching the soul is regarded as an abstract thing, without any conceivable link with the body. In esoteric doctrine, the only rational point of view in this matter, the physical body is a product of the incessant activity of the soul, acting upon the physical through the organism of the astral body, just as the visible universe is but a result of the activity of the infinite Spirit. This is why Jesus gives this doctrine to Nicodemus as the explanation of the miracles he works. It can serve as the key to the spiritual healing practiced by him and by a small number of adepts and saints before as well as after his earthly activity. Ordinary medicine fights the ills of the body by acting upon the body. The adept or saint, as a center of spiritual and fluidic power, acts directly upon the soul of the sick, and, by his astral body, on his physical body. It is the same in all hypnotic cures. Jesus works with the powers which exist in all men, but he functions with strong doses through powerful and concentrated projections. He gives the Scribes and Pharisees his power of healing men's bodies as a proof of his power to forgive or heal their souls, which is his higher purpose.

Thus physical healing becomes the counter proof of moral healing, which permits him to say to the completely restored man, "Stand up and walk!" Modern science seeks to explain the phenomenon which the ancients and men of the Middle Ages called "possession by devils," as a simple nervous disturbance. But this is an insufficient explanation. Psychologists who seek to penetrate further into the mystery of the soul, see in it an intensification of consciousness, an eruption of its latent part. This question is related to the various levels of human consciousness, which sometimes acts on one level, sometimes on another. This activity can be observed in the various somnambulistic states. It also relates to the supra-sensitive world. Hence it is certain that Jesus had the ability to reestablish balance in troubled bodies and to restore souls to their proper state. "Real magic," said Plotinus "is love, with hate as its opposite. By love and hate magicians act through their philters and charms." Love, in its highest manifestation and supreme power, was the "magic" of the Christ.

Many disciples shared in his intimate teaching, but to make the new religion permanent, a group of active chosen ones was needed. They would become the pillars of the spiritual temple he wished to erect. Hence the institution of the Apostles. He did not choose them from among the Essenes because he needed vigorous, free natures and because he wanted to implant his religion in the heart of the people. Two groups of brothers, Simon Peter and Andrew, sons of Jonas on the one hand and John and James, sons of Zebedee, on the other, all four fishermen by calling, and of respectable families—formed the nucleus of the Apostles. At the beginning of his activity Jesus comes to their home at Capernaum on the shore of the Lake of Gennesaret, where they did their fishing. He dwells among them, teaches and converts the entire family.

Peter and John stand out as the two principal figures among the twelve. Peter is the upright of heart, simple, naive and limited, as quick to hope as to discouragement, but a man of action, capable of leading others because of his energetic character and absolute faith. John is the withdrawn, intense nature, filled with such bubbling enthusiasm that Jesus calls him "the son of thunder." John is the intuitive one with the burning soul, almost always turned inward, is generally dreamy and sad, with tempestuous outbursts, apocalyptic furies, but also with depths of tenderness which others are not capable of detecting and which only the Master has seen. John alone, the silent, contemplative one, will understand the Master's thought. He will be the Evangelist of Love and divine Intelligence, the esoteric Apostle *par excellence*.

Persuaded by Jesus' speech, convinced by his works, directed by his great intelligence and surrounded by his magnetic radiance, the Apostles followed the Master from village to village. The popular preaching alternated with the intimate teachings. Slowly he unfolded his thought to them. Nevertheless he still kept a profound silence about himself, his role and his future. He had told them that the Kingdom of Heaven was near, that the Messiah would come. Already the Apostles whispered among themselves, "It is he!" And they repeated this to others. But with gentle gravity, he simply called himself, "The Son of Man," an expression whose esoteric import they did not yet understand, but which in his mouth seemed to mean, "The messenger to suffering humanity." For he added, "Wolves have their caves, but the Son of Man has nowhere to lay his head."

The Apostles saw the Messiah only in terms of the popular Jewish idea, and naively they conceived the Kingdom of Heaven as a political government of which Jesus would be crowned king and they would be the ministers. To combat this idea, to transform it utterly, to reveal to these Apostles the true Messiah, the spiritual royalty, to communicate to them this sublime truth he called "the Father," this supreme power which he called "Spirit," the mysterious force which joins all souls to the Invisible, through his word, his life and his death to show them a true son of God, to leave them the conviction that they and all men were brothers and could rejoin him if they wished, to leave them only after having revealed to them all the vastness of Heaven—this is the prodigious task of Jesus for his Apostles. Will they believe, or will they not believe? This is the question of the drama which unfolds between them and him. There is, however, a more poignant and terrible drama which takes place in the depths of his own being. We shall speak of it later.

At this time a wave of joy submerges the tragic thought in Christ's consciousness. The storm has not yet blown over the Lake of Tiberias. Now is the Galilean springtime of the Gospel; it is the dawn of the Kingdom of God; it is the mystical marriage of the initiate with his spiritual family. The latter travels with him as the procession follows the groom in the parable. The believing followers press close after the beloved Master, on the shores of the blue lake enclosed in its mountains as in a golden cup. They follow him from the cool banks of Capernaum to the orange groves of Bethsaida, to the mountains of Chorazim, where clusters of palms overlook the entire Sea of Gennesaret.

Women have a special place among Jesus' followers. Mothers or sisters of the disciples, timid virgins or repentant sinners surround him in every place. Attentive, faithful, ardent, they perfume his steps with their eternal sadness and hope, like a trail of love. He does not need to prove to them that he is the Messiah. Just looking at him is enough. The strange happiness emanating from his presence, mixed with the note of a divine and inexpressible suffering resounding in the depth of his being, persuades them that he is the Son of God. Long ago Jesus had stifled the cry of the flesh within himself; he had subdued the power of the senses during his stay with the Essenes. In this way he had attained the dominion over souls and the divine power to forgive—that privilege of the angels. He said of the sinning woman who, enveloped in a sea of dishevelled hair, crawled at his feet, while she lavishly spread balm over them, "She will be forgiven much because she has loved much!"

JESUS

This sublime saying contains a complete redemption, for whoever pardons, frees.

Christ is the restorer and liberator of women, whatever Saint Paul and the Church Fathers may have said. In lowering woman to the role of man's servant, these writers have falsified the thinking of the Master. In Vedic times she had been glorified; Buddha deified her. Christ elevates her by restoring her mission of love and divination. The woman initiate represents the soul in mankind, *Aisha,* as Moses called it, that is, the power of Intuition, the loving and seeing faculty. The turbulent Mary Magdalene, whose seven demons Jesus had driven out according to the Biblical account, became his most ardent disciple. It was she, according to Saint John, who first saw the divine teacher, the spiritual Christ, risen from his tomb. Legend has insisted in seeing in this ardent and believing woman Jesus' greatest worshipper, the initiate of the heart, and legend is not mistaken, for her story represents the entire regeneration of woman as desired by the Christ.

It was at the farm at Bethany, with Mary, Martha and the Magdalene that Jesus liked to rest from the labors of his mission and to prepare himself for the supreme tasks. There he freely gave his most gentle consolations and in loving conversations he spoke of the divine Mysteries he did not yet dare confide to his disciples. Sometimes at the hour when the gold of the sunset faded among the olive branches, when twilight slipped between their delicate foliage, Jesus became thoughtful. A shadow fell over his illumined face. He thought of the hardships of his work, the wavering faith of the Apostles, the powerful enemies in the world. The Temple, Jerusalem, mankind, with its crimes and ingratitude, rolled over him like a living mountain.

Would his arms, raised toward Heaven, be strong enough to reduce this mountain to dust, or would he be crushed beneath its enormous weight? Then he spoke vaguely of a terrible trial which awaited him, and of his imminent death.

Struck by the solemnity of his voice, the women did not dare to question him. However unchangeable the serenity of Jesus might be, they understood that his soul was as though closed in the coffin of an unspeakable sadness, which separated him from the joys of earth. They sensed the destiny of the prophet; they felt his unshakable resolution. Why did these dark clouds arise in the vicinity of Jerusalem? Why this burning wind of fever and death, passing over their hearts as over the blighted hills of Judea with their violet, cadaverous hues? One evening . . . a star of mystery . . . a tear shone in Jesus' eyes. The three women trembled and their silent tears flowed in the peace of Bethany. They were weeping for him; he was weeping for all mankind.

42

Conflict With the Pharisees — The Transfiguration

THE Galilean springtime lasted for two years. During this time, at the words of the Christ the radiant lilies of the angels appeared to blossom in the perfumed air and the dawn of the Kingdom of Heaven shone over the attentive crowds. But soon the sky darkened, sinister lightning flashed; everywhere were omens of catastrophe. The storm finally broke over the little spiritual family like one of the tempests which sweep the Lake of Gennesaret, swallowing up the frail boats of the fishermen in its fury. If the disciples were dismayed, Jesus was not at all surprised, for he was expecting this. It was impossible for his preaching and growing popularity not to stir the religious leaders of the Jews. It was also impossible for the conflict between them and him to be other than a decisive one. More important still, light could come forth only from this encounter.

In Jesus' time the Pharisees formed a compact body of six thousand men. Their name *Perishin* meant "the separated" or "distinguished ones." With an exalted, often heroic but narrow, proud patriotism, they represented the cause of national restoration; its existence dated only from the Maccabees. Along with written tradition the Pharisees accepted oral tradition as well. They believed in angels, a life after death and the resurrection, but they drowned these glimpses of esoterism which had come to them from Persia, in the darkness of grossly materialistic interpretation. Strict observers of the Law, but entirely opposed to the spirit of the prophets who put religion in the form of a love of God and men, their piety consisted of rituals and ceremonies, fasts and public penance. On the high Holy Days they were seen walking through the streets, faces covered with soot, praying aloud with a contrite air and distributing alms ostentatiously. In addition, they lived in luxury and eagerly sought for offices and power. They were also the leaders of the democratic party, holding the people in the palm of their hands.

The Sadducees, on the other hand, represented the priestly and aristocratic party. They were composed of families which claimed membership in the priesthood by hereditary right from the time of David. Conservative to the extreme, they rejected oral tradition, accepting only the letter of the Law and denying the existence of the soul and of a future life. They ridiculed the practices of the Pharisees as well as their extravagant beliefs. For them religion consisted only in sacerdotal ceremonies. They controlled the pontificate under the Seleucides, agreeing perfectly with the pagans, even becoming imbued with Greek Sophistry and refined Epicureanism. Under the Maccabees the Pharisees had been evicted from the pontificate, but under Herod and the Romans they had regained their positions. The Sadducees were hard and tenacious men. As priests they were fond of good living, believing only in their superiority while holding but one fixed purpose: to keep the power they held by inheritance.

What could Jesus see in this religion—Jesus the seer of Engaddi, who sought in the social order the image of divine order where justice reigns over life, science over justice, love and wisdom over all three? In the Temple, in the place of supreme knowledge and initiation, he found materialistic and agnostic ignorance using religion as a source of power; in other words, priestly imposture. In the schools and synagogues, instead of the bread of life and the dew of Heaven falling into human hearts, he found a vested morality covered by a formalist devotion; in other words, hypocrisy. Far above them, sitting on a cloud of glory was the all-powerful Caesar, the apotheosis of evil, the deification of matter. Caesar, the sole god of the world at that time, was the only possible master of the Sadducees and Pharisees, whether they wanted him or not. Like the prophets, borrowing an idea from Persian esoterism, was Jesus wrong in naming this reign the rule of Satan, of Ahriman, that is, the dominion of matter over spirit, for which he wished to substitute the rule of spirit over matter? Like all great reformers he did not attack men, who with some exceptions could be excellent, but he fought the doctrines and institutions which shape the majority of mankind. It was necessary for Jesus to challenge, to declare war against the ruling powers of his time.

The struggle took place in the synagogues of Galilee, continuing under the porticoes of the Temple in Jerusalem, where Jesus made long visits, preaching and combatting his adversaries. In this, and in his entire career, Jesus acted with that mixture of prudence and boldness, of meditative reserve and impetuous action which characterized his marvelously balanced nature. He did not take the offensive against his adversaries; he waited for their attack in order to repel it. And he had not long to wait, for from the prophet's beginnings the Pharisees had become jealous of his healing activities and his popularity. Soon in him they detected their most dangerous enemy. Then they approached him with that mocking urbanity, with sharp ill-will, veiled by that hypocritical gentleness which they customarily employed.

As wise teachers, as men of importance and authority, the Pharisees asked Jesus the reason for his dealings with tax collectors and men of low life. Why, also, did his disciples dare to glean wheat on the Sabbath? Why did he tolerate many serious violations against their regulations? Jesus answered them with gentleness and broadmindedness, with tenderness and forebearance. He used words of love. He spoke to them of the love of God which rejoices more at a repentant sinner than at a few righteous men. He told them the parable of the lost sheep and of the prodigal son. Embarrassed, they were silent. But, having come together again, they returned to the charge, reproaching him for healing the sick on the Sabbath. "Hypocrites," retorted Jesus, with a flash of indignation in his eyes, "do you not take the chain from the neck of your cattle to lead them to the drinking-trough on the Sabbath? May not Abraham's daughter be freed from the chains of Satan on that day?" Not knowing what to reply, the Pharisees accused him of driving out demons in Beelzebub's name. Jesus replied that the devil does not drive himself out, and he added that sin against the Son of Man will be pardoned, but not sin against the Holy Spirit, by which he meant that he thought little of the insults directed toward his being, but to deny the Good and the True when it was declared was intellectual perversity, supreme vice and irremediable evil.

This was a declaration of war. They called him a blasphemer. He answered, "Hypocrites!" They called him an imp of Beelzebub. He called them "A generation of vipers." From this moment on, the battle grew more and more vehement, more and more serious. Jesus displayed a terse, incisive logic. His words flayed like a lash and pierced like an arrow. He had altered his tactics. Instead of defending himself, he took the offensive and answered accusations with still stronger accusations, having no pity for vice and hypocrisy. "Why do you transgress the law of God because of your tradition? God commanded, 'Honor your father and mother'; you dispense with honoring your parents if money flows into the Temple! You follow Isaiah only with your lips; you are heartless bigots!"

Jesus never lost his self-control, but he became more excited, more vigorous in the struggle. As they continued to attack him, he took a higher stand as the Messiah. He began to threaten the Temple, to predict calamities which would overtake Israel, to appeal to the pagans, to say that the Lord would send other workers into His vineyard. At this the Pharisees of Jerusalem became deeply worried.

Seeing that they could neither shut his mouth, nor answer effectively, they changed their tactics. They planned to lure him into a trap. Therefore they sent deputations whose purpose was to make him utter heresy, which in turn would permit the Sanhedrin to seize him as a blasphemer in the name of the Law of Moses, or to have him condemned as a revolutionary by the Roman Governor. Hence the insidious question about the adulterous woman and about Caesar's penny. Always seeing through his enemies' schemes, Jesus disarmed them with his answers, which were those of a profound psychologist and skillful strategist.

Observing that these tactics failed, the Pharisees tried to intimidate him by harrassing him at every step. Now the majority of the people, stirred up by the Pharisees, were turning away from Jesus, since it was clear that he would not restore the external kingdom of Israel. Everywhere, even in the smallest villages he met cunning and suspicious faces, spies who were watching him, treacherous emissaries sent to discourage him. Some came and said to him, "Get out of here, for Herod Antipas wants to kill you!" He answered proudly, "Tell that fox that a prophet does not die outside of Jerusalem!" Nevertheless, he had to cross the Sea of Tiberias several times, taking refuge on its eastern shore in order to escape these snares. No longer was he safe anywhere.

While these events were taking place, the murder of John the Baptist occurred. By order of Herod Antipas, he was beheaded in the Citadel of Makerous. It is said that when Hannibal saw the head of his brother Hasdrubel who had been killed by the Romans, he cried out: "Now I know the fate of Carthage!" In the death of his forerunner, Jesus could know his own destiny. He had no illusions about it from the time of his vision of Engaddi; he had begun his work by fully accepting his end in advance. Nevertheless this news, brought by the sorrowful disciples of the preacher in the desert, struck Jesus as a presentiment of his own death. He exclaimed, "They did not recognize him, but they have treated him as they wished. Thus shall the Son of Man suffer at their hands!"

The Twelve were troubled, for Jesus hesitated on his path. He did not wish to let himself be captured, but rather to surrender himself willingly, once his work was finished, and to die as a prophet at the hour he himself would choose. Already followed by his enemies for a year, accustomed to escaping them by circuitous travels, disheartened with the people, whose coldness he sensed after the days of their enthusiasm, Jesus decided once more to flee with his friends.

Arriving at the top of a mountain with the Twelve, he turned around to look for the last time at his beloved lake, on whose shores he had wished to cause the dawn of the Kingdom of Heaven to appear. His eyes rested upon those towns lying at the edge of the water or built in terraces on the mountainsides, partly hidden in their green oases and shining in the golden sunset—all these beloved places where he had sown the Word of Life, he was now abandoning! A foretaste of the future came over him. With a prophetic gaze he saw the country transformed into a desert under the avenging hand of Ishmael, and without anger, but filled with bitterness and sorrow, the words fell from his lips, "Woe to you, Capernaum! Woe to you, Korazin! Woe to you, Bethsaida!" Then turning toward the pagan world, accompanied by the Apostles, he took the road which goes up the valley of the Jordan from Gadara to Cesarea Philippi.

Sad and long was the route of the fugitive band across the great plains of reeds and the marshy land of the upper Jordan, under the burning sun of Syria. They spent the night among herdsmen or with the Essenes who had settled in little communities in this desolate country. The sorrowful, anxious disciples lowered their heads; the sad and silent Master was lost in meditation. He was reflecting upon the impossibility of convincing people of the truth of his doctrine by preaching, of the dreadful schemes of his adversaries. The final struggle was imminent; he had arrived at an impasse. How was he to come out of it? Moreover, his thought dwelt with infinite concern upon his scattered spiritual family, and especially on the twelve Apostles who, faithful and confident, had left all—family, trade, fortune—to follow him, and who, nevertheless, were about to be heartbroken and disappointed in their great hope of the triumphant Messiah. Could he leave them alone? Had the truth sufficiently entered into them? Would they believe in him and in his teaching, in spite of all? Did they know who he really was? Under the influence of this last question, he asked them, "Whom do men say that I, the Son of Man, am?" And they answered, "Some say that you are John the Baptist; others, Jeremiah or one of the prophets." "And you, whom do you say that I am?" Then Simon Peter answered, "You are the Christ, the Son of the living God!"

In Hindu, Egyptian and Greek initiation the term *Son of God* meant *a consciousness identified with divine Truth, and a will capable of manifesting it.* According to the prophets, this Messiah was to be the Son of Man, that is, the Elect of Earth and the Son of God, that is, the Messenger of Heaven, and, as such, having in himself the Father or Spirit, Who rules over the universe through him.

At this affirmation of the Apostles' faith, Jesus experienced tremendous joy. He knew that his disciples had understood. He would live in them, and the link between Heaven and earth would be reestablished. Jesus said to Peter, "You are blessed, Simon, son of Jonas, for flesh and blood did not reveal this to you, but my Father who is in heaven." By this answer Jesus informs Peter that he considers him an initiate in the same sense as himself. Peter has attained this through his inner, profound vision of Truth. This is the real, the only revelation; this is the stone upon which Christ wishes to build his church, "against which the gates of hell cannot prevail." Jesus relies on the Apostle Peter only so long as he has this understanding. An instant later, when he has become the natural man again—fearful and limited—Jesus treats him differently.

When Jesus announced to his disciples that he was going to be put to death in Jerusalem, Peter began to protest, "God forbid, Lord, that this should happen to you!" But Jesus, as if he saw in this movement of sympathy a temptation of the flesh which was trying to shake his great decision, turned around sharply to the Apostle, saying, "Get behind me, Satan! You are an offense, because you cannot understand the things of God, but only those which are of men!" And the firm gesture of the Master seemed to say, "Forward, across the desert!"

Frightened by his solemn voice, by his severe look, the Apostles bent their heads in silence, resuming their way over the stony hills of Gaulonitide. This flight, by which Jesus led his disciples outside Israel, resembled a march toward the riddle of his Messianic destiny, the final solution of which he was seeking.

They came to the gates of Caesarea. The city which had turned pagan since the time of Antiochus the Great, was sheltered in a green oasis near the Jordan, at the foot of the snowy crests of Mount Hermon. It had an amphitheater, and it shone with luxurious palaces and Greek temples. Jesus passed through Caesarea and went to the place where the Jordan arises as a bubbling clear stream from a cavern in the mountain, like life bursting from the deep womb of eternal nature.

A little temple, dedicated to Pan, was there, and in a grotto near the river stood many columns, marble nymphs and pagan divinities. The Jews were horrified at these signs of an idolatrous cult, but Jesus looked at them without anger, and with an indulgent smile. He recognized in them the imperfect effigies of that divine beauty whose radiant archetype he bore in his soul. He had not come to curse paganism, but to transform it; he had not come to pronounce an anathema against earth and its mysterious powers, but to reveal Heaven to it. His heart was large enough, his doctrine broad enough to embrace all peoples, and to say to all cults, "Lift up your heads, and recognize that you all have the same Father!"

Nevertheless, there he was on the extreme boundary of Israel, hunted like a wild beast, pressed upon, stifled between two worlds, each of which rejected him. Before him was the pagan world which did not yet understand him, in which his word was powerless; behind him was the Jewish world, which stoned its prophets and stopped its ears in order not to hear its Messiah. There the Pharisees and Sadducees awaited their prey. What superhuman courage, what extraordinary deed was necessary to break all these obstacles, in order to pass beyond pagan idolatry and Jewish hardness to the very heart of this suffering humanity which he loved with all his being, and to make it hear his word of resurrection?

Then with a sudden turn his thought again followed down the course of the Jordan, the sacred river of Israel; it moved from the temple of Pan to the Temple of Jerusalem; it measured the entire distance which separated ancient paganism from the universal thought of the prophets. Finally, like an eagle returning to its nest, it passed from the distress of Caesarea to the vision of Engaddi! And again he saw surge forth from the Dead Sea that terrible phantom of the cross! . . . Had the hour of the great sacrifice come? Like all men, Jesus had two consciousnesses within him. The earthly one gently comforted him with illusions, saying to him, "Who knows? Perhaps I shall avoid fate!" The other, the divine consciousness, firmly said, "The way to victory passes through the gate of suffering." But was it necessary to obey the latter after all?

In every great moment of his life, we see Jesus withdrawing to the mountain to pray. Did not the Vedic sage say, "Prayer sustains heaven and earth and rules the gods?" Jesus knew this power of powers. Usually he did not allow any companion to share the times when he descended into the arcanum of his consciousness. However, on one occasion he led Peter and the two sons of Zebedee, John and James, to a high mountain in order to spend the night there. Tradition has it that the place was Mount Tabor. There that mysterious scene which the Gospels describe under the name *The Transfiguration* took place between the Master and his three most initiated disciples.

According to Matthew, the Apostles saw the luminous, diaphanous form of the Master appearing in the transparent shadows of an oriental night, his face shining like the sun, his garments radiant as light. Then two forms, which they took for those of Moses and Elias appeared beside him. Trembling they came out of their strange prostration, which seemed to them like both a deep sleep and an intense waking state. Beside them they saw the Master, who touched them in order to awaken them completely. The transfigured Christ was never erased from their memory.

But what had Jesus himself seen, what had he experienced during that night which preceded the decisive deed of his prophetic career? He passed through a gradual disappearance of earthly things under the fire of prayer and an ascension from sphere to sphere on wings of ecstasy. Slowly it seemed to him that through his deep consciousness he was returning into a previous existence, which was entirely spiritual and divine. Far from him were the suns, worlds, earths, whirlwinds of painful incarnations, while in a homogeneous atmosphere was a fluid substance, an intelligent Light.

In this radiance legions of heavenly beings formed a moving canopy, a firmament of ethereal bodies, white as snow, from which emanated gentle rays of light. On the shining cloud where he himself was standing, six men in priestly clothing and of powerful stature are lifting a gleaming Chalice in their united hands. They are the six Messiahs who already have appeared on earth; the seventh is he himself, and this Cup signifies the Sacrifice which he must experience by becoming incarnate on earth in his turn. Beneath the cloud the thunder rolls, a black abyss opens, the circle of generations, the gulf of life and death, the earthly hell appear before him. With a supplicating gesture the Sons of God elevate the Cup. Heaven waits motionless...

With a gesture of acceptance Jesus spreads his arms in the form of a cross, as though he embraces the world. Then the Sons of God kneel, faces to the ground; angels with long wings and lowered eyes carry the shining Chalice upward into the vault of Light. *Hosanna!* rings out from heaven to heaven, melodious and ineffable . . . But without even hearing it, he plunges into the abyss . . .

This is what once took place in the world of Archetypes, in the Bosom of the Father, where the Mysteries of eternal Love are celebrated, and where the movements of the stars pass in waves of living Light. This is what Jesus had sworn to fulfill; this is why he was born, this is why he had struggled upon earth. And now the mighty promise gripped him again at the end of his work, through the fullness of his spiritual consciousness, by means of which he had entered into the revelation of a divine ecstasy.

Impressive vow, dread Chalice! Nevertheless, it was necessary to drink from it. After the rapture of ecstasy, he awakened in the depths of the abyss, at the brink of martyrdom. There could be no further doubt; the time had come. Heaven had spoken, earth cried aloud for help.

Then, slowly retracing his steps, Jesus again went down to the valley of the Jordan and took the road to Jerusalem.

43

Last Journey to Jerusalem — Last Supper — Death and Resurrection

"Hosanna to the son of David!" This cry rang out at Jesus' entrance through the East Gate into Jerusalem; branches of palms were strewn before his steps. Those who welcomed him with so much enthusiasm, hastening from all parts of the city for this ovation, were followers of the Galilean prophet. They greeted the liberator of Israel, who would soon be crowned king. The twelve Apostles who accompanied him still shared this illusion, despite Jesus' express denials. He alone, the proclaimed Messiah, knew that he was walking toward torture, that even his disciples would not penetrate the sanctuary of his thought until after his death. He was offering himself resolutely, with perfect consciousness and a free will. Hence his resignation, his gentle serenity. As he passed beneath the great portal carved in the dark fortress of Jerusalem, the clamor became intensified, pursuing him like the voice of Fate seizing its prey, "Hosanna to the son of David!"

With this solemn entry into Jerusalem Jesus publicly declared to the religious authorities among the Jews that he was assuming the role of Messiah, with all its consequences. The next day he appeared in the Temple, in the court of the Gentiles, and, going to the merchants and the money-changers whose usury and handling of coin profaned the sanctity of the holy place, he spoke these words from Isaiah, "It is written, My house shall be a house of prayer, and you make it a den of thieves!" The merchants flee, carrying with them their tables and money sacks, intimidated by the prophet's partisans who surround him like a solid rampart, but still more by his fiery gaze and commanding gesture. The priests are astounded at his boldness and are terrified at his power.

A deputation from the Sanhedrin comes to him, demanding an explanation, "By what authority do you do these things?" At this cunning question, according to his custom Jesus answered with a no less difficult question for his adversaries, "The baptism of John, whence came it, from heaven or men?" If the Pharisees had answered, "It comes from heaven," Jesus would have said to them, "Then why did you not believe it?" If they had said, "It comes from men," they would have had cause to fear the people who considered John the Baptist a prophet. Therefore they answered, "We do not know." Jesus said, "Then neither shall I tell you by what authority I do these things."

But now, having warded off the attack, he took the offensive and added, "Indeed I tell you that the tax collectors and prostitutes will precede you into the kingdom of God!" Then in a parable he compared them to the evil husbandman who kills the master's son in order to steal the inheritance of the vineyard, and he called himself "the cornerstone which will crush you."

By these deeds and by these sayings it can be seen that on this last journey into the capital of Israel, Jesus had ended his retreating. For a long time the authorities had held the two major points of accusation necessary to destroy him: his threats against the Temple and his affirmation that he was the Messiah. And now his latest attacks exasperated his enemies. From this moment his death, already decided upon by the rulers, was only a matter of time. From the moment of his arrival, the most influential members of the Sanhedrin, the Sadducees and Pharisees, having become reconciled in their hatred for Jesus, agreed among themselves to have "the seducer of the people" die. However they hesitated to seize him in public, because they feared a revolt of the people. Several times previously, soldiers whom they had sent to capture him had returned, converted by his sayings or frightened by his throngs of followers. Several times the Temple guards had seen him disappear out of their midst in an incomprehensible manner. In this same way the Emperor Domitian, fascinated, hypnotized by the Magus whom he wished to condemn, saw Apollonius of Tyana disappear from before his throne, surrounded by his guards!

Thus the struggle between Jesus and the priests continued from day to day with an increasing hatred on their part, and on his, with a vigor, impetuosity and intensity resulting from his certainty of the fatal outcome. It was Jesus' last attack against the powers of his time. He displayed tremendous energy and all that masculine force like armor covering his sublime tenderness, which can be called the Eternal Feminine of his soul. This great combat ended in terrible anathemas against the debasers of religion: "Woe to you, Scribes and Pharisees, who close the Kingdom of Heaven against those who wish to enter! You are fools and blind men, who pay the tithe but neglect justice, mercy and fidelity! You are like whitewashed tombs which appear lovely on the outside but inside are full of dead men's bones and all kinds of offal!"

Having thus branded religious hypocrisy and false priestly authority for centuries yet to come, Jesus considered his struggle ended. He left Jerusalem followed by his disciples, taking the road to the Mount of Olives. From its heights one looked down upon Herod's Temple in all its majesty, with its terraces and vast porticoes, its white marble finish inlaid with jasper and porphyry, its shining roof, overlaid with gold and silver. The disciples, discouraged and sensing a catastrophe, asked him to look at the splendor of the building, and there was a nuance of melancholy and regret in their tone. For they had hoped until the last moment to sit in that Temple like judges of Israel, grouped around the Messiah, crowned pontiff-king.

Jesus surveyed the Temple and said, "Do you see all that? Not one stone will remain upon another." He calculated the duration of the Temple of Jehovah by the moral worth of those who were attacking him. He understood that fanaticism, intolerance and hatred were not sufficient weapons against the battering-rams and battle-axes of the Roman Caesar. With his insight of an initiate becoming more penetrating through that spiritual perception which the approach of death gives, he saw the Judaic pride, the politics of the kings, all Jewish history ending in catastrophe. Victory was not there; it was in the thinking of the prophets, in that universal religion, in that invisible Temple of which he alone had full awareness at that hour. As for the ancient Citadel of Zion and the Temple of stone, he already saw the Angel of Destruction standing at its gates, torch in hand.

Jesus knew that his hour was near, but since he did not wish to let himself be captured by the Sanhedrin, he withdrew to Bethany. Because he had a preference for the Mount of Olives, he went there almost every day to converse with his disciples. From this height there is a magnificent view, which includes the rugged mountains of Judea and Moab with their bluish and purple hues; in the distance is seen a bit of the Dead Sea, like a mirror of lead from which sulphurous vapors escape. Jerusalem spreads out at the foot of the mountain, dominated by the

Temple and the Citadel of Zion. Even today when dusk descends into the gloomy gorges of Hinnom and Jehosaphat, the City of David and of the Christ, protected by the sons of Ishmael, rises in imposing majesty from these dreary valleys. Its cupolas and minarets retain the fading light of the sky, and seem always to be awaiting the Angels of Judgment. There Jesus gave his disciples his final instructions concerning the future of the religion he had come to establish, and regarding the future destinies of humanity. Thus he willed to them his earthly and divine promise, closely linked with his esoteric teaching.

It is evident that the compilers of the Synoptic Gospels have transmitted to us the apocalyptic discourses of Jesus only in a confused form, which makes them almost incomprehensible. Their meaning only begins to become intelligible in the Gospel of John. If Jesus had really believed in his return on the clouds a few years after his death, as naturalist exegisis believes, or yet if he imagined that the end of the world and the final judgment of men would take place in the form conceived by orthodox theology, he would have been merely a very mediocre visionary instead of the initiate sage, the sublime seer, as is proved by each word of his teaching, each deed of his life. It is evident that here, more than elsewhere, his words must be understood in the allegorical sense, according to the transcendant symbolism of the prophets. John's Gospel, of the four Gospels the one which has best transmitted to us the Master's esoteric teaching, imposes on us this interpretation when it reports the words of the Master: "I have yet many things to say to you, but they are beyond your understanding . . . I have told you these things in allegories, but the time comes when I shall no longer speak to you in allegories, but I shall speak to you openly of my Father."

Jesus' solemn promise to the Apostles points to four objects, four growing spheres: planetary and cosmic life; individual soul life; the national life of Israel; the whole human evolution. Let us consider each of these four objects of the promise, these four spheres where Christ's thought radiates before his martyrdom like a setting sun, filling all the earthly atmosphere with its glory, even to its zenith, before illumining other worlds.

1. *The First Judgment* means the ultimate destiny of the soul after death. It is determined by the soul's inner nature and by the acts of its life on earth. I have explained this above with reference to Jesus' conversation with Nicodemus. On the Mount of Olives, speaking on this subject, he says to his Apostles, "Watch that your hearts do not become heavy with cares and pleasures of this life so that this day takes you by surprise." Again he said, "Be ready, for the Son of Man will come at a time you know not!"

2. *The Destruction of the Temple and the End of Israel.* "Nation shall rise against nation . . . You will be given up to the authorities to be tortured . . . Indeed I say to you that this generation shall not pass away until all these things happen!"

3. *The Earthly End of Mankind,* which is not fixed at a definite age, but which must be attained by a series of progressive and successive accomplishments. This goal is the coming of the social Christ, of the divine man on earth; that is, the organization of Truth, Justice and Love in human society, and subsequently the pacification of the peoples. Isaiah already had foretold this distant age in a magnificent vision which begins with the words: "Seeing their works and their thoughts, I come to gather all nations and all tongues together; they shall come and see my glory, and I shall put my sign upon them . . ."

Completing this prophecy, Jesus explains to his disciples that this sign will be the complete unveiling of the Mysteries, of the coming of the Holy Spirit which he also calls the Comforter,

480

"the Spirit of Truth which shall lead you into all truth." "And I shall pray my Father, who will give you another Comforter so that it may remain eternally with you, that you may know the Spirit of Truth which the world cannot receive because it does not see it at all; but you know it because it remains with you and because it will be in you." The Apostles will have this revelation in advance; mankind will experience it later in the course of the ages. But each time that it enters into a consciousness or a group of human beings, it strikes through from top to bottom. "For as the lightning comes out of the east and shines even in the west, so shall the coming of the Son of Man be." Thus, when the central, spiritual Truth lights up, it illumines all truths and all worlds.

4. *The Last Judgment* means the end of the cosmic evolution of humanity or its entry into a definitive spiritual condition. This is what Persian esoterism called the victory of Ormuzd over Ahriman, or of the Spirit over matter. Hindu esotericism called it the complete reabsorption of matter by the Spirit, or the end of a Day of Brahma. After thousands and millions of centuries a time must come when, having gone through series of births and rebirths, of incarnations and regenerations, the individuals who compose humanity will have definitively entered the spiritual state, or have been annihilated as conscious souls by evil, that is, by their own passions which the fire of Gehenna and the gnashing of teeth symbolize. "Then the sign of the Son of Man will appear in the sky. The Son of Man will come on a cloud. He will send his Angels with a great sound of the trumpet, and he will gather together his chosen from the four winds." *The Son of Man*, a generic term, here means mankind in its perfect representatives, that is, the small number of those who have raised themselves to the rank of Sons of God. His *Sign* is the Lamb and the Cross, that is, Love and Eternal Life. The *Cloud* is the image of the Mysteries become translucent, as well

as of subtle matter transfigured by the Spirit, of fluidic substance which is no longer a dense, obscure veil, but a light transparent garment of the soul; no longer a gross fetter but an expression of truth; no longer a deceiving appearance, but spiritual Truth itself, the inner world instantaneously and directly manifested. The *Angels* who gather the chosen are the glorified spirits who themselves have come from mankind. The *Trumpet* which they sound symbolizes the living Word of the Spirit, which reveals souls as they are and destroys all deceitful appearances of matter.

In this way, sensing that he was nearing his death, Jesus opened to the astonished Apostles those great perspectives which from most ancient times had been a part of the doctrine of the Mysteries, and to which each religious founder has always given a personal form and color. To engrave these truths upon their minds, to facilitate their propagation he summed them up in images of extreme boldness and incisive energy. The revelatory picture, the speaking symbol was the universal language of the ancient initiates. Such a symbol possesses a communicative power, a power of concentration and duration which is lacking in the abstract term. In using it, Jesus simply followed the example of Moses and the prophets. He knew that his ideas would not be understood at once, but he wanted to imprint them in letters of fire in the simple souls of his friends, leaving to later centuries the task of generating the powers contained in his speech.

Jesus felt at one with all the prophets of earth who had gone before him and who like himself were messengers of Life and of the eternal Word. In this feeling of oneness and firmness in changeless Truth, before these limitless horizons of heavenly radiance which are seen only from the zenith of First Causes, he dared speak the proud words to his sorrowing disciples:

"Heaven and earth will pass away, but my words shall not pass away!"

Thus the mornings and evenings slipped by on the Mount of Olives. One day, in one of those gestures of sympathy so native to his ardent and impressionable nature, which made him return abruptly from the most sublime heights to earth's sufferings, which he felt as his own, he shed tears over Jerusalem, over the Holy City, and over his people whose terrible destiny he sensed.

Meanwhile, his own destiny was approaching with giant steps. Already the Sanhedrin had deliberated over his fate and had decided upon his death; already Judas Iscariot had promised to surrender his Master. This sinister betrayal was not the fruit of sordid greed but of ambition and wounded vanity. Judas, an individual of cold egotism and absolute positivism, incapable of the least idealism, had become a disciple of Christ only because of worldly speculation. He counted on the immediate earthly triumph of the prophet, and on the benefit which would come to him from it. He had understood nothing of that profound saying of the Master, "Those who would like to gain their life shall lose it, and those who will lose it will gain it."

In his boundless charity Jesus had admitted Judas to the circle of his friends in the hope of changing Judas' nature. When the latter saw that things were turning out badly, that Jesus was lost, his disciples threatened and himself disappointed in all his hopes, his deception turned to rage. The wretched man denounced the one who in his eyes was only a false Messiah, and by whom he considered himself deceived.

With his penetrating insight, Jesus understood what was taking place within the unfaithful Apostle. He resolved to avoid destiny no longer, for he felt its net tightening around him with each passing day. It was the eve of Passover. He ordered his disciples to prepare the meal in the city at a friend's house. He sensed that this would be his last meal, hence he wanted to give it unusual solemnity.

We have reached the final act of the Messianic drama. In order to grasp the soul and work of Jesus at their source it was necessary to describe from within the first two acts of his life, to show his initiation and his public career. The inner drama of his consciousness paralleled the latter. The last act of his life, the drama of the Passion, was the logical consequence of all that had gone before. Since it is known to all, it is self-explanatory, for the nature of the sublime is to be simple, broad and clear.

The drama of the Passion has contributed powerfully to establishing Christianity. It has drawn tears from all men who have hearts, and has converted millions of souls. In describing all these scenes the Gospels manifest an incomparable beauty. John himself descends from his spiritual heights, and his circumstantial account bears the poignant truth of an eye-witness. Each one can relive in himself the divine drama, but no one can recreate it. Nevertheless, in order to complete my task, I must focus the rays of esoteric tradition upon the three principal events by which the life of the divine Master ended: The Holy Supper, the Trial of the Messiah and the Resurrection. If light is shed upon these three it will illuminate all of the Christ's previous career and will cast its radiance over the entire history of Christianity following the Resurrection.

The Twelve, forming thirteen with the Master, had assembled in the upper room of a house in Jerusalem. The unknown friend, Jesus' host, had decorated the room with a rich carpet. According to the oriental custom, the disciples and Master reclined three by three on four large divans in the form of a *triclinia* arranged around the table. When the Passover Lamb had been brought, the cups filled with wine, along with the precious golden chalice, loaned by the unknown friend,

484

Jesus, placed between John and Peter, says, "I have ardently desired to eat this Passover with you, for I say to you that I shall eat no more of it until it is accomplished in the Kingdom of Heaven." After these words, faces grew sad, the air became heavy. "The disciple whom Jesus loved," and who alone guessed everything, inclined his head in silence toward the Master's heart. According to the custom of the Jews at the Passover meal, they ate the bitter herbs, the *haroseth,* without speaking. Then Jesus took the bread and, having given thanks, he broke it and gave it to them, saying, "This is my body which is given for you; this do in remembrance of me." In the same way he gave them the cup after supper, saying to them, "This cup is the new covenant in my blood, which is shed for you."

Such is the institution of the Supper in all its simplicity. It has a much deeper content than is generally known or described. Not only is this symbolic and mystical act the conclusion and summary of all of Christ's teachings, but it is also the consecration and rejuvenation of a very ancient symbol of initiation. Among the initiates of Egypt and Chaldea, as well as among the prophets and Essenes, the fraternal *agape* marked the first step of initiation. Communion in the form of sharing of the bread, the fruit of the wheat, signified knowledge of the Mysteries of earthly life as well as a partaking of the goods of earth and finally a perfect union of the intimately associated brothers. On the higher level, communion in the sharing of wine, the blood of the vine penetrated by the sun, meant a partaking of heavenly goods, the sharing in spiritual Mysteries and divine science. In giving these symbols to the Apostles, Jesus amplified them. For through them, he extends fraternity and initiation, once limited to the few, to all mankind. To these symbols he adds the deepest of Mysteries, the greatest of forces: his Deed of Sacrifice, making of it a chain of invisible but inviolable love between himself and his own. This will give his glorified soul a divine power over their hearts and over the hearts of all men. The cup of Truth coming from the depths of prophetic ages, that golden chalice of initiation which the Essene had offered him in the rapture of his ecstasy as The Son of God—that cup in which he now sees his own blood glow, that cup he now extends to his beloved disciples with the ineffable tenderness of a last farewell.

Do the Apostles understand this? Do they recognize this redemptive thought which embraces the worlds? It shines in the deep, painful look of the Master as he looks from the Beloved Disciple to the one who is about to betray him. No, they do not yet understand. They sigh painfully, as though in a bad dream; a heavy red vapor seems to float in the air and they ask each other whence comes that strange radiance around the head of the Christ. When at last Jesus declares that he will spend the night in prayer in the garden on the Mount of Olives and rises, saying, "Let us go there!"—they do not doubt what will follow. . . .

Jesus has experienced the anguish of Gethsemane. With frightening clarity he has seen the infernal circle about him growing steadily tighter. In face of the terror of this situation, in the dreadful waiting, knowing he is about to be seized by his enemies, he trembles; for an instant his soul shrinks before the tortures awaiting him; a sweat of blood forms itself in drops upon his forehead. Then prayer strengthens him.

Now come sounds of confused voices, lights of torches under the dark olive trees, the clash of arms. It is the soldiers sent by the Sanhedrin. Judas who leads them, kisses his Master so they may recognize the prophet. Jesus returns his kiss with ineffable pity, saying, "My friend, what do you want here?" The effect of this gentleness, of this fraternal kiss, given in exchange for the darkest betrayal, will make such an impression on this hard soul that shortly afterward, seized with remorse and horror at his deed, Judas will commit suicide.

With rough hands the soldiers have seized the Galilean Rabbi. After a brief resistance the frightened disciples flee like a handful of seed scattered by the wind. Only John and Peter remain nearby in order to follow the Master to the tribunal. Their hearts are broken, their souls intent upon his destiny, but Jesus has regained his calm. From this moment on, not a word of protest or complaint will come from his mouth.

The Sanhedrin has assembled hastily for a plenary session. Jesus is led there in the middle of the night, for the tribunal wishes to put a quick end to this dangerous prophet. The sacrificers, the priests in deep red, yellow and purple tunics with turbans on their heads, are solemnly seated in a semicircle. In their midst on a more elevated seat, sits Caiaphas the high priest, wearing the *migbah*. At each end of the semicircle on two small platforms stand the two recorders, one for acquittal, the other for condemnation, *advocatus Dei, advocatus Diaboli*. Dressed in his white Essene robe, Jesus is standing impassively in the center. Surrounding him, bare-armed, fists on hips and with evil expressions, are officers of justice, armed with thongs and ropes. Only witnesses for the prosecution are present, none for the defense. The high priest as supreme judge is the main accuser; the so-called trial is a measure of public safety against the crime of religious treason. In reality however, it is the preventive vengeance of a worried priesthood which feels its power threatened.

Caiaphas rises and accuses Jesus of being a seducer of the people, a *mesit*. A few witnesses taken at random from the crowd, make their deposition, but they contradict one another. Finally, one of them reports the saying, considered blasphemous, which the Nazarene more than once had thrown in the faces of the Pharisees in the porch of Solomon, "I can destroy the Temple and raise it again in three days." Jesus is silent. "You do not answer," says the high priest. Knowing that he will be condemned, not wishing to waste his words, Jesus remains silent. But this saying, even if it were proven, would not justify capital punishment. A more serious confession is needed. In order to draw one from the accused, Caiaphas, the clever Sadducee, asks him a question of honor, the vital question of his mission. Caiaphas well knows that the greatest cleverness often consists in going directly to the essential point. "If you are the Messiah, tell us so!"

At first Jesus answers evasively, showing clearly that he is not fooled by the strategy: "If I tell you, you will not believe me; but if I ask you, you will not answer me." Having failed in his role of examining magistrate, Caiaphas exercises his prerogative as high priest, beginning again with solemnity, "I command you, by the living God, to tell us if you are the Messiah, the Son of God!"

Thus challenged, summoned to retract or to affirm his mission before the highest representative of the religion of Israel, Jesus hesitates no longer. He calmly answers, "You have said it; but I tell you that from now on you will see the Son of God sitting at the right hand of Power and coming on clouds from heaven." By thus expressing himself in the prophetic language of Daniel and the Book of Enoch, the Essene initiate Jehoshoua is not speaking to Caiaphas as an individual. He knows that the agnostic Sadducee is incapable of understanding him. He addresses all future pontiffs, all the priesthoods of the earth, saying, "After my mission, sealed with my death, the reign of religious law without explanation is ended in principle and in fact. The Mysteries will be revealed, and through the human, man will see the Divine. Religions and cults which do not fertilize one another, will be without authority." According to the esoterism of the prophets and Essenes this is the meaning of "the Son sitting at the right hand of the Father." Thus understood, Jesus' answer to the high priest of Jerusalem contains the intellectual and scientific testament of the Christ to the religious authorities of the earth, just as the institution of the Supper contains his testament of love and initiation to the Apostles and to all humanity.

Over and beyond Caiaphas, Jesus has spoken to the world, but the Sadducee, who has obtained what he wanted, no longer listens to him. Tearing his fine linen robe he cries out, "He has blasphemed! What need have we of witnesses? You have heard his blasphemy! What do you think?" A unanimous, ominous murmur arises from the Sanhedrin, "He has merited death!" Immediately vile insults and brutal behavior by inferiors answer the condemnation from above. The soldiers spit on him, strike him in the face, shouting, "Prophet!—Guess who struck you!" Under this outpouring of fierce hatred, the sublime, pale face of the great sufferer again assumes its calm, visionary fixedness. It has been said that there are statues which weep. There are also sorrows without tears, and the silent prayers of victims which terrify executioners and pursue them for the rest of their lives.

But all is not finished. The Sanhedrin can pronounce the death penalty, but in order to carry it out, the secular power and approval of the Roman authority are necessary. The interview with Pilate, reported in detail by John, is no less remarkable than the one with Caiaphas. This strange dialogue between Christ and the Roman Governor, in which the violent interjections of the Jewish priests and the cries of a fanatic mob play the role of the chorus in an ancient tragedy, has the persuasiveness of great dramatic truth, for it reveals the soul of a people, and shows the struggle among three powers: Roman Caesarism, strict Judaism and the universal religion of the Spirit, represented by the Christ.

Pilate is entirely indifferent to this religious quarrel, but is very much annoyed with the affair because he fears that Jesus' death will stir up a revolution among the people. Therefore he questions Jesus with care, extending to him a means of escape, hoping he will take advantage of it. "Are you the king of the Jews?" "My kingdom is not of this world." "Then *are* you a king?" "Yes, I was born for that, and I came into the world to bear witness to the Truth." Pilate no more understands this affirmation of Jesus' spiritual royalty than Caiaphas understood his religious testament. "What is Truth?" asks Pilate, shrugging his shoulders. And this answer of the cavalier Roman skeptic reveals the attitude of pagan society of that time and of all society in decadence. Nevertheless, seeing in the accused only an innocent dreamer, Pilate says, "I find no fault in him." And he proposes to the Jews that he release him, but the mob, prompted by the priests, shouts, "Release Barrabas to us!" Then Pilate, who detests the Jews, gives himself the ironic pleasure of having their so-called king flogged. He believes this will be sufficient for these fanatics, but they become all the more furious, screaming in rage, "Crucify him!"

Despite this manifestation of mob passion, Pilate still resists. He is weary of being cruel. Through his entire life he has seen so much blood flow, he has sent so many rebels to be tortured, he has heard so many groans and curses without being disturbed in the least. But the silent, stoic suffering of this Galilean prophet under the scarlet cloak and crown of thorns arouses a strange fear in him. In a curious, fleeting inner vision, without measuring their significance, he utters the words, *"Ecce homo!* Behold Man!"

The stern Roman is almost moved; he is about to pronounce the acquittal. But the priests of the Sanhedrin, watching him with eager eyes, have seen this emotion and are frightened by it; they feel their prey escaping them. Craftily they confer among themselves. Then, in a single voice they cry out, extending their right hands and averting their heads in a gesture of hypocritical horror: "He has made himself the Son of God!"

John reports that when Pilate heard these words, "he became even more afraid." Afraid of what? What could this expression do to the unbelieving Roman, who with all his heart hated the Jews and their religion, and believed only in the political religion of Rome and of Caesar? Nevertheless, there was a real cause for this fear.

Although it has been given different meanings, the name *Son of God* was quite widely used in ancient esoterism, and Pilate, though a skeptic, had his share of superstition. At Rome, in all the lesser Mysteries of Mithras, into which the Roman officers had themselves initiated, he had heard it said that a Son of God was a kind of interpreter of divinity, and that whatever his nation or his religion, to make an attempt on his life was a great crime. Pilate hardly believed these Persian dreamings, but the saying disturbed him nevertheless, and increased his distress.

Observing him carefully, the priests now throw at the Proconsul the supreme accusation: "If you free this man, you are not the friend of Caesar; *for whoever makes himself king, declares himself against Caesar . . . we have no other king than Caesar!*" This argument is irresistible. To deny God is very little; to kill is nothing, but to conspire against Caesar is indeed the crime of crimes! Pilate is forced to pronounce the condemnation upon Jesus. Thus at the end of his public career Jesus finds himself again facing the master of the world whom he has fought indirectly as a secret adversary throughout his entire life. The shadow of Caesar sends him to the cross. Thus the profound logic of things: the Jews captured him, but it is the Roman specter that kills him, merely by extending its hand. Rome kills the body, but it is he, the Christ glorified, who by his martyrdom will forever take away from Caesar the usurped crown, the divine apotheosis, the infernal blasphemy of absolute power.

Having washed his hands of the blood of the innocent, Pilate utters the terrible words, *Condemno, ibis in crucem.*— Already the impatient crowd is pressing toward Golgotha. . . .

We stand on the barren height, the ground strewn with human bones, overlooking Jerusalem. This place is called Gilgal, Golgotha, the Place of the Skull, a sinister spot, for centuries dedicated to horrible punishments. The mountain is without trees: only gallows grow here. It is here that a Jewish king, Alexander Janneus and his harem had attended the execution of hundreds of prisoners; here Varus had had two thousand rebels crucified; here the gentle Messiah, foretold by the prophets, was to undergo the frightful punishment invented by the atrocious genius of the Phoenicians and adopted by the implacable law of Rome.

The cohort of legionaries has formed a large circle at the top of the hill; with their spears the soldiers scatter the last of the faithful who have followed the condemned one hither. These are the Galilean women; silent, in complete despair, they throw themselves down, their faces to the earth. For Jesus the supreme hour has come. The defender of the poor, the weak and oppressed must complete his work in that condition of abject martyrdom reserved for slaves and thieves. The prophet, consecrated by the Essenes, must let himself be nailed to the cross he had accepted in the vision of Engaddi; the Son of God must drink of the Chalice partly seen in the Transfiguration; he must descend to the depths of hell and of earthly horror.

Jesus has refused the traditional drink prepared by the devout women of Jerusalem, intended to dull the senses of the condemned. In full consciousness he will suffer these agonies. While he is being bound to the infamous gibbet, as rough soldiers with heavy hammer blows sink the nails into those feet adored by the oppressed, into those hands which know only how to bless, a black cloud of heart-rending suffering closes his eyes, stops his throat. But from the depth of these convulsions of infernal suffering, the consciousness of the still living Saviour has but one word for his tormentors: "Father, forgive them, for they know not what they do!"

The bottom of the Chalice now appears; the hours of agony last from noon to sunset. The moral torture increases, and is even greater than the physical torture. The initiate has surrendered his powers, the Son of God is about to be eclipsed; only a suffering man remains. For a few hours he will lose his view of Heaven, in order to experience the abyss of human suffering. The cross stands there with its victim and its inscription, a last touch of irony by the Proconsul, "This is the king of the Jews!"

Now the crucified one sees Jerusalem through a cloud of anguish, the Holy City he wished to glorify, and which had hurled anathemas at him. Where are his disciples? They have disappeared. He hears only the insults of the members of the Sanhedrin, who, thinking that the prophet is no longer to be feared, glory in his agony. "He saved others," they exult, "and cannot save himself!" Beyond these blasphemies, beyond this perversity, in a terrifying vision of the future, Jesus sees all the crimes which unjust rulers, and fanatical priests will commit in his name. They will use his Sign in order to curse! They will crucify with his cross! It is not the dark silence of the heavens veiled from his sight, but the light lost for humanity, which wrings from him the cry of despair, "My Father, why have you forsaken me?" Then the consciousness of the Messiah, the will of his entire life, springs forth again in a final ray of light, and from his soul comes the cry, "Everything is accomplished!"

O Sublime Nazarene, O divine Son of Man, already you are

no longer here! With but a single movement of your wings, in radiant light, your soul has again found your Heaven of Engaddi, your Sky of Mount Tabor! You have seen your Word soaring victorious through all the ages, and you have desired no other glory than the uplifted hands and eyes of those you have healed and comforted. . . . But your last cry, misunderstood by your torturers, caused a tremor to pass over them. Astonished, your executioners, the Roman soldiers beholding the strange radiance left by your spirit upon the calm face of this corpse, look at one another and ask, "Could he have been a god?"

Is the drama really finished? Is the severe though silent struggle between divine Love and death, which beat upon him with help of the ruling powers of earth, ended? Where is the conqueror? Are the victors these priests descending from Calvary, satisfied with themselves, pleased with their deed since they have seen the prophet die, or is the pale, crucified one the victor after all? For these faithful women whom the Roman legionaries have allowed to come near, and who sob at the foot of the cross, for the terrified disciples, who took refuge in a grotto in the Valley of Jehosaphat, all is finished. The Messiah who was to sit on the throne of Jerusalem has perished miserably under the infamous punishment of the cross. The Master has disappeared, and with him hope, the Gospel, the Kingdom of Heaven have vanished. A mournful silence, a deep despair hangs heavily over the little community. Even Peter and John are dismayed. Around them all is dark; not a ray of light shines in their soul. Nevertheless, just as a blinding light followed the intense darkness in the Mysteries of Eleusis, so in the Gospels, this deep despair is followed by a sudden, instantaneous, overwhelming joy. It radiates, it bursts forth like the light of sunrise, and the joyful cry is carried into all Judea: *"He is risen!"*

First it was Mary Magdalene, wandering near the tomb in

the throes of her grief, who saw the Master, recognizing him by his voice as he called her by her name, "*Mary!*" Overcome with joy, she threw herself at his feet. She saw Jesus look at her, make a gesture as if to forbid her to touch him, and then the appearance vanished suddenly, leaving the Magdalene surrounded by the warmth and comfort of a real presence. Then the Holy Women met the Lord, and heard him say, "Go and tell my brothers to go to Galilee, and that they will see me there."

The same evening the Eleven had assembled and the doors were closed. Then they saw Jesus enter, take his place in the midst of them and gently reproach them for their unbelief. Afterward he directed them, "Go into all the world and preach the Gospel to every human creature!" It was strange that as they were listening to him, all of them were as though in a dream; they had completely forgotten his death; they thought him alive, and were convinced that the Master would leave them no more. But just as they were about to speak, they had seen him disappear like a vanishing light. The echo of his voice still rang in their ears. The astonished Apostles went to the place where he had been; a dim light floated there. Suddenly it went out.

According to Matthew and Mark, Jesus reappeared soon afterward on a mountain before five hundred of the brethren who had been called together by the Apostles. He appeared once more to the Eleven. Then the appearances ceased. But the Faith had been created, the Impetus was given, Christianity was alive. The Apostles, filled with the sacred fire, healed the sick and preached the Gospel of their Master.

Three years afterward, a young Pharisee by the name of Saul, violently hating the new religion and persecuting the Christians with all the vigor of youth, was traveling to Damascus with several companions. On the way, he was suddenly surrounded by a light so blinding that he fell to the ground. Trembling from head to foot, he cried out, "Who are you?" And he heard a voice say to him, "I am Jesus, whom you persecute. It is hard for you to kick against the pricks!" His companions, as frightened as he, lifted him up again. They had heard the voice without seeing anything. Blinded by the light, the young man recovered his sight only after three days. . . .

He became converted to the faith of Christ, and is known as Paul, the Apostle of the Gentiles. It is universally agreed that without this conversion, Christianity would have remained confined to Judea and would never have conquered the West.

These facts are reported by the New Testament. However one may minimize them and whatever religious idea or philosophy one may attach to them, it is impossible to regard them as legend or to deny that they are authentic in all essentials. For eighteen centuries the waves of doubt and negation have attacked the rock of this testimony; for the last hundred years, criticism has beaten upon it with all its instruments and weapons. The attack may have succeeded at certain points, but the basic tenets have remained firm.

What is behind the visions of the Apostles?—From the point of view of the conscientious historian, that is, from the authenticity of these facts as spiritual facts, there is no doubt that the Apostles saw these appearances and that their faith in the Resurrection of Christ was unshakeable. If one rejects the account of John because it is said to have been compiled nearly one hundred years after Jesus' death, and considers that of Luke in regard to the appearance at Emmaus as mere poetry, then there remain the simple, positive affirmations of Mark and Matthew, which are the very root of tradition and Christian religion. However, there yet remains something more solid and even more undeniable: the testimony of Paul.

In attempting to explain to the Corinthians the reason for his faith and the basis of the Gospel which he preaches, he enumerates in order the six successive appearances of the Risen Christ: to Peter, to the Eleven, to the five hundred, "the majority of whom," he says, "are still living," to James, to the assembled Apostles, and finally, his own vision on the road to Damascus. Now these facts were communicated to Paul by Peter and by James three years after Jesus' death, and shortly after Paul's conversion on the occasion of his first journey to Jerusalem. Of all these visions, the most unquestionable is not the least extraordinary. I refer to the experience of Paul himself. In his Epistles he constantly returns to it as the source of his faith. Considering Paul's previous psychological condition and the nature of his vision, the latter came to him from the outside, not from within; it is entirely unexpected and electrifying; it changes his entire being. Like a baptism of fire, it penetrates him from head to foot, arrays him in an impenetrable armor, making him the invincible knight of Christ in the eyes of the world.

Thus the testimony of Paul has a double authority, in that it affirms his own vision and corroborates those of others. If one wishes to doubt the sincerity of such affirmations, it would be necessary to reject all historical evidence. With Celsus, Strauss and Renan, one can refuse objective value to the Resurrection, considering it a phenomenon resulting from pure hallucination. But in this case one is forced to attribute the greatest religious revolution of mankind to an aberration of the senses and to a delusion of the mind! Now there is no denying that faith in the Resurrection is the basis of historical Christianity. Without this confirmation of the teaching of Jesus by a radiant Deed, his religion would not even have begun.

This Deed brought about a radical change in the Apostles' souls. From being Judaic, their whole mental outlook became Christian. For the glorious Christ is living, he spoke to them, Heaven opened, the Beyond entered the earth below, the aurora of immortality touched their foreheads, embracing their souls in a fire which never can be extinguished. Above the crumbling earthly kingdom of Israel they have seen the heavenly universal Kingdom in all its splendor. Hence their eagerness for battle, their joy in martyrdom. From Christ's Resurrection comes that overwhelming impulse, that boundless hope which carries the Gospel to all peoples, and eventually to the uttermost parts of the earth. In order for Christianity to succeed, two things were indispensable, as Fabre d'Olivet said: that Jesus was willing to die, and that he had the power to rise again.

In order to grasp the fact of the Resurrection and to understand its religious and philosophical significance, it is necessary to consider only the successive appearances of the Risen Christ, putting aside the idea of the bodily resurrection, one of the greatest stumbling blocks of Christian dogma which, on this point is completely elementary and childish. The disappearance of Jesus' physical body can be explained by natural causes, and it is to be noted that the corpses of several great adepts have disappeared without a trace in as completely mysterious a manner. Among others the corpses of Moses, of Pythagoras and of Apollonius of Tyana disappeared without anyone having been able to discover what became of them. It is possible that the brothers destroyed the Master's remains with fire in order to remove them from the profanations of his enemies. Be that as it may, however, the scientific aspect and the spiritual grandeur of the Resurrection appear only if one understands the latter in the esoteric sense.

Among the Egyptians, the Persians of the Mazdan religion of Zoroaster before as well as after the time of Jesus, in Israel and among the Christians of the first two centuries, the Resurrection has been understood in two ways: the one materialistic, the other spiritual. The first is the popular concept finally adopted by the Church after the repression of Gnosticism; the second is the profound idea of the initiates. In the first sense, Resurrection means the return to life of the material body, in a word, the reconstruction of the decomposed or scattered corpse, which one imagined must occur at the coming of the Messiah or at the Last Judgment. It is hardly necessary to point out the gross materialism and absurdity of this idea.

For the initiate, Resurrection has a very different meaning. It is linked with the doctrine of the threefold constitution of man. It means the purification and regeneration of the sidereal. ethereal and fluidic body, which is the very organ of the soul and, to some extent, the vessel of the spirit. This purification can begin in this life through the inner work of the soul and a certain way of existence, but for the majority of men it is fulfilled only after death, and then only for those who in one way or another have aspired to righteousness and truth. In the other world, hypocrisy is impossible. There, souls appear as they are in reality; they manifest themselves in the form and color of their essence: dark and ugly if they are evil, radiant and beautiful if they are good. This doctrine is expounded by Paul in the Epistle to the Corinthians. He says, "There is a natural body and a spiritual body." Jesus speaks of it symbolically, but with more depth, in the secret conversation with Nicodemus. Now the more spiritual a soul is, the further it will be from earthly atmosphere, the higher the cosmic region which attracts it by the law of affinity, the more difficult its manifestation to men.

As a result, higher souls hardly manifest themselves to men at all except during a condition of deep sleep or ecstasy. Then, the physical eyes being closed, the soul, half detached from the body, sometimes sees souls. Nevertheless it does occur that a very great prophet, a true Son of God appears to his brothers in the waking state in order to convince them by appealing to their senses and imagination. In a similar sense, the excarnated soul succeeds momentarily in giving its spiritual body a visible,

499

even a tangible appearance by means of a specific dynamic which spirit exercises over matter.

Apparently this is what happened in the case of Jesus. The appearances reported in the New Testament belong to either of these categories: spiritual vision or perceptible appearance. It is certain that for the Apostles they were supremely real. The Eleven would rather have doubted the existence of the sky and earth than their living communion with the Risen Christ, for these visions of their Lord were the most radiant thing in their lives, the most profound experiences of which they were conscious.

The Resurrection, understood in its esoteric sense, was both the necessary conclusion to Jesus' life and the indispensable preface to the historical evolution of Christianity. The conclusion was indeed necessary, for Jesus had announced it many times to his disciples. That he was able to appear to them in triumphant splendor after his death was due to the purity, the innate power of his soul multiplied a hundred times by the grandeur of his effort and his fulfilled mission.

Viewed exoterically and from the purely earthly point of view, the Messianic drama ends on the cross. Sublime in itself perhaps, nevertheless this lacks the fulfillment of the promise. Seen esoterically, from the depths of Jesus' consciousness and from the heavenly point of view, there are three high points in the divine Drama: *the Temptation, the Transfiguration* and *the Resurrection*. These three represent *the Initiation of Christ, the Total Revelation* and *the Crowning of the Work*. They correspond to what the Apostles and Christian initiates of the first centuries called *The Mysteries of the Son, of the Father and of the Holy Spirit*.

This is the necessary crowning, as I have said, of the life of Christ, and the indispensable preface to the historical evolution of Christianity. The boat built on the beach needed to be launched upon the ocean. The Resurrection was a great light thrown upon the entire esoteric background of Jesus. It is therefore not surprising that the first Christians were so overwhelmed and blinded by this extraordinary event that they often took the Master's teaching literally, misunderstanding the meaning of his words. But today, now that the human spirit has traveled through ages, religions and sciences, we surmise what a Saint Paul, a Saint John, what Jesus himself meant by the Mysteries of the Father and of the Spirit. We recognize that they contain the highest and truest that the science of the spirit has known. We also see the power of the new amplification the Christ gave to ancient, eternal Truth by the greatness of his love and the strength of his will. Finally, we perceive both the metaphysical and practical side of Christianity, the essence of its power and vitality.

The Brahmins of old found the key to the past and future life by formulating the organic law of reincarnation and the alternation of lives. But because they plunged themselves into the Beyond and into the contemplation of Eternity, *they forgot earthly fulfillment: the tasks of individual and social life.* Greece, originally initiated into the same truths under veiled and more anthropomorphic forms, by its own genius attached itself to the natural, earthly life. This enabled Greece to reveal the immortal laws of the Beautiful by example, and to formulate the principles of the sciences by observation. But, meanwhile, its concept of the Beyond narrowed and gradually darkened. By his broadness and universality, Jesus embraces the two sides of life.

In the Lord's Prayer, summing up his teaching, Jesus says, "Thy kingdom come, *on earth as in heaven.*" And this divine reign on earth means the fulfillment of the moral and social law in all its richness, in all the radiance of the Beautiful, the Good and the True. Thus the magic of his teaching and his power of development—in a certain sense unlimited—reside in the unity of his ethics and his metaphysics, in his ardent faith in eternal life and in his need to begin the latter here on earth by his Deed and his active Love. To the soul overburdened with all the heaviness of earth, the Christ says, "Arise, for your home is in Heaven!—But in order to believe in Heaven and in order to reach Heaven, prove Heaven here on earth in your work and in your love!"

NOTES

Notes

1. This division of mankind into four successive, primitive races was accepted by the oldest priests of Egypt. They are represented by four figures of different types and skin colors in the paintings of the tomb of Seti I at Thebes. The red race bears the name *Rot;* the Asiatic race with yellow skin, *Amu;* the African race with black skin, *Halasiu;* the Lybico European race with white skin and blond hair, *Tamahu*—Lenormant, *History of the Peoples of the Orient*, Vol. I.

2. Refer to the Arabian historians, as well as Abul Ghazi, *Genealogical History of the Tartars* and works of Mohammed Moshen, historian of the Persians. William Jones, *Asiatic Researches* 1. *Discourse on the Tartars and Persians.*

3. *Histoire philosophique du genre humain,* Vol. 1.

4. All who have seen a real sleep walker have been struck by the unusual intellectual excitement which is brought about during sleep. For those who have not witnessed such a phenomenon and who doubt it, we will quote a passage from the famous David Strauss. At the house of his friend, Dr. Justinus Kerner, he saw the famous Clairvoyant of Prevorst and describes her in the following manner:
"Shortly afterward, the seer fell into a hypnotic sleep. Thus for the first time I viewed this unusual state, and, I can say, in its purest and loveliest manifestation. The face bore a suffering yet exalted and tender expression and was as if bathed in heavenly light; *the speech was pure, cadenced and rhythmical, a sort of recitative,* an abundance of overflowing feelings which might have been compared to masses of clouds, sometimes bright, sometimes dark, gliding over the soul, or better still, *to quiet, melancholy breezes caught up in the strings of a marvelous aeolian harp.*" (Trans. by R. Lindau, *Biographie Generale,* art. *Kerner*)

5. Refer to the last battle between Ariovistus and Caesar in the latter's *Commentaries.*

6. *Historie philosophique du genre humain.* Vol. 1.

7. It is noteworthy that the *Zend Avesta,* the sacred book of the Parsis, while considering Zoroaster as the one inspired by Ormuzd and the prophet of God's law, makes him the successor of a much more ancient prophet. Behind the symbolism of the ancient temples one grasps here the chain of the great revelation of mankind, uniting all true initiates. Here is the important passage:

1. Zarathustra (Zoroaster) asked Ahura-Mazda (Ormuzd, God of Light): Ahura-Mazda, holy and most sacred creator of all corporeal beings:

2. Who is the first man with whom you spoke, Ahura-Mazda?

4. Then Ahura-Mazda answered: With the noble Yima, he who was at the head of an assembly worthy of praises, O pure Zarathastra.

13. And I said to him: Watch over the worlds which belong to me, make them fertile in your role of protector.

17. And I brought him the *arms of victory*, I who am Ahura-Mazda:

18. A golden lance and a golden spear...

31. Then Yima raised himself up to the stars in the south, on the path which the sun takes.

37. He walked over this land which he had made fertile. It was one-third larger than before.

43. And the radiant Yima called together the assembly of the most virtuous men in the famous Airyana Vaeja, created pure.
     (*Vendidad Sade,* 2nd *Fargard* Trans. by Anquetil Duperron)

8. The horns of the ram are found on the heads of many human figures carved on Egyptian monuments. This headgear of kings and high priests is the mark of priestly and royal initiation. The two horns of the papal tiara are derived from it.

9. This is how the signs of the Zodiac represent Ram's life, according to Fabre d'Olivet, that thinker and genius who knew how to interpret the symbols of the past according to esoteric tradition: 1. *Aries, The Ram* which is fleeing with head turned backward, indicates Ram's position when leaving his country, his eye fixed on the land behind him. 2. *The Raging Bull* (*Taurus*) stands in the way of his march, but half of his body, held fast in the mud prevents him from executing his plan; he falls upon his knees. These are the Celts, represented by their own symbol, who in spite of their efforts, finally yield. 3. *Gemini* express the alliance of Ram with the Turanians. 4. *Cancer,* Ram's meditations and inner reflections. 5. *The Lion,* his battles against his enemies. 6. *The Winged Virgin,* victory. 7. *The Scales,* the equality of conquerors and conquered. 8. *The Scorpion,* rebellion and treason. 9. *Sagittarius,* the revenge he takes. 10. *Capricorn.* 11. *Aquarius,* the Waterman. 12. The sign of *Pisces* refers to the moral side of his story.
   One may find this explanation of the Zodiac both daring and strange. However, never has any astronomer or mythologist explained to us the origin or meaning of these mysterious signs of the heavenly map, adopted

NOTES

and revered by humanity since the beginning of our Aryan cycle. Fabre d'Olivet's hypothesis at least has the merit of opening new and broad perspectives. I have said that these signs, when read in reverse order in the Orient and in Greece, later marked the ascending steps necessary to reach supreme initiation. Let us remember only the most famous of these emblems: *The Winged Virgin* meant the purity which gives victory; *The Lion,* moral strength; *The Twins,* the union of man and a divine spirit, together forming two invincible fighters; *The subdued Bull,* mastery over nature; *The Ram,* the constellation of Fire or of the universal Spirit, giving supreme initiation through the knowledge of Truth.

10. The Brahmans considered the Vedas their holy books *par excellence.* They found in them the science of sciences. The word *Veda* means *knowledge.* The scientists of Europe have been justifiably drawn to these texts by a kind of fascination. At first they saw in them only a patriarchal poetry; then they discovered in them not only the origin of the great Indo-European myths and our classic gods, but also a wisely organized cult, a profoundly religious and metaphysical system (See Bergaigne, *La religion des Vedas,* as well as the excellent and enlightening work of August Barth, *Les religions de l'Inde.*) The future perhaps still holds a final surprise, which will be to find in the *Vedas* the definition of that secret power of nature which modern science is in the process of rediscovering.

11. What clearly proves that *Soma* represented the absolute feminine principle is the fact that the Brahmins later identified it with the Moon. As the Moon symbolizes the feminine principle in all ancient religions, so the Sun symbolizes the masculine principle.

12. An observation is indispensable here concerning the symbolic meaning of the legend as well as the real origin of those in history who have borne the name, "Sons of God." According to the secret doctrine of India, which was also that of the initiates of Egypt and Greece, the human soul is the child of heaven. Before it was born on earth the soul had a series of corporeal and spiritual existences. The father and mother therefore only engender the body of the child, since his soul comes from somewhere else. This universal law governs everything. The greatest prophets, even those in whom the divine Word has spoken, cannot escape it. And, in fact, from the moment one accepts the pre-existence of the soul, the question of knowing the name of the father becomes secondary. One must believe that this prophet comes from a divine world, and the real Sons of God prove this by their life and death. But the ancient initiates did not believe it necessary to make these things known to the common people. Some of those who appeared in the world as divine envoys were sons of initiates, and their mothers had frequented the temples in order to conceive chosen ones.

13. These are the genii who, in all Hindu poetry are represented as presiding over love and marriage.

14. It is a definite belief in India that the great ascetics can make themselves manifest at a distance in visible form, while their bodies remain plunged in a cataleptic sleep.

15. In ancient India these two functions were often combined. The drivers of kings' chariots were important persons, and often were the monarchs' ministers. Examples of this abound in Hindu poetry.

16. In Brahman initiation this means *Supreme God, God-Spirit.* Each of its letters corresponds to one of the divine qualities, that is, to one of the members of the Trinity.

17. The legend of Krishna helps us to comprehend at its very source the idea of the Virgin Mother, of the Man-God, and of the Trinity. In India this idea appears from the first in its transparent symbolism with its profound metaphysical meaning. In Book V, Chapter II the *Vishnu Purana,* having related the conception of Krishna by Davaki adds, "No one could look upon Devaki because of the light which surrounded her, and those who saw her radiance felt troubled in mind; the gods, invisible to mortals, continually sang her praises, since Vishnu was embodied in her. They would say, 'You are that infinite, subtle Prakriti who once bore Brahma in her womb; you were then the goddess of the Word, the Energy of the Creator of the Universe, and the Mother of the Vedas. O eternal being, who contains in your substance the essence of all created things, you were identical with creation; you were the sacrifice from which all that earth produces originates; you are the wood which in its rubbing engenders fire. Like Aditi, you are the mother of the gods; like Diti, you are the mother of the Datyas, their enemies. You are the light from which the day is born; you are humility, mother of true wisdom; you are the mother of Order; you are Desire from which love is born; you are Satisfaction from which resignation is derived; you are Intelligence, mother of Silence; you are Patience, mother of Courage; all the firmament and the stars are your children, all that exists originates in you. You went down to earth for the salvation of the world. Have compassion on us, O goddess, and show yourself kindly disposed toward the universe; be proud of bearing the god who sustains the world!' "
—This passage proves that the Brahmans identified Krishna's mother with universal substance and the feminine element in nature. They made her the second member of the divine trinity, of the initial unmanifest triad. The Father, *Nara* (Eternal Masculine); the mother, *Nari* (Eternal Feminine) and the Son, *Viradi* (Word-Creator), are the divine qualities. In other words, the intellectual element, the plastic element, the productive element. All three together constitute *natura naturans,* to use Spinoza's term. The organic world, the living universe, *natura naturata* is the product of the Word-Creator who in turn is manifest in three forms: *Brahma,* Spirit, corresponding to the divine world; *Vishnu,* Soul, corresponding to the human world; *Siva,* body, corresponding to the natural world. In these three worlds the male element and the female element (essence and substance) are equally

active, and the Eternal Feminine is seen at the same time in terrestrial, human and divine nature. Isis is threefold in nature, and so is Cybele.

Thus it is clear that the double trinity, that of God and that of the universe, contains the elements and framework of a theodicy and a cosmogony. It is correct to recognize that this basis came from India. All the ancient temples, all the great religions and many outstanding philosophers have adopted it. From the time of the Apostles and during the early centuries of Christianity, the Christian initiates revered the female element in visible and invisible nature under the name of the *Holy Spirit*, represented by a dove, the symbol of feminine power in all the temples of Asia and Europe. If since that time the Church has hidden or lost the key to its Mysteries, their meaning is still written in its symbols.

18. The statement of this doctrine, which later became Plato's, is found in the first book of the *Bhagavad Gita* in the form of a dialogue between Krishna and Arjuna.

19. The *Vishnu-Purana*, Book V, Chapters 22 and 30 speaks of this city in rather clear terms: "Krishna resolved therefore to build a citadel where the tribe of Yadu would find a safe refuge, and which would be such that even women could defend it. The city of Dvarka was protected by raised ramparts, beautified by gardens and fish ponds, and was as splendid as Amarasvati, Indra's city. In this city he planted the Paryata tree, whose sweet scent perfumes the earth afar off. All those who approached it found themselves able to recall their previous lives."

This tree is evidently the symbol of divine knowledge and initiation. We find the same tree in Chaldean tradition. From there it passed to the Hebraic *Genesis*. After Krishna's death the city is submerged, the tree returns to heaven, but the temple remains. If all this has an historic significance, for one who knows the ultra-symbolic and discrete language of the Hindus, it means that some tyrant or other had the city completely destroyed and initiation became more and more secret.

20. Sakia-Muni's greatness resides in his sublime charity, in his moral reform and in the social revolution he brought about through overthrowing the ossified castes. But Sakia-Muni added nothing to the esoteric doctrine of the Brahmans; he only revealed certain parts of it. Its psychology is fundamentally the same, though it follows a different path. (See my article on *La Legende de Bouddha* in *Revue des Deux Mondes*, July 1, 1885)

If the Buddha is not represented in this volume, this is not because we do not recognize his place in the series of the Great Initiates. Rather it is because of the special plan of this book. Each of the reformers or philosophers selected is intended to show the doctrine of the Mysteries in a different aspect and at another stage in its evolution. From this viewpoint, Buddha would represent a needless repetition in connection with Pythagoras, through whom I developed the doctrine of reincarnation and evolution of souls, on the one hand, and on the other, with Jesus Christ, who promulgated for the West as well as the East, the ideal of universal Brotherhood and Love.

As for the book *Esoteric Buddhism* by Sinnet, which in some respects is very interesting, worthy of being read, and whose origin many people attribute to self-styled initiates still living in Tibet, it is impossible for me, until otherwise informed, to see anything in it but a very clever compilation of Brahmanism and Buddhism, with certain ideas borrowed from the Kabbala, Paracelsus, and a few thoughts from modern science.

21. In an inscription of the Fourth Dynasty, the Sphinx is spoken of as a monument whose origin was lost in the darkness of time and which had been found by chance during the reign of this prince, buried in the sand of the desert, under which it was forgotten for long generations. And the Fourth Dynasty carries us back four thousand years before Christ. Let one calculate the antiquity of the Sphinx from this!

22. "Scientific esoteric theology," says Mr. Maspero, "is monotheistic since the period of the Ancient Empire. The affirmation of the fundamental unity of the Divine Being is expressed in formal terms and with great force in the texts which date back to this period. God is the Unique One, Who exists in essence, the only One Who lives in substance, the Sole Generator in heaven and on earth Who is not engendered. Father, Mother and Son at the same time, He engenders, gives birth and exists perpetually; and those three persons, far from dividing the unity of the divine nature, contribute to its infinite perfection. His attributes are immensity, eternity, independence, all-powerful will and boundless kindness. 'He creates his own members, who are gods,' say the old texts. Each of these secondary gods, considered identical with the One God, can form a new type from whom other inferior types emanate in turn and by the same process."— *Histoire ancienne des peuples de l'Orient.*

23. For a long time archeologists have seen in the sarcophagus of the Great Pyramid of Gizeh the tomb of King Sesostus, on the testimony of Herodotus, who was not an initiate, and to whom the Egyptian priests hardly confided anything except trifles and folk tales. The kings of Egypt, however, had their tombs elsewhere. The strange inner structure of the Pyramid proves that it was to be used for initiation ceremonies and secret practices of the priests of Osiris. *The Well of Truth* which we described, the ascending staircase and the room of the arcana are found there. The room called *the King's Chamber,* which contains the sacrophagus, was the one where the adept was led on the eve of his great initiation. These same arrangements were reproduced in the great temples of central and upper Egypt.

24. *The Vision of Hermes* is found at the beginning of the *Books of Hermes Trismegistus* under the name *Poimandres.* Ancient Egyptian tradition has come to us only in a slightly altered Alexandrian form. I have tried to re-

construct this major fragment of Hermetic teaching in the setting of the higher initiation and the esoteric synthesis it represents.

25. These gods had other names in the Egyptian language, but in all mythologies the seven cosmogonic gods correspond in their meaning and attributes. They have their common root in ancient esoteric tradition. Since Western tradition has adopted the Latin names, we use them for greater clarity.

26. There are *Ten Sephiroth* in the Kabbala. The first three represent the divine Trinity, the seven others, the evolution of the universe.

27. These are the Egyptian terms for this septenary constitution of man, as found in the Kabbala: *Chat,* material body, *Anch,* vital force, *Ka,* the ethereal counterpart or astral body, *Hati,* animal soul, *Bai,* rational soul, *Cheybi,* spiritual soul, *Ku,* the divine Spirit.

    One will find the development of these fundamental ideas of esoteric doctrine in the sections on *Orpheus* and on *Pythagoras.*

28. In Egyptian doctrine, man was considered as having consciousness in this life only of the animal soul and rational soul, called *hati* and *bai*. The higher part of his being, the spiritual soul and divine Spirit, *Cheybi* and *Ku,* exist in him in the state of unconscious seed and develop after this life when he himself becomes an Osiris.

29. *Ibrim* means "those of the other side, those beyond, those who have passed the river."—Renan, *Hist. du peuple d'Israel.*

30. Moses' Egyptian first name (Manethon, quoted by Philo).

31. The Biblical account (Exodus 2:1–10) makes Moses a Jew of the tribe of Levi, found by Pharaoh's daughter among the bulrushes of the Nile, where his nurse had placed him in order to touch the princess' heart and save the child from a persecution similar to that of Herod. By contrast, Manethon, an Egyptian priest to whom we owe the most precise information on the dynasties of the Pharaohs,—information confirmed today by the inscriptions on monuments,—states that Moses was a priest of Osiris. Strabo, who obtained his information from the same source, that is, from the Egyptian priests, also confirms this. The Egyptian source has more validity here than the Jewish source, for the priests of Egypt had no interest in making Greeks or Romans believe that Moses was one of them, while the national vanity of the Jews caused them to make the founder of their nation a man of their own blood. The Biblical account recognizes, moreover, that Moses was raised in Egypt and was sent by his government as inspector of the Jews of Goshen. This is the important, major fact which establishes the secret relation between the Mosaic religion and Egyptian initiation. Clement of Alexandria believed that Moses was deeply initiated into the science of Egypt, and, in effect, the work of the creator of Israel would be incomprehensible without this.

32. Later (*Numbers* 3:1) after the Exodus, Aaron and Miriam, Moses' brother and sister, according to the Bible, reproached him for having married an Ethiopian. Jethro, Sephora's father, therefore was of this race.

33. Travelers of recent times report that Hindu fakirs have themselves buried after being plunged into a cataleptic sleep, indicating the exact day when they must be disinterred. One of them, after three weeks of burial, was found alive, safe and sound.

34. The seven daughters of Jethro, of whom the Bible speaks (*Exodus* 2:16–20), evidently have a symbolic meaning, like this entire account which has come to us in a legendary and completely popularized form. It is very unlikely that the priestly ruler of a great temple would make his daughters feed his herds or reduce an Egyptian priest to the role of shepherd. The seven daughters of Jethro symbolize seven virtues that the initiate was forced to acquire in order to open the Well of Truth. In the story of Agar and Ishmael, this well is called "The Well of the Living One Who sees me."

35. The true restorer of Moses' cosmogony is a man of genius almost forgotten today, to whom France will do justice when esoteric science, which is integral and religious science, is reconstructed on its own indestructible foundations. Fabre d'Olivet could not be understood by his contemporaries, for he was at least a hundred years ahead of his time. His universal outlook encompassed in equal degree three faculties whose union creates transcendental intellects: intuition, analysis and synthesis. Born at Ganges (Hérault) in 1767, he undertook the study of mystical doctrines of the Orient after having acquired an extensive understanding of the sciences, philosophies and literatures of the Occident. Count de Gébelin, through his *Primitive World* opened for him the first vistas of the symbolic meaning of the myths of antiquity and the sacred language of the temples. In order to become initiated in the doctrines of the Orient, he learned Chinese, Sanskrit, Arabic and Hebrew. In 1815 he published his major book, *The Hebraic Tongue Restored*. This book includes: 1. An introductory dissertation on the origin of speech; 2. A Hebrew grammar, based on new principles; 3. Hebrew roots viewed according to etymological science; 4. A preliminary discourse; 5. A French and English translation of the first ten chapters of *Genesis,* which contain the cosmogony of Moses. This translation is accompanied by a commentary of the greatest interest. I can only summarize here the principles and substance of this very revealing book. It is permeated with the deepest esoteric spirit and is constructed according to the most rigorous scientific method. The method Fabre d'Olivet uses to fathom the secret meaning of the Hebrew text of *Genesis* is a comparison of Hebrew with Arabic, Syriac, Aramaic and Chaldean *from the point of view of basic common roots,* of which he furnishes us an admirable lexicon supported by examples taken from all the languages, a lexicon which can serve as a key for sacred names among all peoples. Of all esoteric books on the Old Testament, Fabre d'Olivet's gives the surest keys. In addition, he gives an enlightening account of the history of the Bible and the apparent reasons

why its hidden meaning was lost, and even today is utterly unknown to science and official theology.

I shall say a few words about another, more recent work. This is *The Mission of the Jews*, by Saint-Yves d'Alveydre (1884). Saint-Yves owes his philosophical initiation to Fabre d'Olivet's books. His interpretation of *Genesis* is essentially that of the latter's book, *The Hebraic Tongue Restored;* his metaphysics, that of *The Golden Verses of Pythagoras;* his philosophy of history and the general setting of his work are taken from *The Philosophical History of the Human Race.* (These works of Fabre d'Olivet published by Putnam's, N.Y. 1921–9.) From these basic ideas, adding his own materials and shaping them to his liking, he constructed a new building of great richness. His purpose is twofold: to prove that the science and religion of Moses were the necessary result of religious movements which preceded them in Asia and Egypt, which Fabre d'Olivet had already brought to light in his brilliant works; next, to prove that the ternary government by arbitration, composed of three powers, economic, judiciary and religious or scientific, was in every age a corollary of the doctrine of the initiates and a constituent part of religions long before Greece. Such is Saint-Yves' own idea, a pregnant idea worthy of the highest consideration. He calls it *synarchy,* or government according to principles; he finds in it the social, organic law, the sole salvation of the future. It is not our task here to discuss to what extent the author has historically proved his thesis. Saint-Yves does not like to quote his sources, but his book, of unusual value, based upon a vast knowledge of esoteric science, abounds in pages of great inspiration, in great descriptions and in many new ideas. My views differ from his on many points, especially in regard to the concept of Moses to which, in my opinion, Saint-Yves has given too great and legendary proportions. However, beyond this I wish to point to the great value of this extraordinary book, to which I owe much. I would refer the reader also to his *Mission of the Sovereigns* and *True France,* where Saint-Yves did justice, though a bit late, and in spite of himself, to his teacher, Fabre d'Olivet.

36. Spinoza's *natura naturans.*

37. This is how Fabre d'Olivet explains the name *IEVE:* "This name, first of all, incorporates the sign indicative of life when doubled and forming the basically productive root *EE.* This root is never employed as a noun, and is the only one which has this prerogative. From its formation, it is not only a verb, but a unique verb from which the others are only derivatives: In short, the verb *EVE, to be, being.* Here (as can be seen, and as I took care to explain in my grammar) the intelligible sign *VAU* (V) is in the middle of *the root of life.* Moses, taking this verb *par excellence* to form from it the proper noun of the Being of beings, adds to it the sign of potential manifestation and of Eternity *I* and obtains *IEVE,* in which the facultative being is placed between a past without origin, and a future without end. This marvelous name, therefore, means exactly *The Being who is, was and is to be.* (For further details, see Fabre d'Olivet, *The Hebraic Tongue Restored,* trnsl. by Redfield, Putnam's, New York, 1921—Ed.)

38. "*Elohim* is the plural of *Elo*, a name given to the Supreme Being by the Hebrews and Chaldeans, and itself derived from the root *El*, which pictures *elevation, strength* and *expansive power*, and which means in a universal sense, *God. Hoa*, that is, *He*, is one of the sacred names for divinity in Hebrew, Chaldaic, Syriac, Ethiopian, Arabic."—Fabre d'Olivet, *The Hebraic Tongue Restored*, N.Y. 1921.

39. "*Ruah Elohim:* The Breath of God, figuratively indicates a movement of *expansion, dilation*. In a hieroglyphic sense it is the force opposed to that of darkness. Thus, if the word *darkness* characterizes a *compressing* power, the word *ruah* characterizes an *expanding* power. One will find in both words that eternal system of two opposing forces which the wise men and scientists of all ages from Parmenides and Pythagoras to Descartes and Newton saw in nature and called by different names."—Fabre d'Olivet, *Hebrew Tongue Restored*.

40. *Breath . . . Elohim, Light.* These three names are the hieroglyphic résumé of the second and third verses of *Genesis*. The following is the transliteration of the Hebrew text of the third verse: *Wa-iaomer Aelohim iehi-aour, wa iehi aour.* This is the literal translation Fabre d'Olivet gives: "And-he-said (declaring his will) HE-The-Being-of-beings: There-shall-be light; and-there-(shall be)-became light (intellectual elementizing)." The word *ROUA*, meaning *breath*, is found in the second verse. The word *AOUR*, which means *light*, is the word *ROUA* in reverse. The divine Breath, returning back upon itself, created intelligible Light.

41. *Genesis* 2:23. *Aisha*, the Soul, here resembling Woman, is the wife of Aish, the Intellect resembling Man. She is taken from him, she constitutes his inseparable half, his volitional faculty. The same relationship exists between Dionysus and Persephone in the Orphic Mysteries.

42. In the Samaritan version of the Bible, the adjective *universal, infinite*, is added to Adam's name. Therefore this name is a matter of the human species, of the rule of man in all the heavens.

43. In antiquity, words inscribed on stone were considered the most sacred of all. The hierophant of Eleusis read to the initiates from tablets of stone, things which they swore not to repeat to anyone, and which were written nowhere else.

44. Twice an attack on the temple of Delphi was repelled in the same circumstances. In 480 B.C. the troops of Xerxes attacked it and withdrew, frightened by a storm accompanied by flames coming from the sun and the fall of great blocks of rock.—*Herodotus.* In 279 B.C. the temple was again attacked by an invasion of Gauls and Cymri. Delphi was defended by only a small group of Phoceans. The barbarians attacked, but at the moment they were about to enter the temple, a storm broke out and the Phoceans routed the Gauls.

NOTES

(See the excellent account in *The History of the Gauls* by Amedee Thierry, Book II.)

45. According to the ancient tradition of the Thracians, poetry had been invented by *Olen*. This name means *Universal Being* in Phoenician. Apollo has the same root: *Ap Olen* or *Ap Wholen* means *Universal Father*. Originally, in Delphi the Universal Being was worshipped under the name *Olen*. The cult of Apollo was introduced by a reforming priest under the impetus of the doctrine of the solar Word, which then was spreading through all the sanctuaries of India and Egypt. This reformer identified the Universal Father with his double manifestation, hyperphysical light and the visible sun. But this reform was scarcely known outside the walls of the sanctuary. It was Orpheus who gave new power to the solar Word of Apollo by reviving it and vitalizing it with the Mysteries of Dionysius. (See Fabre d'Olivet, *Golden Verses of Pythagoras,* trnsl. by Redfield, Putnam's N.Y. 1925.)

46. *TRAKIA,* according to Fabre d'Olivet is derived from the Phoenician *Rakhiwe,* meaning *ethereal space* or *firmament.* For the poets and initiates of Greece like Pindar, Aeschylus or Plato, the name *Thrace* had a symbolic sense and meant the land of pure doctrine and sacred poetry which stems from it. This word therefore had a philosophical and historical meaning for them. Philosophically it designated an intellectual sphere, the group of doctrines and traditions which trace the origin of the world from a divine intelligence. Historically this name recalled the country and people where Dorian doctrine and poetry, that vigorous offshoot of the ancient Ayran spirit had first developed to flowering in Greece through the sanctuary of Apollo. The use of this kind of symbolism is proved by subsequent history. At Delphi was a group of Thracian priests who were the guardians of the high doctrine. The Council of the Amphyctions was formerly defended by a Thracian guard, that is, a guard of initiate warriors. The tyranny of Sparta suppressed this incorruptible army and replaced it with mercenaries of brute force. Later the verb "to thracize" was applied ironically to those faithful to the former doctrine.

47. Strabo confirms positively that ancient poetry was only the language of allegory. Denys of Halicarnassus confirms this, stating that the mysteries of nature and the most sublime concepts of morality have been hidden beneath a veil. Therefore it is not at all a mere metaphor when ancient poetry was called *the Language of the Gods.* This secret magic meaning which makes for its power and charm is contained in its very name. The majority of linguists have derived the word *poetry* from the Greek verb *poiein, to make, to create.* This is simple etymology, and is very natural on the surface, but hardly conforms with the sacred language of the temples, from which primitive poetry came. It is more logical to recognize with Fabre d'Olivet that *Poiesis* comes from the Phoenician *phohe (mouth, voice, language, speech)* and from *ish (superior being, originating being, figuratively: God).* The Etruscan *Aes* or *Aesar,* Gallic *Aes,* Scandinavian *Ase,*

Copit *Os* (Lord), Egyptian *Osiris* have the same root. (See also, Wadler, Arnold: *One Language, Source of All Tongues,* New York, 1948—Ed.)

48. Bacchus with a bull's face is found in the 29th *Orphic Hymn.* It is a recollection of a former cult which in no way belongs to the pure tradition of Orpheus. For the latter completely purified and transfigured the popular Bacchus into the celestial Dionysius, the symbol of the divine Spirit which evolves throughout the kingdoms of nature. We again find the *infernal* Bacchus of the sorceress Bacchantes in the figure of Satan with a bull's face which the witches of the Middle Ages invoked and worshipped in their nocturnal revels. This is the celebrated *Baphomet,* of which the Church accused the Knights Templars of being a sect, in order to discredit them. (See Henry Milman: *History of Latin Christianity,* on the Knights Templars. —Ed.)

49. A Phoenician word, composed of *aur, light,* and *rophae, healing.*

50. Among the numerous lost books which the Orphic writers of Greece attributed to Orpheus was the *Argonautics* which was concerned with the great Hermetic work; *Demetriad,* a poem on the mother of the gods, to which a *Cosmogony* corresponded; the *Holy Songs of Bacchus* or *The pure Spirit,* which has as its complement a *Theogony,* not to mention other works such as *The Veil* or *The Network of Souls,* on the art of the Mysteries and rituals; *The Book of Mutations,* on chemistry and alchemy; *The Corybantes,* on terrestrial mysteries and earthquakes; the *Anemoscopy,* on the science of atmospheres, a natural and magical botany, etc. . . .

51. Pausanias tells us that every year a procession made its way from Delphi to the Valley of Tempe to pick the sacred laurel. This symbolic custom reminded Apollo's disciples that they were attached to the Orphic initiation, and that the original sign of Orpheus was the ancient, sturdy tree whose young living branches the priests of Delphi always picked.

    This blending of Apollonian and Orphic tradition is to be observed in yet another manner in the history of the temples. In fact, the famous dispute between Apollo and Bacchus over the tripod of the temple has no other meaning. Bacchus, says the legend, gave the tripod to his brother and withdrew to Parnassus. This means that Dionysus and the Orphic initiation remained the privilege of the initiates, while Apollo gave his oracles to the people in general.

52. The cry *Evohe,* which in reality was pronounced, *He Vau He,* was the sacred cry of all the initiates of Egypt, Judea, Phoenicia, Asia Minor and Greece. The four sacred letters, pronounced in the following manner: *Iod (EE) He, Vo, He,* represented God in His eternal fusion with nature; they embraced the totality of Being, the Living Universe. *Iod* (Osiris) meant Divinity, strictly speaking, creative intellect, the *Eternal Masculine,* which is in all things, in all places and above all. *He-Vau-He* represented the *Eternal Feminine, Eve, Isis, Nature,* in all the visible and invisible forms engendered

by it. The highest initiation, that of the theogonic sciences and the theurgic arts, corresponded to the letter *Jod* (EE). Another order of sciences corresponded to each of the letters of *Eve*. Like Moses, Orpheus reserved the sciences which corresponded to the letter *Jod* (*Jove, Zeus, Jupiter*) and the idea of the unity of God, to the initiates of the first class, seeking nevertheless to interest the people in it through poetry, the arts and their living symbols. It is for this reason that the cry *Evohe* was openly proclaimed in the Festivals of Dionysus, where, besides the initiates, the simple aspirants to the Mysteries were admitted.

In this appears all the difference between the work of Moses and the work of Orpheus. Both departed from Egyptian initiation and possessed the same truth, but they applied it in different ways. Moses severely, jealously glorifies the Father, the male God. He entrusts its care to a sacred priesthood and subjects the people to an implacable discipline without revelation. Orpheus, divinely in love with the External Feminine, with Nature, glorifies her in the name of God, who penetrates her and whom he wishes to make burst forth in a divine humanity. And this is why the cry *Evohe* became the sacred cry *par excellence*, in all the Mysteries of Greece. (On *Evohe* see Rudolf Steiner: *Eurythmy as Visible Speech* and *Visible Song.—Ed.*)

53. *The Amphictyonic Oath* of the allied peoples gives an idea of the grandeur and social strength of this institution: "We swear never to overthrow the Amphictionic cities, never to turn aside from the things necessary to their needs, whether during peace or war. If any power dares trouble them, we will move against it and we will destroy its cities. Should the impious steal the offerings from the temple of Apollo, we swear that we shall use our feet, arms, voices, all our strength, against them and their accomplices!"

54. In transcendant mathematics, it is demonstrated algebraically that Zero multiplied by Infinity is equal to One. Zero, in the order of absolute ideas, means indeterminate Being. The Infinite, the Eternal in the language of the temples, was indicated by a circle or by a serpent biting its tail, which meant the Infinite moving itself. And, from the moment Infinity becomes determined, it produces all the numbers it contains in its great unity and which it governs in perfect harmony.

This is the transcendant meaning of the first problem of the Pythagorean theogony, the reason which brings it about that the great Monad contains all the small ones, and that all numbers originate from the great Unity in movement.

55. This doctrine is identical with that of the initiate St. Paul, who speaks of the *spiritual body*. (See Rudolf Steiner: *The Bhagavad Gita and the Epistles of St. Paul—Ed.*)

56. One must place Fabre d'Olivet (*Golden Verses of Pythagoras*) in the first rank of these. This living concept of the forces of the universe permeating it from top to bottom has nothing to do with the empty speculations of the

pure metaphysicians, for example, *thesis, antithesis and synthesis* of Hegel, which are simply intellectual exercises.

57. Certain strange definitions in the form of metaphors which have been transmitted to us and which come from the secret teaching of the master, allow one to surmise the grandiose concept that Pythagoras had of the Cosmos. Speaking of the constellations, he called the Great and Little Dipper: *the hands of Rea-Kybele.* Now, *Rea-Kybele* esoterically means *astral light returning,* the *divine wife of the universal fire,* or *creative spirit* which, in concentrating in the solar systems, attracts the non-material essences of beings, grasps them, and causes them to enter the cycle of lives. He also called the planets *the Dogs of Proserpine.* This unusual expression has no meaning other than an esoteric one. Prosperpine, the goddess of souls, was present at their incarnation into matter. Pythagoras therefore called the planets *Dogs of Proserpine* because they keep the incarnated souls as the mythological Cerberus guards souls in hell.

58. The law is called *Karma* by the Brahmans and Buddhists. (See Rudolf Steiner: *The Manifestations of Karma,* 1910.—*Ed.*)

59. *The Epiphany* or vision from above; the *autopsy,* or direct view; the *theophany,* or manifestation of God, are so many correlative ideas and expressions which indicate the state of perfection in which the initiate, having joined his soul to God, contemplates complete Truth.

60. We shall cite two famous absolutely authentic events of this kind. The first took place in Antiquity, and the hero is the famous philosopher-magician, Apollonius of Tyana

    The Second-sight of Apollonius of Tyana. "While these things (the assassination of the Emperor Domitian) were taking place in Rome, Apollonius saw them at Ephesus. Domitian was attacked by Clement around noontime; the same day at the same hour, Apollonius was making a speech in the gardens near the Xystes. Suddenly he lowered his voice a little, as if he had been gripped by a sudden fright. He continued his speech, but his language did not have its usual power, as happens with those who speak while thinking of something else. Then he became silent, like those who have lost the train of their thought. He cast terrified glances toward the earth, moved three or four steps forward, and cried out, 'Kill the tyrant!' One would have said that he saw, not the reflected image of the event as in a mirror, but the event itself in all its reality. The Ephesians (for all Ephesus went to hear Apollonius' speeches) were struck with amazement. Apollonius stopped, like a man who waits to see the outcome of an uncertain event. Finally he cried out, 'Be of good cheer, Ephesians, the tyrant was killed today! What am I saying?—Today? By Minerva! He was killed at the very instant I interrupted myself!' The Ephesians thought that Apollonius had lost his mind; they indeed hoped that he had told the truth, nevertheless they feared that some danger would result for him from this discourse . . . But soon messengers came to announce the good news and gave testimony in favor of Apollonius' science: for the murder of the tyrant, the day it was consummated, the hour of noon, the author of the murder whom Apollonius had encouraged,—all these details were in perfect agreement with those the gods had shown him the day of his speech to the Ephesians."—*Life of Apollonius* by Philostratus. (See Emil Bock, *The Three Years* for an account of Apollonius of Tyana—*Ed*.)

The Second-sight of Swedenborg: The second event refers to the greatest seer of modern times. One can have reservations regarding the objective reality of Swedenborg's vision, but one cannot doubt his second-sight, attested to by a host of facts. The vision that Swedenborg had at thirty leagues' distance from the fire of Stockholm created an uproar in the second half of the eighteenth century. The famous German philosopher, Kant had an inquiry made by a friend at Gothenburg in Sweden, the city where the event took place, and this is what he writes about it to one of his friends:

"The following occurrence appears to me to have the greatest weight of proof, and to place the assertion respecting Swedenborg's extraordinary gift beyond all possibility of doubt. In the year 1759, toward the end of September, on Saturday, at four o'clock in the afternoon, Swedenborg arrived at Gothenburg from England, when Mr. William Castel invited him to his house, together with a party of fifteen persons. About six o'clock, Swedenborg went out and returned to the company quite pale and alarmed. He said that a dangerous fire had just broken out in Stockholm, at the Södermalm (Gothenburg is about 50 German miles—about 300 English—from Stockholm), and that it was spreading very fast. He was restless and went out often. He said that the house of one of his friends, whom he named, was already in ashes and that his own was in danger. At eight o'clock, after he had been out again, he joyfully exclaimed, 'Thank God! The fire is extinguished, the third door from my house.' The news occasioned great commotion throughout the whole city, but particularly amongst the company in which he was. It was announced to the governor the same evening. On Sunday morning, Swedenborg was summoned to the governor, who questioned him concerning the disaster. Swedenborg described the fire precisely, how it had begun, in what manner it had ceased, and how long it had continued. On the same day the news spread through the city, and as the governor had thought it worthy of attention, the consternation was considerably increased, because many were in trouble on account of their friends and property, which might have been involved in the disaster. On Monday evening a messenger arrived at Gothenburg, who was dispatched by the Board of Trade during the time of the fire. In the letters brought by him, the fire was described precisely in the manner stated by Swedenborg. On Tuesday morning the royal courier arrived at the governor's with the melancholy intelligence of the fire, of the loss which it had occasioned, and of the houses it had damaged and ruined, not in the least differing from that which Swedenborg had given at the very time when it happened; for the fire was extinguished at eight o'clock."—Letter from Immanuel Kant to Charlotte von Knobloch, written at Königsburg. (Quoted in George Trobridge, *Emanuel Swedenborg, Life and Teaching*, page 197-8.—*Ed.*)

61. This idea comes logically from the human and divine ternary, from the trinity of the Microcosm and Macrocosm which we have discussed in the preceding chapters. The metaphysical correlative of Destiny, Liberty and Providence has been admirably deduced by Fabre d'Olivet in his analysis of *The Golden Verses of Pythagoras*.

62. This classification of men corresponds to the four stages of Pythagorean initiation, forming the basis of all initiations up to that of the original Free Masons, who possessed a few bits of esoteric doctrine. (See Fabre d'Olivet, *The Golden Verses of Pythagoras*.)

63. This is the version of Diogenes of Laërte on Pythagoras' death. According to Dicearcus, quoted by Porphyrus, the master probably escaped destruction, along with Archippus and Lysis. But he doubtless wandered from city to city until reaching Metapontus, where he let himself die of hunger in the Temple of the Muses. The inhabitants of Metapontus claim, on the other hand, that the sage, welcomed by them, died peacefully in their city. They showed his house, his seat and tomb to Cicero. It should be noted that a long time after the master's death, the cities which had persecuted Pythagoras at the time of the change, claim the honor of having sheltered and saved him. The cities around the Gulf of Tarentum fought over the philosopher's ashes with the same ferocity that the cities of Iona struggled over the honor of having given birth to Homer.

64. In the language of the temples, the term "son of woman" designated the lower stage of initiation, woman meaning here, nature. Above these were "sons of men" or initiates of Spirit and Soul; "the sons of the gods" or initiates of cosmogonic science, and "Sons of God" or initiates of the supreme science. Pythia calls the Persians "sons of women," designating them thus from the nature of their religion. Taken literally, her words would not have any meaning.

65. "These are still to be seen in Minerva's garden," said Herodotus, VIII, 39. The Gallic invasion which took place two hundred years later was repelled in a similar manner. There again a storm gathers, lightning falls on the Gauls at intervals, the earth trembles under their feet, they see supernatural appearances, and the Temple of Apollo is saved. These facts seem to prove that the priests of Delphi possessed the science of cosmic fire, and knew how to manipulate electricity through secret powers like the Chaldean magi. (See Amedee Thierry, *Histoire des Gaulois*, I, 246).

66. Contemporary science would see in these facts only simple hallucinations or suggestions. The science of ancient esoterism attributed both a subjective and objective value to this kind of phenomenon, which was frequently pro-

NOTES

duced in the Mysteries. It believed in the existence of elemental spirits without an individualized soul and without reason. Half-conscious, they fill the earthly atmosphere and are in some way the souls of the elements. Magic, which is will put into action in the manipulation of secret powers, makes these beings visible at times. Heraclitus speaks of them when he says, "Nature, in all places is full of daemons." Plato calls them *daemons of the elements,* Paracelsus names them *elementals.* According to Paracelsus they are attracted by the magnetic atmosphere of man, are electrified and are capable of assuming all imaginable human forms. The more man is given over to his passions, the more he becomes their prey without being aware of it. The magus alone subdues them and uses them. But they constitute a sphere of deceiving illusions and follies which it is necessary to master and pass upon one's entrance into the spiritual world. Bulwer Lytton calls them "the guardian of the threshold" in his unusual novel, *Zanoni.*

67. This is the tree of dreams mentioned by Virgil in the descent of Aeneus into hell, in the sixth book of the *Aeneid,* which reproduces the main scenes of the Mysteries of Eleusis with poetic amplifications.

68. The gold objects contained in the cist were *the pine cone* (symbol of fertility and generation), *the spiral serpent* (universal evolution of the soul; fall into matter and redemption by the spirit); *the egg* (recalling the sphere of divine perfection, the goal of man.)

69. These mysterious words have no meaning in Greek. This proves that they are very ancient, and come from the Orient. Wilford gives them a Sanscrit origin. *Konx* would come from *Kansha,* meaning *object of the greatest desire; Om* from *Um, the soul of Brahma,* and *Pax* from *Pasha, tour, exchange, cycle.* The supreme blessing of the hierophant of Eleusis means therefore: "May your desires be fulfilled; return to the universal Soul!"

70. How did Jesus become the Messiah? This is the original, most fundamental question in the concept of the Christ, but the problem cannot be solved without intuition and without *esoteric* tradition. It is with this esoteric light, this inner flame of all religions, this central truth of all fertile philosophy, that I have attempted to reconstruct the life of Jesus in broad outline, while taking into account all the previous work of historical criticism which has prepared the way. As far as what concerns the historical and relative value of the Gospels, I have taken the three Synoptics (Matthew, Mark and Luke) as a basis, and John's Gospel as the arcanum of the esoteric doctrine of Christ, at the same time allowing for the posterior composition and symbolic tendency of this Gospel.

The four Gospels, which must be compared with each other, are equally authentic, but in different ways. Matthew and Mark are the valuable Gospels of the letter and fact; the public acts and speeches are found there. Gentle Luke lets the meaning of the Mysteries be partly seen beneath the poetic veil of legend. This is the Gospel of the Soul, of Woman and of Love,

John unveils these mysteries. One finds with him the deep foundation of the doctrine, the secret teaching, the meaning of the Promise, the esoteric reserve. Clement of Alexandria, one of the rare Christian bishops who possessed the key of universal esoterism, has well called it "the Gospel of the Spirit." John has a profound view of the transcendant truths revealed by the Master and a powerful way of summarizing them. His symbol is the Eagle, whose wings fly through space, and whose flaming eye observes the deepest secrets. (See also Rudolf Steiner's book, *Christianity as Mystical Fact and the Mysteries of Antiquity*, as well as his published lecture cycles on the four Gospels. Emil Bock's *Studies in the Gospels* and his *The Three Years* also contain useful material.—*Ed.*)

71. Points in common between the Essenes and Pythagoreans: Prayer at sunrise; linen clothing; fraternal love-feasts; novitiate of one year; three stages of initiation; organization of the Order and community of property arranged by trustees; law of silence; oath of the Mysteries; division of teaching into three parts: 1) science of universal principles or *theogony*, which Philo calls Logic; 2) Physics or *cosmogony;* 3) morality, that is, everything that deals with *man*, the science to which the Therapeuts would be dedicated. (See also Rudolf Steiner's lecture cycle on the *Gospel of Matthew* and Bock's *The Three Years—Ed.*)

72. Points in common between the teaching of the Essenes and that of Jesus: Love of one's neighbor as a first duty; prohibition of an oath in attesting to truth as a witness; hatred of the lie; humility; institution of the Supper borrowed from the love-feasts, but *with an entirely new meaning,* that of Sacrifice.

73. *Book of Enoch,* Chapters 48 and 61. This passage proves that the doctrine of the Word and the Trinity found in John's Gospel existed in Israel long before the time of Jesus, and came from the depths of esoteric prophecy. In the apocryphal *Book of Enoch, The Lord of Spirits* represents the Father; *The Elect,* the Son, the Chosen One; *The Other Force,* the Holy Spirit.

Index

INDEX

INDEX

M

Maccabees, 422–23, 441, 464
Mahabharata, 75, 77, 79
Manu, 134
Marathon, 367, 374
Mary, the Virgin, 425 seq.
Masculine, the Eternal, 68, 192, 315, 508
Melchizedek, 176
Memphis, 142, 178, 180, 270, 277, 282, 293, 414, 416
Mexico, 36, 37
Mignaty, Margarita Albana, 15–18, 20–22, 23
Milon, 363–65
mistletoe, 52, 53, 60
Mithras cult, 125, 491
Moses, 46, 131, 140, 172, 173, 177, 186, 329, 417, 438, 444, 453, 461, 467, 482, 498, 511
Muses, the, 313

N

Neo-Platonists, 269
Nero, 417
Nicodemus, 454–57
Nietzsche, Friedrich, 15, 18
Nile, 131–32, 138, 166, 278
Nimrod, 171
Nineveh, 171, 174
Noel, Festival of, 58–59

O

d'Olivet, Fabre, 39, 43, 48, 167, 498, 506, 512, 517
Ormuzd, 125, 289, 481, 506
Orpheus, 41, 131, 221 seq., 231 seq., 324
Osiris, 125, 131, 137, 138, 140, 143–4, 154, 157 seq., 169, 180, 438

P

Pallas Athene, 374
Paris, 16, 24
Paul, St., 496–97, 499, 501, 517
Pericles, 374
Persephone, 249

Peter, St., 458, 469, 470, 485
Pharisees, 437, 444, 457, 463 seq., 471, 476, 487
Philo of Alexandria, 435
Pindar, 371
Plato, 70, 126, 194, 269, 311, 326, 336, 357, 371 seq., 407, 414
Platonic Academy, 391
Plotinus, 458
Plutarch, 290
Polycrates, 271–2, 277
Pontius Pilate, 441–42, 489–92, 493
Proclus, 407
Purgatory, 324
Pythagoras, 70, 126, 263 seq.

R

Races, origin of, 36 seq.
Ram, Rama, 51 seq., 136, 187
Ramayana, 47–8, 78
Rameses, 141, 178 seq., 182
Renan, Ernst, 19, 497
Rishis 41, 78, 87, 88, 112, 171
Rome, 268, 415, 416, 444, 491

S

Saducees, 437, 464, 471, 477
Samson, 425–26
Samuel, 208, 213, 418, 425–26
Saturn, 159, 324, 329
Saul, 208, 213
Schure, Edouard, biography of, 12 seq.
Science of the Spirit, 30
Scythia, 49, 50
Semites, 50
Sepher Bereshith, 187, 189, 206
Septuagint, 188
Sermon on the Mount, 452–53
Serpent of Eden, 192–93
Shelley, P. B., 18
Sinai, 173, 184, 196, 201 seq., 443
Sivers, Marie von, 23–4
Socrates, 378 seq.
Sodom and Gomorrah, 176, 177
Solon, 268
Sphinx, the, 129 seq., 152, 510
Steiner, Rudolf, 22 seq., 517, 522

INDEX